Decolonizing Afghanistan

Decolonizing Afghanistan
Countering Imperial Knowledge & Power

Edited by

WAZHMAH OSMAN AND ROBERT D. CREWS

DUKE UNIVERSITY PRESS *Durham and London* 2025

Project Editor: Ihsan Taylor
Designed by Matthew Tauch
Typeset in Arno Pro and General Sans
by Westchester Publishing Services

Library of Congress Cataloging-in-Publication Data
Names: Osman, Wazhmah, [date] editor. | Crews, Robert D., [date]
editor.
Title: Decolonizing Afghanistan : countering Imperial knowledge and
power / edited by Wazhmah Osman and Robert D. Crews.
Description: Durham : Duke University Press, 2025. | Includes biblio-
graphical references and index.
Identifiers: LCCN 2025004854 (print)
LCCN 2025004855 (ebook)
ISBN 9781478032601 (paperback)
ISBN 9781478029229 (hardcover)
ISBN 9781478061427 (ebook)
ISBN 9781478094432 (ebook other)
Subjects: LCSH: Political stability—Afghanistan. | Violence—
Afghanistan. | Afghanistan—Politics and government—21st century. |
Afghanistan—History—2021- | Afghanistan—Social conditions—21st
century. | Afghanistan—Population. | Afghanistan—Emigration and
immigration—History—21st century.
Classification: LCC DS371.44 .D436 2025 (print) | LCC DS371.44 (ebook)
LC record available at https://lccn.loc.gov/2025004854
LC ebook record available at https://lccn.loc.gov/2025004855

Cover art: Laimah Osman, *They will be greeted by flowers . . .* , 2011
(detail). Graphite, colored pencils, and watercolor on Arches
Watercolor Paper, 4 × 5 ft. Courtesy of the artist.

Contents

Part 3. The Politics & Optics of Representation: Media & Propaganda

Part 4. Reflecting & Speaking Back to Empire

WAZHMAH OSMAN, HELENA ZEWERI & ROBERT D. CREWS

Introduction

Decolonizing Afghanistan:
A Turning Point

Decolonizing Afghanistan features new scholarship exploring the impact of empire on Afghanistan's past and present. The book traces the ways that imperial violence and its technologies of power have shaped Afghanistan and its diaspora. It also explores how the diverse communities that make up Afghanistan have subverted, resisted, and participated in these colonial projects from the early twentieth century to the present, with a particular focus on the American intervention that began in 2001. In interrogating the relationship between knowledge and power, we examine how knowledge about Afghanistan has framed and legitimated imperial governance. Our authors follow calls within and outside of academia to decolonize knowledge about Afghanistan, to extricate the will to know from the will to conquer. Understanding and questioning imperial knowledge are essential steps toward imagining an Afghan political future beyond empire.

Our approach is to situate Afghanistan and its diasporas within the broader study of colonialism and, thus, of modernity, power, resistance, and globalization in the enduring colonial present. Knowledge about Afghanistan has historically been viewed as valuable when it has served the interests of those pursuing geopolitical, military, and, in more recent decades, humanitarian and development interventions. Moreover, as Benjamin D. Hopkins has observed, Afghanistan "is a place studied . . . to tame it" (2022). Part of this taming has come in the form of treating Afghanistan as a domain that requires diagnosis, a space that suffers from a spectrum of different cultural and political pathologies that render it at best a nuisance and at worst an enduring threat to the global community.

We propose instead to highlight colonialism as the crucial framework for understanding not only the last four decades of foreign involvement in Afghanistan, beginning with the Soviet invasion of 1979—a year that also marked more direct American involvement in the country's political affairs—but also British and Russian colonial excursions and wars from the nineteenth century onward. The neocolonial era continued from the inaugural American military operation of October 2001 through the withdrawal of US military forces in 2021. Situating Afghanistan within colonial studies represents a move to decolonize how we understand the country's past, present, and future. It entails a fundamental rethinking of the value of studying Afghanistan and its diasporas as objects of academic knowledge. Understanding Afghanistan within the broader context of empire and colonialism is a decolonial act because it subverts the notion that Afghanistan is only knowable within the conceptual parameters of military strategy, global security, and policy—and not of empire. When people's histories have been told for them in ways that authorize conquest—of land, culture, history, and personhood—then uncovering the stories that have remained untold or been silenced is a necessary step in undoing colonial erasure.

In this volume, we use colonialism and imperialism as distinct yet related concepts to describe foreign modes of governance over Afghanistan's affairs from the nineteenth through the twenty-first centuries. We understand colonialism as direct control and conquest for the economic, military, and material benefit of the colonizing power. Colonial modes of domination in Afghanistan have involved direct forms of administrative control and economic extraction and exploitation. We take imperialism to be the exercise of power by various states over Afghanistan's sovereignty and political, cultural, and economic futures through more indirect modes of control, including the recruitment of local people and co-optations of institutions tasked with carrying out the empire's blueprint for governance. However, we recognize that colonial and imperial modes of power work together to dominate. US imperial interests benefitted from control over the political affairs of Afghanistan: This control provided strategic military and geopolitical strength as well as tangible material and economic benefits in the form of defense contracts and the creation of NGO and development-related jobs. A further benefit was national security: A key premise of US military intervention was to eliminate terrorist training camps and havens in order to ensure the security of the United States by rebuilding Afghan society—until that was no longer in the interests of empire.

Decolonizing Methodology and the Colonial Archive

As Frantz Fanon ([1967] 2008) proposes, decolonization must entail critically interrogating the whole of a colonial situation. Historian Michel-Rolph Trouillot (1995) writes that to provide a critical history is to dissect "what is said to have happened." For Indigenous scholar Linda Tuhiwai Smith ([1999] 2021), in order to dissect the historical record, we have to center the power disparities between researchers who were historically part of the colonizer class and the colonized subjects of research by asking whom such research has benefited and whom it has harmed. In her foundational book *Decolonizing Methodologies*, she explains how the terms *research* and *history* have become "dirty" words in Indigenous communities because they are "inextricably linked to European imperialism and colonialism" and have caused harm to subaltern communities (Smith [1999] 2021, 1).

Moreover, as scholars of settler colonialism Eve Tuck and K. Wayne Yang remind us in their foundational essay "Decolonization Is Not a Metaphor," because colonialism has real-world consequences for the people subjected to its various regimes of violence, we cannot treat decolonization, or migration, for that matter, as empty signifiers. Rather, we must do the hard work of seriously tracking the colonial past and present by making connections across imperial metropoles to their peripheries and across disciplines and media to uncover colonialism's machinations and recover its subaltern losses and damages (2012). While Afghanistan was never a settler colony, it is important to examine what it means that it has been deeply impacted by the exploits of an empire (the United States, among others) that, in conducting wars and sales of military weapons for wars abroad, seeks to maintain its own economic and political power as a settler colonial society.

When it comes to the study of Afghanistan and its diasporas, there has not been sufficient reckoning with these fundamental decolonizing questions and methodological issues. Likewise, whereas intellectuals and scholars commenting on Latin America, parts of the Arabic-speaking world, and South Asia have long engaged with the problems of colonialism, the history and present of colonialism in Afghanistan and what Anila Daulatzai calls its "discursive occupation" have received far less attention (2008). This is also true for other countries, like Iraq, that have had their societies and infrastructures simultaneously torn apart and selectively rebuilt in the War on Terror. As Iraqi American scholar Zahra Ali writes, "There can be no 'innocent' knowledge produced on Iraq because of this history of destruction, military intervention, and occupation" (2024, 419).

This is in part due to the larger problem of the hegemony of and overreliance on the colonial archives with their imperial languages of English, French, and Russian, among others, which are spoken by many former subjects. These archives are caught up in the perpetuation of top-down imperial narratives that devalue and exclude subaltern voices, especially oppositional ones. They tend to be well funded and maintained in comparison to archives in postcolonial and war-torn nation-states, making them more accessible to researchers.

Conversely, due to colonial violence and extraction, there is a serious lack of archives that document decolonial, postcolonial, or anti-colonial activities and movements and the egregiousness of colonizers. When they do exist, they are underutilized due to a lack of fluency in local languages and their distance from the imperial metropole. Moreover, it is difficult to revise or correct the record of "what is said to have happened" when subaltern artifacts, national documents, and media have been repeatedly looted and pillaged from museums, archives, and libraries—or worse yet bombed, burned, destroyed, or forever lost in the upheaval of war and displacement. This pattern of heritage destruction and extraction is of course not just a relic of the past but has been a key feature of twenty-first-century wars and their spoils in Afghanistan, Iraq, and other sites of the Global War on Terror (Aikins 2021; Bahrani 2023, 2025; Feroozi 2004; González Zarandona et al. 2023; Saleh 2020; Slyomovics 2021; Tarzi 2023).

In the media, in think tanks, and in universities, knowledge on Afghanistan is produced by scholars, policy makers, diplomats, and veterans who tend to have a vested interest in or be materially invested in the imperial project. Often, they reproduce top-down analytical perspectives and grand overarching narratives. They amplify the dominant narratives about Afghanistan by citing one another in an echo chamber, removed from the on-the-ground situation in Afghanistan and the lived experiences of those most affected by these narratives. For example, American "experts" on the region have produced "reams of scholarship on 'tribes' or 'Islamism,' which recycle, at best, British colonial strategies of control and domination" (Ahmed 2011, 65).

Heeding the call of decolonial and feminist scholars, decolonizing scholarship, then, requires centering the voices of indigenous, local, subaltern, colonized, and/or hybrid voices of those who see outside/inside of empire and who thus have produced important knowledge that we can learn from to change the status quo. Therefore, throughout the writing process of this book, we have tried to cite, engage with, feature, and give space to the work of scholars and practitioners who have been excluded or sidelined from the dominant threads of academia, postcolonial theory, and

Afghanistan studies and who are producing work outside the echo chamber of the establishment. This includes both those who have come before us—who have influenced us and whom we build on—and emergent voices.

Afghanistan and Colonialism in Historical Perspective

The exclusion of Afghanistan from the main currents of postcolonial studies and studies of empire is also attributable to a dominant conception across the social sciences and humanities that Afghanistan does not offer a generative example of contemporary colonial dynamics. Westerners and some Afghan nationalists have long claimed that Afghanistan was "never colonized." In a similar vein, nationalists and Orientalists alike have celebrated (or castigated) the country as the "graveyard of empires"—a cliché invoked by former President Joe Biden in announcing the American withdrawal in August 2021 in defense of his assertion that the country had always been stuck in a hopeless condition of ungovernable anarchy. As decolonial studies scholars have begun to demonstrate, however, these tropes elide the fact that multiple colonial forces have shaped Afghan politics, society, and culture throughout the modern era (see Nivi Manchanda's chapter in this volume). To be sure, Afghans avoided the fate of their immediate neighbors in Central and South Asia as they were never fully absorbed by European colonial powers. But colonialism has historically been about far more than physical presence and direct administrative control over a territory's political system, economy, and social life (Veracini 2011).

According to colonial studies scholar Lorenzo Veracini, "Colonialism is primarily defined by exogenous domination. It thus has two fundamental and necessary components: an original displacement and unequal relations" (2011, 1). If we employ this more expansive, multiscalar definition of colonialism, it becomes clear that Afghanistan has in fact been subject to imperial modes of domination. Indeed, beginning in the late eighteenth century, Afghan rulers were forced to surrender territories. From the early nineteenth century, treaties between the British and the Afghan governments during the formation of the early Afghan state reflected a quasi-colonial status. British colonial forces based in India challenged Afghan leaders in two Anglo-Afghan wars that resulted in temporary occupations of Afghan territory and considerable destruction. Emerging on the edges of British and tsarist Russian expansionism in the late nineteenth century, the boundaries of the Afghan state were redrawn by British and Russian cartographers, reshaping it as a colonial frontier with gradations of foreign dominance and authority (Hanifi 2011, 2012; Hopkins and Marsden 2012; Manchanda 2017). London controlled Afghanistan's foreign policy until 1919 when Afghanistan won its independence in the Third Anglo-Afghan War, known as the War of Independence. Postindependence, Afghan leaders joined global anti-colonial movements and joined the United Nations for leverage against future colonial incursions (Leake 2022). Afghanistan became a model for anti-colonialists from across neighboring British India to Egypt who sought to launch their own resistance (Wide 2014; see also Marya Hannun's chapter in this volume) and were thus subjected to colonial surveillance and subterfuge.

At the same time, some Afghan rulers, especially Amir ʿAbd al-Rahman (r. 1880–1901), exploited imperial patronage (including a ten-year sanctuary in Russian-occupied Central Asia) and subsidies and weapons to subjugate populations across the territory that would eventually make up the Afghan state. As Robert D. Crews has noted, the political elite of Afghanistan has had a complicated relationship with foreign empires, both participating in imperial projects and resisting them (2015). Likewise, as we show in this book, some Afghan people have participated in imperial rule while others have challenged it, and perhaps all citizens of an imperial nation are implicated. Furthermore, long stretches of occupation and imperial rule have extended to people's minds and senses of self, whereby some come to internalize racist imperial tropes about themselves and other Afghans (Chiovenda 2019; Masood 2024).

Using complex mechanisms ranging from diplomatic alliances and intermarriage to forced resettlement, mass expulsions, executions, and enslavement, Amir ʿAbd al-Rahman drew on colonial technologies and resources to conquer territory and communities to build the modern Afghan state. This is another key dimension of colonialism in Afghanistan's past, one with an enduring afterlife for communities that have sustained in their collective memory this traumatic period of subjugation. Many Hazara intellectuals today recall the era of Amir ʿAbd al-Rahman as the inaugurating moment of genocide that laid the foundation for more than a century of discrimination and violence whose legacies endure today. Turkic communities in northern Afghanistan have retained similar memories of conquest and loss born in this crucial period of state consolidation (see Zohra Saed's chapter in this volume). As Nazif M. Shahrani has pointed out, this "internal colonialism" was "aided and abetted by old colonialist powers" (2002).

Foreign powers would continue to shape Afghan sovereignty in similarly important ways in the second half of the twentieth and the twenty-first centuries. Local leftists seized power in 1978, and the Soviet Union would oversee the brutal occupation of the country from 1979 to 1989. Washington was already a party to this conflict when it began backing anti-Soviet resistance forces in 1979; in 2001, American forces would be on the ground in Afghanistan launching what would be known in the US as "America's longest war," which inaugurated the Global War on Terror.

Yet what to call this era remains contested: Many critics have labeled it a twenty-year "occupation." But whether we refer to it as an *occupation*, *neo-imperialism*, or *nation-building interventions*, materially speaking, as Wazhmah Osman (2020) has noted, the post-9/11 era is similar to the colonizations of the past in that Afghanistan did not have full sovereignty over its airspace, airwaves, or land. With its powerful military might behind it, the US government had jurisdiction over Afghan airspace above a certain altitude; over Afghan airwaves, as the largest donor of media and communication development aid; and over Afghan land, via its ever-growing military bases and prisons, including secret black sites reminiscent of when most of Afghanistan's affairs were under control of the British Empire until the Third Anglo-Afghan War. Whether or not this moment has even ended is an ongoing point of dispute among Afghan citizens and the diaspora. While the last US military and diplomatic personnel left in August 2021, American power lingers, not least within what the Biden administration called its "over the horizon" capacity to wage war on Afghan territory via satellite surveillance and drone technology, as well as through first the Biden and then the Trump administrations' ongoing control of Afghanistan's finances demonstrated by the withholding of the Central Afghanistan Bank's assets in the Federal Reserve Bank, with half potentially reserved for families of the victims of 9/11.

The Racialized Afghan Other and Failure Tropes: Dismantling Dominant Colonial Historiography and Narratives

In the overlap between academic and policy circles, Afghanistan has frequently been characterized as a "failed," "broken," "fragmented," or "collapsed" nation (Coburn and Larson 2014; Ghani and Lockhart 2008; Rubin 2002). In this respect, Afghanistan is one of numerous parts of the world that Western scholars have characterized as being hopelessly doomed to foreign aid dependency, poverty, sectarianism, and violence—not because of colonial misrule or exploitation but rather because of presumed predispositions to barbarity, militancy, and savagery, which are depicted as innate cultural and racial characteristics. Postcolonial scholars of the Middle East and Asia have debunked these racist portrayals (Abrahamian 2013; Abu-Lughod 1998; Asad 1973; Chatterjee 1997; Elyachar 2025; Fahmy 2009; Mitchell 2000, 2002). Contrary to how Afghan elites—monarchs, governors, mayors, and other politicians across multiple centuries—are represented in the Western academy, they were not monolithic nor all despotic like Amir 'Abd al-Rahman, described earlier. Because he perpetuates dominant racist tropes about Afghans, Amir 'Abd al-Rahman has an overdetermined place in the Western canon and has been portrayed as emblematic of all Afghan leaders.

Starting in the early twentieth century, a number of modernizing Afghan leaders including Amanullah Khan (the grandson of Amir 'Abd al-Rahman), his wife, Queen Soraya, and his father-in-law, Mahmud Tarzi, ushered in rights for women and minorities and the beginnings of print journalism and other media (see Hannun's chapter). In the second half of the twentieth century, playing off decades of competitive schemes between the United States and the USSR, Zahir Shah and his cousin and prime minister, Daoud Khan, launched a series of large-scale public-works programs and ambitious infrastructure projects including funding and developing the arts, education, media, and industrial production. The establishment of a constitutional monarchy in 1964 codified elected parliamentary politics, civil rights, and freedom of speech. Although these new policies and the legislature were often top-down and limited in their capacity, they nonetheless expanded the public sphere and gave rise to ground-up social justice movements and the proliferation of diverse and oppositional media outlets and political parties. Demands for more democracy and parity by women, students, ethnic minorities, and the working class intensified through protests and the media. These movements along with divergent ideologies among the royal family and Soviet subterfuge led to the toppling of the monarchy and the subsequent takeover of the country by USSR-backed communist leaders.

However flawed, this was an era of major political, social, economic, and cultural experimentations and transformations. For example, in her ethnographic and historical studies of radio in Afghan society, Mejgan Massoumi (2021, 2022) writes that for Afghans, the 1960s and 1970s inspired robust sociopolitical movements. Afghans came to see their internal struggles as part of international decolonial, anti-imperial, and prodemocracy movements. Radio broadcast the pulse of these events, revealing the talents of a people responding to these "accidents of history" through music, poetry, and literature. Yet, like most of Afghan history, in the Western canon this era too is commonly subsumed under the rubric of failure, "Third World despotism," and corrupt "rentier state" politicking enabled by imperial financing and patronage networks.

Likewise, we cannot automatically dismiss all the nation-building projects and programs that emerged in the post-9/11 period as imperialist endeavors on the basis that they were financed with international development aid tied to the War on Terror economy. Certainly, the global development infrastructure is deeply entrenched in the hegemonic infrastructure of imperialism and provides a moral cover for imperial violence. Yet, as Osman (2020) has written in her ethnography of post-9/11 media and development, it is important to at least partially detangle the "development gaze" from the "imperialist gaze" because while many development projects were indeed mired in foreign and Afghan corruption and extraction, resulting in power grabbing and the abuse of power (SIGAR 2018; USGAO 2011), some yielded positive results to varying degrees and at various times. For example, despite the continued suppression of anti-imperialist activists, journalists, and whistleblowers on the home front in the West, the internationally funded Afghan media sector boom was largely deemed a success especially in the first decade before violence against frontline media makers significantly increased. Despite pressures and constraints from abroad and within, studies have shown how Afghan media makers used a range of strategies to provide much-needed entertainment and news and information critical of foreign and Afghan elites (Osman 2020; Sienkiewicz 2016).

Development was generative in some instances and sectors not only due to the hard work and ingenuity of Afghans and their foreign collaborators but also because the country's political economy, while mostly funded by US aid, was not solely reliant on it—rather it was international in scope. The dangers of foreign aid and dependency, as Osman (2019b) has shown with regards to Russia and Afghanistan's neighbors to the north, manifest when countries' economic, media, and political systems are unilaterally dependent financially on one powerful donor country, thereby making them vulnerable to imperial coercion and likely to replicate those same kleptocratic patronage networks and imperial authoritarian systems domestically.

Moreover, as prominent decolonial anthropologists have demonstrated, "It is difficult to exoticize others or to maintain fictions of bounded and untouched communities of difference when one includes media [and culture] in one's purview" (Ginsburg et al. 2002). Even the supposed "unruly borderlands" and "savage frontier" between Afghanistan and then British India, long characterized in the Western historical canon as a hotbed of the usual colonial tropes of lawlessness, violence, and seediness, are in fact more complex in their excess and layers (Ahmed 2011; Hopkins 2020; see Manchanda in this volume and 2020). New ethnographic research is demonstrating that the borderlands are teeming with culture and media from around the world. Local bazaars and their shopkeepers and media technicians have become hubs in global circuits of images, sounds, and cosmopolitanism, where new media is translated, marketed, and sold as audio and video CDs, digital files, and other formats (Cooper 2024a; Osman 2020). As shown in Timothy P. A. Cooper's work on Pashto film and music, in these networks of exchange and dissemination borderlands become "interfaces" of communication (2024b). Likewise, recent work along the northern border of Afghanistan, also commonly portrayed as a zone of violence and trafficking, has instead demonstrated the notion of "borders as resources" for cross-border markets, medical infrastructure, and personal reconnections, defining the community relationships between the two sides (Sadozaï 2021).

Yet the dominant colonial mode of thinking about the Afghan past and present reduces all nuances to a simplistic narrative of failure and despotism. The same imperial pundits and scholars who are quick to point out the supposed inadequacies of Afghans in the pursuit to modernize conveniently look the other way or rationalize their own governments' brutal record of repression and anti-democratic activities domestically and abroad, even during highly authoritarian regimes. They "outsource" patriarchy and racism as the domains of the Global South and East (Grewal 2013; Mitra 2020; O'Sullivan 2023; Wardak 2018). Talal Asad explains in his book *Anthropology and the Colonial Encounter* how the West perpetuates its dominance over the Third World by inscribing its power in a universalist language of rights that is asymmetrically and selectively applied (1973). Although US and NATO leaders privileged anthropology as a tool of counterinsurgency, especially from 2009 onward, racist colonial discourse about Afghanistan has pervaded most academic disciplines across centuries and has framed some of the most consequential policy decisions made by foreigners for Afghans over the past twenty years. In this view, the Afghan "other" is defined by a static culture and bound by archaic traditions. Ostensibly mired in backwardness, misogyny, and tribalism, Afghans are represented as fierce, militant, isolationist, and inherently opposed to the forces of cultural exchange, pluralism, and global modernity.

Western mainstream media accounts, including best-selling books, news, network television programs and serials, and Hollywood films, have for the most part reinforced these stereotypes (Bose 2020; Ivanchikova 2019; Osman 2022; Osman and Redrobe 2022; Osman et al. 2021). In this way, popular culture echoes and amplifies the views of fervent imperial war hawks and militant xenophobes on the right and left, for whom nation-building and democracy are a futile enterprise for "backward" people and countries incapable of civilizing and modernizing. Based on their racist ideology, they believe the only way to engage with unruly Middle Eastern and Asian people is through control and force via direct attacks or clandestine coups. On the home front, this dehumanizing rhetoric has led to rampant Islamophobia, hate-mongering, and hate crimes against Muslims and those mistaken for Muslims (Kazi 2019; Kumar [2012] 2021; Kundnani 2014).

The dominant "failed state" paradigm and Orientalist Afghan tropes erase not only historical achievements, such as periods of democratization and modernization, but also the fundamental agency, creativity, and intellect of the Afghan people—thus perpetuating the false notion that first the Soviets and then the United States and its European allies introduced Afghans to democracy and modernization and that the country's failings are entirely the fault of Afghans themselves. Punctuated by Biden's invocation of Afghanistan as "the graveyard of empires," a place that could never be "stable, united, and secure," these very ideas guided Washington's withdrawal from Afghanistan and American resignation in the face of the collapse of the US-backed republic and the return of the Taliban to power in August 2021. Conversely, when scholars take into account local and diasporic political contestations, cultural productions, and social movements, as the writers in this book do, they upend the false binaries and simplistic discourses of progress and failure that undergird imperial humanitarian/human rights intervention.

Afghan Decoloniality in Global
Comparative Perspective

Including Afghanistan in colonial studies, then, is also a decolonial move because it refuses to consider Afghanistan as a political and cultural anomaly. Instead, it situates Afghanistan within a broader conversation on imperialism and sovereignty. Recognizing its meaningful resonances with other contexts makes it possible to draw connections and build transnational decolonial solidarity and futures. As described earlier, throughout most of the modern era, Afghanistan has survived in the face of enormous colonial pressures exerted by multiple states, though it has done so by preserving various aspects of sovereignty as a quasi-colonized state. As a quasi-colonized nation-state with semisovereignty over its own affairs, Afghanistan could be considered an example of what anthropologist and Indigenous studies scholar Audra Simpson has called "nested sovereignty" (2016). "Nested sovereignty" refers to how Indigenous models of self-rule may persist within the broader sovereignty paradigm of the settler colonial state. Over the last forty years, Afghanistan has been subject to what Carole McGranahan and Ann Laura Stoler have termed "imperial formations" (2009, 8). For all of their professed ideological differences, Soviet and US elites facilitated a logic of governance in which the autonomy of Afghans would be, to use McGranahan and Stoler's language, at once "partial" and "deferred." Imagining a break from a past stamped by backwardness and brutality, both the Soviet and US imperial projects promised liberation and the capacity to make (at least some) Afghans modern. Similar to the political contexts analyzed by McGranahan and Stoler, colonizers in Afghanistan envisioned "new subjects that must be relocated to be productive and exploitable, dispossessed to be modern, disciplined to be independent, converted to be human, stripped of old cultural bearings to be citizens, coerced to be free" (2009, 8).

There are several more parallels that could be explored between Afghanistan and contemporary imperial formations and colonial dynamics elsewhere, such as in Haiti (Hudson 2017; Pierre 2023), Puerto Rico (Bonilla and LeBrón 2019), the Pacific Islands (Kim 2023), and Palestine (Ayyash 2019; Erakat 2019; Yaqub 2023). While refusing to make historical equivalences, we suggest that the long histories of colonial rule, experiences of mass displacement, and politically active diasporas in those contexts offer important nodes of comparison. As Jemima Pierre (2023) and Peter James Hudson (2017) have written, the US imperial project in

Haiti has involved the outsourcing of control to other countries in the Caribbean and Latin America. The United States and Canada's backing of a Kenyan ground troop invasion of Haiti is the most recent example of this. The multinational coalition of peacekeeping troops, financial advisors, and humanitarian aid workers has functioned to keep Haiti in dependent relationships and quell more revolutionary efforts toward self-determination. Similarly, imperialism in Afghanistan (while led in the last two decades by the United States) has involved a multinational collective of countries and their aid and military apparatuses providing multilateral cover to the imperial project. Likewise, a multiethnic group of people from the Afghan diaspora have been recruited to do the work of nation-building, in the name of humanitarianism and empowerment. In that sense, the War on Terror was as much about cultivating new political subjects at home and abroad—who could see themselves as empowered and as part of the reconstructed civil society of a "failed state"—as it was about the imperial state winning battles.

The case of Puerto Rico also offers important examples for critically assessing the difficulties of reclaiming sovereignty in contexts of prolonged imperial rule. As Yarimar Bonilla writes, in order to "unsettle sovereignty" and transcend its "constrained forms," it is necessary to question the desire to be included by the empire: "I repeatedly say that when allies feel the need to assert that Puerto Ricans are US citizens, they should instead ask themselves if what really needs to be asserted is that the US is an empire" (2020). As Jodi Kim (2023) has recently shown in *Settler Garrison: Debt Imperialism, Militarism, and Transpacific Imaginaries*, US colonial occupations in the Caribbean and Pacific used inclusive language to justify ongoing rule. These places were situated as part of the "domestic US" as unincorporated territories, and their subjects were referred to as US nationals. Such an arrangement allowed imperial control over certain aspects of life but also ensured the steady flow of labor migration to the US mainland. "Sovereignty" was marked by both selective care and extractivism. Kim's exploration of the US occupation in the Pacific also reveals a form of metapolitical authority through the use of debt imperialism and military dependency to indirectly rule over sovereign nations (2023).

Similar discussions are unfolding regarding which Afghan subjects are deserving of being given refuge by the US government in the aftermath of war. When organizations increasingly use the language of allyship to make the case that Afghans working as interpreters and other military personnel must be given refuge to express gratitude for their service to the US military, what does such a claim imply about other Afghans who had no association with the US government during the war? What "non-allies" are produced in such discourses of inclusion and worthiness? What kinds of conditions do people need to meet in order to be embraced and protected by the empire? Studies have shown that marginalized communities, including the subaltern/colonized, immigrants, people of color, LGBTQ people, and women have used their incorporation into and service to the security state apparatus to improve their second-class status and partial inclusion at the expense of their own and other marginalized communities (Osman 2019c; Puar 2007). The mass displacement wrought by the 2021 military withdrawal affected people from a range of class backgrounds and statuses and shed light on the hierarchies of "grievability" and "suffering" that underpins the US immigration system and war in Afghanistan more generally, hence determining who is viewed as worthy of extraction and refuge (Butler 2009; Fassin 2012). Tausif Noor's, Gazelle Samizay's, and Helena Zeweri's chapters in this volume offer important case studies on how postwithdrawal Afghans and diasporic Afghans have collectively organized and mobilized against these exclusionary and racist systems through art and activism. Paniz Musawi Natanzi has also shown the limits of working within European state institutions of art and culture, which readily fund but also actively censor Afghan creatives who critique NATO's mission in Afghanistan (2024). The limits on free media and public protest in the West are also coming into sharp focus with the violent crackdowns on protestors and firings of critics of the US-backed Israeli genocide in Gaza. Likewise, the rise and spread of anti-immigrant movements across Europe and North America are revealing the limits of even selective care and partial inclusion.

Afghanistan and the Colonial Knowledge Economy: Gatekeeping, Producing, and Censoring

At the root of the various colonial projects that have targeted Afghanistan in the modern era has been the impulse to create knowledge about the country and its peoples that would serve colonial power. Since the early nineteenth century, knowledge about Afghanistan has been entangled with British, Russian, European, and, later, Soviet and American colonial exploits. British colonial authorities claiming expertise about all matters related to Afghans and Afghanistan have left a long legacy that has colored how the world has imagined Afghanistan to the present. "The epistemological impact of British colonialism," argues Shah Mahmoud Hanifi, "determined the categories used to understand Afghanistan" (2012, 89). The career of Mountstuart Elphinstone (1779–1859), a Scottish statesman whose work influenced British colonial knowledge projects, is a good example of how the colonial apparatus appropriates research for its own benefit. As Nivi Manchanda has shown, Elphinstone himself was interested in delineating the similarities between his own Scottish clan and various communities in Afghanistan (2020). However, many of his problematic generalizations about Pashtuns being troublesome and unruly were reappropriated by British diplomats in future colonial missions and used to justify the need for British control. These early racist colonial tropes gained neocolonial currency in the War on Terror, as Pashtuns were recast as "terrorists" and "criminals" by the imperialists, which was then taken up by local "partner governments" in Afghanistan and Pakistan (Durrani 2022; Osman 2020; Wardak 2018).

In the late twentieth century, the USSR, too, generated colonial knowledge about Afghanistan to justify Soviet interventions and rule. Where the Kremlin saw leftist allies whose floundering revolution needed "saving" by Red Army troops in 1979, President Ronald Reagan would frame the Afghan opposition, the mujahideen, as like-minded "freedom fighters." Moscow condemned them as "terrorists," while Washington embraced them as crucial partners in a global cold war. For some of the mujahideen, the lesson of their military victory over the Red Army and the Soviet withdrawal was that jihad (a "holy struggle" or "war" undertaken in the name of Islam) provided a roadmap for the future of Afghanistan—and the world. It is important to note that the United States, Pakistan, and Saudi Arabia— partners in driving the Soviets from Afghanistan—played a key role in fomenting the jihad. They funded madrassas (religious schools), provided textbooks that reified jihad with lessons like "*J* [*jeem* in the local languages] is for Jihad," and indoctrinated poor Afghan orphan and refugee boys in the border towns of Pakistan and Iran in Islamism and militancy. For many observers, the Soviet defeat in Afghanistan appeared to be proof of the failure of Soviet socialism and of the inevitable triumph of "the West." American elites remained confident that the inability of the Soviets to defeat Afghan rebels pointed to flaws in how the Soviets conducted warfare, highlighting their brutal disregard for civilian casualties.

Paradoxically, the Soviet approach to Afghanistan had been built on a very different view of "friendship" between Afghans and themselves (to use the language that framed expert discussions of Afghan politics in St. Petersburg and Moscow; see Robert D. Crews's chapter). Like the British, Russian and later Soviet experts developed a mapping of Afghanistan's diverse populations that drew on contemporary Orientalist tropes and imaginings. Russian and Soviet elites were particularly drawn to understanding—and manipulating—ethnic and religious differences among communities in Afghanistan. Afghanistan appeared to be a potential anti-British ally, with Pashtuns—whom Russian and Soviet observers viewed as innately unruly—seeming to be ripe for incitement to rebellion against British control of the Indo-Afghan frontier. Simultaneously, in the north of Afghanistan they identified non-Pashtun communities who had suffered exploitation by Afghan authorities and who thus seemed amenable to rebelling against the Afghan state itself in the event of necessity. What they imagined to be the "anti-colonial" and "anti-imperialist" instincts of Afghans appeared as a powerful force lying dormant until awakened by Russian or Soviet "friends" during their invasion and ten-year occupation. A sense of failed "friendship," of mutual incomprehension, and of alienation from their ostensible allies and the physical space of Afghanistan ultimately undermined Soviet confidence in their mission and, crucially, fueled a violent hostility toward the Afghan population as a whole.

Beginning in 2001, the US-led Global War on Terror produced its own technocratic experts to explain Afghanistan in ways that facilitated colonial control. From the outset, American officials pledged to avoid the pitfalls that seemed to make the Soviets so unwelcome and to prove that this was a wholly different kind of intervention. The American project produced a wide-ranging interest in the country and an influx across a number of domains—including policymakers, NGO practitioners, aid workers, media makers, and the US military. Yet their multipronged approach and wide-ranging nation-building projects were still undergirded by and viewed through the prism of military, policy, and war. The recruitment of academic knowledge informed counterinsurgency approaches and was essential to projects such as the "Human Terrain System," a technique of mapping Afghan communities based on the proposition that anthropological knowledge was necessary to pacify them. Nomi Stone's ethnography of Iraq War simulation actors sums up the relationship between knowledge about the distant "other" and its military domination. These simulations, Stone writes, "offer another iteration in the long history of the entanglement between militarism and 'culture' and the 'human sciences.' . . . In this history, cultural knowledge has long danced with conflict, from anthropology's colonial beginnings, through World War II, the Cold War, the Vietnam War, and the present" (2022, 8). This is echoed by Morwari Zafar's chapter in this volume, "Operationalizing 'Afghan Culture': Role-Playing and Translation in US Military Counterinsurgency Training," which examines how Afghan Americans and "Afghan culture" were operationalized in US military training in biased ways that presented backwardness, conflict, and terrorism as extensions of Afghan cultural and social values. At the same time, various organizations also utilized academic scholarship (much as Elphinstone's was used) to aid and abet more "benign" projects such as USAID gender-empowerment activities and infrastructural development, some of which proved to be shortsighted and mired in corruption (Kandiyoti 2005; Khan 2015; Osman 2020; SIGAR 2018; see Purnima Bose's chapter).

Research and learning about Afghanistan in the post-9/11 era were thus highly refracted through a military and policy lens and was designed to be useful to think tanks and research institutes that were either formally or loosely affiliated with the US/NATO military and development projects. "As a consequence of the current US-led war in Afghanistan," writes Munazza Ebtikar, "the Anglophone work produced on Afghanistan directly influences the ways in which Washington perceives the country and its inhabitants. The power to represent and theorize about Afghanistan is located in the West, which has produced knowledge to establish economic, political, and cultural power over the region and its inhabitants" (2020). In sum, emissaries of knowledge have always been needed in emergent colonial economies of knowledge production.

Much like during the heyday of colonialism, during the twenty-year Global War on Terror, colonial knowledge abounded. But that abundance of colonial knowledge has also proved dangerously narrow and violently myopic and "produced a more intense silencing of Afghan voices" (Zeweri 2022, 10). Afghans and diasporic Afghans who have not properly expressed their gratitude to the imperial state or, worse yet, have been critical of it have been silenced, censored, and cut off from the comforts and privileges of empire. We see this in the silencing of Afghan and Pakistani activists like Malalai Joya and Malala Yousafzai and women's movements when they break from the imperial feminist "victim/savior" script to hold the US ruling elite accountable for the rise of Islamism and extremism in their homelands (Osman 2019a). Relatedly, the same media pundits and politicians who vociferously clamored on behalf of Afghan women's rights post-9/11, turning the spotlight on Afghan women's plight under the Taliban in their first incarnation, are, postwithdrawal, eerily silent. They have turned their spotlight away from Afghan women's suffering and protest movements against the Taliban 2.0, highlighting the duplicity of the imperial feminist agenda to "save Afghan women" (Osman and Bajoghli 2024). Feminists from the region are caught between fighting local misogynist hardliners, who suppress women's rights in the name of "anti-imperialist" national unity and security, and Western misogynist war hawks, who readily use their activism as a ruse to further their imperial incursions and calls for regime change. That is why, in the case of Iran, where women's rights have been suppressed since the 1979 revolution, Manijeh Moradian has called for an "intersectional anti-imperialism," making connections between domestic and foreign structures of violence (2021, 214–246).

Mechanisms of imperial censorship, erasure, and policing are always evolving and expanding, extending to the study of decoloniality. The same right-wing circles who have been attacking and policing critical race theory (CRT) and diversity, equity, and inclusion (DEI) initiatives are also attacking decolonial studies by trying to ban books, theories, and even the words themselves. They fear historical and present-day truths and calls for justice and parity. When it comes to Afghanistan, the stakes of knowledge production have always been high, as knowledge has directly impacted the ways that imperial powers have engaged in Afghanistan and therefore impacted how Afghan civilians have been treated in the international system.

Decolonial Alternatives and Futures

Our book challenges the dominant narratives that, since 2001, have sought to justify a military-led nation-building project in Afghanistan. One of the central claims made by the military-knowledge-policy apparatus following the American withdrawal from Afghanistan was that this intervention was a more benign form of imperial rule than others (see Wazhmah Osman's chapter in this volume). Yet, in analyzing such claims, we must revisit the question, Whose lives and voices mattered, and whose were sidelined? What kinds of analyses were considered important, and to what end was information mobilized? This means taking an inventory of the recent colonial past and present by revealing their erasures *and* recovering and telling the indigenous, local, and diasporic stories that were never told.

The contributors to this volume do just that: Building on their cultural connections and fluency, they present Afghanistan in terms unfettered by the overlapping hegemony of pundits, politicians, and scholars. In this way, the book represents a critical intervention in knowledge production about Afghanistan. By offering critical perspectives on the nexus of academic and military knowledge production, we show how Afghanistan and its diaspora are and have been a transnational and globally mobile society deeply attuned to global developments, communication technologies, and the flow of ideas and discourses about Afghans and Afghanistan, rather than apolitical subjects who passively accept imperial interventions and knowledge. We explore how Afghanistan and its diasporas remain deeply aware of, impacted by, and still in the throes of colonial and imperial matrices of power.

Indeed, decolonial studies is increasingly moving in the direction of "thinking otherwise," as significantly laid out in other edited volumes and series such as *On Decoloniality* (Mignolo and Walsh 2018) and *Constructing the Pluriverse* (Reiter 2018). For Walter Mignolo and Catherine Walsh, decoloniality must be an affirmative epistemological project that is rooted in highlighting the pluriverse, the many "local histories, subjectivities, knowledges, narratives, and struggles against the modern/colonial order and for an otherwise." In that sense, Mignolo and Walsh seek to highlight movements, efforts, and projects that move beyond "resistance" and toward "re-existence," which they define, borrowing from Adolfo Albán Achinte, as "'the redefining and re-signifying of life in conditions of dignity'" (2018, 3). Likewise, Zahra Ali, referring to her "Critical Studies of Iraq" initiative—but equally applicable to Afghanistan—writes that we need to foster "the development of an independent research agenda [as] opposed to research 'on Iraq,'" one that sustains "critical thinking, social justice, and peace" and imagines a future beyond empire and violence (2024, 421). In an imperial ecosystem where Afghanistan has always been "spoken for" in the words of Nivi Manchanda (see her chapter), criticism featuring the contributions of Afghan heritage scholars, activists, journalists, and artists, as well as other ground-up perspectives that are usually sidelined or silenced by the establishment, like those included in this book, is an affirmative step toward decolonization.

In the analyses developed throughout this volume, we open up intellectual space to think more affirmatively about what decoloniality as a political, epistemological, and cultural project can look like in Afghanistan and its diasporas—a project that values all people and believes that basic human rights to freedom, justice, resources, peace, and life should not be contingent on service and servitude to the imperial state. Part of this epistemological effort is to undo the racist preconception of Afghans and Afghanistan as politically and culturally insular—by contrast, the country's cultural lineages, its political histories, and its many intellectual traditions are shaped by a range of transnational and global encounters, which this volume highlights.

Taking inspiration from Amahl Bishara's analysis of decolonizing anthropology, such work "requires an expansion of the bounds of politics, consideration of who can participate, and reconsideration of what the goals of political action are. It entails working toward liberations that are always plural" (2023, 396). Thus, decolonization also means creating spaces that value a plurality of voices, lived experiences, and positionalities. Due to long-standing global inequalities, almost a half century of war, mass displacement, and precarious access to academic institutions, Afghan-heritage scholars have rarely found it easy to access or navigate institutions that produce, disseminate, and market academic knowledge (Daulatzai et al. 2022). These include but are not limited to universities (as graduate students, faculty), academic journals, policy research institutes, and government agencies. The voices of Afghan nationals, diasporic Afghans, ethnic minorities and sexual minorities, nonacademics, and practitioners who speak critically of the war have been especially marginalized from both public discourse and academic conversations about Afghanistan, while the voices of those who perpetuate the dominant discourse, despite usually having little or no cultural or language fluency or connection, are often exalted and given the platforms to speak for Afghans and determine policy (Daulatzai et al. 2022).

Over the course of the US war and even since the American withdrawal, there have been numerous conferences, symposiums, plenaries, publications, task forces, and other public and private forums at universities and other venues about various aspects of Afghanistan, including women's rights, archives and archaeology, arts and culture, and its political future more broadly, without the inclusion of any Afghan or Afghan diasporic experts. For example, the congressionally mandated Afghanistan War Commission, tasked with assessing the US war in Afghanistan thus far has no Afghan or Afghan American commissioners or academics. Like the many other examples of censorship and erasure shared throughout the volume, these occlusions too are a form of silencing. After all, as scholars of feminist science studies (e.g., Donna Haraway, Sandra Harding, Londa Schiebinger, and Lorraine Daston) and revisionist anthropologists (e.g., Faye Ginsburg) have posited through "standpoint epistemology" and the "parallax effect," different points of view frame and explain the same phenomenon in different ways, sometimes complementary and sometimes not. For example, when it comes to the highly scrutinized gender and sexuality practices and problems of Middle Easterners and Asians, heritage and hyphenated or hybrid scholars have explained and framed hot-button issues like honor (*namus/namoos*), honor killings, homosociality, queerness, *bacha bazi* (pederasty), *bacha posh* (girls dressing as boys), and *baad* exchanges (offering girls in marriage to resolve blood feuds) entirely differently and in more complex and less sensationalistic terms than their Western counterparts (Abdi 2024; Abu-Lughod 1998; Ali 2018; Manchanda 2015; Munhazim 2025; Najmabadi 2005; Osman 2020, 2023; Shakhsari 2012; see Zafar's chapter in this volume).

While pointing to this erasure, we recognize that many non-Afghans, including the ones featured in this volume, have written thoughtfully about the country and that, likewise, some Afghan scholars have fallen into parochialism and bias in their analyses. Our point is not to neatly delineate who can speak but rather to center perspectives that provide alternatives to those traditionally centered when generating knowledge about Afghanistan, be it in academia, policy circles, news, or development. It would be shortsighted to suggest that decolonizing knowledge about Afghanistan begins or ends with the racial and ethnic makeup of those who produce knowledge. As scholars of multiculturalism have written, multiculturalism, while an important tool for expanding whose experiences get to shape policy and discourse, can also fall short of actually overhauling discriminatory and supremacist structures and their underlying premises, by tending to privilege a politics of recognition over a politics of transformation (Hale 2002; Povinelli 2002). At the same time, the right-wing and "nativist" attacks on diversity initiatives in US universities will further decrease the hiring and retention of minority scholars. Put affirmatively, to paraphrase Black and Indigenous feminist activists and scholars, if our oppression is linked then so is our liberation and so let us work together (Angela Davis qtd. in Matthews 2017; Watson 1988). Therefore, creating a just pluriverse requires building solidarity and support across disciplinary, racial, and political divides of decolonial studies, critical race theory, area studies, and Indigenous studies and being in dialogue and learning from one another (Ali and Dayan-Herzbrun 2024; Chakravartty and Jackson 2020; Osman 2019c).

Yet if we continue to privilege the hegemonic discourse of the imperial ruling elite and their sociopolitical industries, they will continue to deal in the usual racial pathologizing and securitized diagnosis, deeming some Afghans valuable and others dangerous to empire, thus dooming Afghanistan to their imperial fantasies of endless wars. Instead, the contributors and editors of this volume, representing a multiplicity of ethnicities, races, and nationalities, offer new analyses, ideas, and case studies to demonstrate that Afghan society and its diasporas are talking back to imperial power and are both envisioning and building a democratic Afghanistan that is part of a global community where everyone has the right to a just and peaceful life: This simple shift in thinking is a decolonial turning point for Afghanistan and Afghan studies.

Volume Overview: Decolonization in Practice

The chapters that follow showcase the many contexts in which various actors have questioned, subverted, and resisted, but also facilitated, colonial power relations. Our authors interrogate the ways in which imperial and colonial projects and imaginaries have historically organized knowledge production about Afghanistan. In particular, they explore the infrastructures, forms of cultural expertise, and technologies that undergirded the US-led War on Terror from 2001 to the present. They also investigate gender politics; the diaspora's use of art, literature, and social media; the relationship between wartime media and propaganda; and the possibilities and challenges of circulating alternative representations of the country and its people in Afghan and diasporic media over the past twenty years.

Decolonizing Afghanistan is organized into four parts. Part 1 examines the historical roots of imperial knowledge production about Afghanistan and how it has manifested in the present. Nivi Manchanda examines the historical mobilization of the tropes of the "graveyard of empires" and "the Great Game" as symptoms of a colonial desire to make sense of Afghanistan while continuing to obfuscate its realities. Robert D. Crews examines the emergence and transformation of the Soviet colonial archive and its consequences for the Soviet war in Afghanistan between 1979 and 1989 and for the post-2001 American project. Wazhmah Osman reckons with the contradictions of the American empire, tracking the United States' rise as an imperial global power, its propensity for violence, and the deployment of its vast development apparatus.

Part 2 explores the impact of the discursive and technological infrastructures of power that unfolded during the War on Terror. In an ethnographic account focusing on the role of Afghan Americans in counterinsurgency operations, Morwari Zafar shows how training exercises enacted with the "imperial gaze" repackaged and reenacted "Afghan culture" as a commodified object of knowledge. Journalist Matthieu Aikins examines how the neo-imperial army distanced itself from the bloodshed of civilian casualties via outsourcing to its network of Western-funded private security contractors and how they in turn undermined state-building. Probing another key aspect of colonial knowledge production, Ali Karimi examines how the United States pursued domination of Afghanistan through biometric technologies of identification, which, he argues, reflected the paradox of "too much information and too little knowledge" characteristic of the operative logics of the American intervention.

Part 3 delves into the politics and optics of representations, exploring the salience of media, propaganda, and public relations to the workings of modern warfare and empire. Starting chronologically, Marya Hannun examines how in the early twentieth century gender politics in postindependence Afghanistan became a key object of not only Western but regional conversations around modernity, coloniality, and anti-coloniality. Shifting to investigate transnational media circulation, Hosai Qasmi explores the ways in which Indian cinema's interpellation of Afghans has not been immune from Orientalizing tendencies. She tracks the rise of epic historical Hindutva films about Afghan invasions and despotism and the ways they perpetuate present-day Islamophobia. Purnima Bose critiques the postwithdrawal narratives about Afghan women and their "development idealism" that have resurfaced across media outlets. She argues that these narratives erase earlier traditions of Afghan women's resistance to the Taliban, create a nostalgic view of US occupation, and universalize the experiences of urban Afghan women. Lastly, Dawood Azami examines how US authorities, as part of their counterinsurgency efforts, and the Taliban, as part of their insurgency efforts, waged battles for "hearts and minds" through a variety of media technologies, including radio, television, and print. Azami shows how marketing the war ultimately proved to be futile in a landscape marked by ongoing dehumanization and the violence wrought against social life.

Part 4 looks at how Afghan literature and art evidence a long and rich lineage of political dissent and resistance to colonial paradigms of knowledge. While many of the authors are intricately connected to the subjects of their research by virtue of their Afghan background, the latter chapters take a more directly autoethnographic approach, and/or focus on more direct responses and reflections from Afghans, which offers novel forms of embodied and experiential understandings of self–other relationships. Helena Zeweri examines Afghan Americans' public critiques of the US immigration system in the aftermath of the evacuations, thereby illustrating how humanitarian crisis can heighten diasporic political consciousness of the effects of imperialism. Sabauon Nasseri examines short fiction written between 2001 and 2021 by Afghan authors who connect the everyday survival strategies during the Afghan Civil War (1992–1996) to those of the post-2001 period. Nasseri's chapter provides a window into how Afghans have conceptualized the interplay of eras marked by successive regimes of occupation and violence. Such writers, Nasseri argues, unsettle the typical historical narrative of Afghanistan that sees it devolve from a Cold War battleground to a terrorist haven, and from a site of communist aspirations to a site of mujahideen resistance and Taliban authoritarianism. Tausif Noor examines how Afghan diasporic artists reflect on the legacy of the US presence in Afghanistan and resist the tropes of Afghans as disempowered and dependent on US military and humanitarian aid. In an autoethnographic reflection, Gazelle Samizay provides an up-close look at how four hyphenated Afghan artists, including her, responded to the postwithdrawal moment. She delves into how this experience of evacuating some Afghans and not others prompted new entry points for art as dissent in the diaspora, specifically critiques of the US immigration system and of global borders more broadly. And in her exploration of the experiences of Uzbek/Turkic minoritized communities, Zohra Saed, building on interviews with her Baba (father), examines the internal and foreign colonialism and injustices that marginalized communities in the north faced and shows the layers of disparate lived experiences at the intersection of gender, class, and ethnicity/race. Finally, in her coda, Paula Chakravartty reflects on the volume as a whole, drawing connections across chapters and highlighting key threads that emerge. She underscores the power of colonial and imperial geopolitics that have produced the conditions for perpetual war and destruction for almost half a century, drawing connections to the imperially sponsored genocide unfolding in Gaza.

Decolonizing Afghanistan focuses not only on the administrative and explicitly violent effects of empire but on how empire impacts people's everyday lives, senses of identity, and the political mobilizations that emerge in the wake of imperial war and withdrawal. In a historical moment in which Afghan nationals, refugees, and diasporic peoples are encountering long-standing as well as new stereotypes about who they are, it is especially important to connect those misrepresentations to early colonial and neo-imperial narratives and missions. Such tropes include the Afghan refugee as a passive suffering subject, Afghan women as only *now* politically conscious, and diasporic peoples and displaced Afghans (specifically former interpreters for the US military) as loyal cultural experts who ideologically believed in the US/NATO war. Long after the US "forever war" and its disastrous conclusion, these reductive characterizations continue to circulate, framing the war as filled with strategic and policy errors while failing to question its premises, its human consequences, or the deeply entrenched ways that the Afghan government and nongovernment actors colluded with US and NATO forces to produce the conditions that led to the Taliban takeover of the government in August 2021. Imperial formations, however, are not failures. They succeeded in the death, destruction, and havoc they have caused in the lives of Afghans all over the world. The authors of the chapters that follow insist it is time to reckon with what has happened.

References

Abdi, Ali. 2024. "The Afghan *Murat*: A Queer Subject at Transnational Crossroads." *Men and Masculinities* 27 (4): 355–374. https://doi.org/10.1177/1097184X241273240.

Abrahamian, Ervand. 2013. *The Coup: 1953, the CIA, and the Roots of Modern U.S.–Iranian Relations.* New York: New Press.

Abu-Lughod, Lila, ed. 1998. *Remaking Women: Feminism and Modernity in the Middle East.* Princeton, NJ: Princeton University Press.

Ahmed, Manan. 2011. "Adam's Mirror: The Frontier in the Imperial Imagination." *Economic and Political Weekly* 46 (13): 60–65.

Aikins, Matthieu. 2021. "How One Looted Artifact Tells the Story of Modern Afghanistan." *New York Times*, updated March 8, 2021. https://www.nytimes.com/2021/03/04/magazine/ghazni-panels-afghanistan-art.html.

Ali, Zahra. 2018. *Women and Gender in Iraq.* Cambridge: Cambridge University Press.

Ali, Zahra. 2024. "Politicizing Ethics: Decolonizing Research on Iraq." *Comparative Studies of South Asia, Africa and the Middle East* 44 (3): 418–422.

Ali, Zahra, and Sonia Dayan-Herzbrun, eds. 2024. *Decolonial Pluriversalism*. Lanham, MD: Rowman and Littlefield.

Asad, Talal. 1973. *Anthropology and the Colonial Encounter*. London: Ithaca Press.

Ayyash, Mark Mohammad. 2019. *Hermeneutics of Violence: A Four-Dimensional Conception*. Toronto: University of Toronto Press.

Bahrani, Zainab. 2023. "Iraq: Creative Destruction and Cultural Heritage in the Warscape." In *The Routledge Handbook of Heritage Destruction*, edited by José Antonio González Zarandona, Emma Cunliffe, and Melathi Saldin, 313–321. London: Routledge.

Bahrani, Zainab. 2025. *War Essays*. London: UCL Press.

Bishara, Amahl. 2023. "Decolonizing Middle East Anthropology: Toward Liberations in SWANA Societies." *American Ethnologist* 50 (3): 396–408.

Bonilla, Yarimar. 2020. "Public Thinker: Yarimar Bonilla on Decolonizing Decolonization." Interview by Ryan Cecil Jobson. *Public Books*, May 27. https://www.publicbooks.org/public-thinker-yarimar-bonilla-on-decolonizing-decolonization/.

Bonilla, Yarimar, and Marisol LeBrón. 2019. "Introduction: Aftershocks of Disaster." In *Aftershocks of Disaster: Puerto Rico Before and After the Storm*, edited by Yarimar Bonilla and Marisol LeBrón, 1–17. Chicago: Haymarket Books.

Bose, Purnima. 2020. *Intervention Narratives: Afghanistan, the United States, and the Global War on Terror*. New Brunswick, NJ: Rutgers University Press.

Butler, Judith. 2009. *Frames of War: When Is Life Grievable?* New York: Verso.

Chakravartty, Paula, and Sarah J. Jackson. 2020. "The Disavowal of Race in Communication Theory." *Communication and Critical/Cultural Studies* 17 (2): 210–219. https://doi.org/10.1080/14791420.2020.1771743.

Chatterjee, Partha. 1997. "Our Modernity." In *South-South Exchange Programme for Research on the History of Development and the Council for the Development of Social Science Research in Africa*, 1–20. Selangor, Malaysia: Vinlin Press.

Chiovenda, Andrea. 2019. *Crafting Masculine Selves: Culture, War, and Psychodynamics in Afghanistan*. Oxford: Oxford University Press.

Coburn, Noah, and Anna Larson. 2014. *Derailing Democracy in Afghanistan: Elections in an Unstable Political Landscape*. New York: Columbia University Press.

Cooper, Timothy P. A. 2024a. *Moral Atmospheres: Islam and Media in a Pakistani Marketplace*. New York: Columbia University Press.

Cooper, Timothy P. A. 2024b. "The Situation of the Interface: Pashto Master Copies and Data Migration in Sharjah." *American Ethnologist* 51 (2): 181–192.

Crews, Robert D. 2015. *Afghan Modern: The History of a Global Nation*. Cambridge, MA: Harvard University Press.

Daulatzai, Anila. 2008. "The Discursive Occupation of Afghanistan." *British Journal of Middle Eastern Studies* 35 (3): 419–435. https://doi.org/10.1080/13530190802532953.

Daulatzai, Anila, Sahar Ghumkhor, and Saadia Toor. 2022. "Grievance as Movement: Conversations on Knowledge Production on Afghanistan and the Left." *Jadaliyya*, October 6. https://www.jadaliyya.com/Details/44486.

Durrani, Mariam. 2022. "The Imperial Optic: Mapping the Impact of the Global War on Terror on Higher Education in the US and Pakistan." *Transforming Anthropology* 30 (1): 66–79. https://doi.org/10.1111/traa.12230.

Ebtikar, Munazza. 2020. "A Critique of Knowledge Production About Afghanistan." Afghanistan Center at Kabul University, February 17. https://acku.edu.af/a-critique-of-knowledge-production-about-afghanistan/.

Elyachar, Julia. 2025. *On the Semicivilized: Coloniality, Finance, and Embodied Sovereignty in Cairo.* Durham, NC: Duke University Press.

Erakat, Noura. 2019. *Justice for Some: Law and the Question of Palestine.* Stanford, CA: Stanford University Press.

Fahmy, Khaled. 2009. *Mehmed Ali: From Ottoman Governor to Ruler of Egypt.* London: Oneworld Publications.

Fanon, Frantz. (1967) 2008. *Black Skin, White Masks.* Translated by Richard Philcox. New York: Grove.

Fassin, Didier. 2012. *Humanitarian Reason: A Moral History of the Present.* Berkeley: University of California Press.

Feroozi, Abdul Wasey. 2004. "The Impact of War upon Afghanistan's Cultural Heritage." Paper published by the Archaeological Institute of America, March. https://www.archaeological.org/pdfs/papers/AIA_Afghanistan_address_highres.pdf.

Ghani, Ashraf, and Clare Lockhart. 2008. *Fixing Failed States: A Framework for Rebuilding a Fractured World.* Oxford: Oxford University Press.

Ginsburg, Faye D., Lila Abu-Lughod, and Brian Larkin, eds. 2002. *Media Worlds: Anthropology on New Terrain.* Berkeley: University of California Press.

González Zarandona, José Antonio, Emma Cunliffe, and Melathi Saldin, eds. 2023. *The Routledge Handbook of Heritage Destruction.* London: Routledge.

Grewal, Inderpal. 2013. "Outsourcing Patriarchy: Feminist Encounters, Transnational Mediations, and the Crime of 'Honour Killings.'" *International Feminist Journal of Politics* 15 (1): 1–19.

Hale, Charles R. 2002. "Does Multiculturalism Menace? Governance, Cultural Rights and the Politics of Identity in Guatemala." *Journal of Latin American Studies* 34 (3): 485–524.

Hanifi, Shah Mahmoud. 2011. *Connecting Histories in Afghanistan: Market Relations and State Formation on a Colonial Frontier.* Stanford, CA: Stanford University Press.

Hanifi, Shah Mahmoud. 2012. "Quandaries of the Afghan Nation." In *Under the Drones: Modern Lives in the Afghanistan-Pakistan Borderlands*, edited by Shahzad Bashir and Robert Crews, 83–101. Cambridge, MA: Harvard University Press.

Hopkins, Benjamin D. 2020. *Ruling the Savage Periphery: Frontier Governance and the Making of the Modern State*. Cambridge, MA: Harvard University Press.

Hopkins, Benjamin D. 2022. Review of *Imagining Afghanistan*, by Nivi Manchanda. *Space and Society*, February 25. https://www.societyandspace.org/articles/review-of-imagining-afghanistan-3.

Hopkins, Benjamin D., and Magnus Marsden. 2012. *Fragments of the Afghan Frontier*. New York: Hurst.

Hudson, Peter James. 2017. *Bankers and Empire: How Wall Street Colonized the Caribbean*. Chicago: University of Chicago Press.

Ivanchikova, Alla. 2019. *Imagining Afghanistan: Global Fiction and Film of the 9/11 Wars*. West Lafayette, IN: Purdue University Press.

Kandiyoti, Deniz. 2005. "The Politics of Gender and Reconstruction in Afghanistan." UNRISD Special Events Paper 4. http://www.unrisd.org/80256B3C005BCCF9/(httpPublications)/3050BE40DA5B871CC125704400534A7A?OpenDocument.

Kazi, Nazia. 2019. *Islamophobia, Race, and Gender Politics*. New York: Rowman and Littlefield.

Khan, Azmat. 2015. "Ghost Students, Ghost Teachers, and Ghost Schools." *BuzzFeed News*, July 9. https://www.buzzfeednews.com/article/azmatkhan/the-big-lie-that-helped-justify-americas-war-in-afghanistan#.scBrrwpQm.

Kim, Jodi. 2023. *Settler Garrison: Debt Imperialism, Militarism, and Transpacific Imaginaries*. Durham, NC: Duke University Press.

Kumar, Deepa. (2012) 2021. *Islamophobia and the Politics of Empire*. Chicago: Haymarket Books.

Kundnani, Arun. 2014. *The Muslims Are Coming! Islamophobia, Extremism, and the Domestic War on Terror*. London: Verso.

Leake, Elisabeth. 2022. "States, Nations, and Self-Determination: Afghanistan and Decolonization at the United Nations." *Journal of Global History* 17 (2): 272–291.

Manchanda, Nivi. 2015. "Queering the Pashtun: Afghan Sexuality in the Homo-Nationalist Imaginary." *Third World Quarterly* 36 (1): 130–146.

Manchanda, Nivi. 2017. "Rendering Afghanistan Legible: Borders, Frontiers and the 'State' of Afghanistan." *Politics* 37 (4): 386–401.

Manchanda, Nivi. 2020. *Imagining Afghanistan: The History and Politics of Imperial Knowledge*. Cambridge: Cambridge University Press.

Masood, Syeda Q. 2024. "Empire and Identity: Racialization of the Afghan Middle Class Under U.S. Occupation." PhD diss., Brown University.

Massoumi, Mejgan. 2021. "The Sounds of Kabul: Radio and the Politics of Popular Culture in Afghanistan, 1960–79." PhD diss., Stanford University.

Massoumi, Mejgan. 2022. "Soundwaves of Dissent: Resistance Through Persianate Cultural Production in Afghanistan." *Iranian Studies* 55 (3): 697–718.

Matthews, Lyndsay. 2017. "Here's the Full Transcript of Angela Davis's
Women's March Speech." *Elle*, January 21. https://www.elle.com/culture
/career-politics/a42337/angela-davis-womens-march-speech-full-transcript/.

McGranahan, Carole, and Ann Laura Stoler. 2009. "Introduction: Refiguring
Imperial Terrains." In *Imperial Formations,* edited by Ann Laura Stoler,
Carole McGranahan, and Peter C. Perdue, 3–42. Santa Fe, NM: School
for Advanced Research Press.

Mignolo, Walter D., and Catherine E. Walsh. 2018. *On Decoloniality: Concepts, Analytics, Praxis.* Durham, NC: Duke University Press.

Mitchell, Timothy, ed. 2000. *Questions of Modernity.* Minneapolis: University
of Minnesota Press.

Mitchell, Timothy. 2002. "McJihad: Islam in the US Global Order." *Social
Text* 70 (4): 1–18.

Mitra, Durba. 2020. *Indian Sex Life: Sexuality and the Colonial Origins of
Modern Social Thought.* Princeton, NJ: Princeton University Press. https://
doi.org/10.1515/9780691197029.

Moradian, Manijeh. 2021. *This Flame Within: Iranian Revolutionaries in the
United States.* Durham, NC: Duke University Press.

Munhazim, Ahmad Qais. 2025. "Homo-Humanitarianism: Queering the
Afghan Crisis and Evacuations." *International Politics,* ahead of print,
January 4, 2025. https://doi.org/10.1057/s41311-024-00659-5.

Musawi Natanzi, Paniz. 2024. "Imperial Art Affairs and War: Afghan Artists,
the Goethe Institute and Censorship in Germany." Conference paper
presented at the British Society for Middle Eastern Studies (BRISMES),
Lancaster University, Lancaster, England.

Najmabadi, Afsaneh. 2005. *Women with Mustaches and Men Without Beards:
Gender and Sexual Anxieties of Iranian Modernity.* Berkeley: University of
California Press.

Osman, Wazhmah. 2019a. "Media and Imperialism in the Global Village: A
Case Study of Four Malalais." In *Global Digital Cultures: Perspectives from
South Asia,* edited by A. Punathambekar and S. Mohan, 280–300. Ann
Arbor: University of Michigan Press.

Osman, Wazhmah. 2019b. "Between the White House and the Kremlin: A
Comparative Analysis of Afghan and Tajik Media." *International Journal
of Communication* 13:619–641. https://ijoc.org/index.php/ijoc/article
/view/7576/2551.

Osman, Wazhmah. 2019c. "Racialized Agents and Villains of the Security
State: How African Americans Are Interpellated Against Muslims and
Muslim Americans." *Asian Diasporic Visual Cultures and the Americas* 5
(1–2): 155–182.

Osman, Wazhmah. 2020. *Television and the Afghan Culture Wars: Brought to
You by Foreigners, Warlords, and Activists.* Urbana: University of Illinois
Press.

Osman, Wazhmah. 2022. "Building Spectatorial Solidarity Against the 'War on Terror' Media-Military Gaze." *International Journal of Middle East Studies* 54 (2): 369–375. https://doi.org/10.1017/S002074382200037X.

Osman, Wazhmah. 2023. "The Dangers of Exaggerating Cultural Difference Between Countries in the News." Paper presented at Center for Media at Risk Colloquium, University of Pennsylvania, October 25.

Osman, Wazhmah, and Narges Bajoghli. 2024. "Decolonizing Transnational Feminism: Lessons from the Afghan and Iranian Feminist Uprisings of the Twenty-First Century." *Journal of Middle East Women's Studies* 20 (1): 1–22. https://doi.org/10.1215/15525864–10961742.

Osman, Wazhmah, and Karen Redrobe. 2022. "The Inclusions and Occlusions of Expanded Refugee Narratives: A Dialogue on *Flee.*" *Film Quarterly* 76 (1): 23–34. https://doi.org/10.1525/fq.2022.76.1.23.

Osman, Wazhmah, Helena Zeweri, and Seelai Karzai. 2021. "The Fog of the Forever War with a Laugh Track in 'United States of Al.'" *Middle East Research and Information Project*, May 26. https://merip.org/2021/05/the-fog-of-the-forever-war-with-a-laugh-track-in-united-states-of-al.

O'Sullivan, Sandy. 2023. "Fucking Up, Fixing Up, and Standing Up (to the Colonial Project of Gender and Sexuality)." *American Ethnologist* 50 (3): 350–355.

Pierre, Jemima. 2023. "To Decolonize, We Must End the World as We Know It." *Sapiens*, January 24. https://www.sapiens.org/culture/to-decolonize-we-must-end-the-world-as-we-know-it/.

Povinelli, Elizabeth A. 2002. *The Cunning of Recognition: Indigenous Alterities and the Making of Australian Multiculturalism.* Durham, NC: Duke University Press.

Puar, Jasbir K. 2007. *Terrorist Assemblages: Homonationalism in Queer Times.* Durham, NC: Duke University Press.

Reiter, Bernd, ed. 2018. *Constructing the Pluriverse: The Geopolitics of Knowledge.* Durham, NC: Duke University Press.

Rubin, Barnett R. 2002. *The Fragmentation of Afghanistan: State Formation and Collapse in the International System.* 2nd ed. New Haven, CT: Yale University Press.

Sadozaï, Mélanie. 2021. "The Tajikistani-Afghan Border in Gorno-Badakhshan: Resources of a War-Torn Neighborhood." *Journal of Borderlands Studies* 38 (3): 461–485. https://doi.org/10.1080/08865655.2021.1948898.

Saleh, Zainab. 2020. *Return to Ruin: Iraqi Narratives of Exile and Nostalgia.* Stanford, CA: Stanford University Press.

Shahrani, Nazif M. 2002. "War, Factionalism, and the State in Afghanistan." *American Anthropologist* 104 (3): 715–722.

Shakhsari, Sima. 2012. "From Homoerotics of Exile to Homopolitics of Diaspora: Cyberspace, the War on Terror, and the Hypervisible Iranian Queer." *Journal of Middle East Women's Studies* 8 (3): 14–40.

Sienkiewicz, Matt. 2016. *The Other Air Force: U.S. Efforts to Reshape Middle Eastern Media since 9/11.* New Brunswick: Rutgers University Press.

SIGAR (Special Inspector General for Afghanistan Reconstruction). 2018. *Promoting Gender Equity in National Priority Programs (Promote): USAID Needs to Assess This $216 Million Program's Achievements and the Afghan Government's Ability to Sustain Them.* SIGAR 18–69 Audit Report. Accessed May 2, 2020. https://www.sigar.mil/pdf/audits/SIGAR-18–69-AR .pdf.

Simpson, Audra. 2016. *Mohawk Interruptus: Political Life Across the Borders of Settler States.* Durham, NC: Duke University Press.

Slyomovics, Susan. 2021. "Repairing Colonial Symmetry: Algerian Archive Restitution as Reparation for Crimes of Colonialism?" In *Time for Reparations,* edited by Jacqueline Bhabha, Margareta Matache, and Caroline Elkins, 201–218. Philadelphia: University of Pennsylvania Press.

Smith, Linda Tuhiwai. (1999) 2021. *Decolonizing Methodologies.* 3rd ed. New York: Bloomsbury.

Stone, Nomi. 2022. *Pinelandia: An Anthropology and Field Poetics of War and Empire.* Berkeley: University of California Press.

Tarzi, Nazli. 2023. "Out of Sight: Iraq's TV Archive Lost to the War." *New Arab,* March 20. https://www.newarab.com/analysis/out-sight-iraqs-tv -archive-lost-war.

Trouillot, Michel-Rolph. 1995. *Silencing the Past: Power and the Production of History.* Boston: Beacon.

Tuck, Eve, and K. Wayne Yang. 2012. "Decolonization Is Not a Metaphor." *Decolonization: Indigeneity, Education and Society* 1 (1): 1–40.

USGAO (United States Government Accountability Office). 2011. *Iraq and Afghanistan: DOD, State, and USAID Cannot Fully Account for Contracts, Assistance Instruments, and Associated Personnel.* GAO.gov. https://www .gao.gov/new.items/d11886.pdf.

Veracini, Lorenzo. 2011. "Introducing: Settler Colonial Studies." *Settler Colonial Studies* 1 (1): 1–12.

Wardak, Lailooma Mayer. 2018. "Exporting Racism: Imperial Interventions and the Occupation with Pashtun Culture." In *Cartographies of Race and Social Difference,* edited by George J. Sefa Dei and Shukri Hilowle, 73–90. Cham, Switzerland: Springer Nature.

Watson, Lilla J. 1988. *The Meeting of Two Traditions: Aboriginal Studies in the University, a Murri Perspective.* Armidale, Australia: University of New England.

Wide, Thomas. 2014. "The Refuge of the World: Afghanistan and the Muslim Imagination, 1880–1992." PhD diss., Oxford University.

Yaqub, Nadia, ed. 2023. *Gaza on Screen.* Durham, NC: Duke University Press.

Zeweri, Helena. 2022. "Between Imperial Rule and Sovereignty: Rethinking Afghanistan Studies." *Interventions* 24 (1): 1–11.

Part 1

Imperial Imaginaries & the Historical Production of Afghanistan as a Diagnostic Object of Global Security

Imperial Misconceptions
The Politics of Knowledge Production

"Graveyard of Empires"

This chapter interrogates the recurring spectacle of Afghanistan within the Western political imaginary, a spectral presence violently reinscribed into global consciousness by the 2001 NATO invasion and the frenetic scenes of withdrawal in August 2021. The bookends of this twenty-year war did not merely generate news; they reactivated a potent and persistent representational schema through which "Afghanistan" is perpetually rendered legible. I focus on the enduring power of a specific triad of imperial tropes—the nation as a "graveyard of empires," a perpetual pawn in a renewed "Great Game," and a timeless space of abject squalor and disease. By excavating the genealogies of these narrative devices, I show how they are driven by a colonial anxiety to make sense of Afghanistan. Ultimately, this chapter contends that these representations enact a form of epistemic violence, caught in a recursive logic that perpetually obscures the very object of its gaze, demonstrating how the work of memory and representation constitutes a critical site of ongoing imperial power.

The euphemistic reference to Afghanistan as the "graveyard of empires" has found a place in most contemporary work on the country. The trope is especially problematic on three counts: (1) It is ahistorical, relying on a selective evocation of history. Related to this ahistoricism, it sets up the past as the "key" to understanding the Afghan present. Simply put, this argument stresses the "unchanging" nature of Afghanistan, harking back to the Anglo-Afghan wars of the nineteenth century as not merely shaping the political exigencies of Afghanistan today but as being preordained and definitive guides to the future. (2) It is geographically or "physically" deterministic: Afghanistan is constructed as a land of unconquerable terrain (but nevertheless simultaneously construed as an object ripe for conquering), its topography menacing and ultimately unassailable. Not only does this present the physical environment as an immutable entity, it also feeds into representations of Afghans as rugged warriors, bred to be weathered and austere. (3) It is racialized: Afghans as inhabitants, creators, and living relics of this graveyard are constructed as inured to hardship, belligerent, and always prepared for combat. Seemingly corroborated with references to *Pashtunwali* as the stagnant "honor code" that instills a desire for revenge, and Wahhabi Islam, which glorifies martyrdom and death in battle, the construal of Afghanistan as the "graveyard of empires" becomes a politically charged trope that others the Afghan populace largely harnessed for the explicit purposes of the myriad colonial projects that have assembled in and around Afghanistan.

In alluding to Afghanistan as the graveyard of empires, the three Anglo-Afghan wars (1839–1842, 1878–1880, and 1919 respectively) and the Soviet invasion of 1979 are adduced as the paradigmatic examples, with occasional reference to Alexander the Great and Chinggis Khan as also having met their match in Afghanistan. An article published in *Foreign Affairs* in 2001 titled "Afghanistan: The Graveyard of Empires" captures the thrust of much work that portrays Afghanistan as the land that has, since time immemorial, been the place where foreign armies "go to die." Milton Bearden (2001), referring to Khyber, opines:

> This spot, perhaps more than any other, has witnessed the traverse of the world's great armies on campaigns of conquest to and from South and Central Asia. All eventually ran into trouble in their encounters with the unruly Afghan tribals. Alexander the Great sent his supply trains through the Khyber, then skirted northward with his army to the Konar Valley on his campaign in 327 B.C. There he ran into fierce resistance and, struck by an Afghan archer's arrow, barely made it to the Indus River with his life. Genghis Khan and the great Mughal emperors began passing through the Khyber a millennium later and ultimately established the greatest of empires—but only after reaching painful accommodations with the Afghans.

While there is some ambiguity about the "defeat" suffered by Alexander and Chinggis Khan in Afghanistan, most Western historiography is relatively consistent in its labeling of the British adventures in Afghanistan as a failure. For instance, Thomas Barfield (2004) takes exception to the graveyard canard, claiming instead that Afghanistan has been a "highway

1.1 Elizabeth Thompson, Lady Butler, *The Remnants of an Army*, 1879. Oil on canvas. The portrait depicts William Brydon and his dying horse, allegedly the sole survivors of the First Anglo-Afghan War.

of conquest" since the beginning of recorded history and that only since the nineteenth century can the country be rightly thought of as the burial ground for imperial ambition. He contests that the territory that now comprises Afghanistan was "easily conquered and ruled" by foreign invaders and posits that the difficulties faced by invading armies, including those of Alexander and Chinggis Khan, were caused by attacks by rival states and not by rebellions carried out by inhabitants (263). Although his history of premodern Afghanistan is therefore "revisionist" in this sense, he nevertheless ends up subscribing to the notion that modern Afghanistan is somehow particularly predisposed to be impervious to foreign rule. He asks, "How is it that a territory that was historically overrun by every major power in premodern times became so indigestible in the last 150 years?" and begins his inquisition with the First Anglo-Afghan War of 1839 (263).

Indeed, this war is seemingly eternally inscribed in Anglophone institutional memory as the time when "a horde of 'pagan savages' with primitive weapons had routed the world's greatest power" (Gentilini 2013, 27). This memory has been pictorially commemorated in a famous Victorian oil painting by Elizabeth Southerend Thompson—better known as Lady Butler—*The Remnants of an Army* (1879), which depicts assistant surgeon in the Bengal Army, Doctor William Brydon, clinging to the mane of a fatigued and dying horse, and advancing solitarily towards Jalalabad fort (see figure 1.1).

This melancholic and elegiac painting is partly responsible for the inaccurate myth that Brydon was the sole survivor of the sixteen thousand soldiers under the command of Sir William Elphinstone. William Dalrymple's recently published historical account, *Return of a King: Battle for Afghanistan*, is an exemplary text in this regard. Elsewhere, Dalrymple (2014) claims that in spite of the many "uncomfortable similarities" between the Soviet invasion of Afghanistan and the current NATO intervention, the real "precedent" for the present war is the First Anglo-Afghan War. He labels this war "arguably the greatest military humiliation ever suffered by the West in the East," in which an "entire army of what was then the most powerful nation in the world was utterly destroyed by poorly equipped tribesmen." Despite acknowledging that he finds the argument that Afghanistan is impossible to conquer historically untrue, Dalrymple nevertheless effectively resuscitates the graveyard myth when he conjectures that "any occupying army here will hemorrhage money and blood to little gain, and in the end most throw in the towel, as the British did in 1842, as the Russians did in 1988 and as NATO will do later this year," and thus also displacing the horrors of imperial conquest for Afghans onto a dubious cost-benefit exercise for empire.

In any event, this first war was a patent triumph for the Afghans, and on all accounts the British Army, or more precisely the East India Company (EIC) army, found itself morally and physically crushed. The Second Anglo-Afghan War on the other hand was a resounding success for the British and the Third at least a tactical victory. This Second Anglo-Afghan War was fought between the United Kingdom and the Emirate of Afghanistan between 1878 and 1880. It ended after the British emerged victorious against the Afghan rebels and the Afghans relinquished all control over their country's foreign relations and ceded various frontier areas to Britain, as laid out in the Treaty of Gandamak, which the new Emir, Yaqub, was forced to sign on May 26, 1879 (Barfield 2023). As part of the agreement, he also had to permit a permanent British mission in Afghanistan. The Third Anglo-Afghan War, fought between the months of May and August of 1919, ended in an armistice that affirmed the validity of the Durand Line as the political boundary between British India and the Emirate of Afghanistan. The Afghans were allowed to resume conduct of their foreign affairs in return for a "promise to not foment trouble" on the border with British India (Barthorp 2002). Given that the British won, at least nominally, two of the three Afghan wars, the popular claim that Afghanistan is either unconquerable or impossible to defeat in battle is uncorroborated at best. Moreover, the reason Afghanistan was never fully colonized—that is, its quasi-coloniality—owed as much to British indecisiveness and lack of interest in the country as it did to any ineradicable difficulties in conquering the country or to the Afghans being a particularly formidable enemy. British oscillation between the "forward" and "close" policies with regard to the frontier was documented at the time, and archival research conducted since reveals the detrimental repercussions this had on both the Afghan polity and on relations between high-ranking individual administrators within the colonial apparatus responsible for dealing with Afghanistan (Barfield 2023; Hopkins 2008).

The graveyard of empires trope is perhaps at its most emphatic and most persuasive when it places the Soviet invasion of Afghanistan, and the nine years that followed, at the core of its thesis. Although Soviet Russia's "Afghan misadventure" was of an entirely different magnitude and intensity from the British forays into Afghanistan, the two nevertheless display elements of commonality and overlap. Before drawing out these parallels, a brief recounting of the buildup to the Soviet invasion is germane to the topic. In 1978 Mohammed Daoud Khan, the president of the newly christened Afghan republic, was murdered in a coup that brought the Marxist People's Democratic Party of Afghanistan (PDPA) to power. One of the two factions of the party, the Khalq, quickly became dominant, sidelined the more moderate Parcham faction, and formed a direct alliance with the Soviet Union, abandoning Afghanistan's erstwhile policy of neutrality. The Khalqis instituted radical land reform, made drastic changes in family law, and transformed the education system. Their allegiance to Marxist political ideology also saw them launch a wholesale attack on Islam, one that alienated large portions of the Afghan population. The ruling Khalq faction faced mass resistance, especially in the countryside, which they met with military force, resulting in the country's provinces erupting in rebellion. What were initially localized uprisings soon spread with a vengeance across the country. The Soviet Union, disenchanted with and untrusting of the Khalqi leadership, after a failed attempt to remove the leadership indirectly, surmised that the safest option was to assume direct control of Afghanistan. Under the premise of restoring stability to Afghanistan, the USSR invaded in December 1979, deposed the ruling Khalq faction, and installed a Parchami, Babrak Karmal, as head of the state (Bradsher 1985; Braithwaite 2011; Kakar 1995; Rubin 1995).

Over the next ten years the Soviets engaged in an extensive war with the Afghan populace. The narrative, hegemonic at least in the West, maintains that this decade is testament to, and exemplary of, the region's propensity for savage internecine warfare, and to the indefatigable warrior spirit of its inhabitants. The Soviet Union, on this account, glibly assumed that it could subdue the population of Afghanistan without much effort and rule the country until a government that was subordinate to Moscow but capable of maintaining order in the country could be established (see Crews, chapter 2 in this volume). Instead, they were confronted with the force of a countrywide jihad, which in the words of one commentator is the "standard occurrence every time Afghanistan tries to change" (Gentilini 2013, 81). The mujahideen are said to have worn down the Soviets through attrition and in the process to have been instrumental in bringing down the behemoth that was the Soviet Union. Therefore, in spite of the Soviet enemy's superior strength, better organization, and greater airpower, the "holy warriors," through grit and determination, and united in the name of God, managed to bring the empire to its knees. The outcome may be seemingly inexplicable given the asymmetry between the fighting forces but is entirely predictable according to the dominant discourse of the graveyard of empires, even for those who are somewhat skeptical of the trope (Grau and Gress 2002; Yousaf 1992)

The conflict has been dubbed "Soviet Union's Vietnam" (Dvoretsky and Sarin 1993), and while the analogy is both flippant and misguided in its privileging of American experience as iconic and paradigmatic, it is also revealing. In the first instance, it places the opposition that the Soviets faced in Afghanistan in context: The mujahideen can be viewed as percipient political agents that resorted to arms in the face of a foreign invasion rather than as Islamic zealots propelled by an innate thirst for blood and violence. The analogies between mujahideen guerrilla warfare and Viet Minh fighters may be firmly embedded in an Orientalist framework that relies on the familiar othering logics of racialization and dehumanization. Nevertheless, the comparison goes some way in debunking the "exceptionalist" myth of an Afghan proclivity to fight without a cause by placing the Afghan resistance within the broader arc of Third Worldist struggle for independence and decolonization. While this narrative may be viewed as problematic in its paternalistic ethnocentrism or indeed in its romanticization of "Third World sensibilities," it nevertheless undermines the standard construal of Afghanistan as unique in its impregnability as well as in its knee-jerk hostility to outside intervention. While foregrounding the Cold War as the frame of reference, the analogy ultimately underscores the oft-misplaced faith that the superpowers had in their own abilities to effect radical change in distant locales during the Cold War. Afghanistan, much like Vietnam, can be viewed as a sobering moment in a tale of imperial hubris.

The graveyard of empires trope also becomes less convincing when one considers the extent of foreign aid, especially that of the CIA, Saudi Arabia, and Pakistan, to the Afghan resistance movement. On the second "Afghanistan Observance Day," March 21, 1983, Ronald Reagan, then president of the United States, remarked: "To watch the courageous Afghan freedom fighters battle modern arsenals with simple hand-held weapons is an inspiration to those who love freedom. Their courage teaches us a great lesson—that there are things in this world worth defending" (Reagan 1983). However, when the CIA provided the now legendary man-portable anti-aircraft missile "The Stinger" to the mujahideen in 1986, Afghan "freedom fighters" became well placed to match the Soviet arsenal. According to conservative estimates, the United States supplied over 250 launcher systems and over five hundred Stinger missiles to the mujahideen, along with specialized training required to operate the system, and also considerably ramped up their project of overall military assistance (Coll 2004). The Stinger changed the balance of power to such an extent that the term "Stinger Effect" has been coined to specifically relay the "game-changing" import of the weapon (Crile 2007). The Soviet-Afghan War was an indubitably asymmetrical one, but the mujahideen—though far from pusillanimous—were nevertheless funded and militarily supported adequately enough to question popular representations of them as unarmed but fierce, and essentially antediluvian, militants operating in isolation.

This history of Soviet involvement in Afghanistan complicates prevailing notions of the country and its denizens as possessing primordial qualities that make them uniquely poised to repel all invaders. Just as a nominally independent Afghanistan served British interests in the nineteenth and early twentieth centuries, the USSR ultimately lacked the will and resources to continue to hold Afghanistan indefinitely. It is not some transhistorical, congenital Afghan predisposition or "antibody" that brought the end of Soviet rule in Afghanistan. The Soviets withdrew because Afghanistan became an increasingly expensive proposition for an empire that was crumbling from within and that had a new leader with a different vision for his country, but only after it had caused widespread damage and destruction to the Afghan state and its inhabitants over the course of a decade (Khalidi 1991). Moreover, the graveyard trope conflates military withdrawal with political and economic withdrawal. Military withdrawal, as is the case with imperialism in general, rarely equates to the transfer of power and autonomy to the colonized. Similarly, although much is made of Afghanistan's harsh climate and unforgiving terrain, the country has a diverse topographical makeup and is bounded by six countries. Occupying a large area at the geographical core of Asia, Afghanistan's deserts, mountains, and steppes have been habitually penetrated by caravans and plundering conquerors (Hopkins 2008, 5). While this variation in terrain, topography, and climate across the country often serves to embolden centrifugal forces, it has not historically precluded occupation.

Critical political geography as a subdiscipline has made crucial interventions in exposing the ways in which the fields of geopolitics and conventional approaches to political geography rely on a racialized ontological framework to make sense of the world. Environmental and geographic determinism has been critiqued as a racialized discourse, especially in treatises on climate, disease, and sanitation in Africa (Sheppard 2011). While precolonial and colonial discourses on the inherently dangerous nature of the "tropics" owing to inclement climatic conditions and their adverse impact on the constitution of the white man have all but disappeared (cf. McClintock 1995), the resort to a vocabulary that relies heavily on the topographical perils and hibernal climes of a region in constructing it as a figurative necropolis is not much different in either tenor or import. Pictorial depictions such as Lady Butler's aforementioned *The Remnants of an Army*—in which a blood-covered frozen wasteland forms the backdrop to Brydon and his horse—among others of this period only seem to validate written and verbal accounts of Afghanistan's treacherous terrain. Compounding the problem are the treacherous, belligerent, and quintessentially inward-looking inhabitants of this land.

The graveyard topos has been resurrected to claim that the war in Afghanistan is "unwinnable" owing to the flinty nature of the country and its people. Policy documents, such as the CATO Institute's white paper on Obama's strategy in Afghanistan, routinely evoke the danger of forgetting that "there's a reason why it [Afghanistan] has been described as 'graveyard of empires'" and that unless America rethinks its operations and scales them down drastically it risks "meeting a similar fate" (Innocent and Carpenter 2009). Cartoons and political satire in the Anglophone press (see figures 1.2 and 1.3) regularly echoed this sentiment at the peak of the intervention, aiming to serve as an admonition against an expansive Afghan strategy.

The graveyard of empires trope, even for those who are more circumspect about the sweeping nature of its generalizations or its applicability before the nineteenth century, is so compelling because it perpetuates the institutionalized convention of superficial engagement with Afghanistan. However, the trope is more than a clever misnomer: It pithily weaves to-

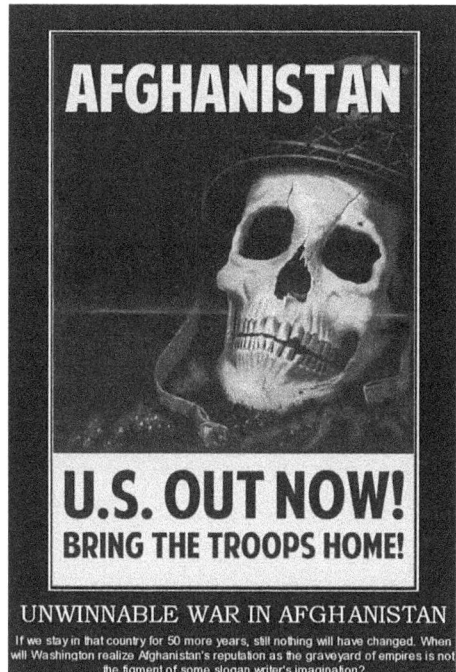

1.2 "Afghanistan: Graveyard of Empires." A satirical movie poster, designed by the website Liberty Maniacs, depicting Afghanistan as a cemetery of imperial ambition.

1.3 "Unwinnable War in Afghanistan." A demand to bring the US troops home from Afghanistan.

gether the skeins of geographical determinism, ahistoricism, and racialized renditions of the Afghan people. It is a profoundly othering discourse, whose most virulent detractors are ironically those that object to the word *empire* as being applicable to the current intervention. Therefore, in contrast to Secretary of Defense Donald Rumsfeld's observation that "several countries have exhausted themselves pounding that country" (Tanner 2009, 292), a reviewer of David Isby's *Afghanistan: Graveyard of Empires; A New History of the Borderland* writes: "The graveyard of empires metaphor indeed belongs in the graveyard of clichés. The Coalition in Afghanistan is not some imperial conquest, is not the Soviets, and is not the Victorian British. Nor do the Afghans perceive it as such" (Cassidy 2011, 153). Afghanistan then remains a graveyard, even if the recent intervention was mislabeled as empire.

This lazy historiography that references past events in a haphazard way is perhaps par for the course when it comes to Afghanistan. This is because it is symptomatic of a long tradition of what can be called imperial negligence—albeit periodically interrupted by moments of perfervid commitment—that continues to govern Afghanistan's interaction with the outside world and to shape the knowledge generated about the country and its people. Even in its more watered-down versions, which argue that Afghanistan is not technically "unconquerable" and instead directs attention to the difficulty in imposing a central government, especially but not only by a foreign power, the trope remains a racialized construction, an ostensible demystification of the Afghan Other that falls back on the civilized/uncivilized bifurcation of the world, for two principal, and mutually constitutive, reasons: (1) Through its selective evocation of history or "racial aphasia" (Thomson 2014) Afghanistan is portrayed as an exceptionally intractable part of the world. This "calculated forgetting" makes it legitimate to claim that Afghanistan was never colonized in spite of multiple sustained efforts. Not only did the British not lose all three Afghan wars, they were also at best halfhearted about making Afghanistan part of the British Raj (Hevia 2012; Hopkins 2008). And while the USSR was more committed to occupying Afghanistan, this commitment wavered in the face both of a dramatic increase in US- and Saudi-led support for the opposition *and* an imploding domestic economy. To question the graveyard of empires trope is to turn attention to the multisited theater of war and the multiple imperial actors who have a stake in Afghan self-determination. And (2), it euphemistically upholds and promulgates the already popular image of Afghans as at once unruly, insulated, backward, and fundamentally untamable people but also as needing to be tamed, in line with an anxious colonial epistemology (see the introduction to this volume). In turn this lends itself to specious reasoning and commentaries on *Pashtunwali*, "warrior masculinities," and "tribal codes," which are rife with ambivalence and continue to plague the study of the region.

At its most potent, in the way that it presents "the past" as the key to Afghanistan's future and present, the graveyard metaphor is actually an extended allegory for the current practices of knowledge production when it comes to Afghanistan. Indeed, after the withdrawal of troops in 2021, the graveyard cliché once more proved to be extremely expeditious—the intervention was doomed to fail from the start, and any deleterious ramifications were certainly not for want of trying on the part of the West but rather due to the uncooperative nature of Afghan society itself. All attempts at understanding colonial intervention fall flat in the face of decades of sedimented knowledges about the innate character of the Afghan state, peoples, and landscape (see the introduction and Osman, chapter 3, in this volume).

The Great Game

Afghanistan's popular reputation as a graveyard of empires finds its academic counterpart in its position in the so-called Great Game, the term given to Anglo-Russian rivalry and jostling for supremacy in Central Asia in the nineteenth and early twentieth centuries. In most modern historiography, Anglo-Russian competition in the region at the time is the master narrative, with the Great Game its central trope or "organizing principle." This metanarrative has also given rise to the geopolitical institutionalization of Afghanistan's position as a "buffer state," the zone that the British had to strategically defend by way of ensuring the Soviet Union did not encroach on its Indian territory. In spite of the relative absence of the *Great Game* as a term in the archives and official correspondence of the time (Allan 2001; Bayly 2016), it continues to be employed widely and has in fact gained currency in the twenty-first century, with multiple scholars increasingly adverting to a "New Great Game" as a way of conceptualizing modern geopolitics in Afghanistan and Central Asia (Ahrari 2002; Mazni 2008; Johnson 2007; Kleveman 2004; Mullerson 2007; Rashid 2002). This New Great Game, according to its semantic engineers, is the contest between the United States and other NATO countries on the one hand and Russia on the other for influence, power, hegemony, and profits in Central Asia and the Transcaucasus, a continuation of old dynamics in a different guise, with Afghanistan's position as a key but truculent potential partner remaining constant (Edwards 2003).

The idea of an enduring antagonistic relationship between Russia and Britain in general, and the metaphoric Great Game in particular, has been the source of fierce contention, and there has been a concerted effort on the part of historians working on Afghanistan to refute what they refer to as the fallacy of the Great Game. Ben Hopkins (2004, 36) observes that the Great Game is the "central conceptual prism through which Afghanistan is currently viewed," a "myth" that "mistakenly over emphasizes the importance of a 'game' which frankly did not exist." Seymour Becker (2012, 65) traces the etymology of the phrase and shows how, for the original architect of the term, Captain Arthur Connolly, the game metaphor "signified a contest in which the Russians were Britain's *potential* opponents, but the

Central Asians were her *immediate* ones," and indeed stressed the importance of Anglo-Russian cooperation in the region. Moreover, for Connolly the "great" game in essence was a noble one with overt "humanitarian associations" and betrayed none of the "uneasy adventurist quality" that is commonly ascribed to the metaphor. This is particularly relevant since most contemporary constructions are based on Peter Hopkirk's (2006) definition of the term, set out in his eponymous book, perhaps the most widely read treatise on the Great Game, as shorthand for a "shadowy struggle for political ascendancy" in Central Asia, especially Afghanistan, between Russia and the United Kingdom. Hopkirk for his part has taken the notion from Rudyard Kipling's *Kim* and like his contemporaries "read[s] the Great Game back into the six decades prior to the publication of *Kim* and forward into the Soviet and post-Soviet era" (Hevia 2012, 12).

James Hevia (2012) in his pioneering study of the British colonial security state examines how the Great Game metaphor and its proponents have obscured the relation between science and empire by relying on Kipling's slightly quixotic rendition of fantasy and romantic adventure as the guiding pillars of Britain's imperial enterprise. Further, as Gerald Morgan (1973, 55–57) insists, the Great Game is a misplaced metaphor that masks and sanitizes the enormous violence that actually transpired in the era, including three British invasions of Afghanistan and recurrent clashes on the northwest frontier. Finally, Martin Bayly (2016) has sought to show how the Great Game as a trope has been both instrumental in and bolstered by the evolution of a certain colonial knowledge community around Afghanistan, one that has retrospectively made a small part of the British narrative of the time into the lynchpin of the "story of Afghanistan."

In light of this sustained scholarly critique of the Great Game metaphor, its continuing use and especially its revival in present literature through the discourse of the New Great Game is striking. On one level, the Great Game is a projection onto a diverse range of events that were conceived differently by the historical actors involved. On another level these actors themselves, not least the British Empire and the Soviet Union, evolved and changed remarkably from when the Great Game supposedly began in the 1830s to when it allegedly ended or was qualitatively transformed after the Bolshevik Revolution in 1917 (Hevia 2012). The Great Game trope is, however, problematic for a multitude of reasons over and above its tenuous historical underpinning. It is emblematic of the ways in which the practices of knowledge production continue both to attempt to render Afghanistan legible and to shroud "it" in a world of mystifying metaphors. Afghanistan is constructed as a pawn in a game of imperial stratagems, deliberately divested of all agency and deprived of a narrative in which the history of Afghanistan is a history of the Afghans (see introduction to this volume). The Great Game narrative continues to exercise such a hold over the Western—and more specifically, the Anglophone—imagination because it sustains and propagates the familiar pigeonholing of Afghanistan as the land of intrigue, possessed of an exotic, unruly mystique over which great powers vie for dominance and paramountcy. Through its persistence, the Great Game conceit typifies the inseparability of power relations from relations of knowledge. More specifically, it forms part of a larger colonial effort to normalize a set of power relations through what Homi Bhabha (1984, 131) calls "the repetition of guilt, justification, pseudoscientific theories, superstition, spurious authorities and classification" as, paradoxically, the only way in which the Other can be made intelligible.

The Great Game also continues to be the abiding narrative because it slots Afghanistan into the established International Relations (IR) *problematique* of the balance of power. In a world of great power politics and competition, Afghanistan occupied a strategic location as a "buffer state," and the metaphor endures because it provides a convenient reduction of Afghanistan's political history to an exoteric idiom (Thomas 2004). The gamification of Afghan history is also a reminder of Afghanistan's position in a hierarchical world of ostensibly sovereign states—its existence is contingent on those who control the material and imaginative resources. The Great Game as a structuring discourse establishes that, in a slightly irreverent paraphrasing of Alexander Wendt (1992), Afghanistan is what great powers make of it. At its most ruthless, the metaphor is another instance of the trivializing and systematic occlusion of Afghan politics, histories, and lifeworlds. The trope rests on the implicit assumption that certain (Afghan) subjectivities are both less important and easily manipulable, and in so doing it constructs Afghanistan as a certain type of "intervenable" space, justifying a set of policies and actions towards it.

Pathology/Disease

Both the Great Game and the graveyard of empires are historical metaphors (purportedly) rooted in particular experiences of Afghanistan's interaction with the outside world. They are crucial elements in the construction of Afghanistan as an imagined political space, or what I call a "discursive regime" (Manchanda 2020), and they are in turn complemented by a litany of other metaphors and tropes that imbue with meaning and make possible this idea of Afghanistan. One such leitmotiv is that of illness or disease. Medical and anatomical metaphors are often utilized in policy and even academic discourse on Afghanistan, contributing a sense of urgency to "our mission" to "save" the country (Savranskaya and Blanton 2009). A *New York Times Magazine* article entitled "Warlordistan" declared in 2003 that the "rebuilding of Afghanistan . . . has so far been a sputtering disappointment" because "like many of its people the nation is missing limbs" (Tanner 2009, 330). In keeping with this spirit, Afghanistan as a nation has been variously depicted as "festering," "pathological," and infested with "cancerous growths" (Farag 2012; Kilcullen 2009; Toynbee 2002). For instance, both *Time* (Thomson 2011) and the *Nation* (Scheer 2006) have labeled Afghanistan "the festering wound," with the former also defining the US war in Afghanistan as "a chronic and oozing pus-filled wound." Richard Holbrooke, Obama's special envoy to Afghanistan and arguably the most important diplomat in the region, has likewise referred to the "festering wound of Afghanistan" (Betizza 2009).

David Kilcullen's argument in his *Accidental Guerrilla*—heralded as a pathbreaking scholarly work of immediate practical consequence—is structured around an extended medical analogy wherein most insurgents suffer from an "accidental syndrome" caused by a "pathological" cycle of infection, contagion, intervention, and rejection. To break this cycle of disease, he proposes an alternate counterinsurgency strategy, one aimed at winning the hearts and minds of the local populace: gentle, culturally sensitive "armed social work" (2009, 30–38). He also advocates for the "persistent presence" of Western troops but cautions that this presence is not a "panacea" (97). Carrying the metaphor forward, he dwells in some detail on what makes Afghanistan such an involuted proposition and on the potential reaction to an ill-conceived intervention:

> It is this interplay between terrain, population, Taliban, and terrorists that makes Afghanistan such a difficult, dangerous, and complicated environment. It also means that Afghanistan . . . is a source of insight into the patterns—global terrorists exploiting accidental guerrillas, societal *antibodies* emerging in response to Western intervention, the risk of playing into the hands of an AQ exhaustion strategy—which I have already described in general terms. (41; emphasis added)

Creating a biopolitical or, in more precise Foucauldian vernacular, a state-racist rift between the "enemy" and the "population," Kilcullen propounds a surgical intervention that is not heavy-handed and expounds on his choices: "More particularly, search-and-destroy operations tend to create a popular backlash and contribute to the 'antibody response' that generates large numbers of accidental guerrillas and pushes the population and the enemy together" (97). This application of a medical lexicon is a key feature of the counterinsurgency literature where the "host nation" goes through a process of remedial care, from a moribund patient to a convalescent and ultimately "self-sufficient" one. The stages are clearly delineated in the widely hailed counterinsurgency manual COIN FM-24 as (1) "stop the bleeding," (2) "inpatient care—recovery," and (3) "outpatient care—movement to self-sufficiency" (US Army and Marine Corps 2007).

Derek Gregory (2008, 4) has shown how this medicinal rhetoric is essentially therapeutic for the American public. It portrays the intervention in Afghanistan as humane and salubrious in an effort to override or mitigate the negative press generated by evidence of torture of detainees in, for instance, Abu Ghraib, and espouses a commitment to and faith in the US armed forces. This is intimately related to my argument that the medicalization discourse used habitually, but by no means exclusively, to describe sociopolitical events and circumstances in Afghanistan is a profoundly dispossessing one and is far from innocuous. The evocative rendering of Afghanistan as being in a state of chronic illness—afflicted and atrophying—is a pernicious political maneuver that sanctions, even demands, certain types of "intervention." The labeling of Afghanistan as "dysfunctional" is yet another tactic to deny the country and its people agency by casting them as hapless patients in need of rehabilitation and normalization (Azoy 2011; Chesterman 2002; Freeman 2002; Mallaby 2002). The "enemy" is a malignant tumor on a decaying body politic, making our incursions not only desirable and indeed noble, but also vitally indispensable. The common-sense refrain then becomes: We *must* save Afghanistan from itself, and by so doing save the world from the deadly effects of potential, nay likely, contagion.

Afghanistan is depicted as the wracked and tortured land of malaise as part of the general process of the displacement of Afghan subjectivity in a colonial strategy of using metaphors, tropes, metonymy, and euphemisms to create identities that can be labeled "actionable," in both senses of the term—that is, as warranting action toward them and as being of practical value (Hafvenstein 2007; Saikal and Maley 1986; Roberts 2001; Suhrke 2008; Wissing 2013). In 2021, Afghan politicians joined a slew of Western commentators to lament the cancer of terrorism, echoing tweets from the

Office of the President of Afghanistan (2019). Indeed, the *metaphoric* is a "process of repression and substitution" through "fixity" (Bhabha 1983), and although it has a long imperial pedigree, it is relied on especially heavily as a tactics of appropriation in making sense of a place that is "almost but not quite" (colonized). The colonial desire for "fixity"—the rigid casting of the Other as visible and knowable—effectuated through the ideological operation of stereotyping continues to plague (if I may) the study of Afghanistan. Colonial economies of knowledge production—like colonial modes of governance in general—depend on strategies that are necessarily reductive, essentialist, and mystifying. When it comes to Afghanistan, however, this economy is buttressed by two centuries of imperial amnesia and lackadaisical interest in the country and its institutions. In line with the spirt of this volume, this chapter is an attempt to put some of the histories and presents of empire in Afghanistan to bed.

Note

This chapter has been adapted from *Imagining Afghanistan: The History and Politics of Imperial Knowledge* (Cambridge: Cambridge University Press, 2020).

References

Ahrari, Mohammed E. 2002. *The New Great Game in Muslim Central Asia.* Honolulu: University Press of the Pacific.

Allan, Nigel. 2001. "Defining Place and People in Afghanistan." *Post-Soviet Geography and Economics* 42 (8): 545–560.

Azoy, Whitney. 2011. *Buzkashi: Game and Power in Afghanistan.* Long Grove, IL: Waveland.

Barfield, Thomas. 2004. "Problems in Establishing Legitimacy in Afghanistan." *Iranian Studies* 37 (2): 263–293.

Barfield, Thomas. 2023. *Afghanistan: A Cultural and Political History.* Princeton, NJ: Princeton University Press.

Barthorp, Michael. 2002. *Afghan Wars and the North-West Frontier, 1839–1947.* London: Cassell.

Bayly, Martin. 2016. *Taming the Imperial Imagination: Colonial Knowledge and Anglo-Afghan Relations, 1808–1878.* Cambridge: Cambridge University Press.

Bearden, Milton. 2001. "Afghanistan, Graveyard of Empires." *Foreign Affairs* 80 (6): 17–30.

Becker, Seymour. 2012. "The 'Great Game': The History of an Evocative Phrase." *Asian Affairs* 43 (1): 61–80.

Betizza, Gregoria. 2009. "Obama, Afghanistan and the Trust Deficit." Aspen Institute, April 29. https://www.aspeninstitute.it/aspenia-online/article/obama-afghanistan-and-trust-deficit.

Bhabha, Homi. 1983. "The Other Question: Homi Bhabha Reconsiders the Stereotype and Colonial Discourse." *Screen* 24 (6): 18–36.

Bhabha, Homi. 1984. "Of Mimicry and Man: The Ambivalence of Colonial Discourse." *October* 28 (Spring): 125–133.

Bradsher, Henry. 1985. *Afghanistan and the Soviet Union.* Durham, NC: Duke University Press.

Braithwaite, Rodric. 2011. *Afgantsy: The Russians in Afghanistan, 1979–89.* New York: Oxford University Press.

Cassidy, Robert M. 2011. Review of *Afghanistan: Graveyard of Empires; A New History of the Borderland,* by David Isby. *Parameters* 41 (3): 153–155.

Chesterman, Simon. 2002. "Walking Softly in Afghanistan: The Future of UN State-Building." *Survival* 44 (3): 37–45.

Coll, Steve. 2004. *Ghost Wars: The Secret History of the CIA, Afghanistan, and Bin Laden, from the Soviet Invasion to September 10, 2001.* London: Penguin.

Crile, George. 2007. *Charlie Wilson's War: The Story of the Largest Covert Operation in History.* London: Atlantic Books.

Dalrymple, William. 2014. "Is Afghanistan Really Impossible to Conquer?" BBC, March 9. https://www.bbc.com/news/magazine-26483320.

Dvoretsky, Lev, and Oleg Sarin. 1993. *The Afghan Syndrome: The Soviet Union's Vietnam.* Novato, CA: Presidio.

Edwards, Matthew. 2003. "The New Great Game and the New Great Gamers: Disciples of Kipling and Mackinder." *Central Asian Survey* 22 (1): 83–102.

Farag, Marwa. 2012. "Eikenberry Assesses U.S. Role in Afghanistan." *Stanford Daily,* January 31. https://stanforddaily.com/2012/01/31/eikenberry-assesses-u-s-role-in-afghanistan/.

Freeman, Christopher. 2002. "Dissonant Discourse: Forging Islamist States through Secular Models—The Case of Afghanistan." *Cambridge Review of International Affairs* 15 (3).

Gentilini, Fernando. 2013. *Afghan Lessons: Culture, Diplomacy, and Counterinsurgency.* Washington, DC: Brookings Institution Press.

Grau, Lester, and Michael Gress. 2002. *The Soviet-Afghan War: How a Superpower Fought and Lost.* Lawrence: University of Kansas Press.

Gregory, Derek. 2008. "'The Rush to the Intimate': Counterinsurgency and the Cultural Turn." *Radical Philosophy* 150 (4): 8–23.

Hafvenstein, Joel. 2007. *Opium Season: A Year on the Afghan Frontier.* Guildford, CT: Globe Pequot.

Hevia, James. 2012. *The Imperial Security State: British Colonial Knowledge and Empire-Building in Asia.* Cambridge: Cambridge University Press.

Hopkins, Benjamin. 2004. "The Myth of the 'Great Game': The Anglo-Sikh Alliance and Rivalry." Occasional paper. Centre of South Asian Studies, University of Cambridge.

Hopkins, Benjamin. 2008. *The Making of Modern Afghanistan*. London: Basingstoke.

Hopkirk, Peter. 2006. *The Great Game: On Secret Service in High Asia*. London: John Murray.

Innocent, Malou, and Ted Galen Carpenter. 2009. "Escaping the 'Graveyard of Empires': A Strategy to Exit Afghanistan." White paper. CATO Institute, September 14. https://www.cato.org/white-paper/escaping-graveyard-empires-strategy-exit-afghanistan.

Johnson, Rob. 2007. *Oil, Islam and Conflict: Central Asia Since 1945*. London: Reaktion.

Kakar, Hassan. 1995. *Afghanistan: The Soviet Invasion and the Afghan Response, 1979–1982*. Berkeley: University of California Press.

Khalidi, Noor Ahmed. 1991. "Afghanistan: Demographic Consequences of War, 1978–1987." *Central Asian Survey* 10 (3): 101–126.

Kilcullen, David. 2009. *The Accidental Guerrilla: Fighting Small Wars in the Midst of a Big One*. London: Hurst.

Kleveman, Lutz. 2004. *The New Great Game: Blood and Oil in Central Asia*. New York: Grove.

Mallaby, Sebastian. 2002. "The Reluctant Imperialist: Terrorism, Failed States, and the Case for American Empire." *Foreign Affairs* 81 (2): 2–7.

Manchanda, Nivi. 2020. *Imagining Afghanistan: The History and Politics of Imperial Knowledge*. Cambridge: Cambridge University Press.

Mazni, Muhammad. 2008. *The New Great Game: Oil and Gas Politics in Central Eurasia*. New York: Raider.

McClintock, Anne. 1995. *Imperial Leather: Race, Gender and Sexuality in the Colonial Context*. London: Routledge.

Morgan, Gerald. 1973. "Myth and Reality in the Great Game." *Asian Affairs* 4 (1): 55–65.

Mullerson, Rein. 2007. *Central Asia: A Chessboard and Player in the New Great Game*. New York: Columbia University Press.

Office of the President of Afghanistan (@ARG_AFG). 2019. "Terrorism is a cancer in the region, and it requires collective efforts to root it out." X (formerly Twitter), February 15. https://twitter.com/ARG_AFG/status/1096330433896300545?lang=en-GB.

Rashid, Ahmed. 2002. *Taliban: Islam, Oil and the New Great Game in Central Asia*. London: I. B. Tauris.

Reagan, Ronald. 1983. "Message on the Observance of Afghanistan Day." Ronald Reagan Presidential Library and Museum, National Archives. March 21. https://www.reaganlibrary.gov/archives/speech/message-observance-afghanistan-day.

Roberts, Nancy. 2001. "Coping with Wicked Problems: The Case of Afghanistan." In *Learning from International Public Management Reform: Part B (Research in Public Policy Analysis and Management, Vol. 11, Part 2)*, edited by L. Jones, J. Guthrie, and P. Steane, 353–375. Leeds: Emerald. https://doi.org/10.1016/s0732-1317(01)11006-7.

Rubin, Barnett. 1995. *The Fragmentation of Afghanistan: State Formation and Collapse in the International System.* New Haven, CT: Yale University Press.

Saikal, Faizal Haq, and William Maley. 1986. "With the Afghan Refugees in Pakistan." *Quadrant* 30 (10): 22–35.

Savranskaya, Svetlana, and Thomas Blanton, eds. 2009. "Afghanistan and the Soviet Withdrawal, 1989: 20 Years Later." Electronic Briefing Book No. 272. National Security Archive, George Washington University, February 15. http://www2.gwu.edu/~nsarchiv/NSAEBB/NSAEBB272/.

Scheer, Robert. 2006. "Meanwhile Back in Afghanistan." *Nation,* January 30. https://www.thenation.com/article/archive/meanwhile-back-afghanistan/.

Sheppard, Eric. 2011. "Geography, Nature and the Question of Development." *Dialogues in Human Geography* 1 (1): 46–75.

Suhrke, Astri 2008. "A Contradictory Mission? NATO from Stabilization to Combat in Afghanistan." *International Peacekeeping* 15 (2): 214–236.

Tanner, Stephen. 2009. *Afghanistan: A Military History from Alexander the Great to the War Against the Taliban.* New York: Da Capo.

Thomas, Raju. 2004. "The South Asian Security Balance in a Western Dominant World." In *Balance of Power: Theory and Practice in the 21st Century,* edited by Michel Fortman, James Wirtz, and T. V. Paul, 305–333. Stanford, CA: Stanford University Press.

Thomson, Debra. 2014. "Through, Against, and Beyond the Racial State: The Transnational Stratum of Race." In *Race and Racism in International Relations: Confronting the Global Colour Line,* edited by Alexander Anievas, Nivi Manchanda, and Robbie Shilliam, 44–61. London: Routledge.

Thomson, Mark. 2011. "The Festering Wound: U.S. Air Strike Kills At Least 25 Pakistani Troops." *Time,* November 26. https://nation.time.com/2011/11/26/the-festering-wound-u-s-chopper-strike-kills-25-pakistani-troops/.

Toynbee, Polly. 2002. "Was It Worth It?" *Guardian,* November 13. https://www.theguardian.com/world/2002/nov/13/afghanistan.comment.

US Army and Marine Corps. 2007. *Counterinsurgency Field Manual: US Army Field Manual No. 3-24; Marine Corps Warfighting Publication No. 3-33.5.* Chicago: University of Chicago Press.

Wendt, Alexander. 1992. "Anarchy Is What States Make of It: The Social Construction of Power Politics." *International Organization* 46 (2): 391–425.

Wissing, Douglas. 2013. "General Malaise." *Huffington Post,* January 19. https://www.huffpost.com/entry/afghanistan-generals_b_2146707.

Yousaf, Mohammed. 1992. *Afghanistan—The Bear Trap: The Defeat of a Superpower.* Havertown, PA: Casemate.

Afghanistan and the Soviet Colonial Archive

The Soviet decision to invade Afghanistan in December 1979 ranks among the most momentous in modern history and continues to cast a deep shadow over the wider region. The Soviet war in Afghanistan (1979–1989) unleashed the staggering destruction of hundreds of thousands of Afghan lives—and the forced displacement of at least five million people.[1] Soviet bombardment devastated the physical infrastructure and natural environment, leaving millions of landmines in its wake. Indeed, mines strewn across the Afghan landscape represent just one of several open-ended legacies of the war (as of 2024, some 20 percent of the country has not been demined, and injuries to children and agricultural workers are a regular occurrence).

The Soviet war has left an enduring impact on the politics of Afghanistan and the globe, yielding multiple afterlives. Beyond the physical ruins and still displaced populations, the conflict has been at the center of conflicting mythologies in the wake of the Cold War. For many Afghan militants as well as for combatants from more than a dozen countries who fought against the Soviets, the war was a noble effort that showed the capacity of Islam to defeat "atheists" and "communists." Their victory, they believed, would inaugurate a new kind of political order around the globe. In Western capitals, by contrast, the Soviet retreat in 1989 seemed to offer confirmation of the inevitability of American-led Western hegemony. The collapse of the Soviet system just two years later further strengthened the idea that the West had "won" the Cold War by ensuring Soviet defeat in Afghanistan.

Viewed from the perspective of the USSR, the war created very different meanings. To be sure, the Soviet invasion and occupation of the country exposed many of the limitations of the Soviet system, including in the military, economic, and ideological spheres (Ro'i 2022). Yet the Red Army's defeat in Afghanistan was not a foregone conclusion. And for just over a decade, the occupying of the country and shoring up the Afghan revolutionary government confronted Soviet state, military, intelligence, and party elites with the challenge of devising a form of control that can best be understood as colonial. This project thus entailed the continuous production of a particular form of knowledge that would enable Soviet rule. The result was a distinctive archive of colonial knowledge that drew on and distilled a lengthy history of engagement with Afghanistan by various Soviet and Russian imperial actors dating back to the eighteenth century.

Two frameworks stand out as essential keys to understanding how the USSR mobilized colonial knowledge in Afghanistan. The first was the idea that Afghanistan was a place where the Soviets would find solidarity, even "friendship," to use the term first employed in 1919—in correspondence between King Amanullah and Vladimir Lenin that formalized the first recognition of Afghanistan's newly won independence by a foreign power— and repeated in subsequent official pronouncements through the 1980s (Lenin 1919). In visual and print media, Soviet and Afghan revolutionary propaganda emphasized the theme of friendship between the two countries, often exemplified by images of individual members of each society collaborating in solidarity, as in figure 2.1.

The second essential element of the Soviet colonial archive in Afghanistan stood in almost direct contrast to the first but nonetheless coexisted and competed with it: This was the preoccupation with Afghanistan, particularly after the first violent confrontations with the Afghan resistance, as a place of singularly uncanny encounters. Red Army soldiers' remembrances frequently recall a profound sense of disorientation, of being uncertain about official narratives of the war and the identity of the "enemy" and unmoored by everything about their time in the country.

Both of these conceptions of Afghanistan were rooted in colonial notions of exceptionalism. On the one hand, Soviet exceptionalism resided in the conviction that Soviet policies were fundamentally different from, and more benevolent than, other states that ruled over vast spaces and heterogeneous populations. The Soviet Union, like the United States, consistently refused to identify itself as an "empire" and repeatedly asserted its anti-colonial identity. At the same time, this understanding of exception was consistent with the Soviet view that in Afghanistan the Red Army and Soviet civilians alike were dealing with a wholly different setting for their

2.1 A Soviet traffic constable and an Afghan soldier guard the high-altitude tunnel of the Salang pass, August 4, 1983. V. Suhodolskiy / Sputnik via AP.

politics. Afghanistan resembled the European colonies characterized by Achille Mbembe as "the location par excellence where the controls and guarantees of judicial order can be suspended—the zone where the violence of the state of exception is deemed to operate in the service of 'civilization'" (2003, 24). In this scenario, Afghanistan was not just an arena in which extreme forms of violence were permitted, even necessary—it was simultaneously an environment stamped by unreason and madness, which spared almost no one.

Making Friends Beyond the Amu River

Intermeshed with Cold War ideology, the Soviets imagined they had a special relationship with Afghans—and thus represented a benign foreign power unlike other empires. Soviet views of Afghanistan in the 1970s and 1980s drew on a generic European Orientalist canon as well as a conception of Russia's unique place in Asia grounded both in the history of the tsarist empire and the emancipatory vision of the Bolshevik party, first enunciated after the First World War, in what they called "the East" (see Nunan

2019). In the nineteenth century, Russian scholars—and European scholars working in Russian imperial institutions such as Johannes Albrecht Bernhard Dorn (in Russian, Boris Andreevich Dorn, 1805–1881)—counted among the pioneers of what would later become "Afghanistan studies." As a St. Petersburg University professor, Dorn published in 1847 the first grammar (in any language) of Pashto (Dorn 1847). In the following year, Alexander Burnes's *Journey to Bukhara*, with one of the most complete accounts of Kabul and its environs, appeared in Russian, reflecting close Russian engagement with British colonial literature (Borns 1848–1849).

As the tsarist empire expanded into Central Asia in the second half of the nineteenth century, frequent interactions between Russian soldiers, diplomats, administrators, traders, travelers, settlers, and subjects of the emergent Afghan state generated particular conceptions of the peoples that inhabited this space. Tsarist and early Soviet ethnographic knowledge has received far less attention than British approaches to Afghanistan. However, from the point of view of the imperial capital of St. Petersburg (and later Moscow), Afghanistan's northern neighbor had distinct advantages. Imperial authorities not only drew on British and other European writings but also produced their own knowledge. This included academic work and what we might call quotidian knowledge based on constant contact with Afghan authorities and communities along the Amu River and, perhaps even more importantly, via interactions with the Afghan diaspora community of exiles, merchants, fugitives, spies, and others who traversed Russian-ruled Central Asia.

The political profile of many of these itinerant figures would prove foundational. Crucially, Russia's Afghan interlocutors included opponents of the ruling dynasties who appealed to tsarist authorities for protection. The future Amir 'Abd al-Rahman Khan (r. 1880–1901) found refuge in the tsarist empire for a decade before he came to power in Kabul. Some of these exiles even sought Russian support against Afghan rivals in laying claim to the Afghan throne. However, nonelites also crossed the border from what would become known as Afghan Turkestan in the late nineteenth century into tsarist territory. Migrating by the thousands between the 1880s and 1900s, these included whole communities of pastoralists, who appealed to Russian officials for safe passage citing persecution at the hands of Afghan officials sent to govern them from Kabul. Jews from Herat also petitioned tsarist officials for permission to migrate to the Russian empire.

Petitions from Afghan subjects seeking safe passage and, in many cases, naturalization as tsarist subjects reinforced the imperial view that Russian expansion was a beneficent, even liberating, force in Asia. For instance, in his account of the Afghan north in 1880, the traveler Boris Tageev (Rustom Bek), a tsarist subject, told Russian readers that Afghan Shia Tajiks expected "liberation" from the "slavery" of their Afghan Sunni rulers (Tageev 1904, 49). Tsarist authorities composed reports on these refugees citing their requests for "rescue from persecution" by Afghan officials. Petitioners, they claimed, saw "our territory" as "the last sanctuary from brutal reprisals."[2] Although such appeals affirmed officials' image of tsarist Turkestan as a refuge for the dispossessed, their approach reflected a cautious appreciation of the wider geopolitical consequences (Crews 2009). In the case of Afghan émigrés, Russian officials feared antagonizing Kabul and generally discouraged flight in large groups across the border. Though they frequently permitted small groups and individual families, in other cases they returned them to Afghanistan or dispatched them on to Persian territory.[3] In some instances, local authorities gave refugees small parcels of land near the border. A number of Afghan notables received stipends in Tashkent or Samarkand, where they were "interned," often with their families. These elders repeatedly offered to join the Russians in waging war against the Afghan state. Russian authorities, in turn, kept them on the payroll as clients in the event they were needed in a time of war—and to forestall the risk of their flight back to Afghanistan. Such payments to Afghan émigré notables continued through 1917.[4]

While tsarist thinking privileged attention to the wider geopolitical context, the imperial discipline of ethnography was yet another lens for understanding subjects of the amir. The inhabitants of Afghan Turkestan appeared familiar in many respects to tsarist observers. The categories "Tajik," "Uzbek," "Turkmen," and "Kyrgyz" were constituent elements of the tsarist project in Central Asia and were thus legible as potential allies or even subjects enjoying protection from the tsar.

However, tsarist authorities regarded the ethnic category "Pashtun" in a very different manner. More than mere objects of ethnographic study, Pashtuns were the focus of various schemes of anti-British incitement in the late nineteenth and early twentieth centuries under both the tsarist and Soviet regimes. They were essential figures in a political myth, born in nineteenth-century military and diplomatic circles, whose appeal straddled the revolutions of 1917 in the Russian empire and the birth of a new Soviet order: Asia, and Britain's Indian subjects in particular, these elites affirmed, looked to Russia for liberation from London's imperialist yoke.

It was Russia's destiny in Asia to act as "defenders of the native population against English domination" (Zagorodnikova 2005, 52).

In this scenario, Pashtuns were amenable, given the right political actions on the part of tsarist and, later, Soviet officials, to act as the avant-garde of this effort. Nikolai Bravin, the first Soviet diplomat in Kabul, a graduate of the Oriental Studies faculty of Petersburg University and former translator at the tsarist consulate in Calcutta, sought in 1919 to open up a corridor through the Pashtun tribal belt from which socialist revolution would spread. The Bolsheviks attracted other like-minded thinkers in colonial Asia. Muhammad Barakatulla, a Muslim Indian nationalist who had appealed to the tsarist government during the First World War as head of a "Provisional Government of India" established in Kabul in 1915, also placed his hopes on the Pashtuns, who would make the victory of the revolution "inevitable." In April 1919 he wrote to Lenin offering aid against "the common enemy of Bolshevism and Islam—England." Requesting money and arms, Barakatulla sought printing presses (with English and Persian type) and paper for pamphlets of a "religious and political character" that would win over the Pashtuns. Barakatulla also shared with Soviet officials an article he had authored in Japan, lauding the martial qualities of the Pashtuns, who, he asserted, had enough "strength and bravery . . . to conquer the world. One should not interfere in their internal affairs but should strengthen in their hearts love of the Afghan state through the bonds of brotherhood in Islam. Just as the Prophet sent preachers to the Arab tribes, so should we send preachers to all the border tribes" (Tikhonov 2005, 36–37).

For the Bolshevik leader Lev Trotsky, this was enough to convince him, in the context of 1919, that "the path to Paris and London lays through the towns of Afghanistan, Punjab, and Bengal." For his part, Bravin sought a million gold rubles, machine guns, and airplanes—as well as the opening of consulates in Jalalabad, Kandahar, Ghazni, and Kaniguram—to incite a massive anti-British rebellion among the tribes. In December, his successor finally made direct contact with frontier Afridis and Waziris, whose "heroic spirit" was supposedly strengthened by news of the Soviet backing (Tikhonov 2005, 39).

In 1919, Lenin's Soviet government was the first to recognize the independence of Afghanistan, an act that Soviet diplomats would tout for decades as a symbol of the special relationship that bound the two states together in "friendship" and anti-colonial solidarity. Although

Central Asians who resisted the imposition of Soviet rule in the early 1920s and collectivization in the late 1920s and early 1930s fled by the tens of thousands to Afghanistan, and King Amanullah touted his Pan-Islamic credentials in the region, extensive cross-border trade and Soviet aid for Afghan infrastructure projects such as roads, airports, dams, and tunnels expanded after the Second World War (Nunan 2016). The Soviet Central Asian republics of Tajikistan and Uzbekistan played an especially important role as showcases of socialist economic, scientific, and cultural development, much of it carried out in languages and articulated through historical and literary references shared with their neighbors (Kalinovsky 2018).

After the April 1978 coup by members of the People's Democratic Party of Afghanistan (PDPA), Soviet advisors anticipated building on the presumed friendship and admiration that they expected to find among Afghan leftists and what they imagined to be more progressive elements in the newly named Democratic Republic of Afghanistan. In addition to ideologically sympathetic military officers corps, urban, secular intellectuals, workers, teachers, and young people were among those whom the Soviets targeted for integration into official organizations modeled on Soviet precedents, including an Afghan version of the Soviet youth organization, the Young Pioneers pictured in figure 2.2.

Differences between Afghan revolutionaries and their mentors in Moscow quickly surfaced, however. Still viewing Afghan politics through inherited ethnographic and geopolitical frameworks, the political aspirations of Pashtuns proved a challenge when revolutionaries such as Hafizullah Amin, who seized control of the revolutionary state in September 1979, lobbied the Soviets for support in creating a "Pashtunistan" and a "Baluchistan." In speaking to his Soviet mentors, Amin insisted that "the territory of Afghanistan must reach to the shores of the Gulf of Oman and the Indian Ocean," adding, "We wish to see the sea with our own eyes" (Mitrokhin 2009, 111). Where Pashtuns once seemed to promise a path toward global revolution, the irredentist activism of Amin and others now struck Moscow as imperiling the broader socialist cause. Critical of the "two hundred-year [policy of] Pashtunization," some Soviet observers warned that the "national question"—obliquely referring to the dominant position of Pashtuns in the revolutionary order—was no less important than "the religious, agrarian, and other" problems facing the revolutionary regime (Shchedrov 1981, 6–7).

2.2 Pioneers at the opening of the House of Soviet Science and Culture of the Union of Soviet Friendship Societies and Cultural Ties with Foreign Countries in Kabul, Democratic Republic of Afghanistan, November 11, 1982. Vladimir Rodionov / Sputnik via AP.

The Soviet Politburo finally opted for a military coup and invasion in December to depose Amin after it had repeatedly rebuffed Afghan revolutionaries' calls for Soviet military intervention over the course of 1979. Officials sent from the USSR sought to mobilize preexisting ideological and cultural ties to shore up the Afghan government while also trying to temper its more radical tendencies. Given Soviet concern that a supremacist ethnic agenda might undermine the socialist project in Afghanistan, non-Pashtun groups who shared a common ethnicity and language with the Soviet Central Asian republics appeared to be fitting targets for initiatives based on past Soviet nationality policies. In the Russian imperial context, Bolshevik leaders had once set out to end what Lenin called "Great Russian chauvinism" and create a "friendship of peoples" in its place. In Afghanistan, the Red Army and Soviet security forces could initially rely on numerous advantages, including a long history of training and equipping the Afghan armed forces and, crucially, reliance on the Soviet Orientalist archive of knowledge about the country and on cadres of experts, including linguists hailing from the Uzbek and Tajik Soviet republics who were familiar with Afghan languages, culture, and society. The Soviets were even able to appoint a party leader and Soviet-style Muslim, Fikriat Tabeev, from the Tatar Soviet Socialist Republic, long a center of Islamic learning with ties to Central Asia and Afghanistan, as ambassador to Kabul ("Posol" 2020). However, as Sabauon Nasseri has shown, Afghan revolutionaries had their own agendas and often clashed with one another and the Soviet advisors who increasingly acted as their "big brother" (2023). Translating Soviet revolutionary precedents to the Afghan setting proved daunting in practice.

Despite a lengthy history of contact and exchange, Soviet advisors struggled to establish a firm grasp on knowledge of Afghan society that could be used to salvage the Afghan revolutionary project. Basic questions of demography were among the thorniest details. Some Soviet experts refuted the long-held Afghan official position that Pashtuns made up an absolute majority in the country. In November 1981, a correspondent for *Pravda* wrote to the Central Committee of the Communist Party in Moscow, asserting that more than half of the country was inhabited by representatives of various "national minorities." He maintained that Pashtuns made up "45 percent" of the total population but only "an insignificant minority" north of the Hindu Kush, a territory encompassing roughly a third of the entire country (Shchedrov 1981, 7–8).

Based on the notion that shared ethnicity would prove a conduit to ensuring political loyalty, this estimation of the ethnic landscape in Afghanistan seemed to play to Soviet strengths. Moscow had ready-made cadres of Soviet Central Asians at the ready to shore up the socialist convictions of populations that Soviet experts understood to be their coethnics. But the idea that one could easily map ethnicity and its political correlations proved unreliable in everyday interactions. Mutual mistrust between Afghan Uzbeks, Tajiks, Turkmen, and others and their Soviet counterparts was a persistent issue. And, despite sharing numerous commonalities on paper, even Soviet Central Asians frequently found Afghans to be far different than what they had expected.

In the judgment of a few dissenting Soviet diplomats and experts such as Vladimir Plastun, the strategy of deploying Central Asian advisors to Afghan government and military personnel on the basis of an assumed solidarity tended to be counterproductive. To Plastun, Soviet citizens from the Uzbek, Tajik, and other republics seemed to lack an authentic understanding of communism to share with their Afghan brothers but nonetheless treated them with condescension. As Plastun recalled in his memoirs, "We noticed this, and the Afghans did too. I saw repeatedly how representatives of the Central Asian Soviet republics landed as advisors in Afghanistan and upon shaking hands with local (Afghan) Tajiks, Uzbeks, Turkmen and Hazaras (but not Pashtuns!) from the official establishment would give them not their palm, but their fingers, which is a sign of disdain" (2016, 168). Shared categories of ethnic classification did not necessarily create a common understanding of how to create a revolutionary society. Ultimately, an even older conception of Afghan politics—long a feature of Russian, Soviet, European, and, later, American views of the country— won out: Like its rivals, Moscow concluded that the "traditional" rulers of Afghanistan were limited to the Pashtuns. Thus they judged that they needed as head of state an ethnically Pashtun ruler as an ally to sustain the revolutionary state and "friendship" with its northern neighbor.

Afghanistan Beyond Reason

By early 1980, Soviet officials had begun to struggle with the realization that academic study of Afghanistan and "the East" was insufficient preparation for a country that seemed to defy the certainties of the Orientalist disciplines. Moreover, Soviets remained dependent on Afghan colleagues to interpret what they encountered. For Vladimir Plastun, an acute illustration of this dynamic was the outbreak of massive protests in Kabul on February 22 and 23, 1980. Soviet officials had no idea why crowds they estimated at some 400,000 people had taken to the streets; Afghan officials were supposedly no help either. They had no answers for their Soviet counterparts. It was only years later, Plastun notes, when he learned that the spark for the event was the shooting of a Soviet soldier at a market where he was shopping. His comrades returned to the scene and opened fire there and in the surrounding neighborhood, shooting as many civilians as they could find (Plastun 2016, 155–165). Soviet propaganda organs countered such episodes of popular resistance by highlighting the recurring "friendship" theme, as in figure 2.3, which purported to portray Afghans, in this case in an apparently rural setting, welcoming Soviet soldiers, here portrayed as including representatives of coethnic solidarity.

Though obscured by such imagery, cycles of miscomprehension and violence are recorded in official Soviet reports and participants'

2.3 Soviet soldiers and Afghan residents, January 6, 1983. L. Iakutin / Sputnik via AP.

memoirs. In contrast to the academic canon of Orientalist certitude, what emerges from these texts is an image of Afghanistan as a place that was unknowable. Its inhabitants were, even years into the war, beyond comprehension.

One issue was the physical setting itself. Strange and menacing, the landscape, flora, and fauna of the country made up a disorienting environment of alienation and confusion. Anonymized interviews of Soviet veterans collected in the relatively open late Soviet era by the journalist Svetlana Alexievich (1992) are especially revealing. As an artillery captain explained to Alexievich about his sense of Afghanistan, "So much of it was exotic, too: the way the morning mist swirled in the ravines like a smokescreen.... There are places there which remind you of the moon with their fantastic, cosmic landscapes. You get the feeling that there's nothing alive in those unchanging mountains, that it's nothing but rocks—until the rocks start shooting at you! You sense that even nature is your enemy" (79). "We went to save lives, to help, to show our love," a nurse recalled. Instead she developed an intense hatred: "Hate for that soft, light sand which burnt like fire, hate for the village huts from which we might be fired on at any moment" (23). Likening the Afghan topography to a surreal dreamscape of despair, a female civilian recalled a nightmare in which she was flying into Afghanistan on a military transport plane: "We can see the mountains through the portholes: then it gets dark. We begin to sink into some kind of abyss: there's a layer of heavy Afghan soil over us. I dig like a mole but I can't reach the light. I'm suffocating" (75). Animals, too, were testimony to the eerie timelessness of the country:

> One morning I lit up a cigarette and there was a lizard, no bigger than a mayfly, sitting on the ashtray. I came back a few days later and the lizard was still sitting there in exactly the same position. He hadn't even moved his little head. It suddenly occurred to me, that's the essence of the Orient! I could disappear and reappear a dozen times, break things up and change things round as often as I wanted, and he'd *still* be in no great hurry to turn his tiny little head. It's the time-scale, you see. It's 1365 according to their calendar. (35)

Ostensibly more familiar creatures did not behave like those at home, either: "The donkeys over there, they lie down during the shelling, and when it's over, they get up again" (4).

Suspended beyond the realm of reason, Afghanistan was a space in which Soviets felt compelled to suspend conventional morality. "What's unthinkable here [in the USSR] was everyday reality over there," a Soviet lieutenant remarked (Alexievich 1992, 111). Violence that would have Soviet citizens jailed made one "a hero for 'punishing bandits'" in Afghanistan (90). "We probably survived by hating," a Soviet nurse remembered, "but I felt full of guilt when I got back home and looked back on it all." She explained, "Sometimes we massacred a whole village in revenge for one of our boys. Over there it seemed right, here it horrifies me" (23).

Some veterans struggled to reconcile their expectation of friendship and gratitude and the everyday violence of the Soviet project. The nurse quoted above confronted this contradiction only after the war: "I remember one little girl lying in the dust like a broken doll with no arms or legs. . . . And yet we went on being surprised that they didn't love us. They'd come to our hospitals. We'd give a woman some medicine but she wouldn't look at us, and certainly never give us a smile. Over there, that hurt, but now I'm home I understand exactly what she was feeling" (23). This vertiginous environment swept over those who passed through the country, undermining soldiers' grip on reality.

The Soviets were fighting "ghosts" (*dukhy*), phantoms who moved in the darkness and across an insurmountable terrain. Red Army soldiers complained that they never saw the enemy clearly. As a Soviet officer told Alexievich,

We killed the enemy wherever and whenever we could, and vice versa. But this wasn't the kind of war we knew about from books and films, with a front line, a no man's land, a vanguard and rear echelons, etc. You know the word *kiriz*? It's the word the Afghans use for culverts, originally built for irrigation purposes. This was a "kiriz war." People would come up out of them like ghosts, day and night, with a Chinese submachine-gun in their hands, or the knife they'd just slaughtered a sheep with, or just a big stone. Quite possibly you'd been haggling with the same "ghost" in the market a few hours before. Suddenly, he wasn't a human being for you, because he'd killed your best friend, who was now just a lump of dead flesh lying on the ground. (111–112)

From the vantage point of an infantry foot patrol or even a helicopter, Afghans remained undifferentiated. In this context, the figure of the "civilian" became obscured. All Afghans might be combatants. Killing individuals "point-blank" was troubling, a Soviet officer observed, but "killing *en masse*, in a group, is exciting, even—and I've seen this myself—fun" (111). Children were no exception. In fact, Afghan children were not *truly* children. Like shapeshifters and specters, they were another unseen threat.

Soviet leaders tried to maintain strict secrecy around their conduct of the war while constantly crafting propaganda to influence audiences at home, in Afghanistan, and across the Cold War divide. The Soviet public was told that the USSR had intervened to honor a treaty of friendship with Afghanistan. In doing so, Moscow was coming to the aid of progressive political forces in Afghanistan and safeguarding the security of the Soviet Union's southern border in Central Asia by fending off the "counterrevolutionary" forces of international "imperialism" and "reaction" backed by the United States. However, the repetition of claims about the successes of the Soviets and their Afghan allies that clearly contradicted the experiences of Soviet personnel in Afghanistan gradually undermined support for the war in some—but not all—quarters. Disillusionment with the callousness of the Soviet system was one response to the war. Cannabis and opium use became a commonplace escape from the war for Red Army conscripts. Most simply focused on survival and on fulfilling the Soviet soldier's "international duty" honorably with the hope of returning home safely alongside one's comrades. Beyond the world of ideological conformity among elites, rank and file members of the Red Army and their civilian counterparts confronted constant disorientation and unease. The enduring trauma of violence that the Soviets perpetrated, suffered, and witnessed in Afghanistan would linger for decades after 1989.

Learning from Empire

The Soviet occupation was more than a black eye for the prestige and legitimacy of the Soviet system, the death knell of the Afghan left, the moment of incubation for Afghan and international Islamist forces, and the transition to a narco-economy. Soviet policies also proved to be what we might call a phantom guide to the American intervention some twelve years later. Numerous scholars have highlighted American reliance on British ideas about Afghanistan (especially in the realm of counterinsurgency) during the US-led war from 2001 to 2021; however, the American empire borrowed from Moscow as well.

Following September 11, 2001, as Washington improvised an attack on Taliban forces then ruling most of Afghanistan, the Soviet experience entered a new phase of interpretation. Soviet failure in Afghanistan became a cautionary tale (what the West should not replicate)—and simultaneously a point of reference for the presumed superiority of the American intervention and the political project that it pursued for the next twenty years. From the invasion of 2001, US policymakers frequently shifted course in Afghanistan, tacking back and forth between contradictory approaches to the insurgency, to the opium economy, and to the corruption of their domestic allies, to name just a few thorny challenges. Yet in doing so, American generals, politicians, and the media who tended to reproduce their points of view constantly made reference to lessons ostensibly learned from Soviet failures. Their understanding of the Soviet experience—rather than the *actual* history of the USSR in Afghanistan—loomed as an omnipresent warning of how *not* to govern Afghanistan. Thus in the twenty-first century, too, Afghanistan remained a site of interimperial knowledge production and transfer.

From the very beginning of the American campaign in Afghanistan, anxiety about replicating the Soviet experience haunted US officials. Less than a year into the war, Defense Secretary Donald Rumsfeld warned in August 2002 that calls for a greater American role in securing the country would risk alienating Afghans: "The result would be that US and coalition forces would grow in number and we could run the risk of ending up being as hated as the Soviets were. In any event, without successful reconstruction, no amount of added security forces would be enough. The Soviets had over 100,000 troops and failed" (2002, 1). By this logic, the Americans could intervene successfully in Afghanistan but only with a "light footprint" designed not to antagonize Afghans. Here "lessons" from the Soviet past pointed to a way to manage an imperial possession, though without an overbearing occupation. This thinking reflected yet another kind of exceptionalism that a confrontation in Afghanistan had given rise to: the belief that the United States could control politics there without resistance.

For their part, a number of Afghan elites allied with Washington reinforced this thinking by citing the Soviet past as a way to highlight the supposedly more benign and humanitarian character of the American war. By such accounts, this was a wholly different kind of intervention. In 2009, for instance, the American commander Stanley McChrystal wrote to his superiors about the status of the war effort and included a quotation from Defense Minister Wardak sharply contrasting Soviet and American approaches: "Afghans have never seen you as occupiers, even though this has been the major focus of the enemy's propaganda campaign. Unlike the Russians, who imposed a government with an alien ideology, you enabled us to write a democratic constitution and choose our own government. Unlike the Russians, who destroyed our country, you came to rebuild" (McChrystal 2009, 4). Of course, not all Afghan elites shared this view. By 2013, a former Democratic Republic of Afghanistan general, Nur ul-Haq Ulumi, had concluded that the American intervention had been far worse for Afghans than the Soviet war (Ulumi 2013).

Just as the Soviet war could in retrospect be used, as Nivi Manchanda shows in her chapter in this book, to reinforce the trope of Afghanistan as a "graveyard of empires," it could serve as a shorthand explanation for the entire trajectory of Afghan history since 1979, including the twenty-year American war. One variation of this line of argumentation has laid all responsibility for war and instability on the USSR without acknowledging the pivotal role of the United States in bankrolling and sustaining the mujahideen who opposed the Soviets and went on to control, if not govern, the country between 1992 and the US intervention in 2001. Zalmay Khalilzad presents this narrative of deflection in his memoir, insisting, "The Soviet invasion and Moscow's brutal tactics created extreme circumstances that the Islamists exploited. Afghan fighters were radicalized, and militants throughout the Muslim world descended on the country. At that time, US policymakers had a limited understanding of the rising Islamist threat. This blind spot enabled Pakistan to cultivate extremists as proxies. Inattentive to the longer-term risks, we went along" (2016, 66).

With greater distance from the events of the American war, however, the notion that the Soviets oversaw an "evil" occupation, while the Americans fought a "good war" (a phrase often used to describe President Barack

Obama's approach) or, from 2021, a mismanaged but necessary and well-intentioned war has become cloudier. As enthusiasm for "war(s) on terror" have waned among much of the public in the United States and elsewhere, space may be emerging for a more faithful accounting of the actual nature of the wars fought in modern Afghanistan. Declassified documents and the proliferation of memoirs have yielded promising leads. Some US military commanders have broken with established orthodoxies and even conceded that American methods were much like those of the Soviets, using these resemblances to critique Washington's policies. General Daniel Bolger, for example, has recalled the early phase of the war as amounting to "a better-executed version of the old Soviet tactics: round them up, kill a lot, and let God sort them out" (2014, 91). By August 2021, moreover, many American elites' view of the Soviet war had shifted once again: The USSR implicitly figured into US President Joe Biden's (2021) claim that the American withdrawal from Afghanistan was justified because the country was "known in history as the 'graveyard of empires'"—and because "no amount of military force would ever deliver a stable, united, and secure Afghanistan." The Soviet war thus continues to loom over international politics in Afghanistan and to shape conceptions and practices of rule and warfare and the sense we make of them.

Notes

1 I use "Afghan" here as a civic (not an ethnic) label to denote populations recognized by successive governments as subjects and, later, citizens of the state of Afghanistan. Translations from publications in Russian are my own, except where noted.

2 See, for example, RGVIA, f. 400, op. 1, d. 2767, ll. 16–16 ob.; and RGVIA, f. 400, op. 1, d. 3692.

3 RGVIA, f. 400, op. 1, d. 2767.

4 RGVIA, f. 400, op. 1, d. 3692, ll. 103–109 ob.

References

Alexievich, Svetlana. 1992. *Zinky Boys: Soviet Voices from the Afghanistan War*. Translated by Julia and Robin Whitby. New York: W. W. Norton.

Biden, Joseph. 2021. "Remarks by President Biden on Afghanistan." August 16. https://bidenwhitehouse.archives.gov/briefing-room /speeches-remarks/2021/08/16/remarks-by-president-biden-on -afghanistan/.

Bolger, Daniel P. 2014. *Why We Lost: A General's Inside Account of the Iraq and Afghanistan Wars*. Boston: Houghton Mifflin Harcourt.

Borns, Aleksandr. 1848–1849. *Puteshestvie v Bukharu: Rasskaz o plavanii po Indu ot moria do Lagora s podarkami velikobritanskogo korolia i otchet o puteshestvii iz Indii v Kabul, Tatariiu i Persiiu, predpriniatom po predpisaniiu vyshego pravitel'stva Indii v 1831, 1832 i 1833 godakh leitenantom Ost-Indskoi kompaneiskoi sluzhby, Aleksandrom Bornsom, chlenom Korolevskogo obshchestva*. Translated by Georg Min. Moscow: V Universitetskoi tipografii.

Crews, Robert D. 2009. "An Empire for the Faithful, a Colony for the Dispossessed." In *Le Turkestan russe: Une colonie comme les autres?*, edited by Svetlana Gorshenina and Sergei Abashin. Special issue, *Cahiers d'Asie centrale* 17/18:79–106.

Dorn, Bernhard. 1847. *A Chrestomathy of the Pushtū or Afghan Language: To Which Is Subjoined a Glossary in Afghan and English*. St. Petersburgh: Printed for the Imperial Academy of Sciences.

Kalinovsky, Artemy. 2018. *Laboratory of Socialist Development: Cold War Politics and Decolonization in Soviet Tajikistan*. Ithaca, NY: Cornell University Press.

Khalilzad, Zalmay. 2016. *The Envoy: From Kabul to the White House, My Journey through a Turbulent World*. New York: St. Martin's.

Lenin, V. I. 1919. "Pis'mo emiru Afganistana Amanulla-khanu." November 27. Electronic Library of Historical Documents [in Russian]. Accessed March 3, 2025. https://docs.historyrussia.org/ru/nodes/30905-pismo -emiru-afganistana-amanulla-hanu-27-noyabrya-1919-g.

Mbembe, Achille. 2003. "Necropolitics." Translated by Libby Meintjes. *Public Culture* 15 (1): 11–40.

McChrystal, Stanley. 2009. "Commander's Initial Assessment." International Security Assistance Force, Kabul, Afghanistan, August 30. National Security Archive, George Washington University. https://nsarchive.gwu.edu /document/24560-headquarters-international-security-assistance-force -kabul-afghanistan-gen-stanley.

Mitrokhin, Vasiliy. 2009. *The KGB in Afghanistan*. Working Paper No. 40. Cold War International History Project, Woodrow Wilson International Center for Scholars.

Nasseri, Sabauon. 2023. "The Red Flower of Life: A History of the People's Democratic Party of Afghanistan, 1964–2020." PhD diss., Stanford University.

Nunan, Timothy. 2016. *Humanitarian Invasion: Global Development in Cold War Afghanistan*. New York: Cambridge University Press.

Nunan, Timothy. 2019. "The Soviet Elphinstone: Colonial Histories, Post-Colonial Presents, and Socialist Futures in the Soviet Reception of British Orientalism." In *Mountstuart Elphinstone in South Asia: Pioneer of British Colonial Rule*, edited by Shah Mahmoud Hanifi, 275–297. Oxford: Oxford University Press.

Plastun, Vladimir. 2016. *Iznanka Afganskoi voiny 1979—1989 gg. Dnevnikovye zapisi i komentarii uchastnika.* Moscow: Institut vostokovedeniia RAN.

"Posol voennogo vremeni: pochemu Tabeev naznachili poslom v Afganistan." 2020. *Tatarstan*, February 28. http://protatarstan.ru/news/pokolenie /pochemu-firkyata-tabeeva-naznachili-poslom-v-afganistane-100-let-tassr.

RGVIA (Rossiiskii gosudarstvennyi voenno-istoricheskii arkhiv [Russian State Military History Archive]), Moscow.

Ro'i, Yaacov. 2022. *The Bleeding Wound: The Soviet War in Afghanistan and the Collapse of the Soviet Union.* Stanford, CA: Stanford University Press.

Rumsfeld, Donald. 2002. Memo to President George W. Bush. Subject: "Afghanistan." August 20. National Security Archive, George Washington University. https://nsarchive.gwu.edu/document/24551-office-secretary -defense-donald-rumsfeld-memo-president-george-w-bush-subject.

Shchedrov, I. 1981. "Dokladnaia zapiska v TsKK KPSS ob Afganistane." November 12. National Security Archive, George Washington University. https://nsarchive.gwu.edu/document/25677-document-95-dokladnaya -zapiska-i-schedrova-v-ck-kpss-ob-afganistane.

Tageev, Boris (Rustom-bek). 1904. *Po Afganistanu: Prikhliucheniia russkogo puteshestvennika.* Moscow: Izdanie D. P. Efimova, B. Dmitrokva, d. Bakhrushinykh.

Tikhonov, Iu. N. 2005. "Bor'ba sovetskoi diplomatii za 'afganskii koridor' v zonu pushtunskikh plemen v 1919–1921 gg. (po arkhivnym materialam)." In *Afganistan i bezopasnost' Tsentral'noi Azii,* edited by A. A. Kniazev, 2:32–51. Bishkek: Ilim.

Ulumi, Nur ul-Haq. 2013. Interview with Robert D. Crews. Kabul, November.

Zagorodnikova, T. N., ed. 2005. *"Bol'shaia igra" v Tsentral'noi Azii: "Indiiskii pokhod" russkoi armii: Sbornik arkhivnykh dokumentov.* Moscow: Institut vostokovedeniia.

The Imperial Gaze and the Development Gaze

Reckoning with the Two Faces of American Empire and Its Afterlives and Deaths

In 2010, during one of my trips to my country of birth, Afghanistan, I sat in the back of an armored vehicle, departing the American embassy in Kabul with some new and old Afghan and American friends. We had attended a showcase of Afghan- and Afghan American–made documentary films, including my own codirected film *Postcards from Tora Bora* (2007, see figure 3.1) and were now making our way through a busy bazaar. A gunner was seated in the center, straddling a large machine gun contraption, with her head half-in and half-out of the middle of the vehicle. As she gazed at the assembled Afghan vendors and shoppers, she casually said, "I want to blow all their heads off." I begin my chapter on decolonizing Afghanistan and the United States with this autoethnographic anecdote because it shows the dehumanizing and polarizing effects of war. These types of on-the-ground experiences capture the everyday effects of living under occupation in ways that detached theorizing never could. They characterize the multiple dimensions of the US war and interventions in Afghanistan and my own intersectional Afghan American position and the contradictions inherent in both. The US embassy, which I would visit for cultural and social events during my fieldwork trips, was an "oasis" in the green zone of Kabul in comparison to other parts of the country, and yet it was under constant attack by Afghan "insurgents." There I met diplomats, media makers, journalists, and members of the military who were doing

3.1 The author in Panjshir Valley, 2004.

incredible work to rebuild Afghanistan as part of a large-scale development apparatus even as others within the same project were actively bombing and destroying other parts of the country. In this chapter, I will track and try to reckon with the contradictions, consequences, and effects of the post-9/11 US imperial project in Afghanistan and offer suggestions for peaceful decolonial futures.

In July of 2019, as the US "forever war" in Afghanistan was hemorrhaging US tax dollars and growing increasingly unpopular and the Trump administration was actively negotiating an exit strategy with the Taliban, then-President Trump in his first term told reporters at a White House meeting, "I could win that war in a week. I just don't want to kill 10 million people. . . . If I wanted to win that war, Afghanistan would be wiped off the face of the earth. . . . I don't want to go that route" (Rupar 2019). As Trump had tested the most powerful nonnuclear bomb, the Massive Ordnance Air Blast (MOAB), known more commonly as the "Mother of All Bombs" on Afghanistan in 2017, his statement, which outraged Afghans around the world, was not the empty, outlandish threat of a movie villain. At the time of his statement, in 2019, the US coalition forces were also dropping a record number of bombs on Afghanistan (UNAMA 2023). He was explicitly communicating that the US government had the military might, technology, and will to bomb Afghanistan into oblivion but that he was exercising restraint. The reason for the restraint—that the US empire is benevolent—is implied.

Trump's admission echoes General James Mattis's earlier remarks to Iraqi leaders following the US invasion of Iraq in 2003: "I come in peace. I didn't bring artillery. But I'm pleading with you, with tears in my eyes: If you fuck with me, I will kill you all" (quoted in Zehfuss 2013, 225). Like Trump, Mattis projected the US military's superior force and capacity for violence, threatening the annihilation of all Iraqis, while also articulating a desire for peace. However, he was more direct in emphasizing that the restraint was contingent on Iraqi cooperation and compliance with the occupation, and not guaranteed even though he, as the commander of the US armed forces, had "come in peace." The Iraqi scholar Kali Rubaii in her assessment of Mattis's statement underscores this point: "The claim of those bearing capacity for lethal violence is that they desire to foster life-sustaining care, under the condition that recipients of that care remain docile and receptive. In this framework of salvation by subjugation, a well-established motif in colonial enterprise, protection and harm run together" (2023).

In his book *Humane: How the United States Abandoned Peace and Reinvented War*, historian Samuel Moyn (2021) illustrates how Barack Obama legitimized the idea of a humane war by emphasizing the precision of drones and the exporting of human rights. The realities of drone warfare, as journalists, researchers, and human rights institutions have shown, is far from humane, not only in injuring and killing civilians but also traumatizing communities subjected to them (Bashir and Crews 2012; Bureau of Investigative Journalism 2015; Gusterson 2019; Hastings 2012; Khan 2021; Osman 2017a).

What is clear in these messages of imperial force coupled with benevolence is their doublespeak. Bilge Yesil (2024) calls this type of political doublespeak "strategic obfuscation" in describing how populist despots operate. Therein lie the two faces and crux of twenty-first-century US empire: its simultaneous propensity for incredible violence and its promises of altruism, care, and humanitarianism, further complicated by the vast development apparatus that the US government and its allies launched in their war in Afghanistan. In fact, not only did the US government spend significantly more in reconstruction efforts in Afghanistan than in previous wars, but more than half of it was funneled through the Department of Defense, which was an unprecedented break from previous development efforts that were led by USAID and other branches of the State Department

(Osman 2020, 77, 98). This merging of the military, diplomatic, and development branches is emblematic of the US war in Afghanistan.

Following the 9/11 attacks on the United States, in October of 2001, the United States initiated Operation Enduring Freedom to militarily remove the Taliban and spent two decades trying to keep them subdued. This was premised on launching a multifaceted development apparatus that would usher in an era of women's rights and democratic civil society in Afghanistan and peace and security globally. By November 2001, the George W. Bush administration was actively trying to convince the American citizenry of the need to save the Afghan people and "bring them into the twenty-first century." Former First Lady Laura Bush famously gave a radio speech in November 2001 about US military interventions as part of a larger humanitarian endeavor to save Afghan women: "Because of our recent military gains, in much of Afghanistan women are no longer imprisoned in their homes. They can listen to music and teach their daughters without fear of punishment. Yet, the terrorists who helped rule that country now plot and plan in many countries, and they must be stopped. The fight against terrorism is also a fight for the rights and dignity of women" (Office of the First Lady 2001), ushering in an era of what Mariella Pandolfi (2010) has called in other contexts of war "the militarized management of humanitarianism." In hindsight, the incredible irony of the US government's August 2021 withdrawal and brokering a peace deal and cease-fire with the Taliban, after spending over a trillion dollars on military and development and partly premising the war on saving Afghan women from the Taliban's misogynist rule, is not lost on the world and especially Afghan women, who are suffering through the Taliban's brutal gender apartheid regime once again (Osman and Bajoghli 2024).

How do we reconcile these contradictions of the US empire in the twenty-first century, distinguish the nation-building projects that were actually generative from those that were not, and make sense of the whole enterprise being discarded? How do we comprehend the sheer violence and carnage of the US and NATO military campaigns and operations in light of their claims of a humane, measured violence? While these discrepancies of US empire may not be reconcilable in the ways that its emissaries purport they are, in this chapter, based on my extensive ethnographic research, comprising multiple in-depth fieldwork trips in Afghanistan, I will track the contours, trajectory, and transmutations of the US government's war directives and development projects across twenty years in order to highlight the key characteristics of twenty-first-century US empire, thereby strategically unobfuscating and unmasking its imperial doublespeak. In doing so I will reckon with its contradictions, duplicities, and ironies, and offer ideas for decolonizing Afghanistan so the country and its people may be free from the endless cycles of imperial wars, sectarian violence, and bloodshed that have consumed them for a half century.

Rebranding Empire as Kinder and Gentler

As postcolonial scholars have shown, the encounter between imperialists and those they colonized has always been complex, and it has changed across the immense geographical areas and vast timespans that empires occupied. Empires have vacillated between exercising their full force and extent of their violence and more hybrid formations wherein select groups of the subject populations are allowed to exercise a degree of agency (see the introduction to this volume for more on empire's "select" and "partial" inclusion). Following the decolonial and independence movements of the 1940s to the 1970s in the Global East and South, wherein people used a variety of strategies to extricate their countries from the rule of the old guard colonial empires stretching from the seventeenth to the twentieth century (namely the British, Russian, Soviet, Dutch, and French), these older empires-turned-nation-states have become cognizant of the importance of not appearing to be imperial aggressors, invading, occupying, and extracting without provocation or a humane pretext. Of course, World War I and World War II were also important lessons in not engaging in xenophobic ethnonationalisms, although with history repeating itself with the rise of anti-immigrant sentiment, Islamophobia, and anti-Semitism in the West and elsewhere, it is questionable whether the lessons were learned. What is clear, though, is that following the world wars, the United States emerged as a world power.

With the collapse of the Soviet Union, precipitated by its ten-year war and occupation of Afghanistan, the United States further solidified its geopolitical position as a superpower. Yet, while there is agreement among Western scholars, policymakers, and others on this, there is—with the exception of decolonial scholars, politicians, and activists—a reluctance in the West and especially in the United States to entertain the notion that the United States, with its unmatched military might, having unleashed wars, military attacks, and economic sanctions across the world with little journalistic or international oversight, has also emerged as an imperial country. Likewise, for Russianists who are still caught in Cold War politics, there is a refusal to use the language of imperialism in their assessment of the Soviet Union's prolonged war in and influence on Afghan politics and society. Recognizing the United States' and the USSR's imperialism would entail those actors admitting their own disciplinary and professional culpability or at least complacency in the workings of empire. Some have gone as far as calling the United States "empire lite," a concept that Canadian academic and politician Michael Ignatieff (2003) introduced in his book *Empire Lite: Nation-Building in Bosnia, Kosovo, and Afghanistan* to describe how the modern empire, namely the US empire, unlike its predecessors, has transformed to be a force of good in the world. While he provides important case studies to support his conceptual framework, that is not the case in Afghanistan. If one closely analyzes the US war in Afghanistan beyond its public relations rhetoric, especially as it progressed, as I do in this chapter, it becomes clear that it was not a "good war."

In the case of the 2003 invasion and subsequent occupation of Iraq, the framework and simulacrum of a good war, predicated on the lie that Saddam Hussein was stockpiling weapons of mass destruction (WMDs), fell apart right away because the evidence that Colin Powell infamously presented to the UN Security Council was revealed to be false. The release of the Abu Ghraib prison-abuse photos and their circulation in US mainstream media in 2004 to international outrage further diminished the image of a good war in Iraq. The Bush administration was quick to reframe the torture as "enhanced interrogation techniques" and as isolated incidents—even though they were part of a larger pattern of torture at US detention centers abroad, including in Afghanistan and Guantanamo Bay.

The idea of the good war and interventions in Afghanistan, on the other hand, was more persistent, stretching across two decades. Beyond misguided retaliation for the 9/11 attacks, the US war was predicated on: (1) removing the Taliban for harboring Osama bin Laden and oppressing Afghan women and ethnic minorities, and (2) bringing democracy, human rights, and nation-building to the country. While cracks in the mission began to appear on the ground in Afghanistan almost immediately, it was not until the second decade of the US war there, when the situation became worse, that it was publicly debated and protested. For the American and Western public, it was only in the latter half of the second decade that the extent of the disinformation campaigns and problems with the war and its interventions were exposed in a series of investigative features in major Western press outlets. That coverage included the 2019 bombshell the "Afghanistan Papers," which, as the Pentagon Papers had for the Vietnam War, further cracked the facade of the good war. Based on more than two thousand pages of internal documents that the *Washington Post* obtained from the Office of the Special Inspector General for Afghanistan Reconstruction (SIGAR) through the Freedom of Information Act (FoIA), the Afghanistan Papers not only revealed that systematic fraud and corruption was prevalent in US development expenditures but also showed widespread disparities, ambiguity, and contention within the government over the central aims and focus of the war. It was a glimpse into the internal workings of the war that showed the idea of the good war was devolving even within the ranks—disillusioned, those involved were no longer sure who the good and bad guys were and where they fit in (SIGAR 2018; Whitlock 2020).

Development and Nation-Building in Afghanistan: The Good

Yet, the notion of a good war in Afghanistan was not only effective because the public relations media and policy campaigns kept the brutalities of the war off the front pages. Some of the many ambitious nation-building and democracy-development projects that the United States, the United Nations, and international community launched and invested billions in had potential and initially did usher in a new era of hope for Afghanistan. That is not to say that they were all generative and successful—far from it. Rather, the legal and political framework for the post-9/11 and post-Taliban transitional government that was laid out in the UN- and US-led Bonn meetings, which was then ratified in a new constitution, had many of the foundations of democracy. The constitution mandated free and fair elections and different branches of the government—consisting of the president's office, two parliaments, and the courts—to check one another's power. The constitution and Kabul-based *loya jirgas* (grand assemblies) that followed also encouraged the creation of political parties and the public to vote across the diverse spectrum of Afghans. Thus, initially political participation was high, and people were highly engaged. Especially in the cities, one could see political campaigns and pictures of candidates across media platforms from flyers plastered all over, to radio and television spots.

The constitution also required that at least 25 percent of both the lower and upper parliaments consist of female MPs, which is more than most first world nations, and that women be represented in other high-ranking government positions as ministers and governors, positions appointed by the president's office. Freedom of speech, assembly, and media was also legislated in the constitution. Although government officials would use article 3 of the constitution—which prohibited anything that was deemed "contrary to the sacred religion of Islam"—to censor, ban, charge, or fine media outlets, media owners in many cases were able to successfully fight the charges in the courts, thus refining the media laws (Osman 2020). With international aid, the media rapidly proliferated with the creation of hundreds of radio and television stations and print publications and internet media. These diverse media outlets enabled Afghan artistry, culture, and journalism to redevelop and flourish again, providing war-weary Afghans with much-needed entertainment *and* a counterbalance to the influence of government, warlords, and foreign interests via news and other informational programming and political talk shows (Osman 2020). Furthermore, as part of the US and UN transitional government mandates, civil society and international watchdog groups such as the Afghanistan Independent Human Rights Commission (AIHRC), the United Nations Assistance Mission in Afghanistan (UNAMA), Nai-SOMA (Supporting Open Media in Afghanistan), and others formed early on to further promote justice and try to safeguard human rights in a variety of ways.

Thus a robust albeit fragile public sphere emerged allowing for important national debates about human rights, democracy, modernity, and Islam. After a bloody civil war and years of sectarian and gender violence, Afghans across the political and religious spectrum had the infrastructure to express and exchange their diverse ideologies and viewpoints, contend with their pluralistic and multicultural citizenry, and seek justice through democratic means. During this time, a sense of pride in the diversity of the country and respect for the rights and equality of all Afghans also developed. Afghan media makers, artists, activists, and others, in conjunction with various civil society organizations, produced and disseminated message and campaigns on human rights, pluralism, and unity through a variety of media and platforms. There were many women's empowerment programs on television and radio stations. The Moby Media Group, which was partially funded by the US government, launched its popular "We Are All Afghan" campaign videos on its Tolo TV and Lemar TV channels. Multiethnic singers and choirs produced new songs such as "Mutahad bashan omagy" (Be united people) and reproduced classic solidarity and peace anthems such as "Dar een watan" (In this country) and "Watan eshque tu eftekharam" (Loving our country is our honor). As I describe in detail in my book, the efficacy of these media products varied dramatically and was hard to quantify (Osman 2020). However, the overall effect was such that even people who held conservative or misogynist positions on women, or bigoted viewpoints about other ethnic groups or *quowms*, had to be mindful at least in the public arena.

For the generations that were born after the 1979 Soviet invasion and occupation of Afghanistan, which threw the country into nearly half a century of war, this was their first glimpse of a semifunctional society where free expression, political participation, and social mobility through educational and work opportunities was somewhat possible. Hence when the US-backed Afghan government and statecraft scaffolding began to crack in its second decade, entirely collapsing with the return of the Taliban in 2021, it was particularly disillusioning, heartbreaking, and surprising for the Afghans who had come of age during this time and wholeheartedly believed in the US-led nation-rebuilding mission to see it all fall apart with the ill-executed exit of the United States/NATO and the international donor community.

The Dark Side of Empire: Twenty-First-Century Imperial Warfare

While that collapse might have been surprising, the large-scale democratic infrastructure project encompassing many different experiments was in fact, from the outset, built with a self-destruct button in place because the larger forces of imperialism, warlordism, and war were at odds with it. For starters, the US-backed Afghan government invited ruthless warlords, many of whom were former mujahideen leaders, to join the ranks of government in spite of massive protests. Some of them were even included in the US- and UN-led transitional government meetings following 9/11. Fearing prosecution for their lengthy records of human rights abuses, many of the warlords and their militias, who had been pushed out by the Taliban, hid or went into self-imposed exile until they were welcomed back with high-ranking government positions, homes, land, and money. At the same time, the Taliban—who had actively fought some of the warlords and their strongmen and removed them and their stranglehold on the population during their own brutal rule in the 1990s—were labeled insurgents and terrorists (see Aikins's chapter in this volume). Furthermore, because the war had to have a central enemy, the Taliban were prohibited from registering as a political party and were outlawed from civil society. Meanwhile, via electoral fraud, corruption, bribery, and sectarianism, the invited warlords used their newfound government positions in the parliament, courts, and min-istries to divert international funding to themselves and grow their bases, thereby making democracy a farcical commodity for sale and continuing to wreak havoc on the population, now from within the government as well.

At the same time, while people in the cities could enjoy the fruits of the international development initiatives to varying degrees, in the provinces, the Afghan National Army, in conjunction with US and NATO forces as part of their counterinsurgency operations against the Taliban, terrorized and traumatized the population along ethnic lines for two decades. Dur-ing Hamid Karzai's presidency, in the first decade of the war, Afghans were subjected to an onslaught of ground attacks and aerial bombardment, over ten thousand night raids (also called "kill and capture raids" and home in-vasions), imprisonment, and other acts of violence resulting in the deaths of countless Afghans, with official estimates going up to a hundred thou-sand, with many not counted (Billing 2022; Crawford and Lutz 2021; for more on night raids, see Azami's and Zafar's chapters in this volume). In the second decade of the war, during Ashraf Ghani's presidency, civilian casualties sharply increased due the US government shifting toward a strat-egy of more lethal force and less diplomacy and development. As reported by the Watson Institute's Costs of War Project, "The United States military in 2017 relaxed its rules of engagement for airstrikes in Afghanistan, which resulted in a dramatic increase in civilian casualties. From the last year of the Obama administration to the last full year of recorded data during the Trump administration, the number of civilians killed by U.S.-led airstrikes in Afghanistan increased by 330 percent" (Crawford 2020). In 2019, while in peace negotiations with the Taliban and seeking an exit strategy, the US coalition forces under the Trump administration dropped a record num-ber of 7,423 bombs on Afghanistan (McCarthy 2020).

Away from the gaze of international media and other oversight and monitoring organizations, the joint Afghan and US/NATO forces also con-tinuously subjected provincial Afghans to a litany of ever-evolving new technologies of war under all four American presidential administrations. Just as Afghanistan had become a laboratory for proxy war, insurgency and guerilla tactics, and weaponry during the Cold War, Afghanistan continued to serve as an imperial laboratory in the War on Terror. This time it was the testing ground for direct and indirect counterinsurgency war against the Taliban and new technologies of warfare, including artificial intelligence and algorithmic and biometric targeting (see Karimi's chapter in this vol-ume). In fact, armed and weaponized drones were first used in Afghanistan in the aftermath of the 9/11 attacks. During his presidency, Barack Obama earned the moniker "Drone King" for deploying more drone attacks on the Middle East and Asia than any other president. Whereas Pakistan and Iran have shot down multiple US drones allegedly in their airspace, the Afghan government and its army, which was funded and trained by the United States, was in a weaker, dependent, subject-colony position in relation to the United States, and therefore was not able to thwart the rising tide of US military operations and killings.

Afghanistan also became the testing ground for other war technology. As mentioned earlier, in April 2017 the Trump administration dropped the Massive Ordnance Air Blast bomb, or "Mother of All Bombs," the largest nonnuclear bomb, on Afghanistan. The US government, in conjunction with the Afghan government, quarantined the impact area, keeping journalists out; hence there was no on-the-ground coverage of the aftermath of the bomb. They released a few seconds of a drone recording of the detonation and claimed that the area was desolate and therefore there were no civilian casualties. The black-and-white aerial footage showed an explosion in a valley by mountains in long-distance wide shot, leaving out all signs of life (see figure 3.2). US network news outlets and major newspapers dutifully showed the video footage or images of it and reported the state-sanctioned message. I along with a few other critical voices challenged the dominant narrative, arguing that valleys in the area are full of life, but in the absence of any independent on-the-ground reporting from before or after the detonation, the true scale of the MOAB's human, animal, and environmental destruction remains concealed and undetermined, at least to the public at large (Ohl 2019; Osman 2017b). Outside of the United States, to their credit, journalists in Afghanistan, including international ones, though kept out of the impact zone, at least reported on how the area was quarantined. As scholars have shown, there is a long history of the US media industry being enmeshed and embedded in the US military industrial complex. What has been called the military industrial media complex (MIMC) often disseminates official government war narratives through its vast infrastructure of news and entertainment while censoring dissenting voices (see, for example, Osman 2019, 2022; Shaheen 2008; Stahl 2010; Wasson and Grieveson 2018).

As Hannah Gurman has documented, entire villages were razed with explosives, and night raids, disappearances, and renditions of suspected Taliban, tearing apart families and communities, especially in Pashtun areas; for every enemy targeted, three civilians were wrongly killed or captured (2013, 4). According to the Costs of War Project, in total an estimated

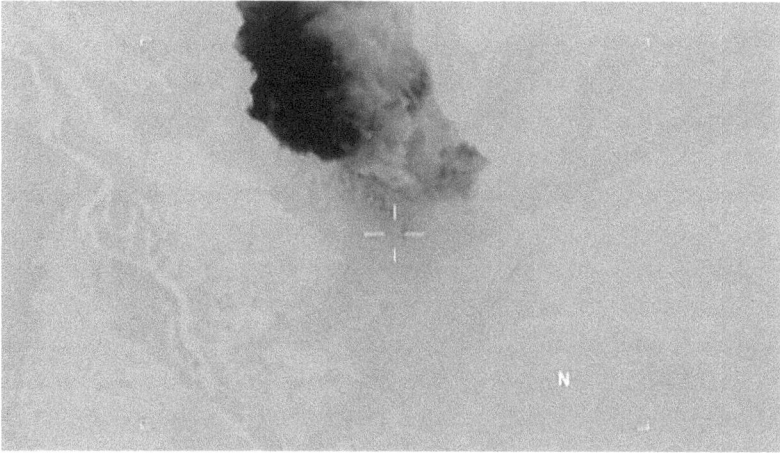

3.2 The Massive Ordnance Air Blast (MOAB) or "Mother of All Bombs" detonating in a valley in Achin, 2017.

250,000 people have been killed in Afghanistan and on its border with Pakistan (Crawford and Lutz 2021), and many others have been maimed. For those living outside of major urban areas and their green zones, the War on Terror became what many have called the War *of* Terror.

Investigative journalistic reports have also revealed extrajudicial and clandestine violence and killings enacted during military operations and in the United States' extensive networks of overseas military bases, prisons, and black sites, carried out through their rendition programs and by the notorious Zero Units and other CIA-trained Afghan militias and squads, as well as private security contractors, working with US special forces (Billing 2022; see also Aikins's chapter in this volume). In response to the International Criminal Court's (ICC) efforts to investigate suspected war crimes, in 2019 the then secretary of state Mike Pompeo threatened sanctions against the ICC—an unprecedented move from a democratic country. The United States and other members of the UN Security Council also regularly use their vote and veto power to maintain their hegemony and those of their allies such as Israel.

While the United States, like the USSR before it, engages in extensive rhetorical clean-up during and in the aftermath of their withdrawals, they do not engage in actual cleanup of its war debris and residuals. In its hasty withdrawal, the United States left behind large quantities of material detritus, everything from plastic bottles to abandoned military vehicles, bombs, landmines, and missiles, and their toxic by-products and residue such as depleted uranium—"imperial remainders" and reminders with their own afterlives, half-lives, and deaths that will not go away (Weyman 2003; Young 2021; see Karimi's chapter regarding US biometric technologies falling into the hands of the Taliban, and Noor's chapter on art and activism in response to imperial debris and waste). In my collaboratively made film *Postcards from Tora Bora* (2007), we documented some of the dangers of these discarded weapons of war, including cluster bombs dropped in canisters resembling food drops. Allowed by the international community and the Afghan government, which was in a subject-colony position, to act with impunity, imperial powers first turned Afghanistan into an experimental testing ground or theater of war and then into a not-so-living museum of war contaminating its once thriving communities, arterial rivers, valleys, and mountains. And yet in the face of death seeping all around them, Afghans are trying to raise awareness, clean up, and live with dignity (see figures 3.3 and 3.4).

How Imperial Violence Undermined Development

Like previous wars, these US-coalition-led military incursions and violence often across ethnic and urban/rural lines sowed the seeds of division. While Afghan reformers (sometimes in conjunction with international collaborators) in different sectors worked tirelessly to create the foundations of democracy, peace, and stability through policies and messages of inclusion, pluralism, and equality (Osman 2020), the US imperial project at large, through covert and overt military operations and outsourcing to private militias, was reanimating sectarian ethnic and gender tensions and retribalizing the country for its own gain. After all, as the old colonial powers knew well, segmented and divided societies, with infighting among the locals, are easier to exploit and rule. Therefore, orchestrating "divide and conquer" strategies was a key feature of British, Russian, and Soviet imperial subterfuge (see the introduction to this volume for details). Likewise, this was to the benefit of Afghan elites and warlords, who were used to profiteering from war economies. By including some people and excluding others, creating haves and have-nots, empire had exacerbated ethnic, urban/rural, gender, and class divides.

As the countryside became more of an incendiary hellscape, naturally the situation of women and girls, the hallmark of Western development, deteriorated, especially outside cities. As high-profile investigative journalistic reports have revealed, while urban women and girls enjoyed a degree of freedom, including access to education and employment, for women

3.3 The OMAR Mine Museum in Kabul houses bombs and
land mines from over fifty countries that have been used in
Afghanistan. From *Postcards from Tora Bora*, © 2007.

3.4 US government poster depicting food drop,
from *Postcards from Tora Bora*, with subtitles from the film, © 2007.

and girls in the rest of the country, who experienced the worst of imperial violence and bombing, life became increasingly untenable (Billing 2022; Gopal 2021; Osman 2020).

However, as corruption and violence spread, civil society began to devolve for people in the cities as well. The main markers of US development's success across all three US administrations—namely, women's rights, civic participation, education, healthcare, the economy, and the mediascape—began to fall apart due to increased corruption, insecurity, and instability. For example, as I have documented in depth in my book, long before the Taliban re-takeover, violence against media makers was a serious problem, resulting in self-censorship. While the internationally funded media sector at first afforded media makers, including women journalists, producers, and presenters, opportunities to improve their sociocultural positions and be active in shaping the public sphere, as violence increased over time, media makers became prime targets of elites within and outside of the government. Frontline journalists and on-air media makers, especially those with high profiles, those from unprivileged socioeconomic backgrounds, and women, were particularly vulnerable to threats and assassinations. Visibility itself became deadly for women who were targeted by patriarchal hardliners and others (Osman 2020).

In the face of mounting evidence of the collapse of the Afghan government and Taliban military gains throughout the country, the US imperial apparatus went into overdrive to defend the success of their projects and absolve themselves of its failures—much like the Soviet imperial apparatus once had. Via its public relations institutions and bureaucratic accounting and bookkeeping practices, US institutions exaggerated to make it seem that human and gender rights, education, and democratic governance were on track and thriving (Khan 2015; Nawa 2006; Osman 2020; SIGAR 2018; USGAO 2011). The simulacra of democracy, through superficial markers and the appearance of progress, supplanted and concealed the failures of the humanitarian/war apparatus and its harsh reality.

While the Afghan government and US-led NATO forces attacked the Taliban via military and media campaigns, the Taliban were also fighting back with counterattacks, improvised explosive devices (IEDs), and suicide bombs and at the same time amping up their own media campaigns to counter the United States and NATO's hearts-and-minds campaigns (see Azami's chapter in this volume). Similar to their tactics during their first ascent to power, the Taliban set themselves up as a counterbalance to US imperialism, the US-led "puppet" Afghan government, the warlords, and their kleptocracy and violence. Yet while civil society activists share their discontent with the US imperial project in Afghanistan, the Taliban are not a viable alternative. After two decades of fighting for their rights as citizens, the public wants no part in a one-party autocratic state (Crews and Osman 2021). This is evident in the protests and social movements in the country led by women, who dared not exit their houses during the first Taliban regime (Akbari and True 2022; Osman and Zeweri 2021; Osman and Bajoghli 2024); ethnic minorities (Ibrahimi 2017); and young people (Bose et al. 2019).

With the ill-executed and ill-fated US withdrawal from Afghanistan, the United States' sense of entitlement in controlling Afghanistan's future is ever present, as demonstrated by the Biden administration's seizure of $7 billion of Central Bank assets, allocating half to relatives of the victims of the 9/11 attacks. At the same time, the US government is allocating the other half to humanitarian efforts in Afghanistan, in addition to providing financial assistance to the Taliban so their government does not collapse (White House 2022).

Conclusion: The Afterlives and Deaths of Empire

So how do we reckon with these glaring and at times shocking discrepancies of US empire? There are a number of conclusions we can draw from the contradictory and ironic actions that characterize US imperial interventions in Afghanistan. Those with a more generous view of the US-led war and interventions interpret the doublespeak and contradictions as anomalies, mistakes, and mere shortsightedness rather than empire working as it was supposed to. Such accounts define the failures of the imperial project and its violence as aberrations and ruptures in an otherwise democratic and judicious system. On the other hand, as decolonial scholars and civil society activists and leaders have been arguing, the broken promises of altruism and the violence of imperialism are very much the norm of US foreign policy, a constitutive part of its ideological and political framework (Aouragh and Chakravartty 2016; Appy 2021; Chakravartty 2019; Elyachar 2005; Lears 2019; Mbembe 2003; Osman 2020; Said 2004). We can further debate whether this regime of "reluctant imperialists" and their counterinsurgency operations have actually been producing more "accidental terrorists" (Kilcullen 2009; Mallaby 2002; see Manchanda, chapter 1, in this volume). Furthermore, as I have shown throughout this chapter, narratives about the humaneness of war are misleading and legitimize the moral premises of waging war (the initial reasons for beginning it) and its ethical premises (how to wage it in a fair way) (Moyn 2021; Osman 2017a; Zeweri and Gregory 2023).

Here, my concepts of the development gaze and the imperial gaze, which I develop in my book (Osman 2020), can help clarify the discrepancies between the US-led coalition's loftier goals of nation-building and war directives. While development is deeply entrenched in empire, including how it has rebranded itself in the twenty-first century, I have also argued that it is important to analyze the efficacy of development projects on a case-by-case basis because the more collaborative, participatory, and ground-up ones were actually generative, including those highlighted throughout this chapter. These programs sustained hope and livelihoods by providing a semblance of a functioning society to a people who have been besieged by almost a century of war. The drive to help and serve others, especially those less fortunate and in need of assistance, was not the problem: It was the imperial infrastructure of war and its politics of discord and division that ultimately destroyed the nation's rebuilding projects from within and outside. This is because the imperial gaze is marked by hubris, mendacity, and racism because it is premised on imperial exceptionalism, manifest destiny, and supremacy.

Existing in their own echo chamber of truths, Western technocrats are are bestowed enormous imperial power and resources to wield their often top-down and detached expertise and war apparatus on the world's most vulnerable people. With the wave of their imperial wand, they can and have entirely remade, transformed, and slashed and burned economies, geologies, histories, and infrastructures of countries in the Global South and East and the lives of their people.

In the case of Afghanistan, whether one frames the imperial gaze in US foreign policy as the shortsighted mistakes of empire that can be rectified— as in, "We can do better next time"—or believes that there are and were intentional flaws and violence built into the system, making it designed for failure, the result was the same: the collapse of Afghan society, the rise of more extremists, and the continuation of cycles of destruction and rebuilding that have become a hallmark of modern US foreign policy abroad. In other words, the short-term rhetorical success of selling the war was paramount. The long-term success of peace and democracy in Afghanistan was inconsequential. Given the long-standing colonial tropes portraying the Afghan people as backward and savage (see the introduction and Manchanda, chapter 1 in this volume), the failures of civil society building in Afghanistan could easily be, and were said to be, the failures of Afghans, thus reifying the US government's altruism and benevolence in attempting to modernize a hopelessly failed state with a long history of barbarity, infighting, and misogyny—while absolving the United States of responsibility for the unnecessary loss and destruction of lives and livelihoods.

Another hallmark of the modern empire, which I have detailed in this chapter, is the bifurcation, fragmentation, and segmentation of society. As Achille Mbembe has articulated about the case of apartheid South Africa and in Israel/Palestine, the occupier splinters society via divide-and-conquer mechanisms, creating parallel infrastructures for the occupier and its emissaries, which are demarcated and removed from the rest of society. While some people, including women, enjoyed the fruits of empire for a limited time, most did not. While some grew rich and lived in relative security, most did not. In Afghanistan, elites living in what was called the "Kabubble," or the imperially protected green zones of Kabul and other urban areas, turned a blind eye to the suffering of their fellow citizens. When attacks occurred, they sequestered themselves in their international security compounds with bunkers, four- and five-star securitized hotels, poppy palaces, and gated communities. Much like during the Soviet occupation of Afghanistan, outside the bubble, resistance grew as society simultaneously began to devolve inside the bubble until the whole foreign-sponsored enterprise burst. When the US-backed Afghan government collapsed in 2021, the imperial elites and those with foreign and dual passports had the privilege to pack their bags and go home (see Samizay's and Zeweri's chapters on the disparities in privilege and discrimination among Afghan refugees in different countries). Military jumbo jets, Chinook helicopters, and private charters were ready to evacuate them. At the same time, the world watched the chaotic, desperate scenes unfolding at the Kabul airport, where Afghan nationals were kept outside the airport gates while some clung onto departing planes and fell to their deaths. And still the afterlives of war continue to wreak havoc on Afghans and Afghan refugees, who still have nowhere to go. They have been internally displaced many times and have been bounced around between neighboring countries for generations. Since 2023, according to the UN International Organization for Migration (IOM), the undemocratic governments of Pakistan and Iran have forcibly deported about 2.5 million (and counting) Afghan refugees, returning them to deplorable and dangerous conditions in Taliban-controlled Afghanistan ("Safety and Shelter" 2025). As citizens of a colonized country that has become a haven for imperial wars, experimentation, and "terrorism," Afghans have become both prey to and pariahs of the international immigration system.

Therefore, in considering what a decolonial future might look like for Afghanistan and the United States—as a political, epistemological, and cultural project—that future must first and foremost be grounded in a shared humanity, one that is truly embedded in an ethics of care and empathy, not profit, expansionism, and geopolitical hegemony. We cannot live in relative peace and prosperity while other people, domestically or internationally, are subjected to sanctions, poverty, bombing, and other imperial violence. As prominent decolonial activist scholars such as Angela Davis, Edward Said, Judith Butler, and Cornel West, among others, have shown, imperial violence and national violence are intricately linked. The imperial gaze traverses globally, moving between its metropole and peripheries to target subaltern people and racialized and sexual minorities, deploying the same technologies of war and subjugation, including policing from above, informational surveillance, prior criminalization, and the carceral state.

Thus, a decolonial future for Afghanistan and the United States is going to be one where everyone is included, a pluralistic society that is part of a global community, what decolonial scholars have termed the "pluriverse" (Ali and Dayan-Herzbrun 2024; Bishara 2023; Reiter 2018). More globally speaking, peace and security is contingent on there being peace and security everywhere, not just at the heart of the empire or the belly of the beast. No matter how many walls and borders are built, troops deployed, and bombs dropped, the world and its inhabitants and ecosystems are holistically connected: We will all suffer the consequences of imperial violence. Moreover, all empires collapse, especially those cloaked by absolute power, impunity, and hubris, who, sequestered in their own echo chambers, have come to believe their own doublespeak and supremacy. We in the United States must come to terms with the fact that we are an imperial nation that wages ill-conceived wars, threatens international justice organizations, and stifles and censors dissenting and independent voices, violently cracking down on anti-war protestors past and present. Taking a line from one of the US government officials who have resigned in protest of the United States sending billions of dollars in weapons and aid to fund the Israeli genocide in Gaza, "We cannot be both against occupation, and for it" (Flanders 2023). Likewise, we can't be both for and against empire.

References

Akbari, Farkhondeh, and Jacqui True. 2022. "One Year on from the Taliban Takeover of Afghanistan: Re-Instituting Gender Apartheid." *Australian Journal of International Affairs* 76 (6): 624–633.

Ali, Zahra, and Sonia Dayan-Herzbrun, eds. 2024. *Decolonial Pluriversalism*. Lanham, MD: Rowman and Littlefield.

Aouragh, Miriyam, and Paula Chakravartty. 2016. "Infrastructures of Empire: Towards a Critical Geopolitics of Media and Information Studies." *Media, Culture and Society* 38 (4): 559–575.

Appy, Christian G. 2021. "Abandoning Afghans from the Start." Review of *The Afghanistan Papers: A Secret History of the War*, by Craig Whitlock and the *Washington Post*. *Boston Review*, October 4. https://www.bostonreview.net/articles/abandoning-afghans-from-the-start/.

Bashir, Shahzad, and Robert Crews. 2012. *Under the Drones: Modern Lives in the Afghanistan-Pakistan Borderlands*. Cambridge, MA: Harvard University Press.

Billing, Lynzy. 2022. "The Night Raids." *ProPublica*, December 15. https://www.propublica.org/article/afghanistan-night-raids-zero-units-lynzy-billing.

Bishara, Amahl. 2023. "Decolonizing Middle East Anthropology: Toward Liberations in SWANA Societies." *American Ethnologist* 50 (3): 396–408.

Bose, Srinjoy, Nematullah Bizhan, and Niamatullah Ibrahimi. 2019. "Youth Protest Movements in Afghanistan." *Peaceworks*, no. 145 (February). https://www.usip.org/sites/default/files/2019-02/pw145-youth-protest-movements-in-afghanistan-seeking-voice-and-agency.pdf.

Bureau of Investigative Journalism. 2015. "Drone Strikes in Afghanistan." Archived at https://web.archive.org/web/20180624010404/https://www.thebureauinvestigates.com/projects/drone-war/afghanistan.

Chakravartty, Paula. 2019. "The Media, 'Race' and the Infrastructure of Empire." In *Media and Society*, edited by James Curran and David Hesmondhalgh, 242–262. New York: New York University Press.

Crawford, Neta C. 2020. "Afghanistan's Rising Civilian Death Toll Due to Airstrikes, 2017–2020." *Costs of War*. Watson Institute, Brown University. https://watson.brown.edu/costsofwar/files/cow/imce/papers/2020/Rising%20Civilian%20Death%20Toll%20in%20Afghanistan_Costs%20of%20War_Dec%207%202020.pdf.

Crawford, Neta C., and Catherine Lutz. 2021. "Human Cost of Post-9/11 Wars: Direct War Deaths in Major War Zones." *Costs of War*. Watson Institute, Brown University. https://watson.brown.edu/costsofwar/files/cow/imce/papers/2021/Costs%20of%20War_Direct%20War%20Deaths_9.1.21.pdf.

Crews, Robert, and Wazhmah Osman. 2021. "The Taliban Wants to Rule Afghanistan Again: But the Country Has Changed." *Washington Post*, July 20. https://www.washingtonpost.com/outlook/2021/07/20/taliban-wants-rule-afghanistan-again-country-has-changed/.

Elyachar, Julia. 2005. *Markets of Dispossession: NGOs, Economic Development, and the State in Cairo*. Durham, NC: Duke University Press. https://muse.jhu.edu/book/69426.

Flanders, Laura. 2023. "'Why I Resigned from the State Department': An Interview with Josh Paul." *Nation*, October 30. https://www.thenation.com/article/society/josh-paul-resignation-interview/.

Gopal, Anand. 2021. "The Other Afghan Women." *New Yorker*, September 6. https://www.newyorker.com/magazine/2021/09/13/the-other-afghan -women.

Gurman, Hannah, ed. 2013. *Hearts and Minds: A People's History of Counter-insurgency*. New York: New Press.

Gusterson, Hugh. 2019. "Drone Warfare in Waziristan and the New Military Humanism." *Current Anthropology* 60 (19): S77–S86.

Hastings, Michael. 2012. "The Rise of the Killer Drones: How America Goes to War in Secret." *Rolling Stone*, April 16. https://www.rollingstone.com /politics/politics-news/the-rise-of-the-killer-drones-how-america-goes -to-war-in-secret-231297/.

Ibrahimi, Niamatullah. 2017. *The Hazaras and the Afghan State: Rebellion, Ex-clusion and the Struggle for Recognition*. Oxford: Oxford University Press.

Ignatieff, Michael. 2003. *Empire Lite: Nation-Building in Bosnia, Kosovo, and Afghanistan*. Toronto: Penguin.

Khan, Azmat. 2015. "Ghost Students, Ghost Teachers, and Ghost Schools." *BuzzFeed News*, July 9. https://www.buzzfeednews.com/article/azmatkhan /the-big-lie-that-helped-justify-americas-war-in-afghanistan#.scBrrwpQm.

Khan, Azmat. 2021. "Hidden Pentagon Records Reveal Patterns of Failure in Deadly Airstrikes." *New York Times*, December 18. https://www.nytimes .com/interactive/2021/12/18/us/airstrikes-pentagon-records-civilian -deaths.html.

Kilcullen, David. 2009. *The Accidental Guerrilla: Fighting Small Wars in the Midst of a Big One*. London: Hurst.

Lears, Jackson. 2019. "Imperial Exceptionalism." Review of *Empire in Re-treat: The Past, Present, and Future of the United States*, by Victor Bulmer-Thomas, and *Republic in Peril: American Empire and the Liberal Tradition*, by David C. Hendrickson. *New York Review of Books*, February 7. https:// www.nybooks.com/articles/2019/02/07/imperial-exceptionalism/.

Mallaby, Sebastian. 2002. "The Reluctant Imperialist: Terrorism, Failed States, and the Case for American Empire." *Foreign Affairs* 81 (2): 2–7. https://doi.org/10.2307/20033079.

Mbembe, Achille. 2003. "Necropolitics." Translated by Libby Meintjes. *Public Culture* 15 (1): 11–40.

McCarthy, Niall. 2020. "Record Number of Bombs Dropped on Afghanistan in 2019." *Statista*, January 28. https://www.statista.com/chart/16079 /weapons-released-by-the-us-coalition-over-afghanistan/.

Moyn, Samuel. 2021. *Humane: How the United States Abandoned Peace and Reinvented War*. London: Verso.

Nawa, Fariba. 2006. "Afghanistan, Inc.: A *CorpWatch* Investigative Report." *CorpWatch*, October 6. https://www.corpwatch.org/sites/default/files /Afghanistan%20Inc.pdf.

Office of the First Lady. 2001. "Radio Address by Mrs. Bush." November 17. Archived at https://georgewbush-whitehouse.archives.gov/news /releases/2001/11/20011117.html.

Ohl, Jessy J. 2019. "The 'Mother of All Bombs' and the Forceful Force of the Greater Weapon." *Argumentation and Advocacy* 55 (4): 322–338.

Osman, Wazhmah. 2017a. "Jamming the Simulacrum: On Drones, Virtual Reality, and Real Wars." In *Culture Jamming: Activism and the Art of Cultural Resistance*, edited by Marilyn DeLaure and Moritz Fink, 348–364. New York: New York University Press.

Osman, Wazhmah. 2017b. "U.S. Drops Its Biggest Non-Nuclear Bomb on Afghans, Already Traumatized by Decades of War." Interview by Amy Goodman. *Democracy Now!*, April 14. https://www.democracynow.org /2017/4/14/us_drops_its_biggest_non_nuclear.

Osman, Wazhmah. 2019. "Racialized Agents and Villains of the Security State: How African Americans are Interpellated against Muslims and Muslim Americans." *Asian Diasporic Visual Cultures and the Americas* 5 (1–2): 155–182.

Osman, Wazhmah. 2020. *Television and the Afghan Culture Wars: Brought to You by Foreigners, Warlords, and Activists*. Urbana: University of Illinois Press.

Osman, Wazhmah. 2022. "Building Spectatorial Solidarity Against the 'War on Terror' Media-Military Gaze." *International Journal of Middle East Studies* 54 (2): 369–375. https://doi.org/10.1017/S002074382200037X.

Osman, Wazhmah, and Narges Bajoghli. 2024. "Decolonizing Transnational Feminism: Lessons from the Afghan and Iranian Feminist Uprisings of the Twenty-First Century." *Journal of Middle East Women's Studies* 20 (1): 1–22. https://doi.org/10.1215/15525864-10961742.

Osman, Wazhmah, and Helena Zeweri. 2021. "Afghan Women Have a Long History of Taking Leadership and Fighting for Their Rights." *Conversation*, October 11. https://theconversation.com/afghan-women-have-a -long-history-of-taking-leadership-and-fighting-for-their-rights-167872.

Pandolfi, Mariella. 2010. "From Paradox to Paradigm: The Permanent State of Emergency in the Balkans." In *Contemporary States of Emergency: The Politics of Military and Humanitarian Intervention*, edited by Didier Fassin and Mariella Pandolfi, 153–172. New York: Zone Books.

Reiter, Bernd. 2018. Introduction to *Constructing the Pluriverse: The Geopolitics of Knowledge*, edited by Bernd Reiter, 1–16. Durham, NC: Duke University Press.

Rubaii, Kali. 2023. "Decentering Death: The War on Terror and the Less-Than-Lethal Paradigm." *American Anthropologist* 126 (3). https://doi.org /10.1111/aman.13870.

Rupar, Aaron (@atrupar). 2019. "Trump casually says that if he wanted to, 'Afghanistan would be wiped off the face of the Earth—it would be over literally in 10 days.'" Twitter, July 22. https://twitter.com/atrupar/status /1153352075016835072.

"Safety and Shelter Elude Afghan Women Returnees from Iran and Pakistan." 2025. UN News, July 3. https://news.un.org/en/story/2025/07/1165331.

Said, Edward. 2004. *Humanism and Democratic Criticism*. New York: Columbia University Press.

Shaheen, Jack. 2008. *Guilty: Hollywood's Verdict on Arabs After 9/11*. Northampton, MA: Olive Branch Press.

SIGAR (Special Inspector General for Afghanistan Reconstruction). 2018. *Promoting Gender Equity in National Priority Programs (Promote): USAID Needs to Assess This $216 Million Program's Achievements and the Afghan Government's Ability to Sustain Them*. SIGAR 18–69 Audit Report. Accessed May 2, 2020. https://www.sigar.mil/pdf/audits/SIGAR-18-69-AR.pdf.

Stahl, Roger. 2010. *Militainment, Inc.: War, Media, and Popular Culture*. New York: Routledge.

UNAMA (United Nations Assistance Mission in Afghanistan). 2023. "Reports on the Protection of Civilians in Armed Conflict." https://unama.unmissions.org/reports-protection-civilians-armed-conflict.

USGAO (United States Government Accountability Office). 2011. *Iraq and Afghanistan: DOD, State, and USAID Cannot Fully Account for Contracts, Assistance Instruments, and Associated Personnel*. GAO.gov. Accessed May 13, 2020. https://www.gao.gov/new.items/d11886.pdf.

Wasson, Haidee, and Lee Grieveson, eds. 2018. *Cinema's Military Industrial Complex*. Oakland: University of California Press.

Weyman, Tedd. 2003. "Uranium Contamination of Afghanistan." Uranium Medical Research Centre. https://umrc.net/wp-content/uploads/2012/06/Uranium-Contamination-of-Afghanistan-Tedd-Weyman-2003.pdf.

White House. 2022. "Fact Sheet: Executive Order to Preserve Certain Afghanistan Central Bank Assets for the People of Afghanistan." February 11. https://www.whitehouse.gov/briefing-room/statements-releases/2022/02/11/fact-sheet-executive-order-to-preserve-certain-afghanistan-central-bank-assets-for-the-people-of-afghanistan/.

Whitlock, Craig. 2020. "Afghan War Plagued by 'Mendacity' and Lies, Inspector General Tells Congress." *Washington Post*, January 15. https://www.washingtonpost.com/investigations/afghan-war-plagued-by-mendacity-and-lies-inspector-general-tells-congress/2020/01/15/c65d0d46-37b5-11ea-bf30-ad313e4ec754_story.html.

Yesil, Bilge. 2024. *Talking Back to the West: How Turkey Uses Counter-Hegemony to Reshape the Global Communication Order*. Urbana: University of Illinois Press.

Young, Sydney. 2021. "Depleted Uranium, Devastated Health: Military Operations and Environmental Injustice in the Middle East." *Harvard International Review*, September 22. https://hir.harvard.edu/depleted-uranium-devastated-health-military-operations-and-environmental-injustice-in-the-middle-east/.

Zehfuss, Maja. 2013. "Staging War as Cultural Encounter." In *International Politics and Performance: Critical Aesthetics and Creative Practice*, edited by Jenny Edkins and Adrian Kear, 221–233. London: Routledge.

Zeweri, Helena, and Thomas Gregory. 2023. "'Outside the Wire': Brereton and the Dehumanization of Afghan Civilians." *Australian Journal of Political Science* 58 (3): 256–271.

Part 2

Infrastructures & Technologies of Empire

Operationalizing "Afghan Culture"

Role-Playing and Translation in US Military Counterinsurgency Training

> You would get attacked in the middle of the woods. You would get attacked in your village. . . . Usually they would come around 4 a.m. or 6 a.m. to pick you up and you'd go with them. They technically couldn't keep you longer than fourteen hours, but that wasn't the case, sometimes it would be seventeen–eighteen hours depending on what they needed. . . . It was really fun! (Zafar 2017, 189)

Such was the experience of Farah, an Afghan American woman who worked part time with a defense contractor as a role-player at military bases in the United States.[1] In 2015, Farah acted out scripted training scenarios created by the US Army to help soldiers gain practical field experience prior to deployment; those trained included the Rangers, the army's most highly trained and specialized soldiers, and those conducting some of the most important missions. The drama unfolded across a vast expanse in a setting that emulated Afghanistan's terrain and life on a forward operating base (FOB).[2] Dotted with mud huts, the set was meant to resemble an archetypal Afghan village (though on occasion it also accommodated representations of rural Iraq) replete with shops and wandering livestock. Soldiers were cast against this backdrop on three-week training exercises to help them anticipate and work through the social and cross-cultural impediments that could hinder their missions. The trainings were designed to help the military feel the pulse of the populations whose hearts and minds would determine the success of counterinsurgency (COIN) efforts in Afghanistan.[3] Alongside US military personnel were Afghan Americans contracted to create a sensory environment akin to living among Afghans. They were hired as actors to lend authenticity to the simulated setting and interactions that defined the Afghan experience. From this encounter emerged a reconstituted image of Afghanistan, one bearing the stamp of American empire.

This chapter explores the content and effect of the narratives that emerged from the US military's encounter with Afghan American contractors within the diaspora and how those narratives deepened the prejudices governing America's posture toward Afghanistan. I argue that such training exercises ultimately perpetuated the imperial gaze that turned Afghan culture and social organization into objects of the imperial project and convenient justifications for America's twenty-year occupation of Afghanistan and its haphazard withdrawal in August 2021. The rewriting of Afghan culture was, therefore, by design, an extended imperial project to render a revised version of Afghanistan. The research for this chapter draws on a four-year ethnographic project for which I conducted interviews and participant observation with and among communities of Afghan American contractors and US military personnel. I situate my observations of predeployment role-playing trainings in the context of the US military-industrial complex, which allows us to situate Afghan American contractors as producers of "cultural expertise" and as active participants in the vast security and foreign policy apparatus scaffolding US imperialism that creates the demand for cultural knowledge as a product. I limit my focus here to the role-playing medium as the most concentrated expression of cultural discourse and performance. The epistemological reductionism that ensues highlights the institutionalized biases that inform the US government's posture toward Afghanistan. Through this relationship, the appropriation, overextension, and paradox of culture becomes apparent in the denouement of the war.

I apply Erving Goffman's theoretical perspectives on framing and self-representation to analyze how knowledge produced by Afghan Americans is communicated to US military personnel as the consumers of such information. These representations channel an understanding of Afghanistan that, although produced with diasporic expertise, often equates to Orientalist renderings that reinforce and are reinforced by the prevailing narratives about Afghanistan—a criticism that substantiates similar findings in other studies of the American military encounter with Afghan Americans (Ferguson 2013; González 2007; Price 2009). Beyond a critique of the weaponization of culture in the military (see Boas 2005; Ferguson 2013; Foucault 1980; González 2007; Price 2009), this chapter uses Goffman's (1959) theater metaphor to capture scenario-based role-playing exercises as performances of knowledge designed not only to simulate the Afghan environment but also to help the military orient itself in a new cultural material reality. I focus in particular on Village Stability Operations (VSOS) as a major part of COIN and posit that the US military's insistence on Key Leader Engagements (KLES) and tribalism conflated the training scenario scripts on which the diaspora's performance was based with the historical and social context of Afghanistan. Whether a more acute reflection of reality would have changed Afghanistan's fate in global politics is arguable. But these new cultural worlds thus generated an archetype that was more rooted in US colonial imaginaries about Afghanistan than in Afghanistan's actual history.

In the years since the US invasion of Afghanistan, Afghan American contractors have been engaged across a spectrum of occupations. Some were role-players on military bases, while others role-played Afghans on various training programs at defense contracting companies in the Washington, DC, area. At the height of counterinsurgency, the US security sector awarded lucrative contracts to private-sector defense contractors, such as Mission Essential Personnel and Science Applications International Corporation, to employ droves of Afghan Americans who could apply linguistic, cultural, and regional expertise in training, advisory, and analysis programs across the portfolio of COIN and counterterrorism operations. My research subjects often applied for these positions with the hope that they would lead to more substantive engagement on US policy in Afghanistan. Many voiced frustration at being limited to short-term contracting roles despite having the knowledge and experience to contribute to technical areas in Afghanistan's state-building. My research and personal experience have demonstrated that the executive positions within the foreign policy and national security domains with actual authority, power, and, therefore, the ability to make significant decisions affecting Afghanistan are very often occupied by White decision-makers or those of European ancestry. Afghan Americans are usually cast in supporting roles, providing information on translating and decoding Afghanistan but rarely having an actual hand—or voice—in its future. There are exceptions. Zalmay Khalilzad, the prominent former US ambassador to Iraq and special envoy to Afghanistan, is a prime example. A trusted agent of US empire, Khalilzad is the embodiment of the "comprador intellectual," whose embrace of political realism and US hegemony facilitated the Taliban's return to power in Afghanistan (Dabashi 2011; Anderson 2005). Whether among the comprador intelligentsia or the short-lived contractor community, colonized forms of knowledge production rattle through the structures of race, belonging, and neocolonialism in Afghanistan (Ebtikar 2020; Manchanda 2020). Edward Said's description of the "Orientalist scholar" precisely characterizes culturally oriented contracting work in support of COIN: "Standing before a distant, barely intelligible civilization or cultural monument, the Orientalist scholar reduced the obscurity by translating, sympathetically portraying, inwardly grasping the hard-to-reach object" (1978, 222). Many contractors I interviewed who sought upward mobility within the US government's policy-planning arenas settled for such opportunities, exercising in hermeneutics what little agency there was to effect peace-building in Afghanistan. In the post-9/11 world, while the landscape of empire influence and intervention has evolved to showcase increasing localization, the transformation is veiled under the pretext of curated "native perspectives" and cultural expertise.

Actors and Agents: Performing Afghanistan in the Theater of Operations

For many of the Afghan American role-players, Afghanistan was a distant memory and one often drawn from the nostalgic recollections of family relations. In her mid-thirties, Farah had lived in the Northern Virginia suburbs since she was a toddler. Her family moved to the United States in 1981 after the Afghan government began persecuting families like hers, who were related to Zahir Shah, the deposed king, or were considered to be royalists. While Farah identifies as "Americanized," she feels strongly connected to her Afghan identity, enough to consider herself an authority on the values and norms associated with Afghanistan's sociocultural context. But her role-playing work was as much a learning experience for Farah as for the US military personnel with whom she interacted. She explained:

> When I got there, at first I was an interpreter with the US Army in army clothes, then I did some role-playing. . . . My Dari is better when I go back-to-back (to the rotations), but it's worse when I'm away longer. . . . Fort

Polk is huge. They have these little villages that they built a couple of years ago during the Iraq War. Like mud huts, fake gas stations, those doors. Some of the writing is in Arabic, they took down and made signs in Dari or Pashto. They'll bring out goats and stuff like that. It's like a movie set. The role-players go and they get their roles like clan leader's wife or mullah's wife or the mullah. . . . I conveyed some of the traditions like how to talk to leaders, not to put . . . what is it? . . . your right or left hand out, or the sole of your shoe, or if you're at someone's house offer to take your shoes off, things like that. When I worked with the FETS [Female Engagement Teams], I'd tell the women, "Don't try to shake hands with the men because they won't" or to have a headscarf on out of respect. Since I didn't grow up in Afghanistan, I had to brush up [on Afghanistan] from family and other Afghans—so they'd tell me, and I probably forgot, "Don't shake hands with your left hand and stuff like that." . . . I'd give them [the US soldiers] a background of why there are so much ethnic issues in Afghanistan, how Afghanistan works, let them know about the different ethnic tribes—just to give them an idea of why there is so much turmoil because they have no clue. (Zafar 2017, 189)

Rotations, as they were called, were twenty-one-day training exercises through which US military personnel and Afghan Americans like Farah would stage a scripted performance. The objective of the training was to equip the US military with enough skills and knowledge to make sense of their encounters in Afghanistan. Similar to previous examples, the irony of the drama was heightened by the fact that some of the Afghan American contractors had no firsthand experience in Afghanistan. The contractors were preparing for roles they had not previously assumed. Yet they were charged with a presentation of Afghan-ness that had to be socially and culturally authentic. Within the reconstructed theater of operations, the relationships among Afghans and with the US military were critical reflections of counterinsurgency and counterterrorism operations in Afghanistan. The expectations of Afghan culture and society among the military drew on conceptions of Afghanistan reconstructed in the diaspora, which were shaped by personal migration trajectories and colonial ideas perpetuated in the media and public discourse. Thus, the reproduced ideas of Afghanistan were scripted into training vignettes and cued the performance of both the US military and Afghan American role-players.

Role-playing often had two overlapping dimensions. In one sense, it was supposed to help the US military personnel anticipate and respond to different operational environments and the populations within them. But beyond that it was also supposed to help inculcate cultural relativism and sensitivity under the umbrella of "cross-cultural competence" or "3C." These efforts derive from a strategic need by the US government and military, as a whole, to redefine military personnel or "warfighters" into "warrior-diplomats" or "cross-cultural experts" who can understand and appreciate the disparities between the United States and the rest of the world (Rasmussen and Sieck 2012, 71). This endeavor requires the mitigation of bias. As "cultural researchers," US military personnel are expected "to frame . . . differences objectively" despite their mandate to fight certain populations (72). The role-playing scenarios create the opportunities to frame—and reconcile—the disparities between Afghan and US culture. But the medium through which such cultural interactions are negotiated creates a subjective experience. This channel of expression encourages producing knowledge that can be readily labeled, categorized, and rearticulated. Role-playing, viewed through Goffman's (1959) idea of performance, is nondiscursive, performed knowledge. In each role-playing performance, the participants enacted a series of roles simultaneously. The medium of role-playing imposed different frames on Afghan Americans that made them enact a range of social identities. US military personnel became students, diplomats, and aspiring anthropologists who were meant to observe and learn. Afghan American contractors were cast as both the experts and the subjects of expertise. Most importantly, the contractors had the ability to not only generate information but influence meaning. They had the power to shape a picture of reality about Afghanistan and direct an understanding of it. The limitations were minimal. As long as the interpretations mapped onto prevailing notions of Afghans or Muslims, Afghan American contractors might have been contested by their own peers, but their analyses would often go unchallenged by their US military counterparts.

In some interviews, US military personnel assumed that their knowledge of Afghanistan, despite several deployments, had little to no value compared to the presumed expertise of Afghan Americans such as Farah. This relationship entrenched the Afghan American contractors' position as both outsiders and insiders of Afghan culture and ushered them into the fold of US militarism. As insiders, they could demystify Afghanistan and speak about it in a way the military could understand. However, the validity of the knowledge they produced and transmitted depended on their role as assimilated migrants, familiar with the culture and values of

America writ large. Based on the perceived biculturality, Afghan Americans were considered sufficiently Americanized to understand and safeguard the US mission—a perception underscored by attaining government security clearances. As people straddling a line between two critical spheres of American power, Afghan Americans' insider-outsider liminality made them invaluable interlocutors capable of giving the US military a competitive edge. A term I heard often in training exercises was *skeleton key*—an allusion to an illusory piece of information that would finally provide the military with a solution to Afghanistan. Thus, the relationship between performing nondiscursive knowledge, producing discursive knowledge, and shaping identity can be expressed in two ways. First, Afghan Americans' representations of their knowledge established them as insiders in America, and secondly as experts with a unique positionality *outside* of American or Western culture. Inside the frame of a reconstructed village, Afghan Americans could position themselves as outsiders and take ownership of the scripts to advise on how authentically they aligned with their perceptions and memories of Afghanistan—despite the fact that the audience of US military service members had more recent experiences in Afghanistan. Assigning the term *expert* to Afghan American contractors significantly bolstered the assumption of the validity and authenticity of the knowledge performed on set by military service members and the defense contracting companies that hired them. The "expert" label also appeared to inflate the contractors' sense of authority, although I ironically found this to be limited among Afghan Americans who had actual, continuous lived experience in Afghanistan. The US military-industrial complex's reliance on authentic knowledge heightened the importance of diasporic expertise and engagement in COIN efforts. As a result, whether constituted as insiders or outsiders, Afghan American contractors maintained their relevance and status as key components of the US political and military strategy in Afghanistan.

During my research, role-playing exercises often featured a village to represent the provincial areas where much of the fighting occurred as well as an emphasis on Key Leader Engagements—or KLEs, as they became commonly known. Goffman's (1959) perspective on the actors, performances, and the stages on which everyday presentations of self occur is helpful in understanding how the medium influenced the knowledge that was produced. Farah and other interviewees, who had served as role-players in the village settings, described the village as a theater. Military officers in charge of creating the setting and directing the play consulted with the actors—the role-players—to assess the accuracy of the material world they were creating to develop an understanding of Afghanistan. Although most Afghan Americans who had experience in such settings with whom I spoke related that they found the artifacts familiar and consistent with their experience, those who had grown up outside of Afghanistan often referred to the same artifacts as "costumes" and "props" and relegated them to "playing" (e.g., "play fighting" when acting out a Special Operations raid on an Afghan household). Suleiman, a former role-player who had moved to America in 1974, described his experience:

> I got to wear a turban and act the part of a tribal elder. I'm Tajik, and that's a more Pashtun thing—the tribal stuff I mean. But it was fun to dress the part of a powerful Afghan khan, and show the Americans how to negotiate with an Afghan. . . . I got to wear a cloak like Karzai does. The Americans loved it. . . . I'd make it tough on them, like if they had raided my house, I would show anger and pound the table or something.

Similarly, a woman to whom he referred me echoed some of his reflections:

> Once I was assigned the role of a village housewife, so I put on a burka and stayed inside the house the whole time. That was boring. The houses were bare and small, and there were, like, farm animals roaming around everywhere. It was freaky. I can't even imagine how Afghans live like that. . . . Another time, they did a play night raid and we had to run around inside the house. I was just in regular Afghan costume, like the pants and dress on top, because the point was that the SOF [Special Operations Forces] guys had to try to engage us without offending our honor because I didn't have a headscarf or burka on. (Zafar 2017, 201)

The reliance on the village and the physical world it invoked created an opportunity for the contractors to develop a collective narrative about Afghanistan, and though any of them could contest the articulations, the process still afforded Afghan Americans a voice in shaping what the military came to understand as Afghan culture and Afghan people, even when they—like the village housewife quoted above—saw the experience of being Afghan as foreign as did their US military counterparts.

Another component of the scenario-based trainings was the focus on KLES. At a time when COIN operations actively referenced anthropology, "rapport building" was widely perceived as the conduit to winning hearts and minds. In both the reconstructed villages and in offices and classrooms where trainings were held, KLES provided an opportunity for mock interactions between US military service members and influential Afghans ranging from tribal leaders and village elders to warlords, government ministers, and three-star generals. An army colonel who directed training exercises noted that "practicing cultural dos and don'ts helps soldiers understand how to interact with Afghan leaders. . . . It helps them build rapport and it helps them avoid the cultural traps that, say, someone without that knowledge, might fall into" (Zafar 2017, 205). One common role-playing scenario was to enact a situation in which a US military service member would engage an Afghan American contractor playing the role of an Afghan National Army officer. The scene and script would focus on the US military providing training and technical assistance to Afghan security forces.[4] Some KLE scenarios anticipated corruption and bribery, not as misconduct but as social customs that enabled US military objectives, particularly for the Special Operations community.[5] US military personnel were drilled with a set of key points about Afghan culture that were supposed to guide their conduct as trainers or mentors to their Afghan counterparts. As Farah's account noted earlier, some of the recommendations were based on perceptions—not firsthand experiences—of Afghan social customs. In other cases, they reified the impressions and assumptions that US military personnel gathered from their deployments to Iraq. Anthropologist Nomi Stone's (2022) account of military simulation sites in Oregon discusses stark parallels—the generic "Middle-eastern village" becoming a referent for any place east of the US capital, enmeshed in the "Global War on Terror." In both instances, the medium of scripting and role-playing circumscribed the knowledge produced because it placed the performance of each actor within a specific frame that was duplicated, without accounting for differences in human behavior and context, in every iteration of the exercise. The reification of professional or personal misconduct, which I will discuss in a proceeding section on corruption and pedophilia (two commonly observed or experienced aspects of military deployments), further complicated the line between a political war and a "clash of civilizations." When the role-players physically performed cultural knowledge, they strengthened and validated ideas by cultivating a particular understanding of Afghanistan and Afghans based on routine interactions. In the KLE trainings I observed, role-playing exercises amplified sociocultural differences but rarely accounted for the disparity in power between the military and the supposed Afghan key leaders. Treating the interactions as cultural negotiations obligated each to roles as "Afghans" and as "Americans," rather than as "subjects" and "occupiers." Thus, once an understanding of local culture was established, it was used to convince Afghans of the judiciousness of the US government's top-down governance and security measures.

At the reconstructed village sites, some KLEs centered on *shuras* and jirgas—assemblies of local decision-makers to develop consensus around issues important to the community. Often, they positioned a high-ranking military officer in a role-playing scenario where he or she would learn to negotiate with a tribal leader or village elder acting in the role of "key leader." Within this frame, the contractors consistently articulated and performed select elements of Afghan culture that resonated with hyper-Orientalized perceptions of Afghans (for example, insisting on drinking green tea to build rapport, while weaving fictional accounts of tribal rivalries). While not all contractors performed in such a manner, many did. Motivated by salaries and recognition as experts, they produced knowledge that was dramatized and compelling, if not entirely accurate. The performances were not just entertaining to the participants: They helped advance the notion that the war in Afghanistan was a cultural one that could be imminently solved with increased cross-cultural understanding, rather than by assuming accountability for post–Cold War politics that had entrenched divisions and instability in Afghan society and the national economy. The reduction of cultural values to practices like breaking bread and drinking tea oversimplified the grievances of local Afghan populations as well. COIN's ambitions did not recognize the limitations of US military personnel, who, trained in and for warfare, had to become social scientists, nation builders, and cultural ambassadors practically overnight. But the task seemed less political given the message conveyed through the role-playing exercises and reinforced in public discourse: that the war in Afghanistan was inherently a tribal or ethnic conflict. The exercises and village scenarios lent credibility to the belief that the war stemmed from a natural proclivity for conflict among Afghans, a myth that has been at the root of creating an Other on which the shortcomings of US strategy can always be pinned.

Afghan Culture as an Antagonist: The Problem of an Ungovernable Other

The cultural explanations for Afghanistan's sociopolitical challenges that circulated during predeployment trainings and consequently among the US public strengthened the West's footprint in Afghanistan. Two major issues—corruption and *bacha bazi*—are at the heart of this discussion. The preoccupation with *bacha bazi*, in particular, in the American security and development worlds served to reinforce biases, implicit or otherwise, between Western and Eastern civilizations and their treatment of human life. American military and development circles understood *bacha bazi* as a condoned cultural practice, as though the sexual exploitation of young children was ritualized rather than stigmatized among Afghans.

The cultural problematization of the Afghan war, as generated through the US foreign policy apparatus, situated Afghans in Afghanistan as victims of their own making. Prior to the withdrawal of the United States, the international community's justification for occupation drew on extant social binaries and divisions between genders and ethnicities to project and decry the future the world could expect if Afghanistan were left to its own devices: a land of lawlessness, violence, and depravity. Forays into human sexual behavior are not uncommon in anthropological discussions on sex and power, particularly from the point of view of Orientalized fetishisms that have constituted the basis for hegemonic interventions in the past (Little 2004; Naber 2012; Said 1978, 1993). In addition to US military leadership, influential US politicians and media personalities touted literature on Afghanistan (both fiction and nonfiction) as objective ground truths that defined de facto social norms. From my observations, they summarily disregarded the subjectivity of the assertions in these texts. Various cross-cultural competence training exercises instructed intelligence analysts, for example, to mitigate their personal biases. However, the same perspective on the effect of bias was infrequently extended to the material products with which they worked. In an interview in 2014, an Army military intelligence officer who had deployed to southern Afghanistan from 2011 to 2012 recalled his ability to apply cultural relativism to his experiences in Kandahar Province. "I can fault the Afghan soldiers all I want for their sexual behavior, but they are doing something that is ingrained in their culture. . . . I may not like it, Americans may not like it, but Afghans don't see it the same way that we do," he related, referencing a controversial report issued by a team from the Human Terrain System (HTS). HTS consisted of often-pseudo social scientists on military fact-finding missions. The report was about the supposed preponderance of *bacha bazi*. Authored by Anna Maria Cardinalli, an HTS social scientist (with a doctorate in theology) and a self-professed military investigator, the report connects the practice of pedophilia in Kunduz Province with "a long-standing cultural tradition in which boys are appreciated for physical beauty and apprenticed to older men for their sexual initiation" and suggests that Western responses consider "whether this can rightly be termed abusive when seen through a lens from within the culture" (2009, 1–2). Such reports romanticized and effectively normalized pedophilia and pederasty, both explicitly outlawed in Afghanistan's constitution. Moreover, they conflated errant sexual crimes with Afghan queer and trans identity. The conflation distorts how Afghan queer and trans populations are represented—or rather, are not represented at all. From the perspective of anthropology, Roberto González and David Price critique the negligent assignment of cultural relativism based on the misattribution of anthropological information. They argue that "the 'anthropological' information provided to the military by HTS frequently stressed such exoticism, while ignoring centuries of contact with the West, legacies of European colonialism, and the inequities of power relations that most anthropological analyses would address" (2015, 5). The Cardinalli report effaced the historical actualities that had given rise to rampant sexual violence. A media article in 2015 accounted for the history of the practice, tracing it to the time of the Soviet invasion and the legacy of the US-supported mujahideen warriors. According to the account:

> Afghanistan's Mujahideen warlords, who fought off the Soviet invasion and instigated a civil war in the 1980s, regularly engaged in acts of pedophilia. Keeping one or more "chai boys," as these male conscripts are called, for personal servitude and sexual pleasure became a symbol of power and social status. . . . When the former Mujahideen commanders ascended to power in 2001 after the Taliban's ouster, they brought with them a rekindled culture of bacha bazi. Today, many of these empowered warlords serve in important positions, as governors, line ministers, police chiefs, and military commanders. (Mondloch 2013)

Cloaking their decision not to take action on matters related to *bacha bazi* as respect for cultural relativism, the American military leadership reinforced the legitimacy of the abuse. Such social issues fell outside of the purview of the military, particularly as their mission was to train, advise, and assist in the tactical and operational aspects of war fighting. Moreover, it is worth noting that the US government had empowered the mujahideen, setting the conditions that enabled their representation as part of Afghanistan's central government.

Corruption, as a concept and practice, was perceived and cast in a way that was similar to the representation of sexual abuse in the last fifteen years of war in Afghanistan. While corruption is endemic to any system in which there are sustained inequalities, the challenges it poses to good governance and stability in Afghanistan are linked to its treatment as a cultural practice. Military interviewees, who had worked on VSOs or directly in training and advisory roles with the Afghan national security forces, cited corruption as a means of "doing business" in Afghanistan. An Army civil affairs officer recalled her experience working with Afghan civilians as well as government and military officials. She observed:

> Everybody was corrupt. They all wanted *bakhshish* [a donation or handout]. Like we would try to set up a *shura* for the villagers and they would demand a *bakhshish*. They were basically charging us a fee for giving *them* money and assistance. At first, when I got there, I was like "How the fuck does that work, if we are supposed to be helping them?" It was just plain stupid. And then I got to understand that it is part of their culture and they don't see it like we see corruption in America. (Zafar 2017, 278)

Other military personnel as well as many of the Afghan American contractors I interviewed or observed in the training workshops consistently reiterated that they saw her position as valid. One thirty-six-year-old Afghan American contractor, who had grown up in America since she was two years old, expressed her frustrations with Afghan culture to a group of Special Operations Forces soldiers: "Corruption is the worst part of Afghan culture. . . . We have some nepotism in America, but in Afghanistan, it's *the* way things are done. . . . Everything is based around patronage networks" (Zafar 2017, 279; emphasis in the original). By drawing a sharp distinction between "us" and "them," she positioned Afghan values in direct opposition to US values of transparency and order. The explicit underlining of the distinction between America and Afghanistan, however, supports an empirical argument for US interventions in Afghanistan. Corruption, as a practice, can also be traced to the vast amounts of money that flooded Afghanistan from international organizations to fund security and development programs. Asma, one of my research participants and a former medical doctor in Afghanistan, explained that prior to the civil war by the mujahideen, "corruption was still an issue but not that much. People investigated corruption and those [who] were responsible got punished. Now with all the money that goes, and without any monitoring of how it is spent and by who, now corruption is a big problem" (Zafar 2017, 279). Asma's remarks are supported by the vast literature on aid inefficiencies and their relationship to corruption, which are not limited to Afghanistan (see Elyachar 2005; Moyo 2009; Nawa 2006; Osman 2020; Van Buren 2011).

The same matrix of contracting and privatization that buttressed knowledge production also contributed to creating a culture of corruption in Afghanistan, exacerbating an issue that was the legacy of the civil war's lawlessness and criminality. But considering corruption an intrinsic part of the culture helps solidify the idea that, like *bacha bazi*, corruption did not evolve from hegemonic military and nation-building interventions. Instead, these elements are assumed to be organic to the Afghan way of life—an idea that is insightfully approached by Wazhmah Osman, Helena Zeweri, and Seelai Karzai (2021) in their critique of an American television show. Centered on an Afghan translator, Al, whose US Army counterpart helps him immigrate to America, the show is replete with moments in which Al's cultural background, and its presumptions, are the punchline to a joke. They observe that when Al's character is pulled over by an American police officer, Al's immediate instinct is to bribe him—an act that draws a laugh track on the episode. In another scene that "reif[ies] the trope of Afghans as sexually repressed and misogynistic," Al can hardly keep his wits together during his driving test when the female driving instructor turns up in shorts. So astounded and flustered is he at the freedom of (white) American women that he drives the car into a tree. The show resonates with the narratives the American audience have come to associate with Afghans because it "reinforces existing imaginaries of Afghanistan as a land of warlords, corruption and unbridled violence." An intensified focus on corruption and sexual violence among Afghans blurs problematic parallels among American or Western communities. As a most recent example, several agents from the US Drug Enforcement Agency are, at the time of writing, under investigation for using the agency's resources for "a worldwide debauchery tour" of "binge-drinking and illicit sex." In contract to narratives about Afghanistan, such behavior in America is written about as a "culture of corruption among U.S. Drug Enforcement Administration agents," limited as a window into a particular organization, not into a people (Goodman and Mustian 2024). Tying together the various strands of the imperial imagination, US President Joe Biden (2021) concluded one of his early press conferences on the withdrawal with an exasperated admission that the United States should no longer be "sacrificing American lives to try to establish a democratic government in Afghanistan—a country that has never once in its entire history been a united country, and is made up—and I don't mean this in a derogatory way—made up of different tribes who have never, ever, ever gotten along with one another." An even perfunctory review of Afghanistan's history negates the prejudiced justification for summarily abandoning America's allies, Afghans who risked their lives to serve with US military and civilian officials.

In conclusion, the devastating aftermath of Afghanistan's collapse to the Taliban regime was in part made possible by a reimagined historiography of the country—a legacy of decades of neocolonial mythmaking designed to facilitate Afghanistan's political and economic exploitation. By promoting cultural understandings of Afghanistan that distort Afghan culture, US policymakers have dismantled the explicitly imperial dimension of America's occupation and instead decry the inability of Afghans to unite and govern themselves. In this chapter, I have focused on predeployment trainings, particularly role-playing exercises, as key elements in reframing an understanding of Afghanistan. I argued that role-playing exercises reengineered Afghanistan as a new cultural world—one developed by and for the US military-industrial complex. As part of the system, the US military and Afghan American contractors assisted in the reproduction of narratives critical to strengthening the projection of America's neocolonial posture toward Afghanistan. Afghanistan's political history, its culture, and its communities have, therefore, become revisions to a new accepted narrative. This emergent story assigns inherent cultural and moral flaws, such as corruption and sexual misconduct, to the Afghan state that excuses America's imperial ambitions and failures. While the commodification of cultural knowledge allowed Afghan Americans to gain salience as its producers, it did little to afford most Afghan Americans, outside of comprador intelligentsia, any meaningful voice in foreign policy decisions related to Afghanistan. Governing Afghanistan's future continues to remain a deeply colonial enterprise, particularly in the distribution of power, authority, and representation.

Efforts to decolonize knowledge within academe must extend to think tanks and government institutions, particularly within spaces of authority and power. It requires little research beyond a functional Boolean search to see that the circles closest to executive political decision-making in US government are starkly white. As I have critiqued elsewhere (Zafar 2023), even a thirty-eight-member study group on the Afghan peace process in Washington, DC, included only two Afghan Americans (US government civil servants accustomed to an uncontested narrative of American political realism) (USIP 2021). The recycling of tokenized Afghan knowledge in the form of the comprador intelligentsia conveys a prosaic gesture of concession—a proverbial checking of the box—without the intent to open up genuine spaces of dialogue and constructive engagement with populations most vulnerable to seismic shifts in global politics. Had the intent of brokering knowledge, particularly cross-cultural understanding, been in earnest, perhaps Afghans would have experienced the contours of US occupation less bluntly. But the US government's curation of data points served an already-established conclusion about Afghanistan as a foregone state rather than as a sincere effort to understand and mitigate the effects of a colonial project. Even the logic of "winning" hearts and minds is predicated on domination and victory, and obfuscates empire-making with state-building on a superficial framework. At best, the reductionism I have outlined in this chapter in the production of knowledge and its profoundly Orientalized imaginary may be a manifestation of an unconscious bias and perceived hierarchy within the US foreign policy and national security spheres. However, the treatment of Afghans, particularly in comparison to Ukrainians in the ongoing Russo-Ukrainian conflict, compounded by the tenor of the US government's posture, including President Biden's caustically racialized commentary, signal a much more nuanced and cultivated sense of institutional discrimination. America's dramatic curtain call in its theater of operations in Afghanistan is more than a somber pause for reflection. It signals the need for a deliberate sustained effort against the inequities of a system predicated on power and privilege.

Notes

1   All quotations are from interviews conducted for my doctoral dissertation (see Zafar 2017).

2   As an extension of larger main operating bases, the FOBS conduct tactical operations in local areas (e.g., FOB Salerno in Khost Province in Afghanistan).

3   COIN defined the US military doctrine in 2009 before it was phased out by 2014. COIN doctrine was premised on understanding local Afghan communities to incentivize their cooperation with US and NATO forces to defeat the Taliban.

4   Such trainings gained even greater traction when counterinsurgency became obsolete and the NATO mission transformed to a train, advise, and assist effort.

5   The acceptance and perpetuation of bribery was not limited to military and/ or military special operations. In fact, when I worked for an international relief and development organization in Kabul, "facilitation fees" appeared as line items in our program budgets. These were monies paid to officials (for example, Afghan governors or the local police) to allow us access to sites or beneficiaries. The payments, having no basis in Afghan social customs, were specifically outside of what was legally obligated in Afghanistan.

References

Anderson, Jon L. 2005. "American Viceroy." *New Yorker*, December 19.

Biden, Joe. 2021. "Remarks by President Biden on the Terror Attack at Hamid Karzai International Airport." White House, August 26. https://www.whitehouse.gov/briefing-room/speeches-remarks/2021/08/26/remarks-by-president-biden-on-the-terror-attack-at-hamid-karzai-international-airport/.

Boas, Franz. 2005. "Scientists as Spies." *Anthropology Today* 21 (3): 27.

Boone, Jon. 2010. "Foreign Contractors Hired Dancing Boys." *Guardian*, December 2. https://www.theguardian.com/world/2010/dec/02/foreign-contractors-hired-dancing-boys.

Cardinalli, Anna Maria. 2009. "Pashtun Sexuality." Unclassified Human Terrain Team AF-6, research update and findings. Public Intelligence. Accessed October 4, 2014. https://info.publicintelligence.net/HTT-PashtunSexuality.pdf.

Dabashi, Hamid. 2011. *Brown Skin, White Masks*. London: Pluto.

Ebtikar, Munazza. 2020. "A Critique of Knowledge Production About Afghanistan." Afghanistan Center at Kabul University, February 17. https://acku.edu.af/a-critique-of-knowledge-production-about-afghanistan/.

Elyachar, Julia. 2005. *Markets of Dispossession: NGOs, Economic Development, and the State in Cairo*. Durham, NC: Duke University Press.

Ferguson, R. Brian. 2013. "Full Spectrum: The Military Invasion of Anthropology." In *Virtual War and Magical Death: Technologies and Imaginaries for Terror and Killing*, edited by Neil Whitehead and Sverker Finnstrom, 85–111. Durham, NC: Duke University Press.

Foucault, Michel. 1980. *Power/Knowledge: Selected Interviews and Other Writings, 1972–1977*. New York: Pantheon.

Goffman, Erving. 1959. *The Presentation of Self in Everyday Life*. New York: Doubleday.

González, Roberto. 2007. "Towards Mercenary Anthropology? The New US Army Counterinsurgency Manual FM 3–24 and the Military-Anthropology Complex." *Anthropology Today* 23 (3): 14–19.

González, Roberto, and David Price. 2015. "The Use and Abuse of Culture (and Children): The Human Terrain System's Rationalization of Pedophilia in Afghanistan." *CounterPunch*, October 9. http://www.counterpunch.org/2015/10/09/the-use-and-abuse-of-culture-and-children-the-human-terrain-systems-rationalization-of-pedophilia-in-afghanistan/.

Goodman, Joshua, and Jim Mustian. 2024. "Takeaways from AP's Investigation into DEA Corruption, Agent Accused of Rape." Associated Press, July 25. https://apnews.com/article/drugs-dea-rape-corruption-fentanyl-opioids-trafficking-b3c2d83139e7cff077cd11401b84c0fa.

Little, Douglas. 2004. *American Orientalism: The United States and the Middle East since 1945*. Chapel Hill: University of North Carolina Press.

Manchanda, Nivi. 2020. *Imagining Afghanistan: The History and Politics of Imperial Knowledge*. Cambridge: Cambridge University Press.

Mondloch, Chris. 2013. "Bacha Bazi: An Afghan Tragedy." *Foreign Policy*, October 28. https://foreignpolicy.com/2013/10/28/bacha-bazi-an-afghan -tragedy/.

Moyo, Dambisa. 2009. *Dead Aid: Why Aid Is Not Working and How There Is a Better Way for Africa*. New York: Farrar, Straus and Giroux.

Naber, Nadine. 2012. *Arab America: Gender, Cultural Politics, and Activism*. New York: New York University Press.

Nawa, Fariba. 2006. "Afghanistan, Inc." *CorpWatch*, October 6. https://www .corpwatch.org/article/afghanistan-inc-corpwatch-investigative-report.

Osman, Wazhmah. 2020. *Television and the Afghan Culture Wars: Brought to You by Foreigners, Warlords, and Activists*. Urbana: University of Illinois Press.

Osman, Wazhmah, Helena Zeweri, and Seelai Karzai. 2021. "The Fog of the Forever War with a Laugh Track in 'United States of Al.'" *Middle East Research and Information Project*, May 26. https://merip.org/2021/05/the -fog-of-the-forever-war-with-a-laugh-track-in-united-states-of-al/.

Price, David. 2009. "Problems with Counterinsurgent Anthropological Theory: Or, by the Time a Military Relies on Counterinsurgency for a Foreign Military Victory It Has Already Lost." Paper presented at the University of Chicago, Department of Anthropology Conference: Reconsidering American Power, Chicago, Illinois, April 24.

Rasmussen, Louise J., and Winston R Sieck. 2012. "Strategies for Developing and Practicing Cross-Cultural Expertise in the Military." *Military Review* (March–April): 71–80

Said, Edward. 1978. *Orientalism*. New York: Pantheon.

Said, Edward. 1993. *Culture and Imperialism*. New York: Alfred A. Knopf.

Stone, Nomi. 2022. *Pinelandia*. Berkeley: University of California Press.

US Department of the Army. 2014. *Insurgencies and Countering Insurgencies*. FM 3-24, MCWP 3-33.5. https://irp.fas.org/doddir/army/fm3-24.pdf.

USIP (United States Institute of Peace). 2021. "Afghanistan Study Group Final Report: A Pathway for Peace in Afghanistan." https://www.usip.org /publications/2021/02/afghanistan-study-group-final-report-pathway -peace-afghanistan.

Van Buren, Peter. 2011. *We Meant Well: How I Helped Lose the Battle for the Hearts and Minds of the Iraqi People*. New York: Metropolitan Books.

Zafar, Morwari. 2017. "COIN-Operated Anthropology: Cultural Knowledge, American Counterinsurgency, and the Rise of the Afghan Diaspora." PhD diss., University of Oxford.

Zafar, Morwari. 2023. "The Old West and The Wild East: Cultural Biases in Contemporary US Afghan Policy." *Journal of Conflict Transformation and Security* 10 (1): 12–24. https://cesran.org/wp-content/uploads/2023/06 /2.pdf.

Shifting Loyalties and Profits

The Rise of Afghanistan's Western-Funded Private Security Contractors

The sudden collapse of the Islamic Republic of Afghanistan in 2021 brought an end to two decades of state-building and development by the US and its allies. Here I explore the remarkable growth of private security companies (PSCs) during the US-led occupation and its relevance for explaining the failure of the Western state-building project. While privatized violence, from Roman mercenaries to Elizabethan privateers, has been a long-standing feature of empire, the scale and rapid growth of the PSC industry in Afghanistan reflected the novel circumstances of a decades-long war intersecting with a global superpower and international markets.

Drawing on fieldwork and interviews conducted between 2010 and 2012 (Aikins 2012), I offer a case study of a large Afghan PSC at the height of the foreign military occupation and describe its links with informal armed groups that formed during the civil war. I argue that the PSC industry provided a means for such groups to avoid disarmament post-2001. By linking these peripheral actors with international rents, the PSC industry empowered them against the central government, incentivizing neopatrimonial strategies of governance by the center that ran contrary to state-building efforts. The upshot is that much of what was often decried as Afghan corruption by international observers was in fact produced by the structure of Western intervention, under which enormous amounts of military and stabilization spending bypassed the central government. In a second case study of Kandahar Province, I show how such international spending was crucial to the political settlement that formed there among republican elites post-2001, resulting in a doubly unstable order, dependent both on foreign rents and patrimonial bargains between periphery and center. In conclusion, I argue that the political economy of the PSC industry described here offers evidence that internal contradictions within the Western state-building project, rather than policy mistakes, or the supposedly traditional nature of Afghan society, best explain its failure and the republic's collapse in 2021.

Afghanistan's Pre-2001 Commander Networks

Conflict is not simply destructive but has transformative effects on social relations and rearticulates political and economic geographies. The decades of civil war and foreign occupation that began with the Communist coup d'état in 1978 gave rise to new forms of armed mobilization in Afghanistan. Historically, social and political organization in Afghanistan were fragmented along lines of solidarity referred to as *qaum* or *quowm*, a versatile term that can refer to tribal, kinship, and ethnolinguistic affiliations (Coburn 2011; Osman 2020; Rzehak 2012). Such *qaum* networks were the principal way that armed resistance to the central government was organized, but they also mediated patronage within a weak rentier state whose strategic position between rival imperial powers allowed it to access foreign assistance—by the 1960s, such grants and loans accounted for 80 percent of Afghan investment and development spending (Rubin 1995, 65).

Beginning in 1978, the Afghan war led to a structural shift in the distribution of foreign patronage favoring peripheral actors, as the United States and Soviet Union funded opposing sides of the war. Amid political and economic fragmentation, a new form of organization called the commander network arose, which linked armed groups of affiliation and solidarity, each led by *komandan* (Roy 1995; Edwards 2002; Dorronsoro 2005). While they traced their roots back to *qaum*-based tribal uprisings and organized banditry, these groups emerged in response to the civil war's widespread insecurity, economic destruction, and social upheaval, and included both progovernment militias and mujahideen insurgents. While commander networks could span regions or the entire country, the armed groups themselves were usually locally rooted. One 1988 study of hundreds of mujahideen units in Afghanistan found that 56 percent contained twenty to sixty men, "about the maximum size for units based on face-to-face interaction." (Rubin 1995, 188).

During the period of superpower patronage, these groups were integrated into larger networks by the seven Pakistan-based mujahideen parties that were given a monopoly of US weapons and aid, by Iranian-supported Shia parties and by the militia programs of the Communist government. It was not unusual, however, for groups to switch patrons over the course of the civil war. Following the withdrawal of Soviet forces in 1989 and the subsequent decline in foreign military aid, these patronage systems broke down and fragmented. In some regions, warlord polities—composed of hierarchical networks centered around military strongmen—emerged, while in others, including Kandahar Province, a state of anarchy reigned as competing commander networks clashed over territory and resources and preyed on the local populations (Giustozzi 2009).

Commander networks thus existed at nested, hierarchical levels but remained fluid, often with multiple or shifting allegiances. The commanders and their men acted as entrepreneurs of violence, seeking patronage and control of logistical routes, border crossings, mines, and drug cultivation areas (Rubin 2000; Goodhand 2005). As time went on, these networks were integrated into a transnational "regional conflict complex" in Southwest and Central Asia (Wallensteen and Sollenberg 1998).

As Jeremy Weinstein (2007) has argued, rebel groups that depend on natural resources or external funding are less disciplined and cohesive than those that emerge in resource-poor contexts. The mutability of commander networks in response to patronage helps explains the instability of political settlements during the war and how swiftly regime changes occurred. Defections by progovernment militias after the cutoff of Soviet aid in 1991 paved the way for the collapse of the Communist regime, and the Taliban's remarkably swift advance three years later was due in part to their co-optation of preexisting commander networks (Sinno 2008). As such, the commanders and their networks were ready to reemerge with the arrival of a new imperial patron in 2001, when they would form the roots of a conflict economy built around the vast inflow of foreign resources.

Private Security and the Failure of Disarmament

The end of the Cold War marked a distinct phase in the development of the global private security industry, one bolstered by trends associated with neoliberalization and the increasing reliance on private contracting by the United States and other governments (Singer 2003; Owens 2008; Chatterjee 2009; Stanger 2009; Abrahamsen and Williams 2011). Though

PSCs were used by the US military as far back as Vietnam, the American-led wars in Iraq and Afghanistan saw a dramatic expansion of the scope and size of their involvement, with companies like Blackwater playing controversial and widely reported roles.

Yet the PSC industries in Iraq and Afghanistan were remarkably different. Although both had a small managerial elite of mostly Western contractors, PSCs in Iraq employed third-country nationals as their workforce, typically South Asians willing to work for lower wages. By contrast in Afghanistan, 95 percent of US-contracted PSC staff were Afghan (Stanger 2009; Schwartz 2011). Moreover, PSCs in Iraq were largely foreign owned and operated, while in Afghanistan the majority of PSCs were either in whole or in part Afghan owned. In other words, the Western-funded PSC industry in Afghanistan was far more integrated with the local economy.

This was the result of the initial US-led invasions that took place in very different ways in each country. In Iraq, the US military deployed nearly half a million personnel and quickly established territorial control with supply routes from existing bases in neighboring countries. International PSCs arrived with the invading coalition forces and preferred to import third-country nationals as guards, as they were considered more reliable than local Iraqi hires (Stanger 2009). In contrast, the campaign against the Taliban in 2001 relied on Afghan militias backed by small units of CIA and Special Forces, and airpower—around 5,500 US personnel took part in the initial invasion, or about 1 percent of the forces used in Iraq (Malkasian 2021, 68). Afterward, the United States sought to avoid a costly military occupation by relying on these local militias, with both the CIA and Special Forces hiring informal armed groups for security and counterterrorism operations. Thus from the beginning of the intervention, commander networks were linked to the Western military through patronage. As Anand Gopal (2017, 38) demonstrates, in the early years prior to the revival of the Taliban insurgency, these groups captured international support by "producing" a resource—namely, Afghanistan's ability to act as a buffer against terrorism, often by falsely accusing rivals of terrorism or by turning in old weapons caches. Counterterrorism operations in the country's periphery thus led to a "rent dispersion," where foreign spending bypassed the central government, while US military patronage also allowed these militias to avoid disarmament (29).

Similarly, but on a larger economic scale, the PSC industry provided both a source of rents and a means to avoid state control for many armed groups. This was less the result of a misguided counterterrorism strategy than an inadvertent outcome of what Mark Duffield (2001) calls "the securitization of aid," where development spending was linked to the military mission and focused on insecure, peripheral areas, with little consideration for its impact on local politics. International PSCs often turned to informal armed groups for staffing and salary levels in PSCs at the time were typically well in excess of police and army salaries, decreasing incentives for former combatants to integrate into the Afghan government (Bhatia and Sedra 2008; Schmeidl 2008, 15). Successful completion of disarmament programs was not a requirement for hiring; indeed, PSCs often sought out individuals or commanders who could supply their own arms (Schmeidl 2008, 13).

For example, US Protection and Investigations (USPI), an American-owned PSC hired by the World Bank and other international donors, paid an Afghan police official from the Jamiat mujahideen party, General Din Mohammad Jurat, who hired informal armed groups (International Crisis Group 2005). One former USPI security contractor described how, working on road projects, he and his colleagues would approach nearby villages and offer cash to commanders in return for a levy of fighters. When the UN formed a guard force for its projects in 2004, the Protective Unit, it also turned to General Jurat, allowing his men to avoid disarmament (Bhatia and Sedra 2008).

When the US military built a base in Shindand District in Herat Province in 2007, security was contracted to an international PSC, Armor-Group, which hired staff from two local, feuding strongmen, Nadir Khan and Timor Shah. The US officer who referred ArmorGroup to the strongmen explained that he wanted to stop the flow of job seekers from the local community who were "bothering us during operations" (US Senate 2010, 9). Nadir Khan proceeded to assassinate Timor Shah in December 2007. The following year, another US-contracted PSC in Shindand turned to a local commander, Abdul Wahab Qattili, who had formerly worked with USPI, and whose militia was affiliated with the regional powerbroker Ismail Khan (US Senate 2010, 38).

By 2008, only 10 percent of the illegal armed groups that were registered with the government had disarmed. Estimates of their numbers countrywide ranged from 120,000 to 180,000 (Bhatia and Sedra 2008, 16; Giustozzi 2008, 218). Of the 25,000 weapons turned in by October 2006, only 7 percent were from the south and southeast, the focus of foreign military operations. Peripheral commanders who captured these dispersed rents made their presence felt in Afghanistan's nascent democracy. While under Afghan law candidates with links to illegal armed groups were banned from standing in elections, thanks to their political influence only 34 out of 1,108 candidates identified with such links were disqualified in 2005; 80 percent of the winning candidates from the provinces and 60 percent in Kabul maintained ties to illegal militias (Bhatia and Sedra 2008, 138). Similar levels of warlord influence were reported in the next election in 2010 (Foschini and Hewad 2010). Although the international community had identified disarmament as a key condition for peace in postconflict situations, its widespread use of informal armed groups and warlords for private security allowed them to reproduce themselves and mobilize.

Case Study: A Jamiat-Linked PSC North of Kabul

This case study is based on a series of interviews conducted in November 2011 with more than a dozen employees of a PSC and its owner (Aikins 2012). The PSC's head office was in the Shomali Plains north of Kabul, in a predominantly rural, ethnically Tajik village noted for its association with prominent Jamiat figures (Coburn 2011). The owner and president of the company was a former Jamiat commander in his mid-forties from the area who rose to minor prominence during the civil war and achieved the rank of brigade commander before leaving during the reforms to the Ministry of Defense in 2005. He was closely linked to current Jamiat power brokers and participated in profitable land grabs in Kabul after 2001. At the time of the interviews, he was an important notable and employer in his home village.

The company was a major player in the PSC industry. It contracted directly with the foreign military for base defense, as well as with transport companies for convoy protection on routes supplying bases in the north and south. While the owner was careful to maintain that his company only employed five hundred men in accordance with the law, his commanders candidly admitted that the company employed close to 4,500 guards. They emphasized the flexible nature of mobilization, saying the company formerly had nine thousand men when there was more business and could get "up to twenty thousand" if need be.

The company was organized hierarchically, with different levels of commanders. They were ranked and paid according to the number of men they commanded, between ten and three hundred. Commanders were responsible for recruiting their own men, which they did through kin and *qaum* networks in their home villages, similar to patterns of mobilization during the civil war. They stressed that PSC employment was highly desirable given the pay and that there was a large pool of willing and unemployed men to draw on. Recruits had to be guaranteed by a relative or village elder, and they received a medical checkup and some basic training. The head trainer was a former Communist officer, chosen for his formal military education.

Guards were mostly in their early twenties, predominantly Tajiks from rural villages in Parwan and Baghlan who were often the sole cash-income breadwinners in their families. They had little to no education or vocational training and most frequently described their reason for joining as there being no other options for work. There was a division of labor between convoy and base guards, with each receiving different training. Base guard duty was seen as less demanding and dangerous. Recruits were responsible for supplying their own weapons, a Kalashnikov-type assault rifle, whose market price—between $500 and $800—was equivalent to several months' salary. Some sold livestock or took out loans to do so.

Commanders in the PSC were often connected to other informal armed groups. For example, one commander's brother was the head of a progovernment militia in his home village. Ammunition was paid for by the PSC but often procured by the commanders themselves. Under new regulations, the government was supposed to sell the PSCs ammunition, but commanders reported frequent shortages, particularly for rocket-propelled grenades and heavy machine guns. As a result, ammunition was purchased from corrupt police and army commanders or "procured from our own villages"—that is, from the black market.

During the Republic, PSCs were frequently linked with smuggling and organized crime. They were blamed for robberies and kidnappings, and the Ministry of Interior had opened several investigations into weapons trafficking (UN Human Rights Council 2010, 24). An Afghan employee at another PSC in Kabul described regular visits from an arms dealer affiliated with Jamiat circles in the Ministry of Defense who sold weapons and ammunitions from Afghan National Army depots. The practice extended to international PSCs as well; one working for the US embassy was reported to have purchased weapons in the Kabul market in 2005 (Bhatia and Sedra 2008, 173).

PSCs and the Surge

As the security situation in Afghanistan deteriorated, the response of the United States and its allies was to invest more troops and money, in a self-justifying cycle of escalating commitment (Surkhe 2011). US troop levels, which had been under 10,000 at the beginning of 2003, climbed to 20,300 by 2006 and were augmented by some 10,000 allied forces from countries including the UK, Germany, France, and Canada. In 2009, seeking to stabilize the Afghan government, US President Barack Obama ordered a surge of forces, with US troop levels more than doubling that same year. By March 2011 there were 99,800 US troops deployed in Afghanistan, along with 41,000 allied troops and another 90,339 contractors employed by the US military—a total force more than double that at the peak of the Soviet occupation in 1983. Operational and maintenance costs of the US deployment grew even more rapidly than troop levels, with war spending rising from $19 billion in 2006 to $118 billion in 2011 (Belasco 2011; Schwartz and Swain 2011).

Estimates of the total number of PSC employees employed at the height of the surge ranged from sixty to eighty thousand. The fifty-two PSCs registered with the Ministry of Interior by 2011 listed some thirty thousand employees, but many PSCs were widely believed to maintain a larger number of personnel than they registered, particularly if they operated outside of Kabul (Schwartz 2011). Afghan officials cited by Susanne Schmeidl (2008, 11) named 90 known PSCs and estimated that there might be up to 140 countrywide.

According to registration figures, 44 percent of those PSCs were wholly Afghan owned. However, as Schmeidl (2008) notes, formal foreign ownership was sometimes a front in order to secure international contracts. Many companies included Afghan silent partners, elites who could mobilize local commander networks and navigate state bureaucracy. Whether Afghan or foreign-owned, a management cadre of expatriate security professionals would interface with the foreign military, bid for contracts, design and manage security, and supervise a larger force of Afghan guards. Increasingly, Afghan-owned PSCs were integrated into international markets and what Rita Abrahamsen and Michael C. Williams (2011) call "global security assemblages." For example, one Afghan PSC, Asia Security Group, was sold to an American company, Amtex Global, while its Afghan owner gained a controlling interest in Amtex, making it one of the first Afghan PSCs to branch out internationally, including into port security contracts in Corpus Christi, Texas.

The massive expansion of the PSC industry was reflected in the extent to which PSCs engaged in combat. Just counting registered PSC personnel, in the first half of 2010, there were more US-employed guards killed in action than US soldiers (235 versus 195), making them nearly three times more likely to die in battle (Schooner and Swan 2010; Schwartz 2011). These figures, along with high-profile battles such as one in Helmand where the Taliban attacked a project employing 1,200 guards, killing twenty-one (Rubin and Sahak 2010), added to the perception that the war was being fought as much by a chaotic and unaccountable army of PSC guards as it was by the US or Afghan government.

Eighty percent of US military supplies reached Afghanistan by land, and the military outsourced security for its convoys to PSCs (US House 2010, 6). The Kabul–Kandahar route, known as Highway 1, became a vital logistical line and was dominated primarily by Afghan-owned companies. The ownership of these PSCs often overlapped with that of the trucking companies (Lister and Karaev 2004). Convoys might include several hundred trucks and would take two to three days to reach Kandahar in southern Afghanistan. Attacks were frequent: Convoy guards accounted for 73 percent of US-employed PSC fatalities from June 2009 to November 2010 (Schwartz 2011, 9). Convoy PSCs frequently retaliated with indiscriminate fire when hit by ambushes or roadside bombs. However, protection payments to the insurgency and other informal armed groups were also common practice. A US congressional investigation found evidence of widespread corruption, abuse, and protection payments to the Taliban; a number of Afghan contractors were detained by the US military, which had been inadvertently funding its own enemy (Aikins 2016).

The convoy business encouraged new alliances across political and ethnic divides. Convoy routes rarely remained within the territory of one commander; for example, taking trucks from Kandahar City to Musa Qala in late 2010 involved paying cuts to the representatives of three different power brokers spread across two provinces. These spatially dispersed rents led to the emergence of new peripheral elites like Matiullah Khan, who became the preeminent power broker in Uruzgan Province through his monopoly of convoy security between Kandahar City and the provincial capital (Derksen 2015). Other power brokers tied to the PSC industry include Abdul Wali Khan, known as Koka, who was formerly the police chief of Musa Qala and controlled lucrative routes to British and American military bases in Helmand, and Pacha Zadran Khan, a major strongman in southeastern Afghanistan.

Case Study: Political Settlements in Kandahar

A growing body of literature has examined political settlements—the distribution of political and economic resources among elites—in post-conflict scenarios (Le Billon 2007; Khan 2017). As Lewis and Sagnayeva (2020) argue, such settlements do not exclude violence and may be maintained through coercive practices and exclusion. In Afghanistan, the post-2001 period was characterized by unstable political settlements at multiple levels (Sharan 2022). As Jonathan Goodhand and David Mansfield (2010, 32) have observed in the case of post-2001 opium trafficking networks, elite alliances became increasingly heterogeneous and based on economic profit. At a central level, the political settlement around the presidency of Hamid Karzai (2002–2014) was embodied by the financial arrangements behind Kabul Bank, which brought actors together from diverse political backgrounds and ethnic groups and collapsed due to fraud in 2010. Unstable political settlements, in other words, are key to understanding the fragility of the Republic. In this section, I describe the elite dynamics and political settlement that emerged in Kandahar Province, a key battleground of the war and a major focus of the PSC industry, and explain their relevance for understanding center-periphery relations in post-2001 Afghanistan.

Kandahar Province, located in southern Afghanistan on the border with the Pakistani province of Baluchistan, has played a crucial role in the country's history. Politics were historically dominated by a tribal aristocracy of landowning khans, predominantly from the three principal tribes within the dominant Durrani confederation—the Barakzai, the Popolzai, and the Alokozai. The Taliban movement also emerged there in the 1990s. Following the US invasion, a power struggle took place between republican elites led by Gul Agha Sherzai, a Barakzai, Mullah Naqib, an Alokozai, and President Karzai, a Popolzai, and his brother, Ahmed Wali Karzai, who established residence in Kandahar City. Authority was not exercised through tribal institutions per se, which no longer existed as an autonomous form of social organization. Rather, tribal elites gained their power through their access to money, private militias, and patronage networks (Jackson 2015).

Sherzai, who arrived with US forces in 2001, enjoyed the initial advantage and seized power as governor. His brother controlled the militia in charge of the airport's perimeter security, and thus access to the US military based there. Sherzai was able to monopolize gravel and labor contracts at the base and kept millions of dollars in customs revenue from the border crossing at Spin Boldak (Chayes 2006; Giustozzi and Ullah 2007). The CIA and US military also relied on a Sherzai-backed militia to pursue members of the Taliban and al-Qaeda (Gopal 2011).

By contrast, the Alokozai, who were given positions in the army and police, were marginalized early on, due in large part to their lack of access to US patronage. Without any US-affiliated militias or PSCs, they were affected disproportionately by disarmament in 2003. The 2nd Corps, which had been given to the Alokozai commander Khan Mohammed, was disbanded and 1,300 soldiers disarmed (Thruelsen 2006, 23). Ahmed Wali, however, was able to cultivate a close collaboration with the United States from the beginning, providing Popolzai recruits for the militia that guarded the CIA and Special Forces' base.

Sherzai's access to peripheral US patronage initially enabled him to defy the center and pose a threat to President Karzai's base of power in Kandahar. In response, the Karzai brothers worked to wrest control of peripheral rents, such as foreign contracting, from Sherzai. Drawing on his experience working for NGOs since the 1980s, as well as his fluent English, Ahmed Wali established himself as a central figure in the distribution of aid in Kandahar. He also led efforts to set up local political bodies, including the Kandahar Municipal Council, the Kandahar Provincial Military Council, and the *eslahi* or reform council, which served as a vehicle to criticize Sherzai's governance (Forsberg 2010, 23). Ahmed Wali leveraged his connections to Kabul through his brother, President Karzai, to facilitate his grip over the south's political economy by monopolizing the official appointments and state regulations essential to doing business in Kandahar. These two approaches were complementary: His dominance of local politics allowed him to become the essential intermediary for international military and development efforts, while his access to international patronage established him as the most powerful local actor.

Sherzai—who did not speak English and had come under increasing international criticism for corruption and his informal style of governance—was ousted as governor in 2005 and was eventually replaced by a succession of Karzai loyalists, including Tooryalai Wesa, an Afghan Canadian and former academic.

International money was the linchpin of the political settlement that President Karzai and his brother forged in Kandahar. Kandahar was a focal point for military operations, and stabilization funds were disproportionately spent there. Control of the PSC industry, and therefore

5.1 Members of a tribal militia commanded by Abdul Raziq at a border crossing in Spin Boldak, Afghanistan, in 2009.

informal armed groups, was crucial to Ahmed Wali's position. Watan Risk Management, another large PSC with numerous contracts in Kandahar, was founded by two Karzai relatives, Rashid and Rateb Popal. And several key Karzai allies dominated the convoy escort business on Highway 1, including Ruhollah, the most powerful commander on the Kabul–Kandahar route.

President Karzai and his brother were thus able to wrest control of these spatially distributed rents from a peripheral actor, Sherzai, and use to them to tie together the province's elites under the center. After Ahmad Wali's assassination in 2011, this political settlement endured under another Karzai ally, the warlord and police commander Abdul Raziq (see figure 5.1). Yet it was doubly unstable, dependent on the distribution of dispersed foreign rents, and contingent on elite bargains in Kabul and Kandahar. After Karzai reached his term limit, and was succeeded in 2014 by Ashraf Ghani, a new power struggle began between center and periphery, as Ghani strove unsuccessfully to control Raziq. This, along with a decline in international spending, fractured Kandahar's political settlement, which ultimately collapsed in 2021 with widespread defection and surrender to the Taliban by progovernment commanders (Aikins 2024).

Peripheral Rents and Neopatrimonial Governance

The center-periphery dynamics described in Kandahar help explain the paradox of state-building in Afghanistan, which is that more international resources did not lead to greater success, as many early critics had argued would happen (Jones 2006; Paris 2006). Afghanistan was indeed an extreme example of a rentier state based on foreign aid, with $9.4 billion in public spending in 2010 compared to only $1.65 billion in revenues (World Bank 2011, 6), but little of this rent was controlled directly by the central government. Two out of three civil servants were paid for directly by international donors, and the international community in effect ran a parallel state, with 77 percent of all aid up to 2009 delivered with little or no Afghan government involvement (World Bank 2011, 10; Poole 2011, 9). As Astri Surkhe (2011) argues, the scale of foreign intervention engendered dependence but not compliance or submission. Rather, Karzai and other elites struggled to wrest control of rents from donors through strategies that undermined state-building, and which can be broadly characterized as "neopatrimonial"—that is, a mixture of bureaucratic and personalized or informal control (Erdmann and Engel 2007).

Afghanistan, with its struggling formal institutions and strong peripheral and external actors typified a type of "weak state" where private accumulation, dispersed rents, and patronage were critical terrain of political struggle (Lund 2006). As William Reno (1999, 7) describes, central actors in weak states in Africa could behave paradoxically, whereby rulers that face the most severe threats from peripheral actors are the most thorough in destroying remaining formal state institutions, "the very tools advocates of reform regard as key to state survival." As the domain of political struggle shifts to capturing private accumulation, the result is what Jean-Francois Bayart calls the "criminalization of the state," whereby state control is rearticulated through informal patronage networks (Bayart et al. 1999). In Afghanistan, Karzai's principal challenge was to manage independent, peripheral elites, and he did so through neopatrimonial methods that consistently undermined institution-building, such as divide-and-conquer strategies (Giustozzi and Orsini 2009; van Bijlert 2009). As David Mansield and Adam Pain (2008) have demonstrated in the case of Afghanistan's opium eradication campaigns, attempts at reform can result in neopatrimonial consolidation by central elites, an example of what Richard Snyder and Angelica Duran-Martinez (2009) call "state-sponsored protection rackets."

As illustrated by the Kabul Bank scandal, which involved extensive capital flight to Dubai and other overseas markets, the resulting corruption was enabled by international institutions and actors, through which both Afghan and expatriate actors profited.

In the case of the PSC industry, the ban on private companies announced by Karzai in 2009 was also used as an opportunity to exert pressure on rival power brokers and international companies while rewarding local allies. For example, of the seven Afghan PSCs who had their licenses revoked, only Watan, owned by Karzai relatives, was able to get its license reinstated on appeal by the Afghan government. Karzai's regulation of the PSC industry can therefore be seen as both an attempt to strengthen the power of central government and an instance of neopatrimonial governance that undermined institution-building and the rule of law, an example of the paradoxical effects of state-building efforts in Afghanistan.

Conclusion: Why Did the Western State-Building Project Fail in Afghanistan?

Explanations for the failure of Western state-building, which culminated in the collapse of the Afghan republic in 2021, can be broadly categorized into three types. The first is the claim that the established recipe for liberal peace-building was not properly applied: for instance, that bureaucratic and interagency disputes hamstrung Western policy (Keane 2016) or that the United States was overly focused on counterterrorism and did not foster a legitimate political system (Murtazashvili 2022). Mistakes were made, in other words, but the project might have succeeded. Yet state-building in Afghanistan failed over a twenty-year period that saw a variety of fully resourced strategies and experiments by Western donors. The second type of explanation for failure argues that the essential structure of Afghan society itself made such a project difficult, if not impossible: Afghanistan's "strong society" led to a weak state (Saikal 2005), and the persistence of informal or traditional social structures in the periphery made neopatrimonial forms of governance necessary (Mukhopadhyay 2014; Malejacq 2020). Such accounts have difficulty explaining the consolidation of central authority under the Taliban in the 1990s—the only period in recent history that Afghanistan did not receive significant external rents. The political economy of Afghanistan's PSC industry described here instead provides evidence for a third type of argument, which holds that the structure of the international intervention, rather than policy mistakes or the nature of Afghan society, provides a better explanation for the revival of warlordism and the failure to forge stable political settlements post-2001 (Surkhe 2011; Gopal 2017). In its reliance on private contracting and security spending that produced dispersed rents and incentivized neopatrimonial governance by the center, the West's intervention carried the seeds of its own defeat.

References

Abrahamsen, Rita, and Michael C. Williams. 2011. *Security Beyond the State: Private Security in International Politics*. New York: Cambridge University Press.

Aikins, Matthieu. 2012. "Contracting the Commanders: The Political Economy of the Private Security Industry in Post-2001 Afghanistan." Master's thesis, New York University.

Aikins, Matthieu. 2016. "The Bidding War: How a Young Afghan Military Contractor Became Spectacularly Rich." *New Yorker*, March 7.

Aikins, Matthieu. 2024. "America's Monster: Who Was Abdul Raziq?" *New York Times Magazine*, May 22.

Bayart, Jean-Francois, Stephen Ellis, and Beatrice Hibou, eds. 1999. *The Criminalization of the State in Africa*. Bloomington: Indiana University Press.

Belasco, Amy. 2011. "The Cost of Iraq, Afghanistan, and Other Global War on Terror Operations Since 9/11." Congressional Research Service, March. https://sgp.fas.org/crs/natsec/RL33110.pdf.

Bhatia, Michael, and Mark Sedra. 2008. *Afghanistan, Arms and Conflict: Armed Groups, Disarmament and Security in Post-War Society*. New York: Routledge.

Chatterjee, Pratap. 2009. *Halliburton's Army: How a Well-Connected Texas Oil Company Revolutionized the Way America Makes War*. New York: Nation Books.

Chayes, Sarah. 2006. *The Punishment of Virtue: Inside Afghanistan After the Taliban*. New York: Penguin.

Coburn, Noah. 2011. *Bazaar Politics: Power and Pottery in an Afghan Market Town*. Stanford, CA: Stanford University Press.

Derksen, Deedee. 2015. *The Politics of Disarmament in Afghanistan*. Washington, DC: United States Institute of Peace. https://www.usip.org/sites/default/files/PW110-The-Politics-of-Disarmament-and-Rearmament-in-Afghanistan.pdf.

Dorronsoro, Gilles. 2005. *Revolution Unending: Afghanistan: 1979 to the Present*. New York: Columbia University Press.

Duffield, Mark. 2001. *Global Governance and the New Wars: The Merging of Development and Security*. London: Zed Books.

Edwards, David B. 2002. *Before Taliban: Genealogies of the Afghan Jihad.*
Berkeley: University of California Press.

Erdmann, Gero, and Ulf Engel. 2007. "Neopatrimonialism Reconsidered:
Critical Review and Elaboration of an Elusive Concept." *Commonwealth
and Comparative Politics* 45 (1): 95–119.

Forsberg, Carl. 2010. *Politics and Power in Kandahar.* Washington, DC:
Institute for the Study of War. http://www.jstor.org/stable/resrep07920.1.

Foschini, Fabrizio, and Gran Hewad. 2010. "The Alchemy of Vetting."
Afghanistan Analysts Network, July 16. https://www.afghanistan-analysts
.org/en/reports/political-landscape/the-alchemy-of-vetting/.

Giustozzi, Antonio. 2008. "Shadow Ownership and SSR in Afghanistan." In
Local Ownership and Security Sector Reform, edited by Timothy Donais,
215–232. Yearly Book Series. Geneva, Switzerland: Geneva Centre for the
Democratic Control of Armed Forces.

Giustozzi, Antonio. 2009. *Empires of Mud: War and Warlords in Afghanistan.*
New York: Columbia University Press.

Giustozzi, Antonio, and Dominique Orsini. 2009. "Centre-Periphery
Relations in Afghanistan: Badakhshan between Patrimonialism and
Institution-Building." *Central Asian Survey* 28 (1): 1–16. https://doi.org
/10.1080/02634930902771466.

Giustozzi, Antonio, and Noor Ullah. 2007. "The Inverted Cycle: Kabul and
the Strongmen's Competition for Control over Kandahar, 2001–2006."
Central Asian Survey 26 (2): 167–184.

Goodhand, Jonathan. 2005. "Frontiers and Wars: The Opium Economy in
Afghanistan." *Journal of Agrarian Change* 5 (2): 191–216.

Goodhand, Jonathan, and David Mansfield. 2010. "Drugs and (Dis)order:
A Study of the Opium Trade, Political Settlement, and State-Making in
Afghanistan." Working Paper No. 83 (series 2). Crisis States Research
Centre, November. https://assets.publishing.service.gov.uk/media
/57a08b2ced915d622c000b5b/WP83.2.pdf.

Gopal, Anand. 2011. "The Battle for Afghanistan: Militancy and Conflict
in Kandahar." New America Foundation, November. https://static
.newamerica.org/attachments/4336-the-battle-for-afghanistan/kandahar
_0.685663454461452584d08faeae6d538b.pdf.

Gopal, Anand. 2017. "Rents, Patronage, and Defection: State-Building and
Insurgency in Afghanistan." PhD diss., Columbia University.

International Crisis Group. 2005. "Afghanistan: Getting Disarmament Back
on Track." Asia Briefing No. 35. February 23. https://www.ecoi.net/en
/document/1027740.html.

Jackson, Ashley. 2015. "Politics and Governance in Afghanistan: The Case of
Kandahar." Working Paper No. 34. Researching Livelihoods and Services
Affected by Conflict. Secure Livelihoods Research Consortium, Overseas
Development Institute, June. https://assets.publishing.service.gov.uk
/media/57a08998ed915d622c0002d1/SLRC-WP34.pdf.

Jones, Seth. 2006. "Averting Failure in Afghanistan." *Survival* 48 (1): 111–128.

Keane, Conor. 2016. *US Nation-Building in Afghanistan*. New York: Routledge.

Khan, Mushtaq. 2017. "Political Settlements and the Analysis of Institutions." *African Affairs* 117 (469): 636–655.

Le Billon, Phillipe. 2007, "Geographies of War: Perspective on 'Resource Wars.'" *Geography Compass* 1/2:163–182.

Lewis, David, and Saniya Sagnayeva. 2020. "Corruption, Patronage and Il-liberal Peace: Forging Political Settlement in Post-Conflict Kyrgyzstan." *Third World Quarterly* 41 (1): 77–95.

Lister, Sarah, and Zainiddin Karaev. 2004. "Understanding Markets in Afghanistan: A Case Study of the Market in Construction Materials." Afghan Research and Evaluation Unit Organization, June. https://areu .org.af/publication/420/.

Lund, Christian. 2006. "Twilight Institutions: An Introduction." *Development and Change* 37 (4): 673–684.

Malejacq, Romain. 2020. *Warlord Survival: The Delusion of State Building in Afghanistan*. Ithaca, NY: Cornell University Press.

Malkasian, Carter. 2021. *The American War in Afghanistan: A History*. New York: Oxford University Press.

Mansfield, David, and Adam Pain. 2008. "Counter-Narcotics in Afghanistan: The Failure of Success?" Briefing paper. Afghan Research and Evaluation Unit Organization, December. https://areu.org.af/publication/822/.

Mukhopadhyay, Dipali. 2014. *Warlords, Strongman Governors, and the State in Afghanistan*. New York: Cambridge University Press.

Murtazashvili, Jennifer Brick. 2022. "The Collapse of Afghanistan." *Journal of Democracy* 33 (1): 40–54.

Osman, Wazhmah. 2020. *Television and the Afghan Culture Wars: Brought to You by Foreigners, Warlords, and Activists*. Urbana: University of Illinois Press.

Owens, Patricia. 2008. "Distinctions, Distinctions: 'Public' and 'Private' Force?" *International Affairs* 84 (5): 977–990.

Paris, Roland. 2006. "NATO's Choice in Afghanistan: Go Big or Go Home." *Policy Options*, December 1. https://policyoptions.irpp.org/magazines /afghanistan-2/natos-choice-in-afghanistan-go-big-or-go-home/.

Poole, Lydia. 2011. "Tracking Major Resource Flows, 2002–2010." Global Humanitarian Assistance, January. https://humanitarianoutcomes.org /publications/afghanistan-tracking-major-resource-flows-2002-2010.

Reno, William. 1999. *Warlord Politics and African States*. Boulder: Lynne Rienner.

Roy, Olivier. 1995. *Afghanistan: From Holy War to Civil War*. Princeton, NJ: Darwin.

Rubin, Alissa, and Sharifullah Sahak. 2010. "Taliban Attack Guard in Deadly Raid." *New York Times*, August 20.

Rubin, Barnett. 1995. *The Fragmentation of Afghanistan: State Formation and Collapse in the International System*. New Haven, CT: Yale University Press.

Rubin, Barnett. 2000. "The Political Economy of War and Peace in Afghanistan." *World Development* 28 (10): 1789–1803.

Rzehak, Lutz. 2012. "Ethnic Minorities in Search of Political Consolidation." In *Under the Drones: Modern Lives in the Afghanistan-Pakistan Borderlands*, edited by Shahzad Bashir and Robert D. Crews, 132–152. Cambridge, MA: Harvard University Press.

Saikal, Amin. 2005. "Afghanistan's Weak State and Strong Society." In *Making States Work: State Failure and the Crisis of Governance*, edited by Simon Chesterman, 193–209. Tokyo: United Nations University Press.

Schmeidl, Susanne. 2008. "Case Study Afghanistan." In *Private Security Companies and Local Populations: An Exploratory Study of Afghanistan and Angola*, edited by Ulrike Joras and Adrian Schuster, 9–37. Working paper. Swisspeace, April.

Schooner, Stephen, and Collin Swan. 2010. "Contractors and the Ultimate Sacrifice." Service Contractor, September. GW Law Faculty Publications. https://scholarship.law.gwu.edu/faculty_publications/125/.

Schwartz, Moshe. 2011. "The Department of Defense's Use of Private Security Contractors in Afghanistan and Iraq: Background, Analysis, and Options for Congress." Congressional Research Service, February. https://sgp.fas .org/crs/natsec/R40835.pdf.

Schwartz, Moshe, and Joyprada Swain. 2011. "Department of Defense Contractors in Afghanistan and Iraq: Background and Analysis." Congressional Research Service, May. https://sgp.fas.org/crs/natsec/R40764.pdf.

Sharan, Timor. 2022. *Inside Afghanistan: Political Networks, Informal Order, and State Disruption*. London: Routledge.

Singer, P. W. 2003. *Corporate Warriors: The Rise of the Privatized Military Industry*. Ithaca, NY: Cornell University Press.

Sinno, Abdulkader H. 2008. "The Taliban's Ability to Mobilize the Pashtuns." In *The Taliban and the Crisis of Afghanistan*, edited by Robert D. Crews and Amin Tarzi, 59–89. Cambridge, MA: Harvard University Press.

Snyder, Richard, and Angelica Duran-Martinez. 2009. "Does Illegality Breed Violence? Drug Trafficking and State-Sponsored Protection Rackets." *Crime, Law and Social Change* 52:253–273.

Stanger, Allison. 2009. *One Nation Under Contract*. New Haven, CT: Yale University Press.

Surkhe, Astri. 2011. *When More Is Less: The International Project in Afghanistan*. New York: Columbia University Press.

Thruelsen, Peter. 2006. "From Soldier to Civilian: Disarmament Demobilisation Reintegration in Afghanistan." DIIS Report No. 7. Danish Institute for International Studies. https://www.files.ethz.ch/isn/20984/RP2006 -7web.pdf.

UN Human Rights Council. 2010. "Report of the Working Group on the Use of Mercenaries as a Means of Violating Human Rights and Impeding the Exercise of the Right of Peoples to Self-Determination: Mission to Afghanistan." June. https://digitallibrary.un.org/record/685301?v=pdf.

US House Subcommittee on National Security and Foreign Affairs. 2010. "Warlord, Inc.: Extortion and Corruption Along the U.S. Supply Chain in Afghanistan." Report of the majority staff. Committee on Oversight and Government Reform, US House of Representatives, June. https://oversightdemocrats.house.gov/sites/evo-subsites/democrats-oversight.house.gov/files/documents/Warlord.pdf.

US Senate Armed Services Committee. 2010. "Inquiry into the Role and Oversight of Private Security Contractors in Afghanistan." S. Rep. 111-345. United States Senate, September. https://www.congress.gov/congressional-report/111th-congress/senate-report/345/1.

van Bijlert, Martine. 2009. "Between Discipline and Discretion: Policies Surrounding Senior Subnational Appointments." Afghanistan Research and Evaluation Unit Organization, May 1. https://areu.org.af/publication/923/.

Wallensteen, Peter, and Margareta Sollenberg. 1998. "Armed Conflict and Regional Conflict Complexes, 1989–97," *Journal of Peace Research* 35 (5): 621–634.

Weinstein, Jeremy. 2007. *Inside Rebellion: The Politics of Insurgent Violence.* New York: Cambridge University Press.

World Bank. 2011. "Issues and Challenges for Transition and Sustainable Growth in Afghanistan." https://thedocs.worldbank.org/en/doc/660161540821419600-0310022018/Transition-in-Afghanistan-Nov-2011.

Tracking and Targeting

The US Surveillance
Infrastructures in Afghanistan

Surveillance was a key part of the US war in Afghanistan. In two decades of occupation (2001–2021), the American military invested enormous resources into building a digital regime of tracking, targeting, and identification unprecedented in the history of war. These infrastructures of militarized knowledge included technologies of both geographical and population surveillance that offered American generals a synoptic view of the country from above and below. Yet despite the deployment of high-tech machines and sophisticated weapons, the American war in Afghanistan failed.

This failure exposed the limits of weaponized knowledge that serves the interest of colonial powers in subjugating the target population. As critical media scholars and scholars of colonial statecraft have shown, the history of surveillance and colonial domination are intertwined, and that relationship has been further strengthened in the digital age (Browne 2015; Hopkins 2020; Zureik 2020; M. Kaplan 1995; Nishiyama 2015; Gregory 2004; Weizman 2017). The US technological experiments in Afghanistan, therefore, can be best understood as part of a larger history of imperial construction of militarized knowledge in the Global South. In this chapter, I explore how the United States pursued its domination of Afghanistan through techniques and technologies of biometric identification.

In 2001, Americans knew little about Afghanistan. The country had been closed off for a quarter of a century (1978–2001) due to a series of political events that led to self-imposed isolation. The events included a Communist coup, the Soviet occupation, a civil war, and the Taliban rule, which all happened in succession. In this period, Afghanistan was not exactly like North Korea, but it was close in terms of connections to the outside world beyond the Eastern Bloc. The country missed all the technological advancements that the world had achieved in this crucial quarter of a century. In 2000, for example, there were only two telephone lines in Afghanistan for international calls, both in the capital, Kabul—one at the Ministry of Communication and the other at the Central Post Office, where people from a handful of Western and neighboring countries could call or receive a call (*Shariat Weekly* 2000). The total number of telephone lines in the country was 35,200 in 2001 (the last year of the Taliban), a slight increase from 21,619 lines in 1978 (the year of the Communist rule). Most of these telephone lines were concentrated in Kabul. In 2001, for example, there was not a single telephone line in the provinces of Bamiyan, Farah, Nimroz, Helmand, Nuristan, and Badakhshan—not even in the government offices (*Annual Statistics Book* 2001, 202–220).

This was the state of information communication infrastructure in Afghanistan at the dawn of the new century. The Afghan state, or what was left of it after two decades of war, was a fragile institution with no functioning component parts. Most importantly, its memory was gone: There was not much of an archive where one could find information about the population. Most people had no identification documents or birth certificates, and the state had no way of knowing who was who (Karimi 2019, 4781–4783). This was the state of government institutions when Americans arrived with the mission to transform the country. They were now in charge of conquering this land, defeating insurgents, and building a functional state in which power would be transferred through free and fair elections. Despite all the costly efforts over the next two decades, the US mission failed. This chapter assesses America's knowledge infrastructure in Afghanistan by focusing on how biometric technology served as an instrument of domination. The purpose of this chapter is first to outline the extent of the American surveillance operations in Afghanistan and then to examine the epistemic contradiction inherent in mass surveillance programs: too much information and too little knowledge.

Machine-Readable Enemy: Biometric Data Collection

The US invasion of Afghanistan was the first major war of the twenty-first century. The use of advanced technologies of surveillance, reconnaissance, and targeting was a key part of Washington's strategy for winning the war. Surveillance, in particular, received a great deal of attention from the American military. Mick Ryan, an Australian general, after the fall of the Afghan government, told the *Economist* (2022): "You could put forward a thesis that Afghanistan was the most densely surveilled battlespace in the history of humankind." He was not wrong. The US military and its NATO partners viewed everyone in Afghanistan as potential targets, and they treated them as such. Drones, blimps, and satellites were watching and listening to them from the air, and biometric systems made them accessible on land. The aerial technologies of surveillance and strike, in particular, gave the US military's knowledge of Afghanistan a vertical nature that according to Lisa Parks (2015), Caren Kaplan (2018), Eyal Weizman (2017), and Derek Gregory (2018), has been the default mode of perception for imperial warfighting and population domination. The purpose of these forms of datafication was to create machine-readable targets and automate the work of identifying enemies.

In 2001, right after the US invasion of Afghanistan, one of the first problems the military faced was managing the large number of suspects that they rounded up. At the time, the US military had no automated record-keeping system to manage the detainees' information. Earlier that year, the Army's Battle Command Battle Laboratory had produced a biometric enrollment device called the Biometric Automated Toolset (BAT). It was already used once in Kosovo to build a database of local laborers that the US peacekeeping mission had hired at their bases (BIMA 2010, 5), but it had not yet been used in a combat setting. In 2002, the army shipped a BAT prototype to Afghanistan, which was used to collect and process the identity of the men detained in the country (Voelz 2016, 185–186). This was the first use case of the new tech during the war.

The use of a cutting-edge technology of identification in Afghanistan was a particularly significant development. The US military wanted to build a database of their own from scratch wherein every bit of data entered was produced by, and met the needs of, the Americans. This is, as other scholars have shown, a feature of imperial domination where the colonial power prefers its own (technological) ways of knowing over the indigenous knowledge practices. This epistemic prejudice often harms the subjugated population by creating what Achille Mbembe calls "necropolitics": a condition of ever-present violence imposed by a colonial power over a colonized people (Mbembe 2003, 12; see also Weizman 2017, 1–16; Osman 2020, 71–72; 2019, 159). Those Afghans who had hopes of using America's advanced digital technology—such as biometric identification—as tools to strengthen state institutions soon realized that the United States was pursuing goals that were not necessarily aligned with the interests of the Afghan people. The Americans had no intention of using their technology outside the military realm. The program's militaristic nature was exposed when people noticed that the Americans only collected the data of Afghan men assumed to be of fighting age—between fifteen and sixty-four (Shanker 2011). Such a program was not intended to build the capacity of the Afghan government to deliver public services.

The biometric program started as an instrument to manage the data of detainees and prisoners, but it quickly expanded. The US military would capture the biometric data of all who joined the Afghan army and police or applied to work as translators or laborers on military bases where foreign forces were housed. By 2012, more than 2.5 million people were recorded in biometric databases in Afghanistan (*Economist* 2012). Additionally, the US military captured the biometric data of almost any random person they encountered during a patrol, especially in rural areas. Indeed, it became an important part of the job of army personnel. American soldiers patrolling outside their bases were tasked with stopping every young man they came across and collecting their biometric data, which included a digital scan of their fingerprints, iris, and face (see figure 6.1). Collecting biometric enrollment data took at least half an hour for each person. One soldier handled the devices and several others stood guard until the complicated data entry was completed. An American soldier once complained: "I thought we were in Afghanistan to jump out of airplanes and kill Taliban. [But in practice,] we were on a beat, like local cops" (Jacobsen 2021, 9).

Identifying the enemy has always been a challenge for occupying forces in Afghanistan throughout its modern history. In the nineteenth century, when the British Empire conquered Kabul, they struggled with the same problem of figuring out who was the enemy. In the Second Anglo-Afghan War (1879–1880), the British paid spies to catch insurgents. They paid members of the public, too, between 50 and 120 rupees if they reported an insurgent. The economic incentive turned people against each other. Many ended up on the gallows and the lucky ones were locked up in a

6.1 US marine Nickolai Bautista, rifleman, Bravo Company, 1st Battalion, 7th Marine Regiment, uses a Biometric Enrollment and Screening Device to capture an Afghan man's iris scan during a mission in Helmand Province, Afghanistan, May 1, 2014. Photo: Sgt. Joseph Scanlan (Wikimedia Commons).

city caravanserai that the British had converted into a prison (Karimi 2020, 625–629). A century later, the Soviet army, who similarly faced public resistance as they occupied Afghanistan (1979–1989), had to come up with a method to distinguish friend from foe. Their puppet regime in Kabul was too weak to carry out this task and, instead, indiscriminately arrested, imprisoned, and killed people en masse to solve their problem, which, unsurprisingly, further escalated the fight against the Communists.

On October 8, 1978, people in Kabul woke up to the walls of the Ministry of Interior plastered with pages of paper. The papers contained the names of some five thousand people the regime had killed. The names were put up by President Hafiz Allah Amin, who came to power as the second Communist president after killing the first one, his predecessor Nur Muhammad Taraki, during a swift coup. Amin claimed that Taraki had killed all the victims whose names were posted on the wall. Many people had loved ones disappeared. A large crowd quickly gathered around the Ministry to look for the names of family members who had gone missing. Every few minutes, an anguished wail would rise from the crowd as someone found the name they had been dreading to find. After a couple of days, Amin took down the lists as it did not earn him popularity as he had hoped ('Azimi 1999, 123–125). The bare walls of the Ministry then only showcased the usual "revolutionary" slogans that at the time were calligraphed everywhere in Kabul. One said: "Those who plot in the dark, will be perished in the dark" (Sadat 2014).

The US military, however, had a technological approach to gathering intel about those who fought against it—this was, after all, a war in the age of the internet. They invested early on in building a digital infrastructure of identification and surveillance to not only know the enemy but keep track of them through telecom and aerial surveillance. Biometric technology, however, was the primary instrument that was used to identify what the enemy looked like—their faces, irises, and fingerprints. The type of detailed information that would make the British and the Soviets jealous. Despite the difference in approach, the task of identifying the population and classifying people into friends and foes remained a key area of concern for colonial governmentality in Afghanistan under all the three occupying armies. The Americans, in other words, were doing exactly what previous occupiers did, but with sleeker—and not necessarily less violent—tools.

Once the US military collected the biometric data, a team used it to create "digital dossiers" for each individual and put certain persons of interest on a watch list. The list was then loaded into handheld biometrics devices such as a BAT or Handheld Interagency Identity Detection Equipment (HIIDE) that could "provide immediate feedback if a unit encounters a potential threat on the battlefield or at a base entry point" (Buhrow 2010, 48). The US forces believed the program was a technology for "protecting the Afghan populace and ensuring that only insurgents are targeted." (Buhrow 2010, 45). The whole program was part of a larger effort to create what the US government called a "social radar" for the purpose of total surveillance (González 2015, 8). Some of America's NATO allies in Afghanistan had national restrictions when it came to collecting private information, but the United States itself imposed few limitations (Buhrow 2010). While biometrics could potentially deny anonymity to insurgents, it was not very helpful in preventing terror attacks (especially on Afghan people) or strengthening the capacity of the Afghan state.[1]

The work was aligned with the American strategy of achieving "identity dominance," defined as the ability "to know whether a person encountered by a warfighter is a friend or a foe" (Woodward 2005, 30). This required the knowledge of a person's biometric data as well as names, aliases, past activities, and communication networks. According to a military handbook, "Every person who lives within an operational area should be identified and fully biometrically enrolled with facial photos, iris scans, and all 10 fingerprints (if present)" (CALL 2011, 31). The war was reduced to surveillance, identification, and tracking. This focus on the datafication of the war was partly the result of media backlash against the military's many mistakes, such as bombing the wrong house or arresting the wrong men (Savage et al. 2022; Sturcke 2008). The military decided that they could fix the problem with better technology. In 2017, US military officials bragged to the *New York Times* about the amount of data they considered before authorizing a strike, including the use of 3D models of targeted houses (Khan and Gopal 2017). This technosolutionist approach to profound ethical and political issues inherent in the occupation was a persistent feature of the US war in Afghanistan. The personal data that the United States collected was used, among other ends, to build secret security watch lists that held enormous power over the lives of ordinary Afghans because of how much US law enforcement agencies trusted these methods. It became common for Afghans to be wrongly denied visas or jobs after their names were flagged on one of the security watch lists (*Economist* 2012).

The Failure of the Biometric State

The US military outsourced part of the task of collecting biometric data to the Afghan government. It provided Afghan military institutions with the necessary technology, which significantly increased the amount of biometric data amassed in Afghanistan. Several military and civilian government institutions started to collect biometric data. The Afghan army and police, in particular, would take any opportunity to capture people's biometric data. They did not leave even the dead alone: On June 21, 2012, Taliban gunmen raided Spugmai, a lakefront restaurant outside Kabul, killing more than twenty of the guests. After a long firefight, the Afghan forces finally gunned them down (Neuman 2012). When the soldiers entered the restaurant, ignoring all the blood and debris, they started to scan the eyes of the dead Taliban militants. They were in a rush because the biometric devices could reliably read the iris scan only up to six hours after death. They managed to identify one of the assailants, whose biometric data had been captured in Logar Province two years prior (*Economist* 2012). The biometric data that the Afghan government collected, most of it in military contexts, was then passed on to several US government agencies including

6.2 It was not only suspects but almost everyone in Afghanistan who could be subject to biometric registration. Here, Staff Sgt. John Silvia (*left*) and Senior Airman Bradley Rae (*right*), both from the 455th Expeditionary Security Forces Group Bravo Sector, US Air Force, are collecting biometric information from local Afghan women receiving medical services at Bagram Airfield, Afghanistan, December 2, 2012. Photo: Senior Airman Chris Willis (Wikimedia Commons).

the Department of Defense, Department of Homeland Security, and the FBI (*Economist* 2012).

In a country at war, with weak civil society institutions and vulnerable people struggling with violence and poverty, digital privacy and data sovereignty were not top priorities for most Afghans. Even the political sovereignty of the Afghan state, largely funded by the United States, was compromised by the American military's frequent disregard for local laws, making data sovereignty for ordinary citizens even less attainable. As Wazhmah Osman has noted, the Afghan government was in a "colony position" and in no way poised to stand up to its benefactors (2020, 67). This was a perfect environment to collect massive amounts of personal data with few legal constraints. The Edward Snowden files, for example, revealed that the National Security Agency recorded almost every phone call in Afghanistan (Nicks 2014). They did so because they could: They saw no barriers. In 2011, Afghanistan became "the only country in the world" to fingerprint and photograph everyone, both on arrival and departure, who passed through their major airport (Nordland 2011). The biometric devices at Kabul International Airport were installed by US financing, and all the data they collected was fed into computers at the US Embassy in Kabul and from there shared with other US government agencies (Nordland 2011). This fetishistic data collection was further accelerated with each Afghan election, which required voters to enroll in a biometric program in order to prevent electoral fraud. Despite the data collection, the program failed to produce transparency in elections.[2]

One justification for the widespread use of biometrics in Afghanistan was the existence of corruption and fraud inside the government. Fraud, especially in the military, was indeed a significant problem and key reason behind the state's fragility. In 2016, according to one estimation, 40 percent of the Afghan security forces supposedly stationed in Helmand Province did not exist (SIGAR 2020, 4). This widespread problem became known as the "ghost" problem: There were ghost soldiers, police officers, teachers, schools, and so forth. These all referred to evidence of systemic corruption created by top-level Afghan officials to defraud international donors. The donors themselves, particularly the Americans, were also contributors to Afghan corruption (Chayes 2021). The corruption was especially bad in the security sector where the US spent between $4 billion and $5 billion a year to sustain the Afghan military (SIGAR 2020, 3). Afghan officials would present fake names to donors and receive funds for the salaries, meals, uniforms, and supplies of those "ghost" soldiers. After the fall of the government, the last minister of finance, Khalid Payenda, revealed that the ghost problem was one of the key reasons the Afghan military collapsed as the actual number of Afghan military personal was just a fraction of what was on paper: "Many of us found out that we never had 120,000 soldiers. We did not have police and army that amounted to over 300,000. That was all a lie; we never reached those levels. My conclusion right now, [is that] at best, [there were] maybe 40 to 50 thousand. The rest were all ghosts" (Payenda 2021).

There was a contradiction at the heart of the Afghan information order: While the United States oversurveilled the country and collected all sorts of information about the place and its people, this did not necessarily mean that the Americans had more knowledge of the place and its people. This dilemma is common in surveillance states. When the state puts the entire population under mass surveillance it ends up amassing so much information that it cannot humanly handle or make sense of it. They end up wasting energy on aimlessly collecting data and archiving it. This problem was revealed by Project Maven. In 2018, the Pentagon awarded Google a contract to build an AI program to sift through all the drone footage it had collected from war zones and identify targets. The contract was canceled after Google employees protested that they were not going to build an AI weapon (Shane and Wakabayashi 2018). In contrast, the type of information that leads to useful knowledge is often the information that states collect with the consent of the population. This includes tax data, census data, house numbering, health data, personal information on passports, and similar surveillance techniques and technologies that are participatory: People knowingly and willingly share personal data with the state. The data collected in a predatory way, like the US mass surveillance in Afghanistan, satisfies neither the state's insatiable thirst for information nor its need for practical knowledge—the kind essential for delivering public services.

In order to fight the corruption in the Afghan government payrolls, Washington turned to digital technology. They wanted to build a digital database of verifiable personal information about each individual who received a salary. At the same time, there was already another effort underway to build a digital personal database in Afghanistan for counterterrorism purposes. Therefore, there were two types of biometric databases that the Afghan government used: those that tracked salaried government personnel, both military and civilian, and those that tracked the members of the public for administrative purposes. The database for the military was called Afghan Personnel and Pay System and was funded by the US Department of Defense. It had data on 700,000 individuals dating back forty years (Bajak 2021). In 2018, an audit found that the system still had many problems with verifying the data, suggesting that payroll corruption—a major form of corruption in the military—was still an issue (Office of Inspector General 2019). This database was located at the Ministry of Defense and only authorized users had access to it. It is probable that the Taliban has since gained control of it.

The Ministry of Interior's biometric database, Afghan-Automated Biometric Identification System, also funded by the United States, was an umbrella project for all civilian biometric collection efforts. For everything from passports to public service jobs and university admission, applicants were required to enroll in the biometric database. Many top officials for years had siphoned off the security sector's budget and one can assume that they were not thrilled to see some technology get in the way of their lucrative schemes. The database was located at the Ministry's General

Directorate of Counter-Crimes, suggesting the American donors of the tech considered biometric, among other things, a crime-fighting technology (O'Brien 2010). In July 2020, two gunmen on a motorbike assassinated Mohammad Anwar Moniri, the director of the biometric center at the Ministry of Interior, outside his home in Kabul (*Ufuq News* 2020). We never learned who were behind the attack.

Selling digital technologies, such as biometric identification, to people in a fragile state with widespread instability and corruption is easy. The public, out of desperation, will embrace any solution that promises to end their problems. This was the situation in Afghanistan when the Americans arrived. The Afghans who supported the American biometric program in the country hoped that the advanced technology would help the Afghan state build capacity to deliver public services. There was, however, a naivety in the belief that Afghanistan's problems were only technological. This was a country under occupation where the state officials felt accountable only to their colonial patrons, not to the public. One cannot expect the rule of law and accountability to exist in such an environment, and, therefore, the idea of building a digital Afghan state run on biometric data was doomed from day one. In a country where foreign soldiers have full authority to take the lives of citizens, national sovereignty and state power have no meaning. Afghanistan's problem was too big to be solved by technology.

Conclusion

Mass surveillance creates only the illusion of knowledge. Despite all the surveillance from land and air, the massive amount of data the Americans collected in Afghanistan could not help them succeed in their mission—nor did it help build a functional Afghan state. The reason was simple: The United States collected the data for its own militarized objectives, not to serve the people of Afghanistan or strengthen Afghan state institutions. As seen in colonial projects across the Global South, imperial powers have historically exercised control through knowledge practices designed for domination. These colonial modes of knowing are fundamentally predatory, excluding subject populations from any meaningful participation in the production of knowledge. This exclusion, as decolonial scholars have noted, is the result of "a hierarchy of superior and inferior knowledge" that is inherent in colonial epistemology

(Grosfoguel 2007, 214). In the case of Afghanistan, the US military spent billions of dollars on high-tech, intrusive surveillance infrastructure but ignored investing in local institutions that could lead to an accountable state based on an impersonal bureaucracy and the rule of law, a state capable of delivering public services and settling disputes. The surveillance data collected by the US military not only failed to help the United States—and the Afghan state—it posed a serious threat to the safety of people in Afghanistan. In 2021, the Afghan government collapsed, and the Taliban took power, again. After two decades of bloodshed, the Americans replaced the Taliban with the Taliban. The new Taliban regime, technologically sophisticated and politically motivated, soon put to use all the surveillance infrastructures that they inherited from the Americans and the Afghan government.

The biometric infrastructures that the US built in Afghanistan harmed the public when the Americans were in the country and continue to harm them after they have left. The biometric databases stored at Afghan state institutions were always risky because of the weakness of the Afghan state and the threat of compromise. The US military, before their withdrawal, erased some of the biometric databases that the Afghan government maintained, especially the ones that stored the private information of the Afghan military personnel (Bajak 2021). The Taliban, however, have long been familiar with the importance of biometric data. They had managed to access the government's biometric devices even before the fall of the state. In some parts of the country, they would stop buses on the highway and subject passengers to biometric screening. In 2017, on one occasion, the Taliban identified ten members of the Afghan security forces on a bus and executed them on the spot (Kakar 2017; see also *Tolo News* 2016). The United States built a sophisticated surveillance infrastructure in Afghanistan that benefited no one, except for the Taliban. The group, according to local media, uses biometric technology to track down former employees of the Afghan government (Human Rights Watch 2022). Americans are gone from Afghanistan, but their legacy lives on.

Notes

1   On biometrics as a technology of identification, see Magnet (2011); Browne (2015); Gates (2011).
2   On this election, see the collection of detailed reports by Afghanistan Analyst Network, an independent think tank in Kabul (AAN 2020).

References

AAN (Afghanistan Analysts Network). 2020. "AAN Dossier XXVII: Afghanistan's Contested 2019 Presidential Election and Its Aftermath." September 29. https://www.afghanistan-analysts.org/en/dossiers /thematic-dossier-xxvii-afghanistans-contested-2019-presidential-election -and-its-aftermath/.

Annual Statistics Book 1380 [in Persian]. 2001. Kabul: Central Statistics Office.

Azimi, Muhammad Nabi. 1999. *Urdu va Siyasat (Dar Sih Dahah-i Akhir-i Afghanistan)*. Peshawar: Mayvand.

Bajak, Frank. 2021. "US-Built Databases a Potential Tool of Taliban Repression." *AP News*, September 7. https://apnews.com/article/technology -business-taliban-c007f85fb1b573c43a4391b947a5dcd4.

BIMA (Biometrics Identity Management Agency). 2010. "Introduction to Biometrics and Biometric Systems." US Army Corps of Engineers. https://www.tam.usace.army.mil/portals/53/docs/udc/training /biometrics%20101.pdf.

Browne, Simone. 2015. *Dark Matters: On the Surveillance of Blackness*. Durham, NC: Duke University Press.

Buhrow, William C. 2010. "Using Biometrics in Afghanistan." *Army Magazine*, February. https://www.ausa.org/sites/default/files/Buhrow.pdf.

CALL (Center for Army Lessons Learned). 2011. *Commander's Guide to Biometrics in Afghanistan: Observations, Insights, and Lessons*. CALL handbook. For official use only. Fort Leavenworth, KS: Center for Army Lessons Learned. https://info.publicintelligence.net/CALL -AfghanBiometrics.pdf.

Chayes, Sarah. 2021. "Afghanistan's Corruption Was Made in America." *Foreign Affairs*, September 3. https://www.foreignaffairs.com/united-states /afghanistans-corruption-was-made-in-america.

Economist. 2012. "The Eyes Have It." July 7. https://www.economist.com /asia/2012/07/07/the-eyes-have-it.

Economist. 2022. "Where to Process Data, and How to Add Them Up." January 29. https://www.economist.com/technology-quarterly/2022/01/29 /where-to-process-data-and-how-to-add-them-up.

Gates, Kelly A. 2011. *Our Biometric Future: Facial Recognition Technology and the Culture of Surveillance*. New York: New York University Press.

González, Roberto J. 2015. "Seeing into Hearts and Minds: Part 1. The Pentagon's Quest for a 'Social Radar.'" *Anthropology Today* 31 (3): 8–13.

Gregory, Derek. 2004. *Colonial Present: Afghanistan, Palestine, Iraq*. Oxford: Blackwell.

Gregory, Derek. 2018. "Eyes in the Sky—Bodies on the Ground." *Critical Studies on Security* 6 (3): 347–358.

Grosfoguel, Ramón. 2007. "The Epistemic Decolonial Turn." *Cultural Studies* 21 (2–3): 211–223.

Hopkins, Benjamin D. 2020. *Ruling the Savage Periphery: Frontier Governance and the Making of the Modern State.* Cambridge, MA: Harvard University Press.

Human Rights Watch. 2022. "New Evidence That Biometric Data Systems Imperil Afghans." March 30. https://www.hrw.org/news/2022/03/30/new-evidence-biometric-data-systems-imperil-afghans.

Jacobsen, Annie. 2021. *First Platoon: A Story of Modern War in the Age of Identity Dominance.* New York: Penguin.

Kakar, Ajmal. 2017. "Taliban Subject Passengers to Biometric Screening." *Pajhwok News Agency,* February 14. https://www.pajhwok.com/en/2017/02/14/taliban-subject-passengers-biometric-screening.

Kaplan, Caren. 2018. *Aerial Aftermaths: Wartime from Above.* Durham, NC: Duke University Press.

Kaplan, Martha. 1995. "Panopticon in Poona: An Essay on Foucault and Colonialism." *Cultural Anthropology* 10 (1): 85–98.

Karimi, Ali. 2019. "Surveillance in Weak States: The Problem of Population Information in Afghanistan." *International Journal of Communication* 13:4778–4794.

Karimi, Ali. 2020. "The Bazaar, the State, and the Struggle for Public Opinion in Nineteenth-Century Afghanistan." *Journal of the Royal Asiatic Society* 30 (4): 613–633.

Khan, Azmat, and Anand Gopal. 2017. "The Uncounted." *New York Times Magazine,* November 16. https://www.nytimes.com/interactive/2017/11/16/magazine/uncounted-civilian-casualties-iraq-airstrikes.html.

Magnet, Shoshana Amielle. 2011. *When Biometrics Fail: Gender, Race, and the Technology of Identity.* Durham, NC: Duke University Press.

Mbembe, Achille. 2003. "Necropolitics." *Public Culture* 15 (1): 11–40.

Neuman, Scott. 2012. "Taliban Attack Kills 21 At Lakeside Resort Near Kabul." NPR, June 22. https://www.npr.org/sections/thetwo-way/2012/06/22/155560427/taliban-attack-kills-18-at-lakeside-resort-near-kabul.

Nicks, Denver. 2014. "WikiLeaks Claims Afghanistan Under NSA Surveillance." *Time,* May 23. https://time.com/109853/wikileaks-afghanistan-under-nsa-surveillance/.

Nishiyama, Hidefumi. 2015. "Towards a Global Genealogy of Biopolitics: Race, Colonialism, and Biometrics Beyond Europe." *Environment and Planning D: Society and Space* 33 (2): 331–346. https://doi.org/10.1068/d19912.

Nordland, Rod. 2011. "Afghanistan Has Big Plans for Biometric Data." *New York Times,* November 19. https://www.nytimes.com/2011/11/20/world/asia/in-afghanistan-big-plans-to-gather-biometric-data.html.

O'Brien, William. 2010. "Conference Maps the Way Ahead for Biometrics in Afghanistan." Press release. US Central Command, October 15. https://www.centcom.mil/MEDIA/PRESS-RELEASES/Press-Release-View/Article/903841/conference-maps-the-way-ahead-for-biometrics-in-afghanistan/.

Office of Inspector General. 2019. "Audit of the Planning for and Implementation of the Afghan Personnel and Pay System DODIG-2019-115." US Department of Defense, August 15. https://www.dodig.mil/reports.html/Article/1937240/audit-of-the-planning-for-and-implementation-of-the-afghan-personnel-and-pay-sy/.

Osman, Wazhmah. 2019. "Racialized Agents and Villains of the Security State: How African Americans Are Interpellated against Muslims and Muslim Americans." *Asian Diasporic Visual Cultures and the Americas* 5 (1–2): 155–182.

Osman, Wazhmah. 2020. *Television and the Afghan Culture Wars: Brought to You by Foreigners, Warlords, and Activists.* Urbana: University of Illinois Press.

Parks, Lisa. 2015. "Vertical Mediation: Geospatial Imagery and the US Wars in Afghanistan and Iraq." In *Mediated Geographies and Geographies of Media,* edited by Susan P. Mains, Julie Cupples, and Chris Lukinbeal, 159–175. Dordrecht, Netherlands: Springer.

Payenda, Khalid. 2021. "The Khalid Payenda Interview (1): An Insider's View of Politicking, Graft and the Fall of the Republic." Afghanistan Analysts Network, September 27. https://www.afghanistan-analysts.org/en/reports/economy-development-environment/the-khalid-payenda-interview-1-an-insiders-view-of-politicking-graft-and-the-fall-of-the-republic/.

Sadat, Mir ʿAbd al-Vahid. 2014. "Ihqaq-i Huquq-i Mardum va Ya Itlaf-i An." *Hod,* August 12. http://howd.org/likene/211-2014-12-08-20-46-00.html.

Savage, Charlie, Eric Schmitt, Azmat Khan, Evan Hill, and Christoph Koettl. 2022. "Newly Declassified Video Shows U.S. Killing of 10 Civilians in Drone Strike." *New York Times,* January 19. https://www.nytimes.com/2022/01/19/us/politics/afghanistan-drone-strike-video.html.

Shane, Scott, and Daisuke Wakabayashi. 2018. "'The Business of War': Google Employees Protest Work for the Pentagon." *New York Times,* April 4. https://www.nytimes.com/2018/04/04/technology/google-letter-ceo-pentagon-project.html.

Shanker, Thom. 2011. "U.S. Military Uses Biometrics to Identify People." *New York Times,* July 13. https://www.nytimes.com/2011/07/14/world/asia/14identity.html.

Shariat Weekly. 2000. "Announcement of the Afghan Wireless Company" [in Persian]. March 5.

SIGAR (Special Inspector General for Afghanistan Reconstruction). 2020. *Quarterly Report to the United States Congress.* Accessed October 15, 2022. https://www.sigar.mil/pdf/quarterlyreports/2020-07-30qr-intro-section1.pdf.

Sturcke, James. 2008. "US Air Strike Wiped out Afghan Wedding Party, Inquiry Finds." *Guardian,* July 11. https://www.theguardian.com/world/2008/jul/11/afghanistan.usa.

Tolo News. 2016. "Taliban Used Biometric System During Kunduz Kidnapping." June 5. https://www.tolonews.com/afghanistan/taliban-used-biometric-system-during-kunduz-kidnapping.

Ufuq News. 2020. "Mudir-i sistim-i bayumitrik-i vizarat-i dakhilah dar Kabul kushtah shud." July 8. https://ufuqnews.com/archives/154005.

Voelz, Glenn. 2016. "Catalysts of Military Innovation: A Case Study of Defense Biometrics." *Defense Acquisition Research Journal* 23 (2): 178–201.

Weizman, Eyal. 2017. *Hollow Land: Israel's Architecture of Occupation*. New ed. London: Verso.

Woodward, John D., Jr. 2005. "Using Biometrics to Achieve Identity Dominance in the Global War on Terrorism." *Military Review* 85 (5): 30–34.

Zureik, Elia. 2020. "Settler Colonialism, Neoliberalism and Cyber Surveillance: The Case of Israel." *Middle East Critique* 29 (2): 219–235.

Part 3

The Politics & Optics of Representation

Media & Propaganda

Modernity and Gender Beyond the European Gaze

International Media Coverage

of Afghanistan and the

Making of News in the 1920s—

King Amanullah and Queen

Suraya's Grand Tour

In 1928, a photograph of the Afghan queen went "viral." The black-and-white studio portrait of Suraya Tarzi (1899–1968) was taken during her travels to England—part of a larger tour that took Suraya and her husband, King Amanullah Khan (r. 1919–1929), from Kabul to neighboring India, on to Egypt, through a slew of European countries, including France, England, Germany, and Poland, the Soviet Union, Turkey, and Iran, before returning them to Afghanistan. In the photograph, Suraya is wearing a sleeveless dress, with an open neckline revealing a richly jeweled necklace. A tiara rests on her hair, which is styled in a neat bob. Long earrings frame her face. Her expression is serious as she looks into the camera.

The image circulated globally. It was reproduced in the new pictorial magazines of Europe, such as the Parisian publication *L'Illustration* (Mar. 24, 1928), which feted the queen after her visit to France. The Turkish paper *Resimli Ay* also printed the image as part of a larger story on the couple amid interest generated by the tour (Edwards 2010). This image and others like it were also rumored to have circulated back to Afghanistan, via

India, and to have contributed to the rebellion that would eventually lead to the monarchs' overthrow in 1929.

The circulation of Suraya's image between far-flung locales, and its representational power, is part of a larger story about the gendered mediation of Afghanistan through the persons of the Afghan king and queen in the interwar era. The couple's travels produced sensational coverage in the increasingly global media landscape of the time. Every move they made after first setting foot in India, at the beginning of their tour, was documented not only in the British press but also in newspapers across South Asia, the Middle East, and North Africa. Developments in photographic printing technologies and the popularization of the genre, combined with increasingly speedy wire services and the translation of texts regionally, generated an international buzz about the monarchs, one that circulated back to Afghanistan through its own burgeoning press.

The grand tour, in part due to the media coverage surrounding it, was a turning point in their reign. When Amanullah had assumed the throne in 1919 and declared Afghanistan's independence from the British, he had instituted a series of constitutional and social reforms, including the opening of schools for girls, attempting to establish a minimum marriage age, and laws circumscribing polygamy. After returning from the tour, Amanullah introduced a second major wave of reforms, prohibiting polygamy for government officials and requiring that they wear suits and ties, but also attempting to reform the religious establishment and changing the weekend from Friday (see Nawid 1999, 140–141). During a series of lectures by the king about these reforms, Suraya and a group of elite women are reported to have removed the thin veils covering their faces (142).[1] In November 1928, uprisings against the monarchs began, leading to civil conflict and their eventual abdication in 1929.

As Senzil Nawid and other historians of the period have noted, notwithstanding the complex web of factors behind Amanullah's overthrow, clerical opposition to his rule was articulated largely in terms of his reforms regarding women's issues and in terms of criticism of the queen (Nawid 1999, 228; Ahmed 2017, 263). Moreover, the circulation of reports on the queen and her unveiled image through the media haunts the historical record until today. In February of 1928, a colonial officer reported that a seditious Afghan trade agent in Quetta was buying copies of the illustrated newspapers depicting the unveiled Suraya and sending them to Kabul to foment unrest, a claim echoed by one of the preeminent Afghan historians of the twentieth century, Ghulam Mohammad Ghobar, in his account of the period (Ghobar 1987, 464; Nawid 1999, 178).

Rather than investigating the role of a newspaper image in bringing down a kingdom, in this chapter I explore how these images came to feature so prominently within both the British and the regional press. This tour was something of a global "media event"—to adopt a term coined for later televised state events. While it was not broadcast in real time, the daily coverage of the king and queen as they moved across the world created a "live and unfolding" story, one that transcended national boundaries, moving across colonial and anti-colonial news networks, which were themselves connected, between London, Delhi, Cairo, and beyond.[2]

Drawing on Stuart Hall's (2021, 119–123) analysis of the news photo, which Hall notes is selected for its "formal news value" but is always "angled" or "interpretively coded," I explore how the photographs and textual descriptions of Amanullah and Suraya were differently encoded across the various contexts in which they circulated. Gender played a crucial role in the process of encoding. Just as dress figured into the "grammar of difference" that marked the colonial encounter elsewhere, the dress of the monarchs figured into colonial representations of Afghanistan as, to borrow from Nivi Manchanda's phrasing, "the disOrient"—a place that did not fall neatly into either metropole or periphery but that still was subsumed by imperial logics (Cooper and Stoller 1997, 3; Manchanda 2020, 3, 19). Others have described this liminal relationship with empire in terms of crypto- or quasi-coloniality: Located on the border of empire, Afghanistan achieved nominal independence at the cost of increased *dependence* on foreign capital and European hegemonic forms of cultural identity (Lanzillo 2022; Hanifi and Hanifi 2021, 78).

The first part of this chapter examines coverage of the monarchs in British newspapers and pictorial magazines to illustrate how the dress of the king and queen, and particularly the veil, were encoded in a way that reinforced an image of Afghanistan as being a space apart, as it did not figure neatly into the geography of empire. Indeed, despite their visual presentation in European dress, captions worked to anchor the monarchs firmly as other. As feminist historians and geographers of South Asia and the Middle East have long argued, gender played a necessary discursive role in maintaining the systems of difference that were crucial to the functioning of empire. Through print media, Afghanistan was made to fit into the textual universe of empire. Moreover, at times, and particularly in its focus on Suraya, the British press offered an early example of gendered (mis)representations of Afghan women in ways that prefigured and bore resemblances to those that accompanied the twenty-first-century neocolonial invasion.

Afghanistan's position vis-à-vis the British imperial order also lent it significance as an anti-colonial space. Newspapers across South Asia, the Middle East, and North Africa were connected to one another as well as to the British colonial press, and these papers, too, documented the rulers as they traversed physical space. If, in British papers, Afghanistan was encoded in disOrientalist terms that underscored the superiority of the British empire and the liminal space of the Afghan monarchs, in the papers of the Muslim societies that were under British colonial rule or mandate, it often was encoded as a "non-imperial counterspace"—a phrase employed by Thomas Wide to describe how Muslim reformers from across the border in British India and as far as Egypt conceived of Afghanistan in its early years of independence as outside of and thus in some ways liberated from the British imperial fold (2014, 107). These newspapers formed part of what Marilyn Booth has described as the "lateral cosmopolitanism" of print culture in the Eastern Mediterranean, which depended on the migration of texts between and across regions of the Middle East and South Asia (2019, 5–6). Afghanistan represented an often forgotten node in this textual universe, and examining examples of Amanullah and Suraya's dress as they were taken up, particularly in the Arabic press, we find stories and images of the monarchs and their attire serving as vehicles to address anxieties about modernity, reform, and the role of Islam in society.

These accounts unsettle the entrenched historiographic notion that Afghanistan was a space apart, insulated from both colonial hierarchies and anti-colonial regional imaginaries. Rather, print culture and print capitalism in the interwar era was a vehicle by which reforms in Afghanistan and its cryptocolonial status influenced conversations and social milieus far beyond its borders.

"An Oriental Touch": Afghanistan in the British Press of the 1920s

In the wake of Amanullah and Suraya's world tour, which began in December of 1927, the *Times* of London sent a correspondent to Kabul. In his dispatch, published one year after the tour had begun, the correspondent marveled at the changes the country had undergone: "Even before King Amanullah returned from his epoch-making trip, Kabul was a place so distinct from any other that it should have an onomatopoeic adjective of its own. The atmosphere cannot be termed Eastern; it bears no resemblance to India; it is cosmopolitan with an Oriental touch, and yet it is neither Eastern nor Western: it is itself and beggars description" ("Europe and After: Life in Kabul," Dec. 19, 1928). What is clear from the correspondent's words is that Afghanistan occupied a befuddling space in the imperial world order precisely because of the reforms instituted in the country after it gained independence. It required its own "onomatopoeic adjective" as neither the term *Eastern* nor *Western* quite fit. It could not be called *Eastern* because, in the eyes of the writer, it bore no resemblance to India, the emblem of the Orient in the British imperial construction of the world. Yet it also could not be deemed *Western* due to its location firmly in the east.

Attempts to situate Kabul in the geopolitics of empire were a common feature in British newspaper coverage of Afghanistan even before Amanullah and Suraya's travels put them on the proverbial map. During the first half of the decade, the *Times* documented Afghanistan frequently.[3] The paper did not have a correspondent based in Afghanistan, so its coverage of the newly independent nation came primarily via India: Through diplomatic cables from the India Office, Reuters dispatches, or the accounts from their own correspondents based in India (and sometimes embedded with the British army on the frontier) ("Plots from Kabul," *Times* [London], Aug. 20, 1919). On occasion, correspondents in Tehran, Simla, and Moscow would read and report on developments in Afghanistan through the new Afghan newspapers that circulated to these locales, as well as through other regional newspapers like *Iran* (in Tehran) and the *Pioneer* (in India).[4] Regular readers of the *Times* before the tour would have most often encountered Afghanistan through its frontier with British India and its border with the USSR—sites of conflict and potential anti-colonial unrest.[5]

Looking to a different periodical, the *Illustrated London News* (ILN), over the same period shows a continuity in how Afghanistan was mediated even in different formats and when presented to different audiences. The ILN was a pictorial weekly, and while it prided itself on circulating across the world, as Patrick Collier has argued, its main material function was "symbolic signification," to make meaning for and thereby shape the tastes of its primary audience: the British middle classes (2016, 44–45). Unlike the *Times*, the ILN documented Afghanistan infrequently in the first part of the decade, but when it did, the coverage was similar to that of the *Times*, focusing on Afghanistan's key location on the border with British India, which was reinforced as a place of "murderous frontier outlaws," the diplomacy around the Anglo-Afghan war, and the "Russian menace" ("The Soviet-Afghan Treaty, A New Russian Menace," ILN, Sept. 25, 1926). Because this was a pictorial magazine, these texts were accompanied by a visual language that told its own story. In one photograph, accompanying an article on Afghanistan's reforms and diplomatic relations with India, Amanullah appears wearing a military uniform while delivering a Friday Sermon. His dress, the paper noted, "indicates the modernising tendency of his rule" ("India's Restless Neighbour: Afghanistan—The Amir Reads Prayers," ILN, Aug. 15, 1925). In 1926, to accompany the signing of the Soviet-Afghan Treaty of neutrality, the paper reproduced several photographs from the American travel writer Lowell Thomas's 1925 book *Beyond Khyber Pass*.[6] In one of these, Amanullah poses with his two young daughters, whom the caption describes as "soon to pass from the sunlight into the shadowed seclusion of a noble harem" ("The Soviet-Afghan Treaty," ILN, Sept. 25, 1926). Through the triangle of headlines, photos, and captions, "formal news" stories about diplomatic or political developments were also opportunities to signify familiar Orientalist tropes (e.g., see figure 7.1).

The world tour was a turning point in British media coverage of Afghanistan in the 1920s as the volume of coverage dramatically increased. This was a "media event" of sorts, to draw on the terminology Daniel Dayan and Elihu Katz use to describe spectacles that are broadcast on television and demand viewers anticipate them and tune in (1992, 2). Of course, it was not actually broadcast in real time (though the couple's time in England was filmed by Pathé News). Nevertheless, the *Times* stoked anticipation for the couple's journey in the months leading up to their trip, which the paper dubbed, in a recurring headline, "The Afghan Royal Visit" (Oct. 3, 1927; Dec. 9, 1927). Once their journey began, each leg was carefully documented with dispatches on "The Afghan Royal Visit," beginning with Karachi (Dec. 13, 1927). In this way, it was more than just a single story but an event intended to capture the attention of and sustain an audience, an event that would reach its climax with their arrival in England.

The newspaper's subsequent coverage underscores the degree to which Amanullah and Suraya were the spectacles of a vociferous media that operated on an imperial (global) scale—in the sense that their every move was documented and circulated back to London. The *Times* ran continuous updates throughout the course of their travels, and when they at last arrived

FIRST STUDIO PORTRAITS OF QUEEN SURYIA:
ENGLAND'S ROYAL GUEST FROM AFGHANISTAN.

Queen Suryia, who arrived in England with King Amanullah on March 15, is the first Consort of an Oriental monarch to visit Europe with her husband. She is a daughter of the Afghan Foreign Minister, Tarzi Khan, and is the only wife of the King, who firmly upholds the ideal of monogamy. Already she has made so immense impression in Rome, Berlin, and Paris by her personal beauty and her adaptability to Western ways. "It is difficult to realise," writes Sir Percival Phillips, who accompanied the Afghan royal party from India to Europe, "that this charming lady has, according to our standards, been virtually a prisoner all her life. She lived in the strictest seclusion at Kabul. The Queen is deeply interested in every aspect of life in Europe, particularly the position of women." In Paris she was hailed as a queen of fashion, and had some fifty dresses made there. "She bids fair," it has been said, "to rival Queen Elizabeth in the number of her gowns."

RIVALLING QUEEN ELIZABETH IN THE SPLENDOURS OF
HER WARDROBE: QUEEN SURYIA OF AFGHANISTAN,
THE CHARMING CONSORT OF KING AMANULLAH.

7.1 Queen Suraya in the *Illustrated London News* (March 17, 1928) during the royal visit to London.

in London, multiple columns of print were devoted to the pair each day. The *ILN* went from the occasional image of or reference to Afghanistan in the preceding years to coverage of the royal couple in every issue during the months of March and April 1928. A hint at the extent to which this journey captured the imagination of the British public can be found in the anecdote of a Harrow couple who were reported to have named their newborn twins Amanullah and Surayya in the wake of the royal couple's visit ("News in Brief," *Times* [London], Apr. 30, 1928).

The Presence (and Absence) of Suraya's Veil

Much like the stories post-2001 that breathlessly marveled at the incongruity of Afghan women running track or winning singing competitions, documentation in the British press of the Afghan monarchs during their tour highlighted the contradictions of a society that fit into the projected category of "traditional" but, through the persons of the monarchs and their modernizing projects, displayed elements of what would be considered "modern," defined from the vantage point of the West.[7] The monarchs' attire, and particularly Suraya's veil, figured prominently into how such contradictions and binaries were reproduced both textually and visually.

The work that gendered representations did in producing and reinforcing divisions between East and West is now well-trodden ground for historians of empire. Edward Said's *Orientalism* and the "long shadow" it cast on feminist scholarship of the Middle East and South Asia has illustrated the degree to which knowledge production from the metropole, and its deployment of gender, undergirded the colonial encounter (Burton 1999, 243–244). Within this postcolonial literature, countless works have been devoted to exploring the colonial obsession with the veil and the reasons for its staying power as a trope and object of focus.[8] The veil continues to play a central role in marking Muslims as "other" in the West, as well as in the discourse of "saving" Muslim and Afghan women into the twenty-first century (Abu-Lughod 2013; Mishra 2007). Rather than recount familiar terrain, tracing the significations of the veil and dress in this specific case reveals how representations of the veil operated to limit the possible interpretations of an independent Afghanistan and its relationship to the changing imperial landscape for a British reading and viewing public.

Meyda Yeğenoğlu has suggested the veil represented the colonial obsession with demasking, with rendering the Other legible because it "attracts the eye, and forces one to think, to speculate about what is behind it" (1998, 44). Notably, in Suraya's case it was not the veil but its absence that was remarked on in the British press. From the very first moments of her stepping onto the ship that set sail from Bombay to Port Said in Egypt, she and Amanullah's sister, Kubra, who were described as having hitherto lived a secluded life, were now depicted as being "permitted to discard their veils in public for the first time" ("From Bombay with King Amanullah," *Times* [London], Jan. 6, 1928). Again, when she arrived in Italy, it was noted prominently in the *Times* that she was "unveiled and dressed in European costume" ("King Amanullah's Tour," Jan. 9, 1928). In anticipation of Suraya's arrival in London, the ILN (Mar. 10, 1928) placed a close-up portrait of the queen on its cover, describing how happily she had "adapted herself to Western ways." The following week, the studio portraits that introduced this chapter were released. Again, the phrase "adaptability to Western ways" was used to describe the queen, and her present appearance was juxtaposed to her previous life in Afghanistan with the words, "It is difficult to realise that this charming lady has, according to our standards, been virtually a prisoner all her life. She lived in the strictest seclusion in Kabul" (ILN, Mar. 17, 1928, 423).

Stuart Hall has written about the purpose of the image caption in terms of "anchorage," to direct the reader to particular understandings or interpretations and away from others (2021, 103). The captions and text surrounding Suraya's dress and comportment worked to anchor an ideological signification under the guise of formal news. As such, describing Suraya as a virtual prisoner in Kabul was not an example of factual reporting. Even before she was officially named queen of Afghanistan, in 1926, Suraya participated in the nation's public life more overtly and explicitly than any of the royal women who had preceded her. She participated in Independence Day celebrations and military events—where she presented soldiers with handkerchiefs and coins (Habibullah 1990, 53). She also served a public diplomatic role. Telegrams she wrote abroad were published in the Afghan newspapers. She was reported on in the press for hosting foreign and Afghan elite women, the wives of ministers and diplomats, and accompanying Amanullah on state business around the country.[9]

Depicting Suraya as a prisoner fit into a larger media narrative in which the action of unveiling was coded as liberation, and Suraya's going west—toward European society—was credited with this liberation. One cannot but hear echoes of this language in Laura Bush's infamous radio address in November 2001, following the initial US invasion of Afghanistan. In her address the then first lady drew a direct line between the so-called War on Terror and the liberation of Afghan women, noting: "In much of Afghanistan, women are no longer imprisoned in their homes. . . . The fight against terrorism is also a fight for the rights and dignity of women." As Lila Abu-Lughod has argued, such uncritical representations of Afghan women as voiceless and in need of saving from their own societies under-girded the US invasion and occupation of Afghanistan (2013, 4). The genre of pulp nonfiction that proliferated in the 2000s depicting Muslim women escaping abusive marriages and confinement by escaping to Europe went hand in hand with magazine covers describing the need for more US troops in the region, accompanied by images of burqa-clad Afghan women or photojournalism depicting their physical abuse. In 1928, the first time an Afghan woman was prominently depicted in the English-language media, we find almost identical language used.

In many ways, the trip was successful. Indeed, the other major emphasis of the press coverage, and the tour more broadly, was on capital: military technologies and industrialization. The news documented a schedule for the monarchs that was packed with military displays and tours of facto-ries. Article after article describes them witnessing the splendors of in-dustrial and military advancement in the metropole.[10] This underscores Afghanistan's cryptocoloniality, as the effort to court industrial investment, on the part of the monarchs, and of European states to compete to impress the king and queen in order to secure development opportunities, con-nected with the monarch's own presentation as modern. Holly Edwards, who has analyzed the visual documentation of Amanullah and Suraya in British and Turkish pictorial magazines, describes the dress of the king and queen on their tour as a kind of "cosmopolitan performance and self-fashioning" and notes the success and agency behind this self-fashioning (2010). Yet, the explicit mention of the veil's absence in articles and photo spreads perpetuated its presence and thus limited, for the reader, the possi-ble significations of Suraya's dress and actions, casting them as exceptional and the product of her travels west. This episode offers a clear example of the colonial feminism applied to Afghanistan in the 1920s, described by Wazhmah Osman in her work on media in the country. As Osman observes, "Even though as part of their 'civilizing mission' agents of the British Empire were actively promoting women's liberation and moder-nity throughout their colonies, they were simultaneously undermining those same principles" (2020, 35). In short, the inclusion of Afghanistan in the international community and in technological advancement involved the reinscribing of Afghan women into Western imperial desires around gender and bodily autonomy.

Afghanistan and the Mediascape of South/West Asia and North Africa

Historians often write of Amanullah and Suraya's travels as a "European tour," but this is an incomplete depiction of their journey (Nawid 1999, 136–137; McChesney 1999, 31; Ahmed 2017, 250). In addition to visiting Europe and the USSR, Amanullah and Suraya traveled to India, Egypt, Turkey, and Iran; met with local residents, religious figures, and state leaders; and interacted with and were reported on by the press in these places. Indeed, the tour was a significant moment that contributed to Amanullah and Suraya's transregional importance across South/West Asia and North Africa.

This "transregion" had a somewhat integrated mediascape and was pivotal to the emergence of the press in Afghanistan, where the local and national newspapers relied on translation and reproduction, or "scissors and paste," primarily from regional neighbors to populate their content (Joshi 2017).[11] As Marilyn Booth has noted of the late Ottoman context, "Newspapers in all languages in the [Ottoman] Empire translated material constantly" (2019, 30). The same can be said for Afghanistan, which was intimately connected, in the early 1920s, to this post-Ottoman print sphere. Beginning in its first issue, *Aman-i Afghan*—a weekly paper published in Kabul from 1920 through 1929—divided the news into the *hawādis dākhiliyyah* (internal news to Afghanistan) and *hawādis khārijiyyah* (external news). The latter section relied primarily on translations and reprints from foreign newspapers, particularly from the Iranian, Egyptian, Turkish, Indian, British, and Russian presses. The paper further divided international news into the subsections of the "Islamic world" and *farangastān*. The papers used the news to celebrate individual states (such as Egypt) fighting for national sovereignty and independence from colonial rule, even as they held them up as part of an integrated region, the "Islamic world," united by a shared Islamic past and their identity as populated primarily by Muslims. The degree to which the Afghan press, and particularly *Aman-i Afghan*, projected a sense of regional spirit was noted in a 1921 *Times* of London article ("The Afghan Press," Aug. 3), which said of Afghanistan's major newspaper, "It would be impossible to gain so clear a reading of the heart of the East from Indian, Persian, Arabian, or Egyptian vernacular press." In truth, these presses were all reflected through their reproduction in the paper, as were the British wire services that were a source of news throughout the region.

One can trace the circulation of the Indian, Persian, and Arabic vernacular presses, as they exchanged content with each other and the Afghan press, during the coverage of the Afghan monarchs on their tour. For example, when Suraya and Amanullah first arrived in India, the Cairo-based newspaper *Al-Shura*—an important paper for the Arab nationalist movement that was read across the Middle East and North Africa—published a speech welcoming the king and queen that had been delivered by representatives of the Jamiat al-Islam in Bombay ("What Did the Indians Say?," *Al-Shura* [Cairo], Jan. 1, 1928, 4).[12] The speech praised educational developments in Afghanistan, relating these to the work being done to educate Muslims in India and asserting that "all true Muslims take pride in your majesties."

Much of the coverage was laudatory, exhibiting excitement at the visiting rulers from an independent Muslim state. *Al-Jami'ah al-'Arabiyah*, a biweekly paper published in Jerusalem, reprinted an article (Jan. 5, 1928, 2) from an Egyptian newspaper about the Egyptian League's reception of Amanullah along with a speech by the monarch proclaiming his pleasure at being "among brothers of the East, like myself" and calling for unity and coalition among the peoples of the East. A women's Urdu-language periodical in Lahore, *Tahzib-i Niswan*, reproduced a long profile of the queen (Jan. 14, 1928) from an Alexandrian paper that discussed her accomplishments on behalf of the Afghan state, her Arab heritage (her mother was Syrian), and her work in the advancement of women's well-being.

While far from a complete survey, such stories emphasized a shared affinity between Afghanistan, India, and the Arab world. They also hint at Afghanistan's regional currency as a nominally independent Muslim state and a potential model for an anti-colonial future. The excited news coverage of the monarchs as they moved west also circulated back to Afghanistan via its own media's reproduction of regional texts. An article in the Kabul-based cultural newspaper *Anis* (Jan. 1, 1928, 9, 12) noted that all of the press in Egypt was writing about Afghanistan's *nahża* (awakening), the new Afghanistan, and the young independent king.

Not all of the news coverage was celebratory. The question of veiling and Amanullah's apparel were remarked on in Indian, Persian, Arabic, and Turkish newspapers. As with the British media, the regional press under review noted the monarchs' choice of clothing and grafted it onto foundational dichotomies between East and West. Yet, whereas the British press juxtaposed, through coding, the incongruity of Suraya's dress in Europe with her imprisonment in Afghanistan and delighted in her appearance unveiled, in the Arabic press coverage surveyed, her appearance—as well as that of Amanullah—were framed with more ambivalence. Rather than projecting an Other, their dress was insistently related back to movements, debates, and anxieties within the society in which the news was being consumed. Moreover, while Suraya's veil, and veiling more generally, was an object of focus, the press was equally if not more concerned with Amanullah's choice to wear a round-brimmed hat. Indeed, the overarching concern displayed in these newspapers is about fashion—and its attendant significance in performing gendered modernity/authenticity—rather than in women's seclusion or relative liberation.

After the establishment of the Turkish Republic, Mustafa Kemal's 1925 law mandating Western-style hats for men in public spaces—in lieu of traditional head coverings—and his discouragement of the headscarf for women placed these already contested sartorial practices center stage, regionally.[13] Sara Rahnama, in her examination of these debates in contemporaneous Algeria, asks us to consider dress as a performance, shifting the discussion away from fixed ideas of tradition versus modernity and toward how dress served as a powerful tool to enact and embody competing visions of the future (2020, 429). Rather than generalizing across these contexts, as the case of Amanullah and Suraya's tour demonstrates, these debates were not only happening in parallel—in places like Egypt, Algeria, Afghanistan, Iran, and India—they were happening in conversation with one another.[14]

The travels of Amanullah and Suraya, like the Turkish republican ban on hats in 1925, served as a catalyst for discussions of the anxieties about change, authenticity, and what the ideal future looked like. In Algeria, Rahnama notes, the press shared news from Egyptian papers about Amanullah's visit to Egypt: His alleged questioning of a scholar at Egypt's Al-Azhar about whether he could pray in a European hat sparked controversy in the Algerian press (2020, 442).

In Palestine, *Al-Jami 'ah al- 'Arabiyah*, the same Jerusalem paper that had written of the Afghan king's affinity with organizers in the East, did not reprint but rather described photographs of Amanullah from an Egyptian pictorial weekly, *Al-Musawar*. Under the headline "From the Wonders of Wonders: The King of Afghanistan's Hat," the article notes that the magazine had featured an image in which Prince Edward of England wore an Indian army uniform and a turban while in another, Amanullah, in Egypt, wore a hat and Western dress, failing to "consider the feelings of his people, the Egyptian people, or the Islamic world" (*Al-Jami 'ah al- 'Arabiyah*, Jan. 16, 1928, 1). The paper interpreted the king's discordant dress as a sign of the strangeness of the times. Looking to the original source of the images in *Al-Musawar*, the photographs of the couple's Egypt visit were "angled" differently with a caption that doesn't mention the king's dress. Notably his dress mirrored that of the Egyptian statesmen surrounding him save for his hat, which he holds in his hand while a few of the men around him wear the fez. The caption does, however, describe the queen's face veil and hat: "To his right is Her Majesty the Queen, wearing a hat and wearing western clothes, with a black mask on her face. . . . Her Majesty the Queen, when she sails to Europe, will remove the veil that she lowered over her face during her stay in Egypt, observing the traditions of its people" (*Al-Musawar* (Cairo), Jan. 6, 1928). Here the queen is praised for observing the traditions of the people, rather than denounced for transgressing them. Both examples illustrate a preoccupation with dress and geography that echoes that of the British press in its attempt to project ideas of modernity and place onto the physical bodies of the monarchs. At the same time, they show how these ideas, while built on particular and gendered binaries, were not fixed but contested.

Amanullah's hat and Suraya's face veil were taken up most substantively by the prominent Islamic reformer in Egypt, Rashid Rida (1865–1935). Rida's periodical, *Al-Manar*, which sought to revive the Islamic *ummah* and sketch out Islam's place in the contemporary world order, had a global readership, spanning Southeast Asia, Syria, Turkey, and Russia (Zemmin 2018, 141). Upon the monarchs' visit to Cairo in January 1928, Rida published an article praising Amanullah's status as an independent Muslim ruler and his reforms in the realm of education, drawing links between the king and Jamal al-Din Al-Afghani (d. 1897)—the intellectual forebear for Rida and other reformers of his generation (*Al-Manar*, Jan. 23, 1928, 781–782). Rida noted with disappointment, however, that Amanullah wore a hat and Suraya went unveiled "in a way that was not widespread

صاحبا الجلالة ملك وملكة الافغان أمام فندق وترباس في الاقصر في ٣٠ ديسمبر (تصوير رياض افندي شحاته)

7.2 Queen Suraya and King Amanullah of Afghanistan in Luxor, Egypt. The photo—one of many in the Arab press documenting their visit—was printed in the Egyptian newspaper *Al Lataif Al Musawara* on January 9, 1928.

in Egypt with the Egyptian queen's maintenance of hijab" (784). By all photographic accounts she wore a hat and a covering over her mouth. Rida used their example to write on the importance of preserving the old even while looking to the new as the key of the strongest civilizations (786). Upon Amanullah's visit to Turkey and his meeting with Mustafa Kemal, Rida stated that Amanullah used to be the pride of Muslims, but now he was "going the way of the Turks," a predicament that Rida clearly saw reflected in his own society: He compared Suraya's dress and interest in shopping to the excesses of khedivial Egypt, harkening back to the recent past rather than alluding to the future. He further accused Amanullah of "following the sunna of the Turk in wearing the hat and other evils that proliferated in the Ottoman and Egyptian states" (*Al-Manar*, June 18, 1928, 227–228). Using the term *sunna* was meant to signify to his readers the transgressive nature of following the example of Mustafa Kemal, instead of that of the Prophet Muhammad.

What Rida called Mustafa Kemal's "atheist" policies contradicted his own ideal of reform with renewal. By mirroring the Turkish ruler in his style, Amanullah too posed a threat to the right path for the future. By discussing the past of khedivial Egypt, Rida was signaling to readers the regressive nature of what were ostensibly modernizing reforms. Meanwhile, the Turkish magazine *Resimli Ay* reproduced Suraya's portrait from the *ILN*, along with a caption supporting the monarch's reforms by likening Afghanistan to the Turkey of the previous decade.[15] In this way, the couple's figures provided publishers with a grammar to relate their own society's past to their ideal visions for the future.

Other articles in the Egyptian press framed the same stories of the king and queen's travels and dress in positive terms for their readers. Unsurprisingly, these articles were more likely to circulate back to Afghanistan through its own press. For example, an article on Queen Suraya and veiling was published in *Al-Siyasah*, a weekly newspaper of Egypt's Liberal Constitutional Party, which in the 1920s supported the reforms in Turkey and had a special section for women readers. This article—which was reprinted in the Afghan cultural newspaper *Anis*—praised Queen Suraya and the great advances in women's education in Afghanistan under the new ruler (Jan. 1, 1928, 12). The discussion featured an interview with an unnamed Afghan minister in which he talked about seclusion (purdah) in Afghanistan. Likening Afghanistan to all Muslim countries, the minister noted with approval that veiling and seclusion were becoming less common among the upper classes, and they were not practiced among the lowest classes. Rather, it was in the middle class that the practices remained stubbornly prevalent.

These dispatches around the king and queen's travels, while only a snapshot, highlight a key and urgent question in the changing, postcaliphate Islamic world about what progress should look like and how tradition and authenticity should be maintained in the face of reform. Depending on the producer of the news, the same circulating stories and images of Amanullah and Suraya directed the reader toward meaningfully different interpretations of progress. Through the ad hoc reproduction of articles and images of the monarchs in multiple nations, sartorial impressions circulated across national boundaries, forming a discourse that touched on class, gender, and the role of religion in "Eastern" society. On a more fundamental level, the regional solidarities and familiarities that show up in the media coverage of the monarchs' travels illustrate how, rather than a space apart, Afghanistan was also related to empire through anti-colonial movements. In other words, the Afghan state in the interwar period might have been defined by its cryptocoloniality vis-à-vis the British Empire and access to global capital. But it was also viewed as a potential site of anti-colonial futures. As reformers debated what the present and future should look like, they projected these visions onto the monarchs in conversations that circulated back to Afghanistan through print networks.

Conclusion

The image of Suraya unveiled and the dress and travels of the king and queen, as they circulated across the interwar mediascape, did not tell a single story. Nor did they tell a simple story. Examining how Amanullah and Suraya's travels were taken up across geographic and linguistic divides illustrates, first and foremost, the degree to which their tour was a media event that reverberated internationally. Afghanistan's status as an independent, cryptocolonial Muslim country bordering an empire influenced how their visual and textual images were encoded.

In the British media, their dress and comportment were depicted as a product of their spatial movement west—in contradiction to their own society. Moreover, in an echo of the twenty-first-century discourse around "saving women," the veil, even in its absence, signified women's need to be freed from their own society. Meanwhile, in the Arab news, as it circulated transregionally, Amanullah's and Suraya's dress provided a grammar for publishers and writers to explore Afghan modernity and how it fit into or threatened their own visions for an independent future. The way the couples' image, and particularly their attire, circulated highlights that such mediations were not unidirectional but played off one another. Gendered representations intersected with available media technologies and systems of translation and transmission in ways that were both global in their reach and contextually specific.

On the one hand, it is difficult to say how the positive depictions of their travels reprinted in the Afghan papers were received by readers in the moment, and accounts of the negative news circulating back to Afghanistan through informal networks are based on scant evidence in colonial archives and oral transmission. On the other hand, even without knowing how it was received, the influence of this media, and particularly the images of the unveiled queen, endures as a subject in oral narrations and Afghan histories until today. These narrations claim the British allegedly circulated these images in Afghanistan to foment unrest against Amanullah. If true, Suraya's image was not only deployed in the metropole to cast Afghanistan as backwards, through representations of its women as only liberated when moving west; this image was also used as propaganda in the periphery—a form of media imperialism that foreshadows later attempts to wage war through print, from the Soviet era to the so-called War on Terror (Osman 2020, 88).

In March 2020, *Time* magazine produced a series on the one hundred most influential women from the past century, designing mock covers in the style of the magazine's covers from the early twentieth century. The cover for the year 1927 was an illustration depicting Suraya's London studio portrait. Nearly one century after the photograph had been taken, the same image of the queen that circulated in 1928 was being "angled" to rewrite history for US audiences. The short paragraph of text accompanying the image praised the queen for her progressive vision, notably recasting this vision using the parlance of the twenty-first-century US-led NATO intervention in Afghanistan, as a call "for women to 'take their part' in nation building" (*Time* 2020). Echoing a previous age, this image continues to circulate and signify a gendered vision of Afghan modernity that reflects the ideological position of its producer.

Notes

1   This is also reported in India Office Records IOR/L/PS/10/1285, October 6, 1928.
2   The tour was also recorded by Pathé News in Britain, whose newsreels were screened every two weeks in theaters (Dayan and Katz 1992, 2).
3   When Arthur Moore, the *Times* correspondent to India, paid a brief visit to Kabul in 1922, the paper framed his dispatch as the first "recorded by any British subject not on the business of either the British or the Afghan Government" ("An Englishman in Kabul," June 2, 1922).
4   See, for example, "Tall Talk in Kabul," *Times* (London), June 22, 1920, 15; "The Afghan Press," *Times* (London), August 3, 1921, 7; "The Ameer's Break with Tradition," *Times* (London), July 16, 1921, 9.
5   This is based on a search of every mention of "Afghanistan" between 1919 and 1929 in the *Times* of London digital archive.
6   David Edwards has written of Lowell Thomas's travels to Afghanistan, within the context of his longer career and celebrity for covering T. E.

Lawrence. See the introduction in David Edwards's (2002) *Before Taliban: Genealogies of the Afghan Jihad.*

7   Rather than downplay the significance of women in post-2001 Afghanistan and their actions, I am interested in how they are covered in the US media as foils to their own society. For examples of this kind of coverage, see Longen (2003) and Associated Press (2008). For a discussion of how this "singular success story" has worked to limit the heterogeneity of Afghan women and society more broadly, see Schmeding (2021, 144–146).

8   See, for example, Ghumkhor (2019) and Yeğenoğlu (1998). For a discussion of the veil as a trope or "zone of theory" in anthropology of the Arab world, see Abu-Lughod (1989, 290).

9   See, for example, *Aman-i Afghan* 5, no. 44 (March 7, 1925), 4.

10   Queen Suraya accompanied the queen of England to a performance of *The Desert Song*, an Orientalist operetta written by Otto Harbach and set in Morocco during the Rif Rebellion of 1925, in which a French general is sent to destroy a band of rebels that is threatening the imperial outpost whose leader is in fact the French general's son, masquerading as a sheikh. In his disguise, he seduces a young French woman ("Two Queens at Drury Lane," *Times* [London], March 16, 1929).

11   For a discussion of the movement behind Mahmud Tarzi's *Siraj al-Akhbar* (published between 1911 and 1919), see Schinasi (1979, 74–76).

12   For a discussion of how the paper circulated in the Gulf, see Rashoud (2016, 83–84); for a discussion of its importance as an archive of Arab nationalism more broadly, see Kawar (2017).

13   For more on the hat law as it was applied and contested in Turkey, see Metinsoy (2021, 234–243).

14   For examples not mentioned directly in the text that illustrate these regional conversations: *Tulu'-i Afghan* reproduced an article from an Iranian paper, *Aftab-i Sharq*, discussing Suraya during her travels. See *Tulu'-i Afghan* (Kandahar) 7, no. 55 (May 1928), 5. Senzil Nawid (1999, 228) points to the depictions of Suraya from *Habl al-Matin* in Calcutta that were reproduced in *Aman-i Afghan*. Holly Edwards (2010) discusses the Turkish press.

15   Holly Edwards (2010) has discussed a translation of a special issue of the Turkish weekly *Resimli Ay* 4, no. 52, in 1928 that was dedicated to the Afghan monarchs and their tour.

References

Abu-Lughod, Lila. 1989. "Zones of Theory in the Anthropology of the Arab World." *Annual Review of Anthropology* 18:267–306.

Abu-Lughod, Lila. 2013. *Do Muslim Women Need Saving?* Cambridge, MA: Harvard University Press.

Ahmed, Faiz. 2017. *Afghanistan Rising: Islamic Law and Statecraft Between the Ottoman and British Empires*. Cambridge, MA: Harvard University Press.

Associated Press. 2008. "First 'American Idol,' Now 'Afghan Star.'" *New York Times*, March 14.

Booth, Marilyn. 2019. "Translation as Lateral Cosmopolitanism in the Ottoman Universe." In *Migrating Texts: Circulating Translations Around the Ottoman Mediterranean*, edited by Marilyn Booth, 1–54. Edinburgh: Edinburgh University Press.

Burton, Antoinette. 1999. Review of *Gendering Orientalism: Race, Femininity, and Representation*, by Reina Lewis, and *Colonial Fantasies: Towards a Feminist Reading of Orientalism*, by Meyda Yeğenoğlu. *Signs: Journal of Women in Culture and Society* 25 (1): 243–244.

Bush, Laura. 2001. "Radio Address by Mrs. Bush." The White House, November 17. https://georgewbush-whitehouse.archives.gov/news/releases/2001/11/20011117.html.

Collier, Patrick. 2016. *Modern Print Artefacts: Textual Materiality and Literary Value in British Print Culture, 1890–1930s*. Edinburgh: Edinburgh University Press.

Cooper, Frederick, and Ann Laura Stoller, eds. 1997. *Tensions of Empire: Colonial Cultures in a Bourgeois World*. Berkeley: University of California Press.

Dayan, Daniel, and Elihu Katz. 1992. *Media Events: The Live Broadcasting of History*. Cambridge, MA: Harvard University Press.

Edwards, David. 2002. *Before Taliban: Genealogies of the Afghan Jihad*. Berkeley: University of California Press.

Edwards, Holly. 2010. "Exiles, Diplomats, and Darlings: Afghans Abroad in the Early Twentieth Century." Paper presented at Archaeologists and Travelers in Ottoman Lands: A Symposium, University of Pennsylvania, March 19–20.

Ghobar, Ghulam Mohammad. 1987. *Afghanistan Dar Masir-i Tarikh*. Kabul: Markaz Nashr-i Inqilab.

Ghumkhor, Sahar. 2019. *The Political Psychology of the Veil: The Impossible Body*. Cham, Switzerland: Springer/Palgrave Macmillan.

Habibullah, Amir. 1990. *My Life: From Brigand to King, Autobiography of Amir Habibullah*. London: Octagon.

Hall, Stuart. 2021. "The Determinations of News Photographs." In *Writings on Media*, 119–123. Durham, NC: Duke University Press.

Hanifi, Jamil, and Shah Mahmood Hanifi. 2021. "Crypto-Colonial Independence Rituals in Afghanistan." *Afghanistan* 4 (1): 70–78.

Joshi, Priti. 2017. "Scissors-and-Paste Ephemerality and Memorialization in the Archive of Indian Newspapers." *Amodern* 7. https://amodern.net/article/scissors-and-paste/.

Kawar, Nawal. 2017. "An Arab Nationalist Survival Against All Odds: Muhammad 'Ali Eltaher," *Four Corners of the World* (blog), Library of Congress, June 16. http://blogs.loc.gov/international-collections/2017/06/an-arab-nationalist-survival-against-all-odds-muhammad-ali-eltaher/.

Lanzillo, Amanda. 2022. "Empire and Dependence in Afghan History." *Jamhoor*, January 27. https://www.jamhoor.org/read/empire-and-dependence-in-afghan-history.

Longen, Jere. 2003. "A First for an Afghan Woman, and Her Time Does Not Matter." *New York Times*, August 4.

Manchanda, Nivi. 2020. *Imagining Afghanistan: The History and Politics of Imperial Knowledge*. Cambridge: Cambridge University Press.

McChesney, Robert. 1999. *Kabul Under Siege: Fayz Muhammad's Account of the 1929 Uprising*. Princeton, NJ: Marcus Wiener.

Metinsoy, Murat. 2021. "Neither Fez nor Hat: Contesting Hat Reform." In *The Power of the People: Everyday Resistance and Dissent in the Making of Modern Turkey, 1923–38*, 234–243. Cambridge: Cambridge University Press.

Mishra, Smeeta. 2007. "Saving Muslim Women and Fighting Muslim Men: Analysis of Representations in the *New York Times*." *Global Media Journal* 6 (11): 1–20.

Nawid, Senzil. 1999. *Religious Response to Social Change in Afghanistan, 1919–29: King Aman-Allah and the Afghan 'ulama*. Costa Mesa, CA: Mazda.

Osman, Wazhmah. 2020. *Television and the Afghan Culture Wars: Brought to You by Foreigners, Warlords, and Activists*. Urbana: University of Illinois Press.

Rahnama, Sara. 2020. "Hijabs and Hats in Interwar Algeria." *Gender and History* 32 (2): 429–446.

Rashoud, Talal al-. 2016. "Modern Education and Arab Nationalism in Kuwait, 1911–1961." PhD diss., SOAS.

Schinasi, May. 1979. *Afghanistan at the Beginning of the Twentieth Century*. Naples: Instituto Universitario Orientale.

Schmeding, Annika. 2021. "Dissolving Gender Difference: Female Teachers, Male Allies and the Creation of Islamic Sufi Authority in Afghanistan." *Afghanistan* 4 (2): 142–169.

Time. 2020. "1927: Queen Soraya Tarzi." March 5. https://time.com/5792702/queen-soraya-tarzi-100-women-of-the-year/.

Wide, Thomas. 2014. "The Refuge of the World: Afghanistan and the Muslim Imagination, 1880–1992." PhD diss., Oxford University.

Yeğenoğlu, Meyda. 1998. *Colonial Fantasies: Towards a Feminist Reading of Orientalism*. Cambridge: Cambridge University Press.

Zemmin, Florian. 2018. *Modernity in Islamic Tradition*. Berlin: De Gruyter.

A Changing Orientalist Representation of Afghans and Afghanistan in Indian Cinema

Indian movies are an essential part of Afghan popular culture. It is safe to say that Indian cinema, particularly Hindi cinema,[1] has been a vital cultural factor in many Afghans' lives. Generations of Afghans have grown up watching Hindi cinema and listening to Indian music before, during, and after decades of war and the destruction of its own media industries. Afghans enjoyed watching Indian movies in theaters during the 1970s and 1980s, via VCRs secretly at home during the Taliban rule between 1996 and 2002, and on satellite and cable TV channels today. The popularity of Indian movies, music, actors, and performers is evident among Afghans as bans and restrictions have failed to erase them from the minds and imaginations of common Afghans (Osman 2011, 2020). Watching Indian movies has also reduced the linguistic gap between Afghans and the Hindi-speaking populations of India. Most Afghans understand Hindi and Urdu, at least at a basic level. Although Hollywood films and other foreign content are gaining popularity among the new generation of Afghans, particularly the diasporic community, Indian cinema is still one of the most popular entertainment mediums for Afghans.

The popularity and interest in Indian movies and music among Afghans have not been one-sided. Afghans have also played an integral role throughout the history of Indian cinema. Whether portrayed accurately or not, Afghan characters have appeared in Indian films and have been consumed by audiences through various tropes and stereotypes that this chapter will explore.

Characters referred to as Pathans have been seen in commercially successful Hindi movies since the early 1900s. Traders from Afghanistan and

Pakistan's Pashtun tribe who traveled to the Indian subcontinent carrying dried fruits, saffron, and horses for sale were primarily referred to as Pathans. Foschini (2012, 21) writes, "The term Pathan came later to indicate a class of people (often suggested as one of the four *Ashraf*, nobles, among Indian Muslims' social groupings) only a part of whom had a real Afghan origin." For the purpose of this chapter, I use *Pathan* how it is used in Indian cinema and Indian society and *Pashtun* in reference to the ethnic group in Afghanistan and Pakistan.

During the prewar years of Zahir Shah and Daoud Khan from the 1950s to the 1970s and again in the 1990s before the rise of the Taliban, Indian movies were filmed in different cities of Afghanistan, such as Bamiyan, Kabul, and Mazar-e-Sharif. Mirroring Zahir and Daoud's policies of friendship with India, Indian cinema initially depicted Afghans in contexts of romance, friendship, and camaraderie. Memorable characters that were portrayed in this light included people like Kabuliwala, a romanticized Afghan character identified as Pathan in the movie with the same title (Gupta 1961), the character of Reshma, an Afghan girl who falls in love with the heir to an Indian businessperson in *Dharmatma* (Khan 1975), and Badshah Khan, a strong and determined Afghan man in *Khuda Gawah* (Anand 1992). In sum, Afghanistan and India have been linked through a long exchange of cinematic culture.

However, in more recent years, with the rise of the ring-wing and anti-Muslim Bharatiya Janata Party (BJP) the depictions of Afghans in Indian cinema have become decidedly worse and more Orientalist, situating Afghans as violent invaders and dangerous terrorists through characters like Sheikh Aslam Khan, an aggressive weapons seller from Kabul in *Baahubali: The Beginning* (Rajamouli 2015), or the character of Abdullah Qazar, an Afghan warlord and insurgent who recruits child soldiers from refugee camps in *Torbaaz* (Malik 2020).

In the twenty-first century, there has also been an increase in the production of period films in Hindi cinema marked by extravagant settings, lavish costumes, and big-budget ensemble casts. Such period films focus on medieval wars between Hindu and Afghan Muslim rulers in the subcontinent and function as the new frontiers in which Orientalist, racist, and highly gendered depictions of Afghans are introduced to movie audiences. These period films often focus on the invasions and despotism of Afghan rulers, juxtaposed with the patriotism and heroism of Hindu warriors. I ask why particular historical narratives of Afghan invasion, incursion, looting, and despotism are now being mobilized. How are colonial and Orientalist images of Afghans furthering Islamophobia? In particular, I focus on the representation of Afghans by analyzing both classic Indian movies such as *Khuda Gawah* (Anand 1992) and *Dharmatma* (Khan 1975), as well as some recent releases like *Kabul Express* (Khan 2006), *Padmaavat* (Bhansali 2018), *Panipat* (Gowariker 2019), *Kesari* (Singh 2019), and *Torbaaz* (Malik 2020).

Orientalism and Islamophobia

According to Todd Green (2019), how Muslims and Islam are imagined and understood is rooted in the colonial enterprise that depicts the West as superior and civilized compared to the "uncivilized" Muslim world. Orientalism, as described by Edward Said (2003), is a discourse of power over the Orient that constructs a dichotomy between "the Orient" and "the Occident," the East and the West. Such representations were not limited to the colonial era but are evident today, particularly post-9/11 (Green 2019, 96–97). While there is a large body of literature that analyzes Hollywood's long history and legacy of racist and Orientalist representations, which have proliferated sharply during the US-led Global War on Terror (e.g., Osman 2019; Shaheen 2001; Shohat and Stam 2014), there is less research on intraregional media vilifications in the global East (Guo 2022; Iwabuchy 2010). This chapter aims to contribute to the latter by examining the role of Bollywood, another major global media industry, arguably just as lucrative and prolific as Hollywood, in creating and disseminating racist imagery of Middle Eastern and South Asian people, with a focus on Afghanistan.

The extension of Orientalist ideas in the post–Cold War era has contributed to Islamophobia today around the globe. There are many common notions between Islamophobia and Orientalism, such as perceiving Muslims and Islam as monolithic, othering Muslims, and distinguishing Muslims as inferior. Orientalism and Islamophobia are not identical concepts but overlapping phenomena (Green 2019, 109).

Contextualizing the discussion on colonialism, Orientalism, and Islamophobia in Hindi cinema, I argue that characterizing Afghan characters as violent killers and identifying them as Muslim functions to serve the Self/Other binary prevalent in India's political landscape, which excludes the Other Muslim population on the basis that they do not fit the norms of Indian society, perceived as Hindu, through focusing on their penchant for violence and despotism. In making this argument, I point to how societies that have been subject to Orientalism are not immune from perpetuating Orientalist conceptions of Others who have been depicted by colonial structures as culturally inferior.

Relationship of Afghans with Indian Cinema

Indian cinema has a noticeable impact on Afghan society, largely due to Afghanistan's proximity to the Indian subcontinent and its long history of transnational cultural exchange. Several celebrities in the Indian film industry, including Amitabh Bachchan, Shah Rukh Khan, Madhuri Dixit, and many more, have devoted followers among the Afghan people. Many Indian filmmakers have also shot their movies in Afghanistan because of its picturesque landscapes and unique architecture. Likewise, Indian cinema has also grasped and utilized elements from Afghan culture in its films. Embroidered *waskat* (a vest worn by men), *buzkashi*, natural landscapes, and musical instruments such as the rebab and setar have been used in Indian movies and music.[2] The rebab and daira have served as key musical symbols of Afghanistan and Afghans.[3]

The tribal versus the modern is a common Orientalist trope. For example, the film *Sholay* (Sippy 1975) features the character of Sambha, a Pashtun tribesman, played by Mac Mohan. Similarly, the film *Kabul Express* (Khan 2006) portrays the experiences of two Indian journalists in Afghanistan who interact with local Pashtun tribesmen. Likewise, Afghan music has been featured in Indian films, with filmmakers drawing inspiration from traditional Afghan folk music (Booth 2016, 315).

The relationship between India and Afghanistan was also defined by colonial geopolitics from the seventeenth century onward. The establishment of an overtly conservative Hindu government in 2014 with Modi coming to power through BJP involved escalating rhetoric between India and its Muslim neighbor Pakistan and a variety of anti-Muslim acts of violence exemplified by the destruction of the Babri Masjid—echoes of Indian politics in the 1990s. As a predominantly Muslim nation, Afghanistan was also seen as culturally and religiously problematic for the Indian audience in light of the politicization of Hindu-Muslim relations.

The Pathan: From Loyal Friend to Threatening Invader

The image of the Afghan in contemporary commercial Hindi cinema has changed from that of a loyal Pathan friend to a violent Muslim invader over the past two decades. Historically, in Hindi cinema, Pathans have been represented as tough but honest men; they are aggressive but stand firm in their friendship. As a popular song from the movie *Zanjeer* (Mehra 1973) says, "Yari hain iman mera yaar meri zindagi" (Friendship is my faith, my friend is my life). However simplistic and Orientalist, Pathans were portrayed sympathetically as strong, honest, kind, trustworthy, and generous men, harking back to Pashtun's own codes of honor, loyalty, and hospitality, which are enshrined in the *Pashtunwali*. Rabindranath Tagore's short story *Kabuliwala* (1892), adapted for film in Bengali (Sinha 1957), Hindi (Gupta 1961), and Malayalam (Siddique–Lal 1994) languages, can be named the contributor to constructing a romanticized image of Pashtun tribesmen.

With the rise of the BJP changing the political landscape and the increasing prevalence of Hindu-nationalist ideologies, representations of Pathans, specifically Afghans, have shifted significantly toward neo-Orientalist representations that feed Islamophobic sentiments prevalent in India (Amarasingam et al. 2022, 3). As Foschini (2012) asserts, the war in Afghanistan and growing international traffic in narcotics and weapons smuggling into the Mumbai underworld, in which Pashtuns were involved, also had a part to play in the negative perceptions of Afghans. Whether the public perception of Afghans changed first because of the news stories or Bollywood film scripts is hard to determine, but in either case Pathans ultimately became "bad guys." Once honest friends, Pathans eventually became mafia lords, invaders, and villains.

One popular movie filmed in Afghanistan was *Khuda Gawah* (Anand 1992), with the famous Indian actor Amitabh Bachchan in the lead role as an Afghan man (figure 8.1). *Khuda Gawah* was filmed in Kabul and Mazar-e-Sharif, with scenes featuring *buzkashi* and events unfolding in historical Afghan sites. It is a film in which India's most famous living actor takes on an altruistic Afghan role.

Khuda Gawah narrates a story in which a headstrong Pathan, Badshah Khan, is loyal but aggressive and is tamed by the Indian legal system. He is commitment-driven and stands by his word, all the while being a passive subject who is slandered and cannot prove himself innocent. Badshah Khan, played by Bachchan, travels from Afghanistan to India to fulfill his promise to his love interest, Benazir, played by Sri Devi, of finding her father's killer. Badshah Khan fulfills his promise by finding and executing Habibullah (the killer). Ranveer Singh, an Indian cop, captures Badshah Khan and confronts him. When confronted by the cop Ranveer Singh, Badshah Khan pledges to return within a month to face sentencing for killing Habibullah, once he fulfills his promise of marriage to Benazir. After returning to India, he surrenders himself to Ranveer Singh, whom he addresses as "Rajput Khan," and is jailed for five years.

Ranveer Singh is a Rajput, a member of a patrilineal clan of the Indian subcontinent historically associated with the warrior class. Badshah Khan's reference to Rajput Ranveer Singh as Rajput Khan is a display of utmost respect for his loyalty to his country and his work. By adding "Khan" to his name, Badshah Khan emphasizes that Khans are noble and loyal individuals, just like Rajputs. This honorary title of "Khan" is a significant and respectful acknowledgment of Ranveer Singh's noble character. Despite the conflicts between Badshah Khan and Ranveer Singh, based on their principles, they show deep respect for each other because of their noble identities as a Pathan and a Rajput. However, the idea of the Self and the Other is visible in Badshah Khan and Ranveer Singh. Badshah Khan is characterized as a savage noble and an aggressive lawbreaker, while Ranveer Singh is portrayed as a civilized noble, a cultured individual, and an honest representative of his country's legal system.

The storyline further explores Badshah Khan's daughter's journey to India to look for him, ultimately leading to her marriage to an Indian policeman, implying a remarkably colonialist subtext. The idea that a strong Pathan's daughter who travels alone from Afghanistan to India in search of her father ends up marrying an Indian policeman reinforces that although she is strong, she needs a savior in the Indian policeman, historically cast as corrupt and dangerous in Bollywood films.

Despite their wholesome message and portrayal of Afghans in a relatively positive light, the above-discussed Hindi films employ a variety of stereotypes. Afghans are portrayed as fierce and fearless warriors and identified with stereotypical clothing and physical attributes, such as turbans and beards. Such features can reinforce oversimplified images of Afghan identity that adhere to extreme and traditional values, especially regarding gender roles and social norms. This can lead to an oversimplified and one-dimensional representation.

A Pathan character is often exoticized, portrayed as mysterious, alluring, and different. It is also important to note that classic Hindi movies

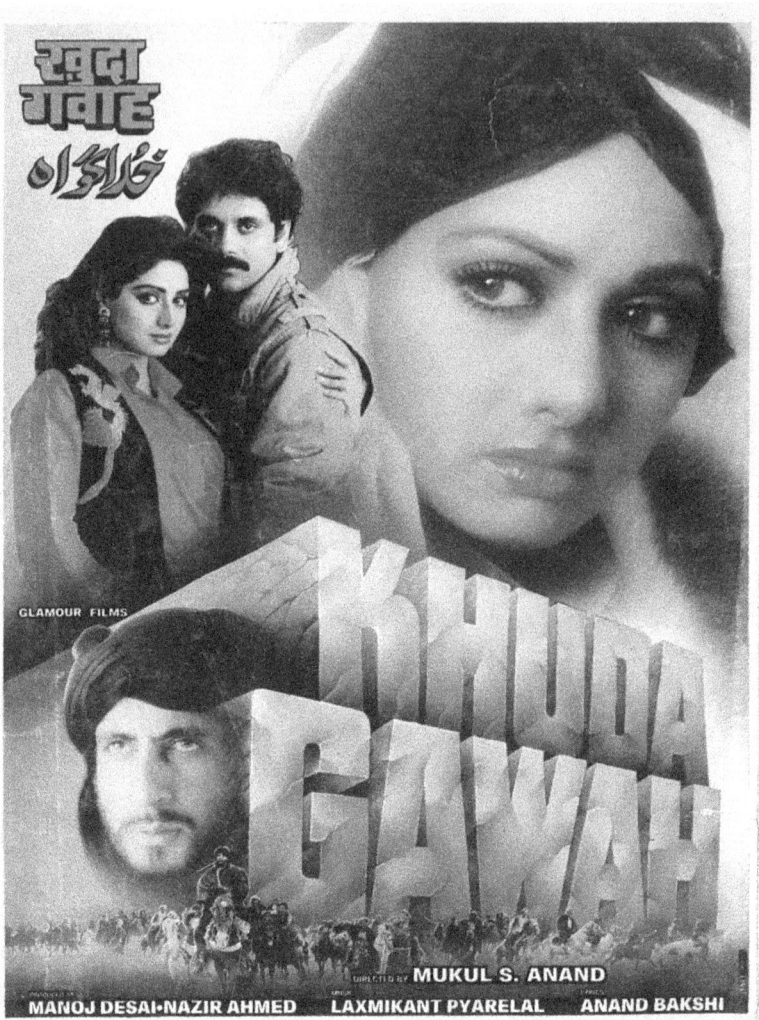

8.1 *Khuda Gawah* (1992) movie poster.

like *Khuda Gawah* maintain the binary divide between both nations and cultures but also romanticize and exoticize the Pathan characters, focusing on their loyalty and faithfulness. A Pathan is portrayed with overly high-lighted and exaggerated characteristics to deepen the divide between Af-ghan and Indian culture, offering an Orientalist gaze.

Additionally, the 2006 movie *Kabul Express* was arguably the turn-ing point in the direction of Orientalist representations of Afghans from the exotic, brave, and commitment-driven Other to the violent, barbaric,

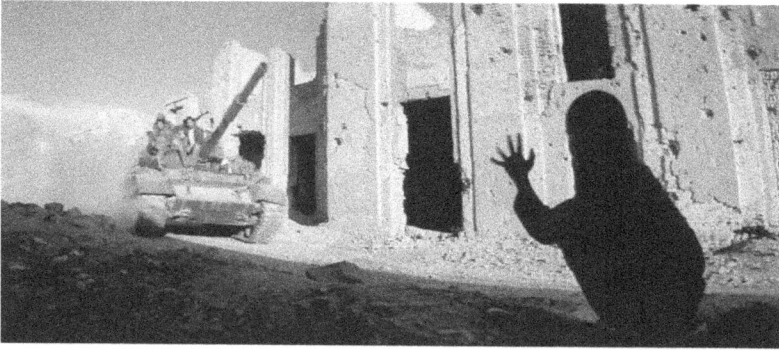

8.2 Jai and Suhel on a military tank in *Kabul Express* (2006).

and inhumane Other who, as a Muslim, is anti-national, insurgent, and potentially terrorizing. The movie claimed to portray the actual conditions of Afghanistan and its people in the aftermath of the war unleashed by the Americans and their allies. However, the Hamid Karzai government of Afghanistan quickly banned the movie despite its strong support during the filming process and condemned India for the biased depiction of Afghans.

The movie displays the ruins and destruction of decades of war and poverty. Commencing with the arrival of the Indian journalists Suhel and Jai by military helicopters in the middle of nowhere and then being escorted to their hotel, "The Kabul Hotel," a completely destroyed building, via a military tank (figure 8.2). During this scene, Jai asks, "Yaha taxi nahi hoti kya?" (Aren't there any taxis here?). Contrary to this portrayal, Afghanistan possesses functioning airports, including one in Kabul, and taxis are one of the common modes of transportation in Kabul and many other cities.

Likewise, in one of the scenes, when Jai and Suhel are out for dinner, food, tea, and weapons are displayed on tables. In the same scene, some Afghan men, after hearing the news of the Taliban's defeat by the Northern Alliance on the radio, start firing in the air as a gesture of celebration. This is not to deny that individuals did have access to weapons; however, such practices were not as omnipresent as portrayed within the film's narrative. Similarly, celebratory air firing is customary but not so pervasive or prevalent that it can be done anywhere at any time, especially in the cities.

The film continues to depict Afghanistan with many inaccuracies and frequent deployment of hackneyed cinematic tropes, including displays of bombed-out landscapes, military vehicles and weapons, women in burqas, and children disabled due to decades of war and militarization. Without political or historical contextualization, these depictions essentialize the image of Afghanistan as a dangerous and precarious place that is intrinsically associated with war and violence. The most intriguing cultural aspects revolve around the mindset of Suhel and Jai, who are part of the "modern world" and experience a profound sense of alienation in Afghanistan's "nonmodern" environment.

Kabul Express and movies representing Afghans post 9/11 take on a complex Orientalist and neo-Orientalist approach to portraying Afghanistan and Afghans. On the one hand, these movies show the country through the figure of the Pathan as passive and tamable. This, coupled with public proclamations by the actors and crew about Afghanistan's natural beauty and cultural warmth, gives moviegoers the impression that Afghanistan is a hospitable place that is ripe for Indian cinematic forms of knowledge production and cultural representation. Afghanistan's natural beauty and hospitality are waiting to be discovered by Indian audiences and ready to be consumed by moviegoers. On the other hand, such films associate the underdeveloped and destroyed parts of the country with decades of war and unstable governance.

Similarly, if the camaraderie and hospitality of Afghans are emphasized, their aggression and fierceness are also exaggerated in relation to their religious and ethnic identities, thus feeding into Islamophobic narratives of the threatening and potentially insurgent Muslim Other that threatens Hindu identity. These Islamophobic narratives are situated within the subtext of Hindu majoritarianism and its monocultural agenda, which signifies Muslims in a reductionistic manner as terrorists, religious extremists, anti-Hindu, and traitors.

Orientalist Representations of Afghans in Hindi Films

The marginalization of Muslims in Indian media has been profoundly shaped by India's current political scenario. The objective of the BJP, the current ruling party of India, is to create a Hindu nation, marginalizing those of other ethnicities, religions, and castes, particularly Muslims (Shani 2021, 264). Representations of Muslims in the context of India are enriched by Orientalist discourse (Patel 2022, 84).

8.3 *Panipat* (2019) movie poster.

Indian movies, in terms of representations of Afghans, can be divided into two major categories: historical epics and representations of contemporary Afghanistan as a dystopia. First are historical references to events between Afghan and Hindu rulers in movies like *Padmaavat* (Bhansali 2018), *Panipat* (Gowariker 2019), and *Kesari* (Singh 2019). Most of the movies are based on historical events that, while based on history, are not accurate in their representation of imperial wars between the rulers of both nations. In these movies, one side is portrayed as the patriotic hero and the other side is the villain and invader. In this case, Afghan rulers are often portrayed as brutal, cruel, and barbaric invaders, whereas Hindu Marathas and Sikhs are portrayed as patriotic heroes defending their land, prosperity, and honor (see, for example, figure 8.3).

The second category portrays the present-day situation of Afghanistan and the Afghan people in movies like *Torbaaz* (Malik 2020) and *Code*

Name: Tiranga (Dasgupta 2022). These movies portray Afghans as passive victims of their own culture and Afghanistan as the epicenter of terrorism and the most dangerous place on earth. Contemporary representations of Afghans, therefore, span representations of them as aggressive, brutal, dishonest, and as invaders, or as passive victims who need to be saved, reproducing the Orientalist stereotypes that dominated from periods of European colonialism to the War on Terror in the post-9/11 era. Framing Afghans as violent aggressors or passive victims functions to reinforce Indian superiority, thus reproducing the Self/Other binary.

Even more innocuous films, such as *Dharmatma* (Khan 1975), which was filmed in Bamyan, Afghanistan, during Mohammed Daoud Khan's presidency, perpetuate Orientalism's discourses by homogenizing Afghanistan's heterogeneous cultures and customs. The movie is about an idealistic and righteous son of a wealthy Indian businessman, Ranbir, played by actor Feroz Khan, who doesn't want to follow in his father's footsteps due to his criminal activities. Ranbir decides to leave India and move to Afghanistan, where he falls in love with an Afghan nomad, Reshma, or, as referred to in the movie, a "Khana Badosh," played by the famous actress Hema Malini. Although Reshma's character is portrayed as an Afghan girl, her costumes represent nothing like traditional Afghan outfits mainly worn by Afghan nomads (*Kuchis*). Her attire mostly resembles Indian apparel.

Furthermore, Reshma is seen riding a camel when she comes to meet Ranbir, the lead male character, right before their wedding. There are two issues with this particular scene: First, camels are only one mode of transportation in Afghanistan that is more common in the rural areas. Second, the scene portrays Afghanistan through a Western framing of the East, incorporating racial and ethnic stereotypes emblematic of Orientalism. A quintessential example is the association of camel riding and extensive deserts. Western literature and media have historically relied on these symbols of camels and deserts to represent the Middle East and Arab nations. Similarly, costumes worn by male characters representing Afghan men are a mix of Afghan and Middle Eastern. Representations of Afghan characters are based on Western interpretations and integrate different cultures into a single identity. By doing so, they reduce the rich tapestry of cultures within the wider region to simplistic and exoticized imagery. In essence, the film's incorporation of such imagery reinforces the Orientalist gaze prevalent in Western depictions of the East for centuries.

Roger Benjamin (1997, 46) suggests that Orientalism is the process of producing a mirage and that the Orient itself is a place with all the appeal and resonance of myth, a place magnificent because so few people had been there. Arguably, not many Indian viewers in 1992 would have traveled to Afghanistan. The movie serves as a source of exoticism for many Indians and a source of imagining the Other: the other art, the other food, and the other South Asian.

Furthering Islamophobia Through Cinema: Hindu Nationalism and Identity Politics

The connection between politics and cinema cannot be overlooked, as films have often served as propaganda tools, given their unique ability to create the illusion of reality (Kohli and Dhawan 2020). Global media has associated Muslims with barbarism and extremism by constructing them as polar opposites of members of "normative" societies. This is in line with Orientalism's emphasis on the discourse of differentiation that constructs polarizations and binaries that function to marginalize Muslims (Abbas 2017, 134; Osman 2022, 370). Although it is important to note that Hindutva (Hindu nationalism) and Orientalism are two distinct concepts, they overlap in their normalization of Islamophobia and othering. While Orientalism is about essentializing the East as an Other to the colonial West, Hindutva is premised on othering Muslimness as alien to the Hindu nation.

We should not neglect the role of popular culture in identity politics. Popular culture binds us by defining who we are and what makes us different from others through storytelling. A growing body of scholarship studies the popular culture–world politics continuum, which links popular culture with political identity (Grayson et al. 2009; Hall 1997). The consensus is that popular culture is far greater than just a momentary distraction from reality where "the political" is customarily conducted. Because popular culture and consumerism are so closely related, they have significant political influence (Grayson et al. 2009, 159). It is, therefore, essential to note that Indian movies are released globally and have billions of viewers worldwide. Indian cinema has a significant economic and political impact. It is a medium of entertainment through which distinct political views are projected and promoted, usually those of the ruling classes. Media scholars and anthropologists have demonstrated Indian media's deep embeddedness and complacency with the Hindu right and the dangers it poses to minorities (e.g., Appadurai 2006; Mankekar 1999; Rajagopal

2001). Indian films are an insight into the country's political landscape. According to Vijay Mishra (2002, 217), during the 1940s through 1960s, the All-India League of Censorship, a de facto vigilante Hindu nationalist group, actively hindered any perceived attempts by Muslims and Parsis to promote an assumed anti-Hindu agenda. Their aim was to cleanse the Indian "film industry from all its non-Hindu elements."

In the 2020s, we have witnessed the glorification of India's Hindu history, which often represents a new version of political and historical truths that fit the current dominant narrative. The current ruling party in Indian politics promotes the nationalist narrative, increasing the Hindutva viewpoint. Likewise, Hindu honor, historical Hindu icons, and Hindu suffering in the past have become popular subjects for films and filmmakers (Rajendran 2022). Hindutva, as an ideology, is premised on othering by promoting Hindu hegemony and marginalizing other identities, including Dalits, Christians, feminists, and Muslims, in particular (Waikar 2018, 162). Hindutva's claim that Muslims are outsiders in India is further reinforced by highlighting Hindu honor and demonizing Muslim identity. Such representations not only promote Hindu hegemony but perpetuate the Eurocentric colonial perspective.

Making films like *Padmaavat* (2018), *Kesari* (2019), and *Panipat* (2019) is an attempt to conflate religion with nationalism, thereby misrepresenting a particular group and history (Rajendran 2022)—in this case, the Afghans, who are predominantly Muslims. Several studies have argued that Muslims in Indian cinema are represented as the Other (e.g., Islam 2007; Kazmi and Kumar 2011; Niyaz Ahmad 2021; Kumar 2013). As Sanjeev Kumar (2016, 235) argues, a category of Hindi cinema has exhibited an overt majoritarian bias toward Muslims. According to him, there is a particular set of films that provoke the cultural agenda of Hindu majoritarianism by misrepresenting Muslims and their actions to promote discourses concerning the contemporaneous Hindutva dominant culture (247). He further draws on Giacomo Lichtner and Sekhar Bandyopadhyay's (2008) notion of historical wars to assert that a "section of Indian cinema constantly perpetuates the cliché of inherently arrogant Muslims and the supposedly tolerant Hindus" (Kumar 2016, 241–242).

Afghan characters are often used to paint Muslims negatively, furthering the Hindutva agenda based on colonial and Orientalist narratives. Prejudices about Muslims have existed in post-partition India. Frequent references to historical Afghan figures such as Ahmad Shah Durrani, Allaudin Khilji, and Sultan Mahmood Ghaznavi as medieval Muslim plunderers are a strategy to further the polarization and to inject mistrust of Muslims. While not justifying the historical acts of aggression, incursions, and attacks that Afghans indeed carried out on Indians and India, films such as *Panipat* and *Kesari* simplify the conflict over power between Hindus and Afghan Muslims by overlooking the political, geographical, and economic complexities of that time. In contrast, as villains, Afghans are portrayed in a historical context, rationalizing the present-day Hindu-Muslim conflict. Historical Afghan-Hindu wars depicting violent Afghan rulers are mainly used as a proxy to strengthen the argument that Muslims are a threat to the Hindu nation and that the conflict is not merely a present-day issue but rather has historical roots. Likewise, Said (2003) argues that the West constructs the Orient as the Other to justify its colonial control, economic exploitation, and imperial ambitions. Packaging hypernationalism as entertainment, these films depict Afghans as Muslim villains whose defeat rests in Hindu pride.

Frank Tomasulo (2013), in his essay "The Mass Psychology of Fascist Cinema," discusses how the content of the documentary film *Triumph of the Will*, directed by Leni Riefenstahl (1935), socially and psychologically diffused a meaning beneficial to the Nazi agenda. He states, "Hitler repeatedly stressed that one could not sway the masses with arguments, logic or knowledge, only with feelings and beliefs" (Tomasulo 2013, 101). Tomasulo further discusses Hitler's portrayal in the film as a messiah and savior of the nation and the combination of religious imagery with patriotic feelings and nationalistic ideals (83). A similar trend is seen in the recent historical Indian movies depicting Afghan and Hindu rulers. There are not only inaccurate and incomplete representations of history but also a cinematographic combination of religious imagery, patriotism, and nationalist fervor to emotionally appeal to the target audiences.

All Muslims of the region, including Indian Muslims, are cast as foreigners. As Maidul Islam (2007, 410) argues, "The politics-film connection cannot absolutely be denied but is very much part of a lively debate that has to be properly dealt with in theorizing the questions of Muslim representations and the political issues of secular-communal categories." Indian cinema is being used as a medium to further the political narratives of the state. As Pranav Kohli and Prannv Dhawan (2020, 21) state, "Erasing the complexity of medieval politics as exemplified in [the] constant internecine conflict between medieval monarchs, these films homogenize Hindu monarchs by juxtaposing them against Muslim 'invaders.'"

The argument here is not that these historical wars were not violent but that Afghan violence is intrinsically associated with their Muslim identity.

Constructing a demonized image of Afghans is, in a way, a disavowal of Muslims and strategically locates the problem elsewhere rather than revealing exclusionary practices by the current right-wing ruling party in India. Furthermore, audiences are fed a simplified narrative of history, ignoring and overlooking the complexities of medieval politics. Hindi cinema's period films represent complex medieval histories through the lens of religious conflict that furthers the "clash of civilizations" (Huntington 1997) discourse. Images of the "Other Muslim" as a dangerous terrorist in the West or an anti-national actor in India speak the same Orientalist narrative.

Conclusion

Representations of Afghans as brutal invaders using the debris of history are problematic and dangerous for the ways in which they fuel Islamophobia and incite violence and discrimination. Whereas Indian cinema is a global entertainment industry that reaches audiences worldwide, Afghanistan's cultural institutions, including its media industry, have been repeatedly destroyed due to almost half a century of wars (Osman 2020). Bollywood (like Hollywood) uses its global representation might to reinforce religious biases, fuel religious conflict, and further other a group already facing global prejudices. Indian cinema's twenty-first-century trend of demonizing and othering Afghans as barbaric Muslim invaders further feeds the colonial narrative of "us versus them" rather than challenging it. It constructs a monolithic image of Afghans and Muslims. Depicting medieval wars between Afghan and Hindu rulers as violent attacks against the Hindu nation argues that this is due to an inherent quality in Islam and that, by extension, all Muslims and Afghans are prone to violence because they are fundamentally the same.

Film has traditionally been India's principal window for viewing historical and contemporary social issues and entertainment across the country. It has been a powerful medium for conveying political and social messages to the public. Constant representations of Afghans as violent, barbarous invaders also erase the long history of goodwill and peace agreements between India and Afghanistan in cultural, social, political, and economic domains.

Furthermore, it is essential to note that such representations can inextricably link Afghans and Afghanistan to violence and barbarism and fuel foreign policies of many countries toward them, particularly at a time when Afghan immigration has taken a surge once again post–Taliban takeover.

Studies have shown that representations of out-groups in media affect the public's perception and behaviors toward those out-groups (Haynes et al. 2016, 19; Saleem et al. 2016, 604), as well as shape policies that impact members of the depicted out-group (Ramasubramanian 2011, 509; Mastro and Kopacz 2006, 319). Hindi films' ability to frame, portray, and disseminate information to the public through how Afghans are portrayed is crucial to their sociopolitical positioning. Little empirical research has examined coverage of Afghans in Indian cinema or evaluated its effects on public attitudes and foreign policies impacting Afghans globally. Moreover, there is little available information on aggregated attitudes toward Afghans worldwide for scholarly examination. Thus, there is a need for more empirical research to understand how representations of Afghans in Indian cinema affect public and political attitudes toward Afghans and what the consequences of these effects are.

Yet, without a doubt, media reinforce stereotypes and shape our consideration of a particular community or group. This othering can have real consequences ranging from negative perceptions to discrimination and violence against vilified groups (Said 2003; Shaheen 2001; Osman 2019). Such representations adopt an Orientalist framework to help audiences contemplate why "they" hate "us" and to legitimize discrimination and prejudices toward Muslims and Afghans. However, in reality, undetected Orientalist and neo-Orientalist frameworks are at the center of such perceptions. Afghans, as Muslims, are represented as both a threat to India's existence and as victims of radical Islam themselves. Highlighting and critiquing such misrepresentations and exploring the impacts of Orientalist and neo-Orientalist frameworks in entertainment is crucial. Equally essential is showing resistance in the wake of such portrayals. It is not just about how "Orientals" and their lands are represented but also about how their counterparts in the surrounding region see them, which has a detrimental effect on their lives.

Notes

1   Hindi cinema, popularly known as Bollywood and formerly as Bombay cinema, refers to the film industry based in Mumbai, producing motion pictures in the Hindi language (Granti 2013, 2).
2   Buzkashi is the national sport of Afghanistan in which horse-mounted players attempt to place a goat or calf carcass in a goal (Azoy 2012).
3   Daira is an Afghan musical instrument similar to the hand drum or frame drum.

References

Abbas, Tahir. 2017. "Islamophobia and Its Discontents." In *Islam and Postcolonial Discourse*, edited by James E. McClung and Esra Mirze Santesso, 133–146. Abingdon: Routledge.

Amarasingam, Amarnath, Sanober Umar, and Shweta Desai. 2022. "'Fight, Die, and If Required Kill': Hindu Nationalism, Misinformation, and Islamophobia in India." *Religions* 13 (5): 380. https://doi.org/10.3390/rel13050380.

Anand, Mukul S., dir. 1992. *Khuda Gawah*. Glamour Films.

Appadurai, Arjun. 2006. *Fear of Small Numbers: An Essay on the Geography of Anger*. Durham, NC: Duke University Press.

Azoy, Whitney G. 2012. *Buzkashi: Game and Power in Afghanistan*. Long Grove, IL: Waveland.

Benjamin, Roger. 1997. "The Oriental Mirage." In *Orientalism: Delacroix to Klee*, edited by Salomon Reinach, 7–31. Sydney: The Art Gallery of New South Wales.

Bhansali, Sanjay Leela, dir. 2018. *Padmaavat*. Paramount Classics, Paramount Pictures, Bhansali Productions, and Viacom 18 Motion Pictures.

Booth, Gregory D. 2016. "Musicking the Other: Orientalism in the Hindi Cinema." In *Music and Orientalism in the British 1780s–1940s Empire*, edited by Marthin Clayton and Bennett Zon, 315–335. London: Routledge.

Dasgupta, Ribhu, dir. 2022. *Code Name: Tiranga*. T-Series Films, Reliance Entertainment, and Film Hangar.

Foschini, Fabrizio. 2012. "Afghanistan in World Literature (III): Kabuliwalas of the Latter Day." Afghanistan Analysts Network, March 30. https://www.afghanistan-analysts.org/en/reports/context-culture/afghanistan-in-world-literature-iii-kabuliwalas-of-the-latter-day/.

Gowariker, Ashutosh, dir. 2019. *Panipat*. Ashutosh Gowariker Productions and Vision World Films.

Granti, Tejaswini. 2013. *Bollywood: A Guidebook to Popular Hindi Cinema*. London: Routledge.

Grayson, Kyle, Matt Davies, and Simon Philpott. 2009. "Pop Goes IR? Researching the Popular Culture-World Politics Continuum." *Politics* 29 (3): 155–163. https://doi.org/10.1111/j.1467-9256.2009.01351.x.

Green, Todd H. 2019. *The Fear of Islam: An Introduction to Islamophobia in the West*. Minneapolis, MN: Fortress.

Guo, Yao. 2022. "Understanding Transcultural Communication and Middle East Politics Through Al Jazeera Practices." *Journal of Transcultural Communication* 2 (2): 202–217. https://doi.org/10.1515/jtc-2022-0018.

Gupta, Hemen, dir. 1961. *Kabuliwala*. Bimal Roy.

Hall, Stuart. 1997. *Representation: Cultural Representations and Signifying Practices*. London: Sage.

Haynes, Chris, Jennifer Merolla, and Karthick S. Ramakrishnan. 2016. *Framing Immigrants: News Coverage, Public Opinion, and Policy*.

New York: Russell Sage Foundation. http://www.jstor.org/stable/10.7758/9781610448604.

Huntington, Samuel P. 1997. *The Clash of Civilizations and the Remaking of World Order*. New York: Touchstone.

Islam, Maidul. 2007. "Imagining Indian Muslims: Looking Through the Lens of Bollywood Cinema." *Indian Journal of Human Development* 1 (2): 403–422. https://doi.org/10.1177/0973703020070208.

Iwabuchi, Koichi. 2010. "Globalization, East Asian Media Cultures and Their Publics." *Asian Journal of Communication* 20 (2): 197–212. https://doi.org/10.1080/01292981003693385.

Kazmi, Fareed, and Sanjeev Kumar. 2011. "The Politics of Muslim Identity and the Nature of Public Imagination in India: Media and Films as Potential Determinants." *European Journal of Economic and Political Studies* 4 (1): 171–187.

Khan, Feroz, dir. 1975. *Dharmatma*. Feroz Khan.

Khan, Kabir, dir. 2006. *Kabul Express*. Yash Raj Films.

Kohli, Pranav, and Prannv Dhawan. 2020. "Bollywood: 'Othering' the Muslim on Screen." *Frontline*, March 21, 2009. https://frontline.thehindu.com/arts-and-culture/cinema/article31007504.ece.

Kumar, Sanjeev. 2013. "Constructing the Nation's Enemy: Hindutva, Popular Culture and the Muslim 'Other' in Bollywood Cinema." *Third World Quarterly* 34 (3): 458–469. https://doi.org/10.1080/01436597.2013.785340.

Kumar, Sanjeev. 2016. "Metonymies of Fear: Islamophobia and the Making of Muslims Identity in Hindi Cinema." *Society and Culture in South Asia* 2 (2): 233–255. https://doi.org/10.1177/2393861716643874.

Lichtner, Giacomo, and Sekhar Bandyopadhyay. 2008. "Indian Cinema and the Presentist Use of History: Conceptions of 'Nationhood' in *Earth* and *Lagaan*." *Asian Survey* 48 (3): 431–452.

Malik, Girish, dir. 2020. *Torbaaz*. Clapstem Entertainment and Rahul Mittra Films.

Mankekar, Purnima. 1999. *Screening Culture, Viewing Politics: An Ethnography of Television, Womanhood, and Nation in Postcolonial India*. Durham, NC: Duke University Press.

Mastro, Dana E., and Maria Kopacz. 2006. "Media Representations of Race, Prototypicality, and Policy Reasoning: An Application of Self-Categorization Theory." *Journal of Broadcasting and Electronic Media* 50 (2): 305–322. https://doi.org/10.1207/s15506878jobem5002_8.

Mehra, Prakash, dir. 1973. *Zanjeer*. Asha Studios, Chandivali Studio, Filmistan Studio, R. K. Studios, and Swati Studios.

Mishra, Vijay. 2002. *Bollywood Cinema: Temples of Desire*. New York: Routledge.

Niyaz Ahmad, Mohammad. 2021. "What It Means to Be a Muslim Living in India: Insights from Experience and from Bollywood Movies." *American Journal of Economics and Sociology* 80 (3): 949–963. https://doi.org/10.1111/ajes.12416.

Osman, Wazhmah. 2011. "'Trashy Tastes' and Permeable Borders: Indian Soap Operas on Afghan Television." In *Soap Operas and Telenovelas in the Digital Age: Global Industries and New Audiences*, edited by Diana Rios and Mari Castañeda, 237–256. New York: Peter Lang.

Osman, Wazhmah. 2019. "Racialized Agents and Villains of the Security State: How African Americans Are Interpellated Against Muslims and Muslim Americans." *Asian Diasporic Visual Cultures and the Americas* 5 (1–2): 155–182. https://doi.org/10.1163/23523085-00501008.

Osman, Wazhmah. 2020. *Television and the Afghan Culture Wars: Brought to You by Foreigners, Warlords, and Activists*. Urbana: University of Illinois Press.

Osman, Wazhmah. 2022. "Building Spectatorial Solidarity Against the 'War on Terror' Media-Military Gaze." *International Journal of Middle East Studies* 54 (2): 369–375. https://doi.org/10.1017/S002074382200037X.

Patel, Ismail Adam. 2022. "Islamophobia in India: The Orientalist Reformulation of Tipu Sultan—The Tiger of Mysore." *Islamophobia Studies Journal* 7 (1): 82–95.

Rajagopal, Arvind. 2001. *Politics After Television: Religious Nationalism and the Reshaping of the Indian Public*. Cambridge: Cambridge University Press.

Rajamouli, Srisaila Sri, dir. 2015. *Baahubali: The Beginning*. Arka Media Works.

Rajendran, Sowmya. 2022. "How Blockbuster Films Are Aiding the Hindutva Nationalism Project." *News Minute*. April 6. https://www.thenewsminute.com/article/how-blockbuster-films-are-aiding-hindutva-nationalism-project-162635.

Ramasubramanian, Srividya. 2011. "The Impact of Stereotypical Versus Counterstereotypical Media Exemplars on Racial Attitudes, Causal Attributions, and Support for Affirmative Action." *Communication Research* 38 (4): 497–516.

Riefenstahl, Leni, dir. 1935. *Triumph of the Will*. Reichsparteitag-Film.

Said, Edward. 2003. *Orientalism*. London: Penguin.

Saleem, Muniba, Grace Yang, and Srividya Ramasubramanian. 2016. "Reliance on Direct and Mediated Contact and Public Policies Supporting Outgroup Harm: Reliance on Direct and Mediated Contact." *Journal of Communication* 66 (4): 604–624.

Shaheen, Jack. 2001. *Reel Bad Arabs: How Hollywood Vilifies a People*. Northampton, MA: Olive Branch.

Shani, Giorgio. 2021. "Towards a Hindu *Rashtra*: *Hindutva*, Religion, and Nationalism in India." *Religion, State and Society* 49 (3): 264–280. https://doi.org/10.1080/09637494.2021.1947731.

Shohat, Ella, and Robert Stam. 2014. *Unthinking Eurocentrism: Multiculturalism and the Media*. 2nd ed. New York: Routledge.

Siddique–Lal, dirs. 1994. *Kabooliwala*. Kavya Chandrika.

Singh, Anurag, dir. 2019. *Kesari*. Dharma Productions, Zee Studios, and Cape of Good Films.

Sinha, Tapan, dir. 1957. *Kabuliwala*. Charuchitra.

Sippy, Ramesh, dir. 1975. *Sholay*. United Producers and Sippy Films.

Waikar, Prashant. 2018. "Reading Islamophobia in Hindutva: An Analysis of Narendra Modi's Political Discourse." *Islamophobia Studies Journal* 4 (2): 161–180.

Tomasulo, Frank P. 2013. "The Mass Psychology of Fascist Cinema: Leni Riefenstahl's *Triumph of the Will*." In *Documenting the Documentary: Close Readings of Documentary Film and Video, New and Expanded Edition*, edited by Barry Keith Grant and Jeannette Sloniowski, 81–102. Detroit, MI: Wayne State University Press.

Withdrawal Narratives
Afghan Women, Time, and
Developmental Idealism

In this chapter, I analyze American print media narratives about the hasty departure of the United States from Afghanistan in August 2021. My title is deliberately provocative to underscore the fact that gender informs several of the salient and contradictory narratives currently circulating in public discourse in the aftermath of the US/NATO withdrawal from Afghanistan. This chapter concentrates on the following two narratives: (1) Afghanistan is going back in time and (2) Afghanistan is *not* going back in time. The status of Afghan women is central to both narratives, which are underwritten by what demographer Arland Thornton calls "developmental idealism," a way of understanding social relations and categorizing the world that is structured according to time and social indices in which some societies are deemed "modern" and "advanced" whereas others are characterized as "backwards" and "stunted" based on the status of women and family structure (2005, 3). US withdrawal narratives replicate the teleological nature and temporal structure of developmental idealism, framed as the loss of girls' and women's rights under the Taliban. In spite of having different temporal alignments, withdrawal narratives construct Afghanistan as a premodern society with atavistic social norms.

I begin by summarizing the major presuppositions of developmental idealism and the discourse of "saving Afghan women." I then analyze the content of sample withdrawal narratives, paying particular attention to the recurring tropes of dreams about Afghan women's futures and the generational reproduction of ideology. Finally, I conclude by sketching some of the consequences of using narratives of temporal regression and progression as explanatory frameworks to understand the status of Afghan women. These narratives, I contend, efface earlier forms of Afghan women's resistance to the Taliban (1996–2001), construct a nostalgic view of the US occupation, universalize the status of some urban Afghan women as representative of all women, conflate different historical eras of Taliban rule, and implicitly suggest that the United States is a feminist utopia. They obscure an investigation into the material conditions of Afghan women's lives and discourage an exploration of cracks and fissures within the governing Taliban that could prove consequential for those under their authority.

My chapter contributes to the project of decolonizing knowledge about Afghanistan through close readings of print media to show how common perceptions about the status of Afghan women depend on axioms related to gender, time, and developmental idealism. As I explain, developmental idealism itself dates back centuries; as the reigning scholarly orthodoxy for hundreds of years, it provided the ideological underpinnings for imperialism and created the discursive space for fashioning Afghan women into contemporary objects of rescue. Their varied and continuous resistance to repression over multiple eras constitutes an important corrective to the imperial archive and aids in decolonizing received wisdom about their lives.

Developmental Idealism and Women as Civilizational Indices

Developmental idealism has become the dominant concept in socioeconomic development projects, part of the common sense of scholars, governments, and aid workers, many of whom place programs directed at girls and women at the center of their agenda. Key tenets of developmental idealism include shared ideas that all societies follow a teleological progression from traditional and less developed to modern and more developed; that modernity and development exist in a dialectical relationship to each other; that all individuals have the right to live in free societies where consent is the glue fastening social relations; and that modern political systems are both desirable and attainable (Thornton 2005, 2001; Allendorf and Thornton 2019).

According to Thornton, the definitions of "modern societies" and "modern political systems" are based on what social scientists erroneously equated solely with Northwest European societies.[1] Scholars described modern societies as containing "many nuclear households," having self-choice marriage, lower and planned fertility, and "a high regard for women's autonomy and rights," among other characteristics. In contrast, "traditional societies," they claimed, have a preponderance of extended families, arranged marriages, high fertility, and limited roles for women. Some of the unconscious assumptions girding attitudes toward political systems in developmental idealism are the association of "modern political systems" with "freedom, liberty, and the consent of the governed" and the understanding of "traditional political systems" as hierarchical and dominated by rules that regulate individual and group behavior. For centuries, "modernity" has been equated with Western societies while "tradition" has been projected onto non-Western societies (Thornton 2001, 454–455).

Thornton argues that social scientists "read history sideways" by confusing geographic distance with historical time (2005, 4). European scholars did not conduct historical research on their own societies; they drew on cross-cultural data from other societies gained through colonization and their own travels. These scholars erroneously assumed that the nuclear family structure and self-choice marriages prevalent in Northwest European societies were the result of "a great family transition" and that an extended family structure was widespread in that region prior to this time.[2] Encountering extended families and arranged marriages in non-Western societies, these scholars supposed that such societies offered a glimpse of their prehistory. That is to say, social scientists "believed they could read the history of the European past in the non-European present" (Thornton 2001, 450–451).

Scholars working in other disciplines have also identified the tendency of Westerners to view Third World societies as snapshots of premodern Europe. Literary critic Anne McClintock theorizes this dynamic in colonial discourse, naming it "anachronistic space" (1995, 41). Analyzing the "distancing devices" anthropologists employ in their study of other cultures, Johannes Fabian has remarked on the "persistent and systematic tendency" of anthropologists to situate societies under study "in a Time other than [the anthropologist's] present" (1983, 31). These insights yield a succinct formulation: To travel across distances to the Third World is to travel back in time to Europe's past. Together, Thornton, McClintock, and Fabian enable us to see how the positing of the simultaneous existence of different temporalities in individual societies around the globe exists in an overarching development narrative in which *all* societies largely follow the same pathway to modernization and traverse similar stages of development in the inexorable march toward progress. Past, present, and future are conflated in a simultaneity of time nonetheless figured within a teleological narrative of development.

Within the general disavowal of temporal simultaneity, the status of women has become a dominant trope to periodize history, particularly the history of conflict in Afghanistan, which is implicitly organized into the Soviet occupation (higher status of women in urban areas); civil war (mixed status of women); 1990s Taliban (repression of women); US occupation (liberation of women); and 2020s Taliban (repression of women). Since the colonial era, the figures of the Third World girl and woman have been important signifiers of a particular culture's civilizational maturity mobilized to justify foreign intervention. We judge the sophistication of societies on the status of their women and the relative freedoms they enjoy. In other words, the status of women functions as an index of modernity. In South Asia, which includes Afghanistan, the British justified colonization in the nineteenth and early twentieth centuries by claiming that they were uplifting oppressed native women from abhorrent practices such as suttee (that is, burning widows on their husbands' funeral pyres), dowry, and child marriage. Colonial officials cloaked the economic and military violence of imperialism as a benevolent form of gender uplift. By legislating against certain native practices, they purported to usher South Asians into modernity and model the gender norms of Western societies, the majority of which had not yet granted women suffrage.[3] Gayatri Spivak, in her now famous essay titled "Can the Subaltern Speak?," formulated this colonial reform enterprise as "white men saving brown women from brown men" (1988, 297). Following 9/11, postcolonial feminists in the United States such as Lila Abu-Lughod (2002) and miriam cooke (2002) drew on this formulation to describe the North American invasion of Afghanistan.

Recall in 2001 that the United States commenced its bombing campaign against Afghanistan, branding it as retributive justice for 9/11 and a humanitarian intervention aimed at saving Afghan women from the Taliban. Earlier in 1997, the Feminist Majority Foundation had launched a campaign against "gender apartheid in Afghanistan" (Feminist Majority Campaign 2023). After September 11, 2001, then Senator Hillary Clinton and former Secretary of State Madeleine Albright joined the feminist chorus and clamored for military action to save Afghan women from the Taliban. According to Rafia Zakaria, leaders of the Feminist Majority were present at the White House and State Department when the administration announced its intention to invade Afghanistan. Such a demonstration of support for military action from North American women substantiates

Zakaria's ironic characterization of this conflict as "the first feminist war" (Strainchamps 2021; see also Basu 2010, 40).

Elsewhere, I have written about the limitations of using Spivak's formulation of "white men saving brown women from brown men" as a heuristic for understanding the US intervention. This discourse of gendered rescue elides important distinctions between imperial regimes in terms of territorial ambitions, economic motivations, and the deployment of military force. It also constructs the American armed services specifically and the United States more generally, as unambiguously "white" and male, while too easily racializing multiple Afghan ethnicities as "brown" (Bose 2020, 60–63). The transposition of Spivak's formulation of the nineteenth century to the twenty-first century obscures important distinctions between British imperialism and its successor, the American empire. In addition, it misleadingly implies that women in the United States have a high status and do not face violence or discrimination.

But for now, let us borrow Spivak's important insight that British imperial discourse constructed native women as victims of men in their societies. This construction of South Asian women has become ubiquitous over a century and a half and is part of the North American common sense of women in this region of the world. We saw its ongoing endurance following the 2001 fall of the Taliban in the well-intentioned rush by NGOs, international organizations, and governments to invest in development schemes targeting Afghan girls and women for different forms of aid (Daulatzai 2006, 2008; Rahmani 2012; Zeweri 2017). Through her ethnographic research, anthropologist Anila Daulatzai demonstrates how the "figure of the war-destitute, dependent and subjugated widow," in particular, "has emerged as the paradigmatic object of intervention for the many international aid agencies that currently work in Afghanistan" (2008, 430). Overall, the number of NGOs active in Afghanistan rose from 158 in 2000 to 617 in 2014, the majority of which were devoted to education, health, and vocational training (Mitchell 2017, 5).[4] As anthropologist Helena Zeweri has pointed out, "The focus on humanitarianism quickly expanded to the provision of long-term empowerment programs for women in particular," which emphasized neoliberal values of "self-sufficiency" and individual "responsibility" (2017, 446). Since 2001, the United States has invested more than $780 million "to encourage women's rights" (Fassihi and Bilefsky 2021). In the ensuing two decades, Afghan women have entered the workforce, become politicians, teachers, journalists, and doctors, started businesses, and joined the police and military forces. According to a World

Bank study, women accounted for 22 percent of the labor force in 2019, which was an increase of 7 percent since 2009 (Huylebroek et al. 2021). These professional opportunities primarily accrued to women from higher socioeconomic backgrounds and dominant ethnic groups who lived in cities; many of these women resided in Kabul (Das 2022, 110). Participation in the employment sector aside, all Afghans, women and men alike, had to contend with quotidian violence emanating from the Taliban, various security forces (US, NATO, and Afghan), and their allies among the warlords (Joya and O'Keefe 2009).

Withdrawal Narratives:
"Afghanistan Is Going Back in Time"

With the ascendancy of the Taliban in August 2021, women are confronting vulnerabilities that both are new and complicate historically existing ones. The Taliban initially sought to present a more moderate face to the world aimed at gaining international legitimacy and attracting foreign aid. Several Taliban officials claimed that women would be allowed to study, work, and participate in government. Zabihullah Mujahid, a Taliban spokesperson, gave his assurances that "there will be no violence against women. No prejudice against women will be allowed, but the Islamic values are our framework" (Fassihi and Bilefsky 2021).

Belying those promises are the Taliban's subsequent actions and their curtailment of girls' and women's rights. Shortly after taking power in August 2021, the Taliban closed women's health clinics in Kandahar. In September 2021 itself, the Taliban sent home female government municipal workers and cautioned others against appearing in public alone. Their gunmen prevented female students and professors from entering the university in Herat. The Taliban warned female students at Kabul University not to leave their dorms unless they were escorted by a male guardian, ostensibly for their own safety. Until December 2022, however, women were permitted to study in gender-segregated classrooms, as long as they were clothed in appropriate Islamic attire; yet female students were restricted from pursuing studies in engineering, agriculture, veterinary science, and economics (Huylebroek et al. 2021).[5] On December 20, 2022, the Taliban rescinded the right of women to attend universities. Female anchors have been banned from state television and, in May 2022, ordered to cover their faces on private outlets (Cunningham 2021; Faizi and Paimani 2022). On

July 4, 2023, the Ministry for the Prevention of Vice and Propagation of Virtue issued a one-month deadline to shutter beauty salons, eliminating one of the few remaining venues for women's employment (Reuters 2023). In cities across Afghanistan, women protesting the restrictions on their mobility and aspirations have been harassed and beaten. Such restrictions serve to circumscribe girls and women in the home, reminding us how such feminized spaces can function simultaneously as sanctuaries and prisons. The Taliban have not named a single woman to their cabinet or appointed any woman to a position of authority in their government (Huylebroek et al. 2021).

Together these restrictions on girls and women have resulted in headlines such as "For Afghan Women, Taliban Stir Fears of Return to a Repressive Past" (*New York Times*); "Afghan Women Fear Return to Restrictions of the Past Amid Taliban Control" (*USA Today*); and "Afghan Women Fear Return to 'Dark Days' Amid Taliban Sweep" (Associated Press) (Fassihi and Bilefsky 2021; *USA Today* 2021; Karam and Seir 2021). These headlines employ repetitive vocabulary; you will have noticed that all three headlines use "return" and "fear," and allude to "restrictions" or "repression" or "dark days," words that appear in many other stories from the print media. Metaphors of lightness and darkness in these stories function as shorthand to signify modernity and tradition that are respectively aligned with enlightenment values and medieval ignorance.

Many of the stories also stress a transgenerational "death of dreams" in their emphasis on the loss of female aspirations for the future, especially in relation to the restrictions on girls' education. For example, a representative headline in the *Washington Post* reads "As the Taliban bars some girls from school, their mothers' dreams are also shattered" (Raghavan 2021). The article quotes a fifteen-year-old who reveals that the termination of her education means the end of her ability to self-actualize. "It makes me feel hopeless," she explains. According to this article, the person who best understands the girl's despair is her mother. The Taliban's education restrictions are "not only suffocating this generation of Afghan girls but also triggering déjà vu for the previous generation. Many of their mothers were children or teenagers during the Taliban regime between 1996 and 2001 and subjected to harsh Islamic codes that deprived women of virtually every basic right" (Raghavan 2021). The vocabulary of a "death of dreams" signals the complete demise of futurity for girls and women that has been already predetermined by gender.

The repetitious vocabulary, the similar content, and the temporal structure of these stories characterize one of the salient narratives of the US withdrawal that currently circulates in the media, a narrative of temporal regression, which can be baldly stated as "Afghanistan is going back in time."[6] This narrative posits Afghanistan as an atavistic land where Afghan women are victims of archaic forms of violence at the hands of Afghan men; in effect, girls and women are represented as objects of native patriarchy, which is the familiar signifier of colonial-era civilizational inferiority. To paraphrase Zeweri, the focus on Afghan women's disempowerment evidences "a hyper-recognition that Afghan women's lives are marked by culturally sanctioned forms of oppression"; "the only way they are knowable is through the extent to which they are at risk of reliving these forms of oppression" (2017, 445). By projecting the future of daughters as a version of their mothers' pasts, the narrative of temporal regression denies women their agency and precludes the possibility of resistance and, ultimately, social change. The biological reproduction of generations is mapped onto social relations, thus naturalizing a historically specific form of women's oppression in ontological terms.

Some of the articles that subscribe to the narrative of historical regression—whether implicitly or explicitly—credit Western intervention for the improvements in the status of women during the twenty-year US occupation of Afghanistan. For example, the *Washington Post* article on the shattering of daughters' and mothers' dreams cited earlier asserts it was "the Western presence," "billions in aid," and "vocational training in empowerment programs set up by the United Nations and other aid organizations" that "ushered" in the "new freedoms" for Afghan women (Raghavan 2021). Echoing this sentiment, along with the ubiquitous references to dreams in other media stories, in the *Washington Post Live* on September 1, 2021, New Hampshire Senator Jeanne Shaheen attributes the "benefits" that accrued to Afghans to "the United States and other NATO countries' involvement," which led to improvements in "healthcare, the school system, the ability of women and girls to pursue their dreams and opportunities, [and] the success of so many men in Afghanistan because of that support from the women in their lives." Noticeably, these statements construct the gains in the status of women as sole achievements of Western entities such as international organizations and military bodies (e.g., NATO). With the exception of functioning as the helpmates of their male relatives, Afghan women are consequently denied any agency in the improvement of their quality of life. They emerge as passive objects of

9.1 "Back to square one for women's rights in Afghanistan,"
Anne Derenne, July 8, 2021.

history rather than as full-blown subjects and authors of their life circumstances in their own right. The illustration "Back to square one for women's rights in Afghanistan" (figure 9.1), published on the Cartoon Movement website, metaphorically condenses Afghan women into a game piece, dangling in the air as she awaits her placement on the board game of women's rights, presumably determined by the powerful arm of Afghan patriarchy. In the foreground of the illustration, a die features the stars and stripes, an indictment of the United States for its role in playing with the lives of Afghan women by gambling with their rights.

This construction of the nonexistence of agency contrasts starkly with the reality of Afghan women's resistance that has assumed a variety of forms over different historical eras. From the legendary women of earlier centuries such as Shah Bori (sixteenth century), Nazauna (eighteenth century), and Malalai of Maiwand (nineteenth century), who took up arms against foreign occupiers, to young women such as Nahid-i-Shahid (twentieth century), the courageous sixteen-year-old who organized public demonstrations against the Soviet occupation and was murdered for her activism, Afghan women have risked their lives fighting foreign invaders (Arbabzadah 2008; Zeweri and Osman 2022). Following the Soviet withdrawal, they have resisted a succession of repressive regimes: warlords, Taliban, US and NATO forces, and the Karzai and Ghani administrations. As elsewhere in the world, the organized women's movement spans the ideological spectrum (conservative, liberal, socialist, religious, and secular) and encompasses a variety of agendas (educational, entrepreneurial, medical, humanitarian, journalistic, and legislative, to name a few) (Zeweri and Osman 2022). The Revolutionary Association of the Women of Afghanistan (RAWA) is perhaps the best-known organization, but it is not the only one advocating for women's rights. Young Afghan Women Movement, Women for Afghan Women, Young Women for Change, Afghan Women Right Organization, and the Afghan Women's Network, along with groups active in the Afghan diaspora, educate, agitate and organize for the attainment of basic rights and the opportunity for a dignified life. (The Afghan Women's Network, an umbrella group, claims a membership of 125 organizations [Afghan Women's Network 2022].)

Developmental idealism serves as a palimpsest for the narrative of temporal regression in several ways. First, the narrative of temporal regression shares the idea prevalent in developmental idealism that the status of Afghan women indexes an earlier premodern historical era. Media articles that feature the temporal regression narrative offer an unstated acknowledgment of the simultaneous existence of societies at different stages of development in which the status of women in the United States presents an implicit foil to Afghanistan. Hence, the time of North American modernity is simultaneous with the time of Afghan tradition in the larger matrix of global time. Second, the temporal regression narrative takes developmental idealism's valuation of modernity, women's rights, and autonomy as an axiom; not only are these values desirable and attainable but they should be normative. A deviation from such norms represents a regression, a temporal slide into an era of barbarism and primitive gender relations. Third, the very naming of the backward slide of women's rights suggests that the narrative of temporal regression shares liberal imperial feminism's investment in the overarching teleology of women's progress and advancement, crucial tenets of developmental idealism.

Withdrawal Narratives: "Afghanistan Is *Not* Going Back in Time"

The Afghanistan-is-going-back-in-time narrative exists in conjunction with its polar opposite, a progressive temporal narrative of women's empowerment, the narrative that Afghanistan is *not* going back in time. In this withdrawal narrative, girls and women are subjects of history rather than its passive objects. Key aspects of this narrative involve the idea that twenty years have increased the consciousness of girls and women as a result of both educational and experiential opportunities in ways that cannot be reversed, and that the media has an important role to play in the dissemination of egalitarian gender ideology. While some articles attribute the heightened awareness and expectations to Western intervention (that is, the US military invasion, along with Western NGOs and international organizations), others credit the egalitarian commitments of Afghan girls and women and the lessons daughters have learned from their mothers in another version of the generational reproduction of gender ideology in the home. References to dreams and futurity also crop up in the progressive temporal narrative, constructing the present as a temporary setback in the long march of women's attainment of rights and happiness, the result of US intervention and a crucial component of the teleology of developmental idealism.

In the *Dallas Morning News*, literary critic, author, and former senior advisor to the Karzai administration Homeira Qaderi identifies mothers as the locus for changes in social attitudes toward rights. "Do Afghan women accept today's unchanged Taliban?" she rhetorically asks. "The short answer is an unequivocal and emphatic no." She explains: "The new generation of Afghan women is very different from their mothers' generation. Our mothers were exhausted from the civil strife and foreign wars, they didn't have the strength to stand up to the Taliban or the voices to speak up. But those same mothers have raised extremely strong and capable daughters who are well aware of their social responsibilities and are aware of their rights" (Qaderi 2021). Although Qaderi characterizes the older maternal generation as too tired and weak to resist the 1990s iteration of the Taliban, another interpretation is possible. Sociologist Elaheh Rostami-Povey astutely observes that "survival strategies are deeply embedded in the material conditions of life" (Rostami-Povey 2003, 269). Building on Rostami-Povey's insights, in a comment posted to the Verfassungsblog on October 9, 2021, postcolonial scholar Shaimaa Abdelkarim coined the term "tactical cunnings" to signify the "actions that sustain the capacity to resist, when such resistance is conceived as impossible in the humanist and gendered framework" that "portrays Afghan women as victims in their social relations." This older generation of women chose tactical cunning, channeling their energy into nurturing the knowledge of rights and resistance in their daughters. The reference to "social responsibilities" in Qaderi's quotation indicates that mothers inculcated not just individual empowerment in their daughters but a collective obligation to work for the common good. While their resistance might not have taken the form of public challenges to Taliban authority, these women, individually and in concert with organizations such as the National Union of Women of Afghanistan, Women's Association of Afghanistan, and the Women's Vocational Training Centre, ran underground schools and clandestine vocational programs in their homes (Rostami-Povey 2003, 269–271). Indeed, as a teenager, Qaderi herself taught basic literacy classes in an underground school for refugee children from 1993 to 1997 (Simon 2020). The imparting of feminist consciousness by mothers to their daughters in this era of Taliban repression gives new meaning to the term *home front*, often used in relation to conflict zones.

Qaderi emphatically rejects the narrative of regressive temporality, noting "Afghan women will not accept a school-burning misogynistic Talib. The Taliban have repeatedly failed in the eyes of Afghan women, especially when it comes to gender equality and human rights. The rallying cry of Afghan women is that peace with the Taliban, without their guaranteed commitment to women's rights, amounts to a declaration of war against women. Afghan women have come a long way, they have sacrificed a lot, and they are not going back to the dark ages" (2021). In a *New York Times* article on August 17, 2021, reporters Farnaz Fassihi and Dan Bilefsky also emphasize the sentiment that history cannot be reversed: "For a new generation of Afghan girls who grew up going to school and nurturing unfettered dreams, the Taliban era is ancient history, and turning back the clock is nearly incomprehensible." Here again we hear the familiar refrain equating the loss of women's rights with a retreat from modernity.

If Qaderi describes an older generation of Afghan women who know the repressive capabilities of the Taliban all too well, Shukriya Barakzai, who helped write Afghanistan's post-2001 constitution and served two terms in Parliament, explains the potential for resistance among a new generation of Afghan women who lack memories of life under the Taliban: "'They are full of energy, hope, and dreams. They are not like me, as I was 20 years back. They're more alert. They're communicating with the world. It's not [the] Afghanistan that was burned in a civil war. It's a developed, free Afghanistan, with the free media, with women.' The Taliban is taking territory, Barakzai says, 'but not the hearts and minds of people'" (Addario 2021).[7]

As these quotations illustrate, the progressive temporality narrative (Afghanistan is *not* going back in time), like the temporal regression narrative (Afghanistan is going back in time), also periodizes Afghan national history in terms of generations of women. This narrative, however, insists that the generation of girls and women who have come to consciousness in the last two decades is qualitatively different from their mothers, in spite of having learned from them, precisely because these young women have been shaped by their education and active participation in the public sphere. Three points seem significant. First, several of the quotations imply that this generation of young women will be more effective because they do not have memories of life under the previous Taliban. Karl Marx once observed that people make history constrained "under circumstances, given and transmitted from the past" ([1869] 1963, 15). In the absence of memories of the Taliban, these young women, in the eyes of their older country women, have escaped the nightmarish weight of the traditions of dead generations that Marx believed could compromise the potential of revolutionary movements. When confronted with the full awfulness of gender restrictions, the quotations imply, the lack of prior memories will generate resistance because young women will refuse to submit to forms of repression that are completely alien to their imagination.

Second, the quotations also insinuate that women who lived under the first era of Taliban rule in the 1990s were not committed to a gender egalitarian society. This assumption is underwritten by a logic that elides differences in the political and legal order between the two eras of Taliban governance, figuring these historically distinct regimes as one and the same. While the post-2021 Taliban numbers some Afghans who were active in the 1990s in its ranks, it also consists of new faces and, thus, is not identical to the earlier regime. The post-2021 Taliban additionally operates in a very different legal, juridical, technological, and geopolitical context that has to contend with the aftermath of decades of war, including twenty years of US and NATO occupation, within a larger framework of cultural and economic globalization. Given the vastly changed contexts between then and now, earlier forms of women's resistance in the 1990s will of necessity be different than those today.

Third, related to the changed historical context, ideology and its dissemination through new media technologies have emerged as an important part of the terrain for the struggle for women's social, political, and economic rights. Sociologist Keera Allendorf points out that "global cultural scripts" have aided in the dissemination of "egalitarian gender ideologies through the world" by the mechanisms of schooling, international organizations, and media, among other institutions and groups (Allendorf and Thornton 2019, 225). The dissemination of egalitarian gender ideology and its association with the good life, she observes, can be a self-fulfilling prophecy as ordinary people in societies dubbed "traditional" embrace the participation of women in the labor force and expand women's access to control over their reproduction (225–226). Barakzai asserts that Afghanistan will *not* go back in time because young women today know how to communicate with the world and they are media savvy. The younger generation has been exposed to the global cultural scripts of gender egalitarianism, in part, through their media consumption.

Recall that when the Taliban were in power in the late 1990s, they had banned television, cinema, and cassette recorders; nonetheless, cassettes, VCR tapes, and DVDs circulated clandestinely on the black market (Osman 2020, 167). During the US occupation, the United States and other international organizations helped underwrite and create a lively mediascape among Afghans, which nonetheless has sometimes confounded the intentions and expectations of their foreign donors. In *Television and the Afghan Culture Wars*, media scholar Wazhmah Osman (2020) argues that since 2001 television has functioned as the Afghan public sphere, providing Afghans with a "space" to debate contested issues such as democracy, women's rights, modernity, and the role of Islam in national life. As she details, female anchors, television personalities, and artists have modeled new roles for girls and women often at great cost to their personal security given that some are targeted for assassination. In addition, international development groups focused on television broadcasting and sports have helped the diffusion of global cultural scripts. Osman maintains that television counters hegemonic perspectives in two important ways: "First, as an institution, it enables local Afghans to 'talk back' to the international community that has Afghanistan in its sphere of influence and discourse. Second, it provides a platform for television producers to act as local reformers, presenting indigenous modernities and cultural practices that challenge local conservative groups that have enlarged their power base as a result of more than four decades of war" (174).

Just as it would be difficult for the Taliban to cut off television and radio programming altogether and ban satellite television and foreign broadcasts in Afghanistan, it would be nearly impossible for them to prevent footage and reports of life under their regime from being aired abroad. One remembers the bravery of RAWA activists in the late 1990s, who captured clandestine film footage from under their burqas of the Taliban executing women in Ghazi Stadium and smuggled it out of the country. While that footage was relatively challenging to shoot given the difficulty of procuring video cameras in the 1990s, the wide availability of cell phones in the 2020s facilitates the ability of Afghan women, following the US withdrawal, to document and narrate their diverse experiences. My point is to emphasize these larger geopolitical factors—including globalization and innovations in media technology—to make some forms of resistance more visible today. That is to say, we cannot assume that contemporary young women are more feminist or politically inclined than the previous generation of Afghan women in the 1990s; however, we should recognize that this current generation of women has the means of self-representation and the technological know-how to insert their narratives into the global public sphere. According to the progressive temporality narrative, young Afghan women's knowledge of media, their desire to participate in the political and cultural spheres, and the creation of their own content will contribute to the effort to focus international attention on the Taliban and women's resistance against them, making it extremely difficult for Afghanistan to turn back the clock of history.

Why Withdrawal Narratives Matter

Developmental idealism informs both withdrawal narratives I have described. The Afghanistan-is-going-back-in-time narrative posits society under the Taliban as a return to a primitive, anti-modern era. The Afghanistan-is-*not*-going-back-in-time narrative borrows the idea of development, figured as the advancement in girls' educational achievement and women's participation in the workforce, as "unending progress toward wealth, health, and power" toward the realization of a modern society (Thornton 2005, 454). If the temporal regression narrative presents an ongoing justification for "humanitarian intervention" across historical periods that has been aligned with a conservative and imperial foreign policy agenda, the progressive temporal narrative offers a more palatable and optimistic prognosis for Afghanistan by being in tune with a liberal world view that believes in the ultimate success of individuals acting in concert with one another to change an oppressive status quo. The progressive temporal narrative, in other words, holds out an optimistic vision of a happily-ever-after for Afghan women who have encountered but will eventually overcome the patriarchal obstacles of history.

Scholars who work on developmental idealism often clarify that they are *not* rendering a judgment about its positive valuation of modernity; rather, their interest is in providing a meta-analysis of development discourse to highlight how taken-for-granted assumptions may themselves be products of empirically suspect scholarship and ethnocentric biases. In the case of developmental idealism, the claims that European scholars made about gender roles, family structure, and great demographic shifts in Northwest Europe are not supported by historical evidence. Yet I suspect that I am not in a minority of feminists who assesses the status of women in terms of our ability to exercise autonomy and choice in our lives, over the professions we pursue, our domestic arrangements, our sexuality, and our reproductive decisions. To my mind, belief in the value of gender progress raises a logical question. Namely, if we believe that egalitarian gender roles are good for women, why should it matter if US withdrawal narratives about Afghanistan recycle the assumptions of developmental idealism?

By way of conclusion, let me outline four reasons why it matters that these temporal narratives have acquired so much explanatory currency. First, both of these withdrawal narratives—Afghanistan is going back in time and Afghanistan is *not* going back in time—misleadingly suggest that life under US occupation for Afghans was ideal. We risk forgetting that Afghanistan's security situation has been dismal for the entire twenty years of the occupation; US and NATO troops were not able to guarantee the safety of civilians, and, indeed, they often subjected civilians to violence, sometimes as the unintended consequences of military actions and at other times as deliberate targets. Of further concern, Western security forces were often aligned with warlords and members of their militias who had been incorporated into the Karzai and Ghani governments. A resurgent Taliban had shared the conflict landscape with al-Qaeda and Islamic State offshoots, who were at war with one another. There was also widespread distrust of government security forces and the Afghan Local Police because of their responsibility for human rights violations and extrajudicial killings. Less than a decade into the US occupation, Afghan Parliament member Malalai Joya warned that "the dark minded forces in [the] country are gaining power with every allied air strike that kills civilians, with every corrupt government official who grows fat on bribes and thievery, and with every criminal who escapes justice" (Joya and O'Keefe 2009, 4–5).

Exacerbating the anarchic security situation, the lack of physical infrastructure made conducting business at any scale larger than the local level challenging. As Daulatzai has lamented, the influx of aid workers, international security forces, and contractors had increased inequality by squeezing Afghans out of the market for housing and making goods and services unaffordable for many (Daulatzai 2008, 304). Widespread corruption and fraud were aspects of daily life under the American occupation. Furthermore, Afghans of all genders lacked access to such basic necessities as nutritious food, healthcare, sanitation, clean water, and adequate housing, all of which the United States failed to deliver in twenty years of occupation (Bose 2020, 90).

A second reason that both temporal narratives matter is they implicitly universalize the status of *some* urban Afghan women as the condition of *all* Afghan women. Outside urban areas of the country, however, the condition of Afghan women under the US occupation had not significantly improved. In 2020, Afghanistan placed 169 out of 189 countries on the United Nations' Human Development Index, which ranks countries based on their literacy rates, life expectancy at birth, and standard of living (Javaid 2020). Afghanistan came in second on the Thomson Reuters Survey of the World's Most Dangerous Countries for Women in 2018, seventeen years into the US occupation (Goldsmith and Beresford 2018).[8] Thomson Reuters ranked Afghanistan first in discrimination, health, and nonsexual violence against women and seventh in both sexual violence and human trafficking. These sobering statistics undermine the perception that Afghan women had racked up major gains during twenty years of American occupation.

A third reason that both temporal narratives matter is their tendency to collapse historical differences between the Taliban of 1996–2001 and the Taliban of 2021. In the early days following the US withdrawal, US commentators confidently asserted that the Taliban of today are not the Taliban of yesterday. Unlike the Taliban of yore, we were told, the Taliban today are skilled negotiators, savvy with social media messaging, and concerned with international opinion (Greenberg 2021). Some have commented on the fissures among moderate and extremist Talib, which Osman links to media exposure: "This Taliban generation, like the rest of the Afghan population, also grew up with mobile phones, hundreds of radio and televisions stations, and the extensive media bazaars of Pakistani border cities like Peshawar and Quetta that have become hubs for pirated content from around the world" (Osman 2022, 140). She cites recent examples of Taliban officials taking to the airwaves to present a more moderate face by cooking during a segment of a Pashto-language television program and by a willingness to discuss, on a different political talk show, the legalization of gay marriage in some Western countries even as this Taliban official condemned marriage equality overall (Osman 2022, 140).

Along with becoming adept with their media usage, the contemporary Taliban have gained experience in administration. They have pioneered a "hybrid" form of governance in the territories they held prior to their takeover of Kabul, consisting of arrangements with local government officials and NGOs in rural areas to deliver healthcare services, oversee education, and "regulate communications and electricity" (Jackson 2018, 5).[9] Ashley Jackson succinctly concluded in 2018 that Taliban governance extended far beyond their formal control of territory; their "governance," she writes, "does not come after the capture of territory, but precedes it" (5). Yet since those early months of the Taliban's assumption of power, the analytic pendulum seems to have swung in the other direction, with a loose consensus emerging among talking heads that the Taliban have not "changed." This view is hard to reconcile with reports describing an administrative infrastructure that has been two decades in the making that regulates health, finance and taxation, justice, and education (11–22).

Whether or not the Taliban have been substantively transformed, I cannot say. But the narrative of temporal regression precludes the possibility of asking if differences inhere between then and now, and, if so, what the significance of these differences might mean for the present and future status of Afghan women. Potential differences between historical regimes matter from a policy perspective that is concerned with optimizing developmental efforts targeted at Afghan girls and women. At a more basic level, differences between the two Taliban eras expose the specific political and material conditions under which women struggle at particular historical moments. It is simply not the case that the US occupation has served a pedagogical function of inducting Afghan women into a feminist modernity and given them the tools to resist the Taliban. Afghan women's resistance instead has taken different forms that are shaped by the political regimes and historical contexts in which they live. The challenge of struggling for gender equality is to identify and navigate historically different matrices of power. The assumption that the Taliban of today are largely unchanged from their precursor incarnation obstructs inquiries about the nature of historical differences between the two regimes and their impact on women by taking this discussion off the table altogether.

Finally, the fourth reason that these temporal narratives matter is that they construct the United States as a feminist utopia, a construction that is

9.2 "Did you say theocracy?" May 15, 2022. © Chappatte in NZZ am Sonntag, Zürich, https://www.chappatte.com.

incorrect to say the least. The 2018 Thomson Reuters Survey of the most dangerous places for women, which I cited earlier, ranks the United States as the tenth most dangerous country for women, primarily because of the risks that American women face for sexual violence and the lack of justice they receive in rape cases (Goldsmith and Beresford 2018). (In fact, the US military is a particularly treacherous for servicewomen, of whom approximately 25 percent experience sexual assault and more than 50 percent are sexually harassed [Koehler 2021].) Published on the Chappatte Globecartoon website, Patrick Chappatte's cartoon "Did you say theocracy?" draws parallels between Afghan and American women and their lack of bodily autonomy, specifically referencing how American women's lack of access to abortion has been sanctified by the Supreme Court (figure 9.2). The cartoon's caption alludes to the overrepresentation of conservative Catholics among the justices, in effect constructing them as the American Taliban.

For decades the highly organized and influential American right wing has chipped away at women's rights to control reproduction and they have redoubled their attacks on the rights to sexual and gender autonomy. Emboldened by a Supreme Court majority secured through dubious congressional maneuvers that render the court illegitimate, the erosion of women's rights has been enshrined in law with the overturning of the fifty-year-old *Roe v. Wade* decision, which guaranteed women access to abortion. As David Finkel (2023) notes, the assault on women's rights by a Supreme Court that is largely out of sync with public opinion cannot be disarticulated from other worrisome developments on the slide to authoritarianism in the United States. The onerous restrictions on voting and outright attempts in state legislatures to overturn election results, the extent to which Republican politicians lie and cheat to achieve their ends, and the deputizing of right-wing vigilantes to police the behavior of women today (and, perhaps, the behavior of others tomorrow) demonstrate that the degradation of women's rights is at the center of the reactionary agenda to roll back the human and civil rights of everyone.[10]

Withdrawal narratives that are based on an Orientalist temporality impede an analysis of the here-and-now of Afghan women's experience. Feminist solidarity requires those of us on the outside to facilitate the mobility of narratives across borders, those stories of heroism and resistance that are being written and enacted daily by Afghan women within the borders of Afghanistan. They are not going back in time so much as they are courageously confronting the present and plotting a better future.

Notes

I have had the opportunity to present portions of this chapter to audiences at Purdue University Fort Wayne and the Indian Institute of Technology Delhi, and I have benefited from the discussions in those venues. Thanks to Steve Carr and Jayan Thomas for invitations to speak at Purdue and IIT-D. Naz Pantaloni helpfully assisted with tracking down permissions. I am also grateful to Keera Allendorf, Srimati Basu, Mona Bhan, and, especially, Helen Zeweri for their comments and suggestions on an earlier draft of this essay. I take full responsibility for its contents.

1   By "Northwest Europe," Thornton (2001, 450) primarily means England and Northwest France.

2   Thornton defines an "extended family" as units comprised of parents living with two or more married children (2005, 51). Not until the 1960s did scholars start to dig into the archives, consulting and interpreting records as far back as the 1300s, only to discover little evidence that joint families were common in earlier centuries. On the contrary, historians found that late and self-choice marriages were normative, and women had a higher status in Northwest Europe than was previously thought. All these traits

had been equated with modernity (Thornton 2001, 451–452; see also Thornton 2005, 4–5).

3 A rich body of feminist scholarship treats these issues. See Lata Mani's (1998) *Contentious Traditions: The Debate on Sati in Colonial India*; Sumit Sarkar and Tanika Sarkar's (2008) *Women and Social Reform in Modern India: A Reader*; Tanika Sarkar's (2001) *Hindu Wife, Hindu Nation: Community, Religion, and Cultural Nationalism*; Kumkum Sangari and Sudesh Vaid's (1990) *Recasting Women: Essays in Indian Colonial History*; and Mrinalini Sinha's (2006) *Specters of Mother India: The Global Restructuring of an Empire*.

4 David F. Mitchell defines NGOs "as independent, nonprofit organizations engaged in humanitarian, development, human rights, or advocacy work," which "excludes professional associations, commercial entities, for-profit development companies, nonprofit research institutions (e.g. universities and think tanks), all United Nations personnel, governmental aid organizations (e.g. United States Agency for International Development and German Technical Cooperation Agency), inter-governmental aid organizations (e.g. International Organization for Migration), and hybrid organizations (e.g. the International Committee of the Red Cross)" (2017, 1).

5 For more on restrictions placed on women in higher education, see BBC (2022).

6 Wazhmah Osman makes a similar observation about characterizations of Afghanistan as being stuck in the past; she writes that "the dominant image of the country as forever static and unchanging is so ingrained and rigidly fixed in the minds, policies, and theories of Western technocrats that there is no room for deviance from these preconceived notions" (2022, 135). My point, however, is slightly different: I am arguing that withdrawal narratives figure time not as stasis but as regression, moving in a backward direction.

7 Barakzai's reference to "hearts and minds" demonstrates how the rhetoric of the Global War on Terror has become associated with women's rights. But as Mona Bhan (2014) shows, the phrase has a longer lineage that is not exclusively tied to the United States' counterinsurgency efforts. See her account of such strategies by the Indian Army in their occupation of Kashmir, *Counterinsurgency, Development, and the Politics of Identity in India: From Warfare to Welfare?*

8 The poll was based on interviews with 548 experts on women, ranging from academics, development specialists, aid workers, healthcare staff, and NGO personnel, among others.

9 These arrangements span the range of collaboration to coercion. This excellent study is based on interviews with 162 informants culled from Taliban administrators, government officials, and NGO workers.

10 For more information on the aftermath of the overturning of *Roe v. Wade*, see Dianne Feeley's (2023) "Before and After Roe."

References

Abu-Lughod, Lila. 2002. "Do Muslim Women Really Need Saving? Anthropological Reflections on Cultural Relativism and Its Others." *American Anthropologist* 104 (3): 783–790.

Addario, Lynsey. 2021. "The Taliban's Return Is Catastrophic for Women." *Atlantic*, August 16.

Afghan Women's Network. 2022. "About Us: AWN History." https://web.archive.org/web/20170802095134/http://www.awn-af.net/index.php/cms/content/68.

Allendorf, Keera, and Arland Thornton. 2019. "New Research on Developmental Idealism." *Sociology of Development* 5 (3): 225–228.

Arbabzadah, Nushin. 2008. "The Fighting Women of Afghanistan." *Guardian*, September 30.

Basu, Srimati. 2010. "V Is for Veil, V Is for Ventriloquism: Global Feminisms in *The Vagina Monologues*." *Frontiers: A Journal of Women Studies* 31 (1): 31–62.

BBC. 2022. "Afghanistan: Taliban Ban Women from Universities Amid Condemnation." December 21. https://www.bbc.com/news/world-asia-64045497.

Bhan, Mona. 2014. *Counterinsurgency, Development, and the Politics of Identity in India: From Warfare to Welfare?* Abingdon, UK: Routledge.

Bose, Purnima. 2020. *Intervention Narratives: Afghanistan, the United States, and the Global War on Terror*. New Brunswick, NJ: Rutgers University Press.

cooke, miriam. 2002. "Saving Brown Women." *Signs: Journal of Women in Culture and Society* 28 (1): 468–470.

Cunningham, Erin. 2021. "Taliban Bars Female News Anchors from State Television, Reports Say." *Washington Post*, August 20.

Das, Devaleena. 2022. "A Transnational Feminist Perspective on the US-NATO Military Withdrawal from Afghanistan: In Conversation with Malalai Joya." *Feminist Formations* 34 (3): 106–126.

Daulatzai, Anila. 2006. "Acknowledging Afghanistan: Notes and Queries on an Occupation." *Cultural Dynamics* 18 (3): 293–311.

Daulatzai, Anila. 2008. "The Discursive Occupation of Afghanistan." *British Journal of Middle Eastern Studies* 35 (3): 419–435.

Fabian, Johannes. 1983. *Time and the Other*. New York: Columbia University Press.

Faizi, Waheed, and Farkhunda Paimani. 2022. "Taliban Want to Erase Women from Media, Afghan Journalists Say." VOA, May 20. https://www.voanews.com/a/taliban-want-to-erase-women-from-media-afghan-journalists-say/6583256.html.

Fassihi, Farnaz, and Dan Bilefsky. 2021. "For Afghan Women, Taliban Stirs Fears of Return to a Repressive Past." *New York Times*, August 17.

Feeley, Dianne. 2023. "Before and After Roe: Scary Times, Then and Now." *Against the Current*, no. 223 (March–April). https://againstthecurrent.org/atc223/before-after-roe-scary-times-then-now/.

Feminist Majority Campaign. 2023. "Stop Gender Apartheid in Afghanistan: Campaign for Afghan Women and Girls." Feminist Majority Foundation.

Accessed April 1, 2023. https://feminist.org/our-work/afghan-women
-and-girls/.

Finkel, David. 2023. "Women's Rights, Human Rights." Editorial. *Against the
Current*, no. 223 (March–April). https://againstthecurrent.org/atc223
/womens-rights-human-rights/.

Goldsmith, Belinda, and Meka Beresford. 2018. "Exclusive: India Most Dangerous Country for Women with Sexual Violence Rife." Reuters, June 26.
https://news.trust.org/item/20180612134519-cxz54/.

Greenberg, Jon. 2021. "What We Know About Today's Taliban." *PolitiFact*,
September 1. https://www.politifact.com/article/2021/sep/01/what-we
-know-about-todays-taliban/.

Huylebroek, Jim, Wali Arlan, and Rick Gladstone. 2021. "Taliban Seize
Women's Ministry Building for Use by Religious Police." *New York Times*,
September 17.

Jackson, Ashley. 2018. "Life Under the Taliban Shadow Government."
Report. Overseas Development Institute, Embassy of Denmark, Kabul,
June. https://cdn.odi.org/media/documents/12269.pdf.

Javaid, Arfa. 2020. "Human Development Index 2020." *Jagran Josh*, December 31.
https://www.jagranjosh.com/general-knowledge/humah-development
-index-ranking-1608992272-1.

Joya, Malalai, and Derrick O'Keefe. 2009. *A Woman Among Warlords: The
Extraordinary Story of an Afghan Who Dared to Raise Her Voice*. New
York: Scribner.

Karam, Zeina, and Ahmad Seir. 2021. "Afghan Women Fear Return to 'Dark
Days' Amid Taliban Sweep." Associated Press, August 13.

Koehler, Robert. 2021. "Women's Rights: Afghanistan and Beyond." *CounterPunch*, September 24. https://www.counterpunch.org/2021/09/24
/womens-rights-afghanistan-and-beyond/.

Mani, Lata. 1998. *Contentious Traditions: The Debate on Sati in Colonial India*.
Berkeley: University of California Press.

Marx, Karl. (1869) 1963. *The Eighteenth Brumaire of Louis Bonaparte*. New
York: International Publishers.

McClintock, Anne. 1995. *Imperial Leather: Race, Gender and Sexuality in the
Colonial Contest*. New York: Routledge.

Mitchell, David F. 2017. "NGO Presence and Activity in Afghanistan,
2000–2014: A Provincial Level Data Set." *Stability: An International Journal of Security and Development* 6 (1): 1–18. https://www.doi.org/10.5334
/sta.497.

Osman, Wazhmah. 2020. *Television and the Afghan Culture Wars: Brought to You
by Foreigners, Warlords, and Activists*. Urbana: University of Illinois Press.

Osman, Wazhmah. 2022. "Transformations in Afghan Media and Culture
Through Cycles of Upheaval." *Current History* 121 (834): 135–140.

Osman, Wazhmah, and Helena Zeweri. 2011. "Afghan Women Have a Long
History of Taking Leadership and Fighting for Their Rights." *Conversation*, October 11.

Qaderi, Homeira. 2021. "Afghan Women Are Not Going Back to the Dark Ages." *Dallas Morning News*, September 9.

Raghavan, Sudarsan. 2021. "As the Taliban Bars Some Girls from School, Their Mothers' Dreams Are Also Shattered." *Washington Post*, September 23.

Rahmani, Roya. 2012. "Donors, Beneficiaries, or NGOs: Whose Needs Come First? A Dilemma in Afghanistan." *Development in Practice* 22 (3): 295–304.

Reuters. 2023. "Taliban Order Closure of Beauty Salons in Afghanistan." *Guardian*, July 4.

Rostami-Povey, Elaheh. 2003. "Women in Afghanistan: Passive Victims of the Borga or Active Social Participants?" *Development in Practice* 13 (2/3): 266–277.

Sangari, Kumkum, and Sudesh Vaid. 1990. *Recasting Women: Essays in Indian Colonial History*. New Brunswick, NJ: Rutgers University Press.

Sarkar, Sumit, and Tanika Sarkar. 2008. *Women and Social Reform in Modern India: A Reader*. Bloomington: Indiana University Press.

Sarkar, Tanika. 2001. *Hindu Wife, Hindu Nation: Community, Religion, and Cultural Nationalism*. Delhi: Permanent Black.

Shelton, Tracey. 2023. "The Afghan Taliban Have Changed 'Drastically' Since They Were Last in Power 20 Years Ago, Experts Say." *ABC News*, August 21. https://www.abc.net.au/news/2021-08-17/afghan-taliban-evolved-since-20-years-ago/100379358.

Simon, Scott. 2020. "Homeira Qaderi Reflects on Motherhood in Her New Memoir." *Weekend Edition*, National Public Radio, November 28.

Sinha, Mrinalini. 2006. *Specters of Mother India: The Global Restructuring of an Empire*. Durham, NC: Duke University Press.

Spivak, Gayatri. 1988. "Can the Subaltern Speak?" In *Marxism and the Interpretation of Culture*, edited by Carey Nelson and Lawrence Grossberg, 271–313. Urbana: University of Illinois Press.

Strainchamps, Anne. 2021. "How Afghanistan Became America's 'First Feminist War.'" *Wisconsin Public Radio*, October 1.

Thornton, Arland. 2001. "The Developmental Paradigm, Reading History Sideways, and Family Change." *Demography* 38 (4): 449–465.

Thornton, Arland. 2005. *Reading History Sideways: The Fallacy and Enduring Impact of the Developmental Paradigm on Family Life*. Chicago: University of Chicago Press.

USA Today. 2021. "Afghan Women Fear Return to Restrictions of the Past Amid Taliban Control." August 17.

Zeweri, Helena. 2017. "The Specter of Failure: Rendering Afghan Women as Sites of Precarity in Empowerment Regimes." *International Feminist Journal of Politics* 19 (4): 441–455.

Zeweri, Helena, and Wazhmah Osman. 2022. "Afghan Women: Always Resisting Empire." *Against the Current*, no. 216 (January/February). https://againstthecurrent.org/atc216/afghan-women-always-resisting-empire/.

The Second Front

The Taliban Information Operation and the Battle for Hearts and Minds in the US/ NATO War in Afghanistan (2001–2021)

By the time the truth arrives, the lies would have destroyed the villages.
—PASHTO PROVERB

If the truth sounds like a lie, don't say it.
—DARI/PERSIAN PROVERB

If they don't believe your true word /
Swearing to the truth of what you say is useless.
—KHUSHHAL KHAN KHATTAK (1613–1689), PASHTO
WARRIOR POET AND TRIBAL CHIEF

Information warfare and strategic communication have been part of conflict throughout human history. In an asymmetric conflict, the war of information and ideas is often more important to the insurgent than the action itself. In recent history, a number of conflicts have become synonymous with the advent of new tools and technologies used in information warfare and to influence strategies. The Spanish-American War (April 21–August 13, 1898)—which ended Spanish colonial rule in the Americas and resulted in the United States' acquisition of territories in the western Pacific and Latin America—has long been referred to as the first "media war" as the US military action was precipitated by media involvement. The main media tool of that war was newspapers that ran sensationalist articles while correspondents were sent to the region to witness and report on the war firsthand (Townsend 2019).

Six decades later, in the 1960s, the US war in Vietnam earned the reputation of being the "first television war," as it became the subject of large-scale TV news coverage. Hundreds of accredited journalists covered this war for US wire services, radio, and television networks (Braman 2003). The Yugoslavian Civil Wars of the 1990s have been described as the "first internet war" as they coincided with the adoption of the internet and the birth of online news outlets (Keenan 2001). However, since internet penetration and public access to it was very limited in the 1990s, calling the Yugoslavian Civil Wars the "first internet war" seems a bit of a stretch.

Therefore, I argue that it was the twenty-first century's Global War on Terror (GWOT) that coincided with the true internet era, a time when the internet became widely available to the public for general use. As the US-led war in Afghanistan that started on October 7, 2001, was the first and main battlefield of the GWOT, it deserves the title of the "first internet war." This war truly showed the internet's full potential to cover war in depth and in real time. I posit that this was also the "first social media war" as individuals on the ground were able to share real-time reports from the frontlines and the sites of attacks. Anyone with a smartphone could collect and instantly transmit information like "war correspondents." They could also post updates and share videos on various social media platforms during military operations, making it possible for people anywhere to virtually experience elements of combat. The war in Afghanistan was also the "first tri-media war," involving radio/audio, TV/video, and print/text.

In fact, the US-led invasion of Afghanistan in 2001 started with the launch of broadcasts in Pashto and Dari languages from a flying radio station using EC-130E aircraft. As the Taliban had banned the internet and television when they were first in power (1996–2001), Radio Afghanistan, which the Taliban had named Radio Voice of Sharia (Da Shariat ẓhagh in Pashto, Sadā-e Shariat in Dari), was the only national radio station in the country. Taking down the transmission towers of the Taliban government's Radio Voice of Sharia was one of the first steps in the United States' military campaign that began on October 7, 2001, aimed at denying the group the means to communicate with the public. Meanwhile, a large number of radios were dropped and distributed for free by the United States and other coalition partners, as well as international nongovernmental organizations across the country. Various departments in the Afghan government also distributed radios among the public as part of its public awareness and information campaign.

Later, the US-led International Security Assistance Force (ISAF) developed its own well-funded and robust media sector. A national radio station in Dari and Pashto, called Sada-e-Azadi (The voice of freedom), was launched with a network of FM stations across Afghanistan as part of the US/NATO campaign to win hearts and minds. It also launched a newspaper with the same name; it had the widest national circulation (500,000) and was distributed for free in the main urban centers of Afghanistan. The radio and the newspaper both served as major tools of the US-led international coalition for public and cultural diplomacy in Afghanistan.

However, the US-led international coalition and the Afghan government it supported had many other media and propaganda outlets aimed at vilifying "the enemy," winning the war of narratives, and portraying a positive image of itself. The role of the media and its use as part of information warfare was evident from the onset of the conflict and remained so until the end. The explosion of media and digital connectivity was one of the most significant aspects of post-2001 Afghanistan—with most Afghans, for the first time in history, gaining access to the internet as well as a wide range of television channels and a broad network of FM radio stations. According to a report by the Special Inspector General for Afghanistan Reconstruction (SIGAR), the US Agency for International Development (USAID) spent approximately US$220 million between 2002 and 2021 "on media-focused programs to build and promote a free press in Afghanistan. (SIGAR 2023, 39).[1]

The US/NATO invasion of Afghanistan, which started following the 9/11 attacks in 2001, eventually became the longest war in US history, lasting nearly two decades (October 7, 2001–August 30, 2021), and spanned four US presidencies. America's war in Afghanistan was longer than World War I (1914–1918), World War II (1939–1945), and the American Civil War (1861–1865) combined. It was also longer than the Vietnam War, where the US armed forces fought for over nineteen years (November 1, 1955–April 30, 1975). Meanwhile, it was the first time that the North Atlantic Treaty Organization (NATO) ever invoked the treaty's Article 5—the Alliance's collective defense clause stating that an attack on one member nation is an attack on all. It paved way for NATO's participation in the war in Afghanistan and eventual deployment on the ground as part of the International Security Assistance

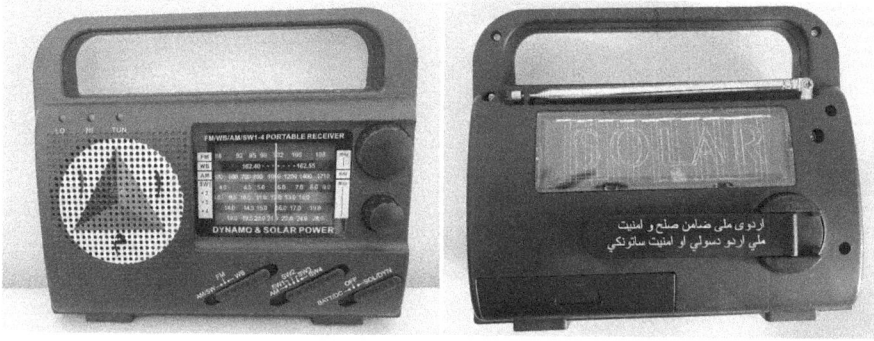

10.1 A radio with the Afghan National Army emblem during the Republic (2001–2021). The text on the back, in Pashto and Dari, says, "National Army, guarantor of peace and security."

Force (ISAF) and Resolute Support (RS) missions. It was NATO's biggest military mission since its creation in 1949 (Azami 2021, 227).

War of Words

Slogans, symbols, and labels are important elements of a propaganda war. As the war in Afghanistan progressed, the use of terminology and negative labeling of "the enemy" became intense and innovative. Both the Taliban and the government in Kabul (the Islamic Republic of Afghanistan) claimed to be the legitimate representatives of Afghans, the country's true protectors, and the real defenders of the life and dignity of its people. The insurgents and the counterinsurgents tried to show they had the public's backing and the upper hand on the battlefield and implied they were on the right side of history. Meanwhile, they competed for the support and trust of the population and sought to isolate "the enemy." They also strove to damage the credibility and prestige of the opposite side by exposing and exploiting their follies and vulnerabilities.

The Taliban tried to discredit the Afghan government by calling it a "puppet regime" and an "illegitimate" government as, according to them, it was dependent on the support of the "infidel countries" that had toppled the government of the "Islamic Emirate of Afghanistan"—the name the Taliban use for themselves and their government. The Taliban also accused the Afghan government officials of being "traitors," "collaborators," and "corrupters" for being part of a non-Muslim US-led alliance.

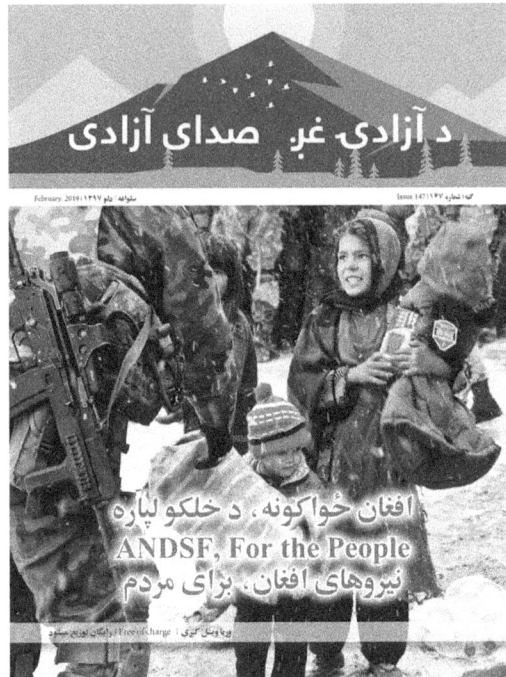

10.2 The February 2019 issue of the US-led military's fortnightly newspaper in Pashto, Dari, and English, named *Sada-e-Azadi* (The voice of freedom).

They called the United States and NATO—the main backers of the Afghan government—"occupiers," "infidels," "crusaders," "aggressors," "invaders," and more (Azami 2009b; Azami 2010).

In their information warfare, the Taliban mainly focused on highlighting their opponents' mistakes and mismanagement. They exploited the shortcomings in the counterinsurgents' tactics and public relations machine, which proved to be more instrumental in losing public trust than the insurgents' narrative and propaganda campaign itself. Unlike the US and Afghan government's message, the Taliban's message was simple and based on the three C's of effective communication: It was generally concise, clear, and consistent.

The Taliban also capitalized on a sense of alienation among the general public, fostered mainly by bad governance as well as military operations resulting in civilian casualties, arbitrary arrests, the mistreatment of local populations, and disrespect to local culture. The Taliban emphasized local concerns such as the loss of livelihood and violations of honor and local traditions, including house and personal searches. The killing of civilians, especially women and children, in air strikes, search operations, and night raids; the detention of innocent Afghans based on incorrect intelligence; and the lack of sensitivity to local culture, especially during night raids with soldiers kicking in the doors of houses and immediately searching inside even if there were women there, allowed the Taliban call to reach receptive ears.

In addition, the Taliban used to good advantage events outside Afghanistan, especially in other theaters of wars where the United States or its allies had a role in the abuse of Muslims, such as the mistreatment of detainees in Iraq's Abu Ghraib prison by the US military personnel and the Israeli government's operations in Gaza. Moreover, the stories of imprisonment and sometimes abuse by American hands of the Afghan detainees also made a big impact. This was truer in the case of those detained in the US military prison at Guantanamo Bay, Cuba, where the Afghan prisoners made the largest single group of the nearly fifty nationalities involved and labeled as "unlawful combatants" by President George W. Bush (Azami 2014). The pictures of blindfolded, hooded, and kneeling shackled detainees wearing orange suits and held in open-air wire cages in Camp X-Ray (which I later visited myself for the making of a BBC documentary) as well as stories of former inmates, both oral and written, circulated in Afghanistan (and the rest of the Muslim world) caused huge damage to America's reputation.

After the release of each Afghan prisoner from Guantanamo, a stream of visitors came to their homes where they told and retold their ordeal. Some Afghan ex-Guantanamo detainees even wrote books (in Pashto and later translated into other languages including Dari and Urdu) that became bestsellers, detailing what they endured in the notorious US detention facility (Azami 2009a). The Taliban sang chants about what they termed the "cruelty" and "inhumanity" of the Americans, and mullahs (clerics) in the mosques and people in private discussed the Americans and their "inhuman" conduct. The Taliban repeatedly highlighted those issues to discredit the United States' claim to be a human rights champion and to garner moral support and donations from the wider Muslim world (Azami 2012, Azami 2010, Azami 2009b).

The Afghan government and its US/NATO allies took the propaganda war right back to the Taliban, labeling the insurgents "terrorists," "miscreants," "mercenaries," "enemies of the people," "enemies of the homeland," "enemies of Islam," and "enemies of the prosperity and development of Afghanistan." Pointing to the militants' sanctuaries in Pakistan, the Afghan government authorities also called the Taliban "Pakistani stooges" and "pawns of the Pakistani security establishment," a charge repeatedly denied by both the Afghan Taliban and Pakistan.

Meanwhile, the Afghan government and its foreign backers blamed the Taliban for continuing the war and killing civilians with suicide bombings, improvised explosive devices (IEDs), and car bombs, and for destroying public infrastructure such as schools, clinics, roads, and bridges. Moreover, the United States and its foreign allies portrayed themselves as the true friends of Afghanistan and constantly reminded the Afghans that their militaries were in their country to protect them from the harms of "violent extremists" and "terrorists." They also presented the billions of dollars they were spending on Afghanistan's development and reconstruction as evidence of being sincere and trustworthy partners of the Afghans.

As part of their competition for strategic advantage, the Taliban, the United States, and the US-backed Afghan government made full use of the contemporary information environment to establish, shape, or challenge a specific narrative. In addition to using their own media outlets, social media platforms (such as Facebook, Twitter/X, YouTube, and Whats-App), and other public relations tools, the insurgents and counterinsurgents tried to influence the media, feeding stories to journalists and even misleading them through cooperation and co-optation as well as intimidation and intimation. Truth and accuracy were frequently sacrificed in favor of speed as the two sides tried to dominate the airwaves and the internet. Both sides exaggerated their "achievements" on the battlefield, often inflating casualty figures to demoralize their opponents and to show their own strength and efficacy. In the first years of the US-led war, I once asked a spokesperson for the US-led military coalition why the number of Taliban fighters they claimed to have killed in military operations was almost always in round figures of forty, fifty, sixty, or eighty and not one less or one more. Each side issued statements regularly about the effectiveness of its military operations and enemy losses. The casualty figures of the opposite side were so inflated over the course of the two-decade-long war that if the number of people both sides often claimed to have killed is added up, it would have been more than half of the total population of Afghanistan.

War of Fatwas

The "war of fatwas" (religious edicts) was another important facet of the campaign to win hearts and minds and delegitimize the opponent. In traditional Afghan society, religious scholars or clerics, who usually use the honorific prefix of *mullah*, *mawlawi*, or *maulana*, have significant influence, with people often seeking their advice. Both the Taliban and the US-backed Afghan government needed a religious cover to justify their struggle and legitimize their cause in the eyes of the wider public, which made clerics useful for both sides (Azami 2013).

The Taliban—the Pashto plural form of the Arabic word *Talib* that literally means "seekers [of knowledge]" but is generally used for religious students—described themselves as being at the vanguard defending Afghanistan's independence and its "original Islamic values." They claimed their armed struggle was based on Islamic Sharia and believed they were engaged in an armed jihad or holy/religious war to liberate their Muslim country from the "occupation of infidel powers." The Taliban tried to legitimize their actions through fatwas issued by ulema (religious scholars) who supported their cause and called the Western troops "crusaders" and "occupiers." Those fatwas not only "justified" the war in Afghanistan as a religiously legitimate armed struggle but also sanctioned tactics such as suicide bombing and the killing of people on charges of "spying" and for "collaborating" with the Afghan government and the United States.

These fatwas were disseminated broadly—read in mosques as well as madrassas (religious seminaries) in several parts of Afghanistan and Pakistan to members of the public and religious students. Taliban leaders and pro-Taliban mullahs also read and quoted these fatwas in their speeches uploaded to the internet or recorded on CDs and DVDs. Some were printed for distribution among the people. Moreover, many leading Pakistani Islamists, most notably Deobandi clerics based in various madrassas in Pakistan, issued their own fatwas to justify the Taliban war in Afghanistan. As many Afghan Taliban members—including some of their leaders—studied in various Pakistani madrassas, they were direct or indirect disciples of these clerics who consistently maintained that the war in Afghanistan was an Islamically mandated jihad. Meanwhile, "internet mullahs"—mostly foreigners pretending to be Islamic scholars and preachers giving sermons and speeches and issuing fatwas online—also became a favorite source of information and indoctrination who not only provided religious justification for the war but also encouraged the people in general to join the insurgency. In time, in Afghanistan itself, many mullahs in certain parts of the country became more vocal and bolder by openly and regularly denouncing Western forces and the Afghan government for operations resulting in civilian casualties and for violating cultural norms. The Afghan government officials allied with the US/NATO forces were accused of deceit and treason and were labeled American stooges.

On the other hand, the Afghan government repeatedly mobilized religious scholars inside the country to delegitimize the Taliban's war and tactics on religious grounds. It also encouraged mullahs to speak out against the Taliban's violence, especially their use of suicide bombings and land mines/IEDs and the civilian casualties they caused. During the two-decade-long war, the Afghan government convened several gatherings of religious scholars that issued fatwas and statements declaring the Taliban insurgency and war tactics "cruel" and "un-Islamic." Those progovernment clerics also issued fatwas justifying the presence of international forces under a United Nations mandate and repeatedly called on the Taliban to stop fighting and join the peace process. Moreover, they denounced the Taliban's call for armed jihad against the Afghan government, arguing that it had been legitimately elected, the president and other officials were Muslims, and the laws of the country were based on Islam (Azami 2013).

As part of the strategy to increase social pressure on the Taliban, the Afghan government and its foreign allies also sought the help of religious scholars in other Muslim countries, including Saudi Arabia and Egypt, asking them to issue fatwas delegitimizing the Taliban's war and denouncing their tactics, especially suicide bombings, on religious grounds. In early 2018, the top US/NATO commander in Afghanistan, General John Nicholson, announced a multipronged approach involving a combination of religious, social, diplomatic, and military pressure. Referring to a 2018 international conference in Jakarta, Indonesia, of Muslim religious scholars on the war in Afghanistan, he added that "there will be religious pressure applied to the Taliban with the ulemas hosted in Indonesia and elsewhere to strip away the religious legitimacy for jihad in Afghanistan" (VOA 2018). In mid-2018, Afghanistan's National Ulema Council, the largest religious body in the country, organized a gathering in Kabul that it said was attended by around two thousand clerics from various parts of the country. The declaration they issued proclaimed the war in Afghanistan and suicide bombing forbidden. They also called the war in Afghanistan unjust and contrary to Sharia (*Tolo News* 2018a).

Meanwhile, the United States used its influence abroad to increase social and religious pressure on the Taliban. In July 2018, US Secretary of Defense James Mattis expressed his gratitude in a letter to the Saudi crown prince, Mohammad Bin Salman, for his willingness to magnify the importance of peace and reconciliation in Afghanistan. His letter came on the eve of another International Ulema Conference on Afghanistan Peace and Security, jointly organized by Saudi Arabia and the Organisation of Islamic

Cooperation (OIC). The two-day conference in Saudi Arabia's twin cities of Jeddah and Mecca was "aimed at assisting efforts to achieve peace and stability in Afghanistan and to condemn terrorism and violent extremism in all their forms and manifestations within the framework of the teachings of the true Islamic religion" (*Tolo News* 2018b). The declaration of the conference called on the Taliban to heed the Afghan government's call to avoid violence, stop fighting, and sit down to negotiations to discuss the peace and security of the country without preconditions. The declaration added that "we hereby affirm that the suicide attacks targeting innocent people and fighting among Muslims are all acts that are prohibited by Allah and His Messenger" (OIC 2018).

The Taliban dismissed the "progovernment" gatherings of clerics, including those in Jeddah and Jakarta, and deemed their declarations foreign and US propaganda. They also warned religious scholars to be aware of "the nefarious agendas of the occupiers and their puppets." The Taliban convened their own meetings of religious scholars to issue counter-fatwas. In early August 2018, the Taliban publicly shared the eleven-article declaration in Pashto language issued by what they called a "grand gathering" of more than four thousand religious scholars, spiritual leaders, teachers, madrassa students, and a large number of tribal elders of Afghanistan in support of the armed resistance. Article 2 of the declaration said that "the ongoing sacred struggle against the American occupiers and their allies is a true jihad; its help and support is the obligation of every Muslim."[2] In the introductory remarks to the text of the declaration, the Taliban labeled the participants of the pro-Afghan government meetings in Indonesia, Kabul, and Saudi Arabia as gatherings of the "so-called religious scholars" that are propagated "by the occupiers and their puppet government." Meanwhile, they called the religious scholars who supported their armed struggle Afghanistan's "notable and respectable [religious] scholars and the true representatives of the pulpit and the mosque" (Alemarah 2018).

The Taliban tried to monopolize the religious narrative and presented themselves as the only true and authoritative voice on the religion and religious issues in Afghanistan. They had little tolerance for those clerics who opposed the Taliban's point of view. They ran a systematic campaign to silence Afghan clerics who spoke against the Taliban's strategy, war tactics, and ideology. A number of religious scholars who had condemned and/or challenged the Taliban by calling their insurgency un-Islamic and unlawful were killed. Several of those targeted were members of the progovernment National Council of Ulema, and the Taliban publicly accepted responsibility for many of those attacks. The Taliban condemned those clerics and accused them of "justifying foreign occupation and creating discord within the Muslim community." They also criticized such religious scholars for leading people astray and weakening the morale of their fighters. In some areas, the Taliban even warned clerics not to offer prayers for dead members of the Afghan security forces. Many religious scholars had to leave their villages and towns fearing reprisals for speaking against the Taliban or not cooperating with them to propagate their narrative (Azami 2013).

Cultural Awareness and the Violation of Cultural Norms

Generally, integrating cultural awareness and sensitivity into an overall hearts-and-minds strategy is a major factor for both the insurgency and counterinsurgency. In an insurgency, violating local cultural norms is a sure path to failure, and calling attention to these missteps was one of the most effective tools to discredit the opponent. In the conflict in Afghanistan, both sides developed tactics and strategies that exploited breaches of cultural customs in order to win public support, isolate the enemy, and delegitimize the opponent's cause. Historically, Afghans have generally followed their traditional rules of warfare in their intra- and intertribal feuds as well as in armed conflicts with foreign invaders. Over the course of centuries, they had developed their own culture of war and rules of the game. However, the Afghan culture of war underwent dramatic and unprecedented changes during the US/NATO combat mission in Afghanistan (2001–2021).

The US/NATO and its Afghan allies had a huge advantage in the strategic communications arena. They had far more resources and brainpower as well as a variety of sophisticated technological tools at their disposal to run a relatively effective hearts-and-minds campaign. As part of the media battlefront, the United States invested heavily in strategic communications to spread "good news stories" and "positive information" in various languages across Afghanistan. The United States and the Afghan government also ran proactive campaigns to confront Taliban propaganda and expose vulnerabilities and contradictions in the insurgents' tactics and strategies. In the context of exploiting the violation of cultural customs, the Afghan government and its US/NATO allies focused more on the Taliban's targets and war tactics. While the Taliban accepted responsibility for relying on some formerly taboo tactics, the Afghan

10.3 The front cover of the October 2014 issue of the Taliban's bilingual (Pashto and Dari) magazine, *Tsrak* (Trace/ clue). The headline of the editorial, in Pashto, reads: "Won't it be a stupidity to expect good from a system founded on corruption and treachery?"

government seized the opportunity to frame them as acts against the Afghan culture and Muslim faith.

Historically, mosques, *hujras/kotas* (male guest houses and meeting or gathering places) and jirgas (traditional tribal councils/meetings) had been immune from attacks. Similarly, the killing of women and children and attacks on the enemy during cultural celebrations—like the Muslim festival of Eid and weddings—and funeral ceremonies are against the letter and spirit of the traditional code of war and peace. However, such local principles were repeatedly violated during the two-decade war. In addition, the culture of *melmastiya* (hospitality)—a pillar of the Pashtun code and way of life generally known as *Pashtunwali*—was abused and violated by both the guests and the hosts on many occasions. Traditionally, when a meal is shared, the guest remains indebted, and never causes any harm, to the host. In turn, the guest is entirely safe under the host's protection. However, in a series of incidents, attackers pretending to be guests killed their hosts in their compounds (mainly through poisoning or shooting), and guests were also targeted in their hosts' compounds.

The suicide attack tactic was another deadly innovation in post-2001 Afghanistan. Despite a long history of wars and invasions, suicide attacks were never a part of the Afghans' warrior tradition. This tactic—adopted from Iraq's theater of war—first emerged as a regular deadly reality of Afghan life in 2005. The religious justification for suicide attacks remained controversial among many Afghan clerics and foreign Muslim religious scholars with many viewing it as a sin, like taking one's own life. Initially, there were different opinions about the religious legality of this tactic among religious scholars even within the Taliban.

However, the Taliban finally embraced suicide bombing—which they termed a *fidāyi* (self-sacrificing) or *istishhādi* (self-martyrdom) act—as an effective war tactic and portrayed it as the "ultimate sacrifice for the sake of faith." Religious scholars associated with the Taliban issued fatwas deeming it not only a religiously permissible but also a highly rewardable deed in Islam. Pro-Taliban clerics promoted suicide attacks in their sermons and encouraged the youth to volunteer for what they called the worthiest act of service and sacrifice. The number of people ready to carry out suicide attacks gradually increased in Afghanistan (as well as Pakistan). In early 2008, one Taliban spokesman claimed that they were overwhelmed with volunteers for suicide attacks, including women, such that they "[could not] provide enough [suicide] vests" (ICG 2008, 24).

Meanwhile, female suicide bombing, which was even a bigger taboo in conservative Afghan society, was also quietly introduced in the country after a few such attacks in Iraq and Pakistan. First reported in 2010, there were a few incidents in Afghanistan where women reportedly carried out suicide attacks. On several occasions, both the Taliban and the Afghan government confirmed the attacker to be a girl or woman.

The first publicly acknowledged female suicide attack in Afghanistan was carried out in eastern Kunar Province bordering Pakistan on June 21, 2010, when a woman targeted a joint check post of Afghan and foreign forces, killing two US soldiers as well as Afghan civilians (US Army 2010; UNAMA 2011a, 5, 10). The Taliban's main spokesman, Zabihullah Mujahid, told the media that the perpetrator was a resident of Kunar who "herself volunteered for this mission because she had lost family members in the war." He added that the attacker "went through some training" and that new female volunteers would be welcomed (Reuters 2011; UNAMA 2011a, 5, 10). In its 2010 annual report, the United Nations Assistance Mission in Afghanistan (UNAMA) also called it "the only documented case of a suicide attack conducted by a female" (2011a, 10). Nearly six months later, on December 4, a female suicide bomber reportedly killed forty-five people in an attack at a World Food Program (WFP) ration distribution point in the adjacent tribal agency of Bajaur on the Pakistani side of the Durand Line. Officials said that most of the victims belonged to a local tribe, which had raised a *lashkar* (tribal militia) against militants in their areas (*Dawn* 2010).

The second known female suicide bombing in Afghanistan was carried out almost a year after, again in Kunar Province. The perpetrator was reportedly an eighteen- or twenty-year-old girl attacking an international military convoy escorted by Afghan forces in Marawara District on June 4, 2011 (*Pajhwok* 2011; UNAMA 2011b, 5). The third relatively widely known female suicide attack took place again in Kunar Province on October 29, 2011, when the attacker detonated her explosives near the building of the Afghan intelligence agency, the National Directorate of Security (NDS), killing herself and wounding several NDS personnel (BBC 2011; *Khaama Press* 2011). The Taliban claimed responsibility for this attack too through a statement which said that "the successful *istishhādi* attack was carried out by a heroic mujahid sister who was wearing an explosive vest" (Alemarai 2011b).[3] Although female suicide attacks did not become popular and were quickly phased out, presumably for cultural and religious reasons, the frequency of male suicide bombing attacks increased with the passage of time. Between 2005, when the Taliban started regularly using suicide bombers, and their return to power in August 2021, the group carried out hundreds of suicide attacks in Afghanistan.

A few months after reestablishing their government in Afghanistan, the Taliban's acting interior minister, Sirajuddin Haqqani, hosted a ceremony in the prominent Intercontinental Hotel in Kabul in mid-October 2021 to honor suicide bombers. He praised their sacrifices and met with families (fathers, brothers, uncles, and sons) of some of those who had carried out such attacks during the previous fifteen years (Gibbons-Neff et al. 2021; VOA 2021). In May 2022, Sirajuddin Haqqani (known in the West as the leader of the Haqqani Network) revealed in a speech to a large gathering of Taliban members that under his supervision alone 1,050 individuals had carried out such attacks in Afghanistan (BBC Pashto 2022).

The Taliban's reliance on suicide bombing continued even after their transformation from an insurgency to a government. The Taliban also displayed their suicide bombers and arsenal of explosives-laden suicide vests in their victory parade in Kabul in 2021. In addition, the Taliban government officials announced the formation of a new "martyrdom brigade" made up of suicide bombers (Siddique 2021). Although the authorities did not reveal the numerical strength of their suicide bomber force, saying they "did not see it necessary," the formation of these units is part of a strategy to rebrand suicide bombers as elite fighters ready to sacrifice their lives for the protection of their government. This is the first time in the history of Afghanistan that suicide bomber forces have been included in the military and security forces' organization.

During the Taliban insurgency, the Afghan government officials and progovernment religious scholars condemned the group for adopting and popularizing suicide attacks in Afghanistan. They argued it was no different from suicide in other contexts, a practice forbidden in Islam. They also pointed out to the collateral damage and the killing and injuring of innocent bystanders, including women and children, caused by such attacks (*Tolo News* 2018a).

The other tactic exploited by the Afghan government in its information warfare against the Taliban was the "turban bombing"—a suicide attack using explosives hidden in the traditional headdress (called *langota, lungai,* or *pagrai* in Pashto) referred to in the West as a turban. Turbans are objects of respect for Afghans (and other Muslims) and were usually not searched at security checkpoints. This too was a new phenomenon in Afghanistan, begun in around 2010, and the tactic claimed the lives of many prominent Afghan politicians, tribal elders, and government officials. For example, on July 14, 2011, a suicide bomber detonated explosives hidden in his headdress inside a mosque in Kandahar during the funeral ceremony for Ahmad Wali Karzai, the assassinated head of the Kandahar Provincial Council and brother of Afghan President Hamid Karzai, killing four people, including the provincial head of the ulema council, Mawlawi Hikmatullah Hikmat. On July 27, 2011, a suicide bomber killed the mayor of Kandahar City, Ghulam Haidar Hamidi, in his office after detonating the device rigged to his turban. On September 20, 2011, an attacker in the guise of a Taliban peace messenger killed the head of Afghanistan's High Peace Council, Professor Burhanuddin Rabbani, in his home in Kabul by exploding the bomb hidden in his turban. Such tactics raised the ire of many Afghans, who called it a violation of the Afghan war culture and a betrayal of local traditions.

Exploiting US/NATO's Follies and Vulnerabilities

The Taliban based their information campaign mainly on two pillars: skillfully exploiting incidents in which their enemy "violated" Islam and Islamic principles and cultural norms, and holding themselves up as protectors of Islam, Afghan nationalism, and culture. They propagated slogans of armed jihad, stating that "Islam and Muslims were under attack" and that Afghanistan was occupied by an "alien and infidel power" that was "violating the Afghan culture" and "disrespecting Islamic norms." They rarely missed an opportunity to amplify reports of and expose cultural violations, bad governance, or harm to the lives, dignity, and property of Afghans in military operations by the Afghan government and US/NATO forces.

In addition to civilian casualties in military operations (some of which even targeted weddings and other social gatherings and civilian buildings), and injustices (ranging from house searches, insults, and arbitrary arrests to damages to property and livelihoods), the violation of Afghan culture and the privacy of homes proved to be among the highly alienating tactics that gradually turned many Afghans away from the Afghan government and its US/NATO allies (Azami 2021, 237). As will be outlined, lack of cultural awareness and repeated violations of local norms and traditions made the counterinsurgents (US/NATO) their own worst enemies. Although the US/NATO claimed it had made doctrinal and strategic-level progress toward integrating cultural awareness into counterinsurgency, repeated tactical mistakes over two decades gave the insurgents ample opportunities to exploit the counterinsurgents' vulnerabilities and push people away from them, thus undermining the overall US-led mission in Afghanistan. The first Pashto radio messages and propaganda leaflets associated with the US information and psychological campaign, released in October 2001, included several grammatical, spelling, and pronunciation mistakes—similar errors would continue throughout the war.

As evident from several incidents that took place mainly during the second decade of its Afghanistan mission, the United States' information warfare remained abysmally poor, and it did not learn sufficiently from previous mistakes. In September 2017, US forces dropped controversial leaflets in Afghanistan's Parwan Province, which is close to Kabul and was home to the biggest US military base in the country. The leaflets showed the section of the Taliban's flag that contains a Quranic passage known as the *Shahāda*—the declaration of Muslim faith that is the basic pillar of Islam—superimposed on the side of a white dog (referencing the Taliban's white flag which features the *Shahāda*), an animal generally considered unclean by Muslims, being chased by a lion (an apparent reference to the US/NATO forces). The text written in Pashto above the images urged people to report insurgents to the authorities: "Take back your freedom from the terrorist dogs and cooperate with coalition forces so they can target your enemy and eliminate them."

However, the leaflets backfired, provoking widespread condemnation in Afghanistan, and contributed to losing the support and trust of many people. The act not only damaged the United States' reputation among many Afghans and the wider Muslim community, it increased the risk of a backlash against international forces, including insider attacks on foreign forces by members of the Afghan security forces, generally known as "green-on-blue attacks." Seizing the moment, the Taliban reacted promptly by issuing a statement saying that the leaflet showed US hatred of Islam and announcing that it had launched a suicide attack near the entrance to Afghanistan's biggest US military base, Bagram Airfield, in revenge. The Taliban statement added that the leaflet made clear "that this war is between Islam and unbelief" (*New York Times* 2017). A senior US commander in Afghanistan apologized for the leaflet in a statement calling it "highly offensive" and adding, "We have the deepest respect for Islam and our Muslim partners worldwide" (*New York Times* 2017).

What was surprising was that it was not the first time US forces had caused cultural or religious offense in Afghanistan. A decade earlier, in August 2007, a similar incident involving the *Shahāda* printed on footballs meant to be gifts for children prompted similar demonstrations, as protesters accused the Americans of insulting Islam. The footballs, dropped from helicopters, displayed flags from various countries, including the Saudi Arabian flag, which features the *Shahāda*. Demonstrators were angry that the US forces had a verse of the Quran, which also contains the names of Allah and Muhammad, on something meant to be kicked—and saw it as an insult to Islam and Muslims. At the time, a spokeswoman for the US forces in Afghanistan said distributing the footballs was an effort to give a gift that Afghan children would enjoy, adding that "there was something on those footballs we didn't immediately understand to be offensive and we regret that as we do not want to offend" (Leithead 2007).

The leaflets distributed in September 2017 were more ironic for the fact that US forces had already spent sixteen years fighting and running a hearts-and-minds campaign. It was hard to believe that any member of the foreign forces in Afghanistan, especially those who ran the information operation, would not know how offensive and counterproductive disrespecting Islamic norms could be or how much it would contribute to stoking anti-foreigner sentiment. It was even more surprising that, just like the first leaflets dropped in the very beginning of the US invasion of Afghanistan in 2001, there were several grammatical and spelling mistakes in the Pashto text on these September 2017 leaflets.

A few months later, in January 2018, video footage showing a US service member firing into the cab of a civilian truck as the two vehicles passed one another on a road in Afghanistan was anonymously uploaded on a social media platform (YouTube) under the title "Happy Few Ordnance Symphony" before it was quickly removed. The troops seen in the video, apparently shot in 2017, wore uniforms typical of US Special Operations Forces and were seen firing machine guns, grenade launchers, rockets, miniguns, and mortars and calling in air or artillery strikes. Set to music, the video was a combat montage that some US troops created to share among themselves, including footage shot from helmet-mounted video cameras (Morgan 2018).

The timing of the uploading of this grim video and the distribution of insulting leaflets could not have been worse for the United States, as these missteps took place when the Trump administration's newly announced strategy for Afghanistan—pledging "to fight and to win"—was in full swing and the Taliban were under extreme military pressure. These acts supported the Taliban narrative and strengthened the resolve and motivation of the Taliban fighters against what they saw as an enemy of their religion and people. The Taliban used such material to show the public that the United States was not there to help but to destroy their religion and people. This also made it easier for the insurgents to gain considerable public support and recruit fighters among ordinary Afghans.

The incidents involving the violation of cultural norms were not unique to the Trump administration (2016–2020), as many others had happened previously with seemingly no lessons learned in between. In January 2012, a video of four US Marines urinating on the bodies of dead "Taliban fighters"—with one of the Marines saying, "Have a great day, buddy"—was posted on public video-sharing websites and went viral instantly. The video showed such a desecration, a possible war crime, that it provoked anger and condemnation in Afghanistan and around the world, raising fears that the images could further incite anti-American sentiments. President Karzai condemned the act and demanded justice and accountability. The Taliban, meanwhile, pointed to the images as evidence of brutality and disrespect, a message with broad appeal in Afghanistan. Such images and incidents surfaced at a time when tensions between President Karzai and the Obama administration were already high, mainly due to the US war strategy and counterproductive tactics, including civilian casualties and home raids. Karzai had been a vocal critic of the US military's conduct during the war and its disregard for Afghan culture, arguing that such acts would strengthen the anti-government narrative (Bowley and Rosenberg 2012).

The next month, in February 2012, disturbances and countrywide protests began after local Afghan laborers discovered charred copies of the Quran as they collected rubbish at the biggest US-run Bagram military base, about an hour's drive from Kabul. According to Afghan workers who witnessed the event, a dump truck escorted by a military vehicle drove up to the landfill and unloaded bags of books including the Quran and threw them into a pit for incineration. Two bags of books the US soldiers had already thrown into the pit had begun to burn before the local Afghan workers became agitated and forced the US soldiers to draw back (BBC 2012; RFE/RL 2012; Rahimi and Rubin 2012).

The news of the incident spread like wildfire throughout Afghanistan. At least thirty people died and dozens were injured in days of countrywide protests and anti-American demonstrations. While condemning the burning of the Quran and calling for calm, the Afghan president, Hamid Karzai, demanded the investigation and prosecution of those involved in the incident (BBC 2012; RFE/RL 2012; Rahimi and Rubin 2012). On the other hand, the Taliban said in a statement quickly emailed to the media that the incident had offended "one billion Muslims around the world" and called for violence: "Our brave people must target the military bases of invader forces, their military convoys, and their invader bases" (RFE/RL 2012; Rahimi and Rubin 2012). The top US and NATO commander in Afghanistan, John R. Allen, was forced to apologize for the incident; President Barack Obama also apologized to President Karzai. While confirming the "inappropriate treatment of religious materials, including the Koran, at Bagram Airbase," US Defense Secretary Leon Panetta promised measures "to ensure that we take all steps necessary and appropriate so that this never happens again" (BBC 2012). The full extent of the problem became clear a few months later when it was revealed that possibly as many as one hundred copies of the Quran had been consumed in the fire (Martinez 2012).

A couple of years earlier, in 2009, the US military had to deny that its soldiers tried to convert Afghans to Christianity after a video shot a year earlier appeared to show military chaplains stationed in the main US air base at Bagram discussing how to distribute copies of the Bible printed in Afghanistan's main languages of Pashto and Dari. A US military spokesperson at Bagram Air Base confirmed the Bibles were sent through private mail to an evangelical Christian soldier and that they were collected before they could be distributed (Al Jazeera 2009; Reuters 2009). It was another highly sensitive issue in a conservative Muslim society, as trying to convert Muslims to another faith is not only a crime in Afghanistan but is usually punishable by death under Islamic law. The Taliban presented such incidents as "proof" of what they called the United States' "proselytizing agenda" and a Western plot to destroy the Afghan culture and religion (Alemarah 2011a).

Similar incidents also took place during the Bush administration (2001–2009). For example, in October 2005, Australian media broadcast a film that appeared to show a US psychological operations team burning the bodies of two "Taliban fighters" in the southern Kandahar Province and using their charred and smoking corpses to taunt nearby Taliban fighters. According to the foreign reporter embedded with the US team, American soldiers faced the bodies toward Mecca (the holiest of Muslim cities and religious centers, toward which the Muslims turn five times daily in prayer) in a deliberately provocative move, set them on fire, and then broadcasted over a loudspeaker toward a village thought to be harboring Taliban fighters and sympathizers the following message: "Attention, Taliban, you are all cowardly dogs. You allowed your fighters to be laid down facing west and burned. You are too scared to come down and retrieve their bodies. This just proves you are the lady boys we always believed you to be." As the Islamic tradition calls for remains to be washed, prayed over, wrapped in white cloth, and buried within twenty-four hours, the alleged act provoked widespread anger across the country and the Afghan government demanded that those responsible be punished. As usual, the US military issued a statement saying that "this alleged action is repugnant to our common values" and added that it had "directed an investigation into circumstances surrounding this allegation" (*Guardian* 2005).

Insults to Afghan culture and violations of religious norms as well as the killing and abuses of civilians by foreign soldiers and their Afghan partners came at a huge cost to the overall US-led mission and resulted in losing the trust and good will of many people that had been painfully won through information operations as well as financial aid and reconstruction projects. More importantly, Afghans usually did not see the United States and other coalition partners punishing those involved in such acts, which further damaged the United States' narrative that it stood for justice, fairness, human rights, and human dignity. Moreover, such incidents repeatedly put the Afghan government in an awkward position and undermined its authority and religious credentials, thus damaging many Afghans' trust in the government. These acts also discouraged those Taliban who were inclined toward negotiations from reconciling and joining the peace process. Overall, these incidents served as gifts to the Taliban, allowing them to win hearts and minds, recruit more fighters, and convince many Afghans of the authenticity of their narrative and the legitimacy of their resistance.

Conclusion

The US-led war in Afghanistan (October 7, 2001–August 30, 2021) was unique for its length and extent, but also for unfolding as the internet and social media became widely available, making it the "first internet war," the "first social media war," and the "first tri-media war" involving the use of audio/radio, TV/video, and print/text simultaneously. Although information warfare and strategic communication have been part of conflict throughout human history, the second front of the war in Afghanistan was more challenging and complicated due to these advancements in communication technology and the nature of the conflict itself. The US/NATO forces, the US-backed Afghan government, and the Taliban increasingly invested more time and resources to win the hearts and minds of the public. Although the United States and the Afghan government had comparatively more resources and expertise, their strategic communication was confusing, contradictory, and, at times, even counterproductive; the opposite of the three C's the Taliban largely pursued in their communication strategy: concise, clear, and consistent. The Afghan government and its foreign backers, mainly the United States, on the whole proved unable to exploit the Taliban's weaknesses and mistakes properly and consistently. However, the biggest flaw in the US information warfare was to become its own worst enemy: its lack of cultural awareness and repeated violations of local norms and traditions, which affected both its military and information operations. Insults to Afghan culture and violations of religious norms as well as the killing and abuses of civilians by US/NATO soldiers came at a huge cost to the overall mission. They also repeatedly put the Afghan government in an awkward position and undermined its authority and religious credentials. Moreover, such acts discouraged even those Taliban who were inclined toward negotiations and joining the peace process.

Although the Taliban had banned the internet and television when they were first in power (1996–2001), their approach to the internet, television, and other relevant platforms changed after the toppling of their regime in 2001. They started using the internet skillfully and established "virtual sanctuaries" in the form of multilingual websites as part of their information warfare. They used a combination of Afghan nationalism, Islamic ideology, and appeals to cultural norms and history to win over popular opinion. Compared to the counterinsurgents, the insurgents' media and propaganda activities were more direct and focused and, with the passage of time, became increasingly sophisticated. The Taliban rarely missed an opportunity to exploit the mistakes, missteps, and weaknesses of the United States and the Afghan government. As I observed firsthand throughout the two-decade-long war, the repeated mistakes made by the United States and its foreign allies, as well as the US-backed Afghan government—and their exploitation by the Taliban—played a more effective role in alienating the Afghan public at large than the Taliban's propaganda itself.

Notes

Epigraph 1: "Chi rishtiya rādzi, darwāghu ba kali wrān kaṛi wi"

[چي رشـتيا راخي، درواغـو بـه كـلي وران كـري وي].

A popular Pashto proverb translated into English by the author.

Epigraph 2: "Rāsti ke ba darogh mānd, magoi"

[راسـتی کـه بـه دروغ مـاند، مگـوی].

A popular Persian/Dari proverb translated into English by the author.

Epigraph 3: "Chi bāwar di pa rishtiya khabara na kā / wa hagho wa ta ba tsa khwre sawganduna."

[چـي بـاور دي پـه رشـتيا خبـره نـه کا / و هـغو وتـه به څـه خـوري سوگنـدونه]

(Khattak 2018, 626). The Pashto verse has been translated into English by the author.

1   For more information on US/NATO and Taliban/insurgent media, propaganda, and the role of international funding in shaping the US Forever War, see Osman (2020) and Sienkiewicz (2016).

2   The declaration (dated August 5, 2018) with a brief introduction was sent to the media by the Taliban's main spokesman, Zabihullah Mujahid, on August 7, 2018, and was published on the same day on the group's official website, Alemarah, titled, "Da hiwād ulamāi kirāmu pa stara ghonda ki da jihād himāyat wakaṛ" (The country's respected [religious] scholars declared support for jihad in a grand gathering). The Taliban spokesman's statement did not specify the location of this gathering. But a Taliban-linked website, Nunn Asia, said it was held in Kuchlak, a small town near Quetta, Pakistan. See Nunn Asia (2018). The quotations from Alemarah and Nunn Asia websites have been translated from Pashto into English by the author.

3   The Taliban's statement in Pashto was published on their website at the
time, Alemara1 (on October 29, 2011—the day of the attack), but this
website was later closed.

References

Alemarah. 2018. "Da hiwād ulamāi kirāmu pa stara ghonda ki da jihād
himāyat wakaṛ" [The country's respected (religious) scholars de-
clared support for jihad in a grand gathering]. Taliban's statement
published on the group's official website. August 7. https://www
.alemarah.af/news/highlights-of-the-country-and-the-world
/%D8%AF-%D9%87%DB%8C%D9%88%D8%A7%D8%AF
-%D8%B9%D9%84%D9%85%D8%A7%D8%A1
-%DA%A9%D8%B1%D8%A7%D9%85%D9%88
-%D9%BE%D9%87-%D8%B3%D8%AA%D8%B1%D9%87
-%D8%BA%D9%88%D9%86%DA%89%D9%87-%DA%A9%DB%90
-%D8%AF-%D8%AC/.
Alemara1. 2011a. "Pa afghanistan ki da masihiyat dāmuna" [Traps of Chris-
tianity in Afghanistan]. Taliban's commentary in Pashto on their official
website. October 17. http://www.alemara1.com.
Alemara1. 2011b. "Self-Martyrdom Attack on the Intelligence Agency
Office Caused Heavy Losses to the Enemy." Taliban's statement in
Pashto language. October 29. http://alemara1.com/index.php?option
=com_content&view=article&id=18777:2011-10-29-08-31-35&catid
=1:news&Itemid=51.
Al Jazeera. 2009. "US Burns Bibles in Afghanistan Row." May 22. https://
www.aljazeera.com/news/2009/5/22/us-burns-bibles-in-afghanistan-row.
Azami, Dawood. 2009a. "Guantanamo Memoirs Prove Bestsellers." BBC,
February 23. http://news.bbc.co.uk/1/hi/world/south_asia/7905643.stm.
Azami, Dawood. 2009b. "Taliban Slick Propaganda Confronts US." BBC,
August 3. http://news.bbc.co.uk/2/hi/south_asia/8176259.stm.
Azami, Dawood. 2010. "Taliban Harness Power of the Web." BBC, March 17.
http://news.bbc.co.uk/1/hi/world/south_asia/8570742.stm.
Azami, Dawood. 2012. "Taliban Poetry and the Lone Fighter." BBC, July 10.
https://www.bbc.co.uk/news/world-asia-17905361.
Azami, Dawood. 2013. "The 'Dissenting' Clerics Killed in Afghanistan." BBC,
November 19. https://www.bbc.co.uk/news/world-asia-22885170.
Azami, Dawood. 2014. "Life After Guantanamo Prison." BBC, February 25.
https://www.bbc.co.uk/news/magazine-26257747.
Azami, Dawood. 2021. "Hybrid Insecurity and Actors and Factors in the
Conflict in Afghanistan." In In Search of Peace for Afghanistan, edited by
Jawan Shir Rasikh, 218–246. Kabul: Kakar History Foundation.
BBC. 2011. "Afghanistan: Suicide Attack Kills 13 Foreign Personnel." Octo-
ber 29. https://www.bbc.co.uk/news/world-south-asia-15504922.

BBC. 2012. "Afghan Koran 'Burning': US Apologises." February 12. https://www.bbc.co.uk/news/world-asia-17116595.

BBC Pashto. 2022. "Sirajuddin Haqqani: 'Yawāzi zuma la lāsa yaw zar aw pindzos istishhādiyān ter shawi di'" [Sirajuddin Haqqani: "One thousand and fifty martyrdom operators have passed through my hand alone"]. February 23. https://www.bbc.com/pashto/afghanistan-60497072.

Bowley, Graham, and Matthew Rosenberg. 2012. "Video Inflames a Delicate Moment for U.S. in Afghanistan." *New York Times*, January 12. https://www.nytimes.com/2012/01/13/world/asia/video-said-to-show-marines-urinating-on-taliban-corpses.html.

Braman, Ed. 2003. "To What End? War Reporting in the Television Age." *RUSI Journal* 148 (6): 26–30. https://doi.org/10.1080/03071840308446942.

Dawn. 2010. "Woman Suicide Bomber Strikes at WFP Centre; 45 Killed." December 25. https://www.dawn.com/news/593552/explosion-in-bajaur-agencies-khar-head-quarter-several-injured.

Gibbons-Neff, Thomas, Sharif Hassan, and Ruhullah Khapalwak. 2021. "Taliban Honor Suicide Bombers' 'Sacrifices' in Bid to Rewrite History." *New York Times*, October 23. Updated November 3, 2021. https://www.nytimes.com/2021/10/23/world/asia/afghanistan-taliban-suicide-bombers.html.

Guardian. 2005. "US Soldiers 'Desecrated Taliban Bodies.'" October 20. https://www.theguardian.com/world/2005/oct/20/usa.afghanistan.

ICG (International Crisis Group). 2008. "Taliban Propaganda: Winning the War of Words?" Asia Report No. 158, July 24.

Keenan, Thomas. 2001. "Looking like Flames and Falling like Stars: Kosovo, 'the First Internet War.'" *Social Identities* 7 (4): 539–550. https://doi.org/10.1080/13504630120107692.

Khaama Press. 2011. "Female Suicide Bomber Kills 1 in Eastern Kunar." October 29. https://www.khaama.com/female-suicide-bomber-storms-government-building-in-kunar-122/.

Khattak, Khushhal Khan. 2018. *Da Khushhāl Khān Khattak Diwān* [Collection of poetry of Khushhal Khan Khattak]. Edited by Habibullah Rafi. Kabul: Aman Book Publishing Institute.

Leithead, Alastair. 2007. "Anger Over 'Blasphemous' Balls." BBC, August 26. http://news.bbc.co.uk/1/hi/world/south_asia/6964564.stm.

Martinez, Luis. 2012. "No Criminal Charges for Soldiers in Koran Burning." *ABC News*, August 27. https://abcnews.go.com/Blotter/criminal-charges-soldiers-koran-burning/story?id=17090174.

Morgan, Wesley. 2018. "Military Investigating Shooting in Newly Leaked Afghan Combat Video." *Politico*, January 10. https://www.politico.com/story/2018/01/10/military-investigating-shooting-afghanistan-battlefield-video-276534.

New York Times. 2017. "U.S. General in Afghanistan Apologizes for 'Offensive' Leaflet." September 6. https://www.nytimes.com/2017/09/06/world/asia/afghanistan-taliban-leaflet-us-apology-dog.html.

Nunn Asia. 2018. "Dini ālimānu da tālibānu pa mlātaṛ aw ishghāl par zad prekṛalik khpor kaṛ" [Religious scholars issued declaration in support of the Taliban and against the occupation]. Taliban-linked website's article in Pashto. August 7. https://www.nunn.asia /126670/%d8%af%db%8c%d9%86%d9%8a-%d8%b9%d8%a7%d 9%84%d9%85%d8%a7%d9%86%d9%88-%d8%af-%d8%b7%d8% a7%d9%84%d8%a8%d8%a7%d9%86%d9%88-%d9%be%d9%87 -%d9%85%d9%84%d8%a7%d8%aa%da%93-%d8%a7%d9%88 -%d8%a7%d8%b4%d8%ba%d8%a7/.

OIC (Organisation of Islamic Cooperation). 2018. "Declaration International Ulema Conference for Peace and Security in Afghanistan." July 11. https://www.oic-oci.org/topic/?t_id=19804&t_ref=11394&lan=en.

Osman, Wazhmah. 2020. *Television and the Afghan Culture Wars: Brought to You by Foreigners, Warlords, and Activists.* Urbana: University of Illinois Press. https://muse.jhu.edu/book/81069.

Pajhwok. 2011. "Teen-Age Girl Carried Out Kunar Attack: Taliban." June 4. https://pajhwok.com/2011/06/04/teen-age-girl-carried-out -kunar-attack-taliban/.

Rahimi, Sangar, and Alissa Rubin. 2012. "Koran Burning in NATO Error Incites Afghans." *New York Times,* February 21. https://www.nytimes.com /2012/02/22/world/asia/nato-commander-apologizes-for-koran-disposal -in-afghanistan.html.

Reuters. 2009. "U.S. Military Says Afghan Bibles Have Been Destroyed." May 5. https://www.reuters.com/article/us-afghanistan-proselytising-sb -idUSTRE5441JH20090505.

Reuters. 2011. "Woman Was Behind Afghan Suicide Attack: Ministry." June 22. https://www.reuters.com/article/world/woman-was-behind -afghan-suicide-attack-ministry-idUSTRE65L164/.

RFE/RL (Radio Free Europe/Radio Liberty). 2012. "Taliban Calls for Violence over Koran Burnings As Protests Continue." February 23. https:// www.rferl.org/a/taliban_call_for_violence_against_westerners_koran _burning/24493308.html/.

Siddique, Abubakar. 2021. "As Taliban Attempts to Transform from Insurgency to Government, Suicide Bombers Remain Key to Its Strategy." RFE/RL, November 4. https://www.rferl.org/a/taliban-suicide-bombings -afghanistan/31546216.html.

Sienkiewicz, Matt. 2016. *The Other Air Force: U.S. Efforts to Reshape Middle Eastern Media Since 9/11.* New Brunswick, NJ: Rutgers University Press.

SIGAR (Special Inspector General for Afghanistan Reconstruction). 2023. "High-Risk List: Report Highlights Major Sources of Risk to U.S. Assistance Efforts in Afghanistan." April 19. https://www.sigar.mil/Portals/147 /Files/Reports/High-Risk-List/High-Risk-List-2023.pdf.

Tolo News. 2018a. "Afghan Clerics Declare Current War Un-Islamic." June 4. https://tolonews.com/afghanistan/afghan-clerics-issue-joint-fatwa-call -ongoing-war-illegal.

Tolo News. 2018b. "Mattis Sends Letter to Saudi Prince About Afghan Peace." July 10. https://tolonews.com/index.php/afghanistan/mattis-sends-letter-saudi-prince-about-afghan-peace.

Townsend, Sarah J. 2019. "Money Mazes, Media Machines, and Banana Republic Realisms." *American Literary History* 31 (4): 687–714. https://doi.org/10.1093/alh/ajz040.

UNAMA (United Nations Assistance Mission in Afghanistan). 2011a. *Afghanistan Annual Report 2010: Protection of Civilians in Armed Conflict.* Kabul, Afghanistan, March. https://unama.unmissions.org/sites/default/files/engi_version_of_poc_annual_report_2011.pdf.

UNAMA (United Nations Assistance Mission in Afghanistan). 2011b. *Afghanistan Midyear Report 2011: Protection of Civilians in Armed Conflict.* Kabul, Afghanistan, July. https://www.ohchr.org/sites/default/files/Documents/Countries/2011MidyearUNAMAReport_2011.pdf.

US Army. 2010. "Combined Forces Conduct Air Assault, Secure Chenar." July 24. https://www.army.mil/article/42803/combined_forces_conduct_air_assault_secure_chenar.

VOA (Voice of America). 2018. "Nicholson: US Planning Religious, Diplomatic, Military and Social Pressure on Taliban." March 19. https://www.voanews.com/a/john-nicholson-us-religious-diplomatic-military-social-pressure-taliban-afghanistan/4305595.html.

VOA (Voice of America). 2021. "US-Wanted Taliban Leader Praises Suicide Bombers, Doles Out Rewards to Heirs." October 19. https://www.voanews.com/a/us-wanted-taliban-leader-praises-suicide-bombers-doles-out-rewards-to-heirs-/6277407.html.

Part 4

Reflecting & Speaking Back to Empire

Between Humanitarian Aid and Political Critique

Afghan American Mobilizations
Post-Evacuations

On August 15, 2021, the Taliban captured Kabul, Afghanistan, marking the end of its military campaign and takeover of the central government. Shortly thereafter, the Biden administration shifted its initial plan to withdraw the US military from Afghanistan from September 11 to August 31. In the days after, 76,000 people scrambled to get on government-chartered flights to transit countries like Qatar, Uganda, and Albania, while hundreds of thousands found themselves stuck in place as they attempted to apply for humanitarian visas to nearby countries like Tajikistan and Uzbekistan, and distant ones like the United States, Canada, the UK, and Australia (Kessler 2022). This period marked a devastating moment for many in the global Afghan diaspora and a uniquely significant turning point for Afghan Americans. As citizens of the country that inaugurated the military invasion of Afghanistan in October 2001 and the "Global War on Terror" (GWOT), young adult Afghan Americans have had a complicated relationship to the US imperial state over the last twenty-four years. Some had friends and family members who were internally or externally displaced, killed, or impoverished as employment opportunities waned during the later years of the war, while others witnessed their relatives and friends experience socioeconomic and professional mobility in the new war economy, including in the saturated NGO and development landscape.

Within the borders of a post-9/11 United States, Afghan Americans themselves confronted a paradoxical situation. On the one hand, they were hailed by the US state as potential cultural experts who could provide valuable cultural knowledge to the US military-humanitarian apparatus as it led a large-scale reconstruction effort. On the other hand, they were socially marginalized by increasing anti-Muslim racism and xenophobic laws and policies like the Patriot Act and the National Security Entry-Exit Registration System (NSEERS) program. As argued by cultural anthropologist Morwari Zafar (2016; see also Zafar's chapter in this volume), Afghan Americans have had a complicated relationship with the GWOT in that recognition and visibility have coincided with human tragedy in Afghanistan. From 2001 to 2021, those in the diaspora found themselves having to navigate between what sociologist Neda Maghbouleh (2017) has described (in relation to the Iranian American diaspora) as invisibility and hypervisibility. Post-9/11, Afghan Americans transformed from an invisible minority to what anthropologist Nadine Naber (2012) has described (in the context of the Arab American diaspora) as a "problem minority" reduced to either the figure of the oppressed Muslim woman or the terrorist male threat. Situated within the paradoxes of an imperial state that has afforded recognition but enacted violence, offered professional opportunities in the war economy but practiced racialized discrimination, many in the US Afghan diaspora have ambivalently participated in policy conversations and public critiques of the US-led war.

In recent years, however, diasporic voices have been more outspoken about the many ways that Afghan life has been rendered ungrievable during the GWOT (Gregory 2012; Zeweri and Gregory 2023). Critiques have also highlighted the notable absence of Afghanistan within academic, media, and even activist conversations about the US military invasion of Iraq (Daulatzai et al. 2022; see the introduction). While the two wars were waged under very different premises, they were both framed as altruistic and virtuous wars designed to defeat al-Qaeda and all forms of terrorism authorized by a global Islamic fundamentalist ideology. As Wazhmah Osman has written, "From its outset, the War on Terror was framed by a massive policy/media apparatus as a 'good war' . . . render[ing] a complex, messy, prolonged, and multipronged military apparatus stretching across vast space and time into a legible singular logic of a just and necessary global war" (2022, 369).

While the realities of war were understood and felt by many in the diaspora since the beginning of the GWOT, the crisis of displacement in August 2021 foregrounded how American empire functioned to control mass migration and Afghan mobilities. By focusing on the public critiques Afghan American community organizers made during and in the aftermath of the withdrawal, this chapter argues that humanitarian aid efforts in the context of mass displacement and prolonged imperial intervention can create the seeds for anti-war critique.

By examining narratives from an activist group that emerged shortly before the withdrawal, my analysis seeks to move beyond the idea of Afghan life as existing in a static and perpetual state of humanitarian crisis. Instead, this chapter thinks about Afghan life as politically agentive and deeply conscious of the roots of injustice. Anthropologist Didier Fassin defines humanitarian government as the "deployment of moral sentiment" in order to enact change. Fassin views humanitarian government as a limited form of action that cannot fully address injustice (2011). In this chapter, I offer an example in which moral sentiment actually becomes the starting point for addressing injustice. Describing humanitarian sentiment as incapable of addressing injustice does not always apply when such sentiment emerges at a collective breaking point after a group has experienced and witnessed ongoing and cumulative forms of imperial violence. I posit that Afghan American community organizer experiences supporting evacuation efforts did not deploy moral sentiment in a vacuum but in the wake of decades of witnessing the human tragedies of war and living with its consequences, including displacement and the fragmentation of their social ties therein. I ask, therefore, how does the process of witnessing the suffering of mass displacement from a diasporic vantage point produce the collective will to address injustice?

It is important to establish the caveat that Afghan American public activism in the post-2021 moment is not homogeneous. Some collectives that emerged after the withdrawal believed the US/NATO project in Afghanistan was morally justified and, while poorly executed, ultimately led with noble intentions. Other collectives critiqued American immigration policy for not recognizing the contributions that Afghan refugees could make to the American economy and society, thus reproducing the idea that displaced people need to prove their worthiness of refuge by demonstrating their labor potential, a paradigm that organizes many Global North state approaches to refugee resettlement and integration (Gowayed 2022). Others used the language of "allyship" to convey that Afghan nationals who served as interpreters for the US military should be prioritized for resettlement because they had already proven their loyalty to the United States, suggesting a hierarchy of not only suffering (Fassin 2011) but also loyalty to and labor for the imperial state.

This chapter specifically focuses on the narratives of two community organizers whose critiques denormalize the notion that imperial wars necessitate political expediencies that produce mass displacement and reinforce securitized borders. It is important to note that such critiques are not necessarily rooted in a politics of open borders or no borders. Such organizers believe in the importance of the imperial host state as a source of governance, social welfare, and human rights for displaced people. In that sense, their politics emphasizes the nation-state as the purveyor of mobility, legal status, and rights. The argument of this chapter is thus a modest one: activist narratives in the aftermath of the withdrawal contain within them the seeds for future forms of collective action that frame war as both a problem of occupation and a problem of mass displacement. Afghan American community organizers' experiences supporting the displaced revealed to them that displaced people are also part of the human collateral of American empire. In witnessing the humanitarian crisis of the evacuations, community leaders were galvanized to mobilize, using social media platforms and in-person protests to hold government bureaucracies accountable for long wait times for visa applications like humanitarian parole, P-1/P-2 visas, and Special Immigrant Visas (SIVs).

This chapter contributes to emergent scholarship on Afghan diasporic life that turns attention to forms of collective action and diasporic subjectivity shaped by multiple geographies of displacement (Oeppen 2010; Olszewksa 2015; Rostami-Povey 2007; Shahimi et al. 2023). In doing so, it centers political dissent in addition to taking seriously the suffering and trauma of the lived experience of displacement. Studies of Afghan life must be approached from an intersectional lens, keeping in mind the multiple subject positions that produce a unique experience of diasporic subjectivity, including race, ethnolinguistic background, class, gender, sexuality, religion, citizenship status, and ability, among other positionalities. As sociologist Saugher Nojan has argued in a study of Afghan American Muslim refugees' experiences of racialization, it is both religion and ethnic background, as well as historical experiences of imperialism and immigration, that have produced Afghan American Muslims as subjects who are marginalized in specific ways (2022).

To be an Afghan American diasporic subject is to have experienced a wide spectrum of discrimination and privilege in the United States relative to both US-based minorities and other displaced Afghan communities throughout the world. The experiences of Afghan refugees in Pakistan and Iran, for example, should not be conflated with those of second-generation Afghan Americans or more recently arrived immigrants, socially, materially, or culturally. Afghan Americans also have a distinct experience of marginalization relative to other Muslim American and South Asian groups in post-9/11 America. This is due in large part to the ways in which the diasporic elite in particular were encouraged by the US state to participate in the broader military-humanitarian-development regime being established in Afghanistan, and in domestic initiatives designed to sell the occupation as a morally legitimate and necessary one. Political dissent within the diaspora should be thought about as a question of power and privilege. For example, many US-based community leaders have benefited from being US citizens, which affords them the privilege of not having to worry as much (relative to more recently arrived communities) about the consequences of speaking out against the US government. Many community leaders have also had access to educational and professional mobility that affords them the money, time, social networks, and cultural capital to be able to organize political protests and initiatives.

These forms of privilege and recognition have coexisted with racialized and gendered discrimination and violence. As scholars of the GWOT Morwari Zafar (2016), Sunaina Maira (2009), Khaled Beydoun (2018), and Purnima Bose (2020) have documented, many in the Afghan American and South Asian community confronted anti-Muslim racism after the events of 9/11. Others confronted the stereotypes of "terrorist" or "religious extremist" for males, while females who were visibly Muslim or who identified as Afghan were consistently called on to answer questions about the state of women in the Southwest Asian and North African region. Still others had to confront the burden of speaking for all Afghans and Muslims, seen as people who were simply vectors of cultural knowledge and expertise by virtue of being born into an Afghan or Muslim family.

Thus, this chapter, in foregrounding a very select sliver of narratives in the immediate aftermath of August 2021, does not represent or speak for any one community's experiences. It gives one example of how diasporic people mobilize not as cultural experts but as politically conscious citizens who are aware of the American landscape and continue to consider the United States' fraught history of imperial intervention. They are deeply connected with other members of a global Afghan community who care about and are connected to Afghanistan in various ways. Insights from two community leaders show that humanitarian crises can be the impetus for long-term diasporic mobilization. In this case, the humanitarian crisis of 2021 became the point of departure for a broader political critique of the laws and policies that justify the wars that contribute to mass displacement.

Much literature in the anthropology of diasporas focuses on diasporic political mobilization as emerging after a humanitarian crisis. But what do we make of situations in which diasporas use humanitarian aid to enact political critique? Studies in the anthropology of humanitarianism have examined how humanitarian aid is used to address short-term crises without addressing the broader political issues that underlie such crises (Redfield 2013; Ticktin 2011). Peter Redfield has written that humanitarian organizations like Doctors Without Borders try to avoid getting involved in political issues but cannot do so completely when the crises they are addressing are produced by long-standing political conflicts or government policies (2013). In other cases, humanitarian approaches to displacement are far from neutral (Feldman 2018; Garelli and Tazzioli 2017). Sienna Craig has shown that humanitarian aid can be used toward political ends by the Tibetan diaspora through carrying out responsibilities that the state refuses to undertake (2011). Erica Caple James argues that humanitarian interventions in Haiti cannot be detached from politics because they are rooted in long colonial and imperial histories. The diaspora's involvement in humanitarian aid leads to larger political discussions about the future of Haiti as an imperial colony (2010). Ilana Feldman's work on humanitarian aid in Palestinian refugee camps shows how refugees think about aid as both opening up and limiting political possibilities for Palestinian return (2018), while Nell Gabiam has shown how the present-focused temporality of humanitarian aid in UN Relief and Works Agency camps can keep the urgency of the Palestinian cause alive more than long-term empowerment programs (2012). In sum, whether or not humanitarian intervention becomes a tool for social justice depends on the cumulative set of historical issues such interventions are responding to.

In this chapter, I argue that humanitarian aid efforts can be politically galvanizing for diasporic peoples, especially when they unfold outside the formal infrastructures of humanitarian aid. Providing aid under urgent conditions without the support of the state that has contributed to the conditions of crisis, coupled with witnessing a pattern of imperial violence, can produce the starting point for sustained forms of political mobilization. As Yarimar Bonilla and Marison LeBrón have analyzed, the aftermath of Hurricane Maria in Puerto Rico marked a new wave of political mobilization in the Puerto Rican diaspora marked by new modes of questioning the geopolitical power dynamics that sustain the imperial relationship between the island and the United States (2019). Diasporic vantage points of humanitarian crises are also, then, witnessings of how the imperial core manages the human fallout of prolonged occupation and can prompt a deeper questioning of its political conditions of possibility.

Afghan American Political Participation: Beyond "Conflicting Identities"

Studies of Afghan American diasporic life have tended to focus on how diasporic subjects navigate the challenges of being American and Afghan, what some have called a hyphenated identity (Aseel 2003; Sadat 2007). In these studies, diasporic Afghans are depicted as constantly having to navigate the conflicting demands of culture and American society, creating the impression that Afghan Americans live in insulated communities whose concerns are not shaped by their local and domestic political issues. The framework of conflicting identities also leaves little room to understand Afghan American civic and political engagement outside of an ethnocentric and insular community framework. However, more recent literature has put into question the binary of Afghan versus American identity through positing that diasporic Afghans inhabit intersectional subjectivities that are shaped by the changing political and social landscape of their countries of residence and/or citizenship and their transnational connections to Afghanistan, whose future has become entangled with US and broader geopolitics (Hakimi 2023; Nojan 2022; Rokay 2021; Zafar 2016). The complication of the dual-identity binary can also be portable to other contexts in which Afghan migrants have resettled. As Zuzanna Olszewska has written, Afghan refugees in Iran experience their identities in complicated ways that are not captured by the dual-identity narrative. Rather, their identities are also shaped by how they are interpellated by other people and institutions (2015).

Scholarship on political and social life in the Afghan diaspora is spread across multiple disciplines (history, anthropology, literary studies, and area studies) (Ahmed-Ghosh 2015; Green and Arbabzadeh 2012; Hanifi 2016; Oeppen 2010; Olszewska 2015; Rostami-Povey 2007; Zafar 2016). Other groundbreaking ethnographic and historical studies have looked at how social and political consciousness in Afghanistan is shaped by a range of institutions, including broadcast media and radio, humanitarian aid, development, and prolonged occupation (Massoumi 2022; Osman 2020; Qasmi 2020). However, there is minimal literature on how Afghan diasporic humanitarian mobilization has been used to address timely political and social issues within the diaspora. Taking cues from historian Robert D. Crews's idea that Afghanistan is a global nation whose diaspora has "inhabited all parts of the globe far beyond the borders of their country" (2015, 1), this chapter examines how those who live outside Afghanistan's borders think about the role their country of residence plays in the lives of those who remain in a place they feel deeply connected and committed to. In doing so, it contributes to ongoing discussions of diasporic identity formation and political mobilization in the Global North in the wake of mass displacement and imperial violence (Bonilla and Rosa 2015; Maira 2016; Naber 2012).

Methods

This chapter is based on an ongoing ethnographic and historical project that examines Afghan American political movements as of the beginning of the GWOT. It also draws insight from projects I carried out from 2008 to 2010, from 2014 to 2016, and from 2021 to the present. The insights from this chapter are based on my analysis of the advocacy work of community organizers who joined to form Afghans for a Better Tomorrow (AFBT), an organization that emerged shortly before the US withdrawal. The analysis is based on interview insights and traces how organizers' approaches and critiques changed over time. Some of the insights also stem from my own involvement in supporting nationals evacuated in 2021, the exchanges I had with these organizers, and the observations I made of how their organization evolved in the months that followed. The analysis represents one sliver of community organizing, since AFBT supports a left-leaning progressive platform on a range of issues that go well beyond immigration. For example, AFBT has led initiatives around climate justice from an intersectional perspective, and the founders themselves have a background in racial and social justice organizing in the United States. The insights from these community leaders are not meant to produce a positivistic generalization about Afghan American political mobilization or Afghan diasporic political life. They serve, rather, to present: (1) an example of diasporic subjects as politically agentive and (2) an example of how humanitarian aid can open up political engagement.

From Humanitarian Aid to Policy Advocacy

In the spring and summer of 2021, several organizations led by Afghan Americans were created and expressly dedicated to evacuating Afghan nationals. They quickly launched websites, social media accounts, and online fundraisers designed to help nationals who were stuck in the country with little food and money, confronting a collapsing economy and potential global isolation, and who were attempting to be admitted onto US-chartered flights out of the country. In large part, facilitating the mobility of Afghan nationals who sought entry into the United States fell on the diaspora, as US government institutions failed to provide timely and efficient processing for those desperate to flee. Organizations like the Afghan Diaspora Hub, AFBT, Afghans Empowered, and the Afghan American Foundation began to evacuate loved ones, friends, and ordinary people who reached out through emails, WhatsApp, Signal, Facebook, and Instagram with messages seeking help. In this humanitarian crisis, social media platforms became critical tools for communicating about the most efficient pathways to temporary refuge in countries near and far. As they mobilized to facilitate movement out of the country, some community leaders began to more publicly and directly critique the withdrawal, the slow processing times, and the war more broadly.

Afghans for a Better Tomorrow formed in May 2021, after the Biden administration announced that the United States was planning a military withdrawal from Afghanistan. One of the founders of AFBT, Tameem,[1] had been a community organizer several years prior, mobilizing local communities around labor rights and anti-war protests. Influenced by the Palestinian resistance movement and the Black civil rights movement in the United States, Tameem believed that the GWOT and the various cycles of displacement it produced therein were reflective of systemic global inequalities that had deeply colonial roots and impacted a range of racialized and minoritized communities including but not limited to Afghan refugees. Prior to AFBT, Tameem was an organizer with a diasporic organization that focused on civic education for first and second generation Afghan American youth on issues of national and global importance, including environmental justice, climate change, civil rights, and immigrants' rights. Tameem's desire to address injustice was also shaped by his work as a journalist who covered the Black Lives Matter movement in 2020. Having come of age after the events of 9/11, Tameem had come to see how pressing social and economic injustices cut across multiple racialized minorities.

In August, Tameem came to play a critical role in helping people evacuate Afghanistan. Drawing on his network of journalist contacts from years prior, he came to serve as an important source of information to a network of Afghan Americans seeking to help family and loved ones escape via Kabul's Hamid Karzai International Airport (HKIA). At the time, leaving via a US or other NATO-power chartered flight from HKIA was the only viable way out of the country since land borders had limited openings and other airports were rendered nonfunctional. Tameem also served as an important source of information for how people seeking to flee and the diaspora could navigate the minefield of US immigration bureaucracy, which now confronted an unprecedented number of requests for humanitarian visas and temporary forms of admission.

As weeks passed, Tameem began to see that simply requesting evacuation through an online form made available to Afghan nationals by the US embassy in Kabul (which shut down its physical offices and began to operate from the Kabul airport), was a futile effort, as hardly any requests received replies. Tameem and another AFBT member with whom I spoke, Neelab, began to realize that getting on US embassy evacuation lists and the manifest lists of both government and private NGO-chartered flights yielded little success. AFBT organizers completed spreadsheets with evacuees' information, while also keeping up to date on the latest invitations by congresspeople's offices via Twitter, Instagram, and Facebook, to complete evacuation request forms (usually a Google form or an Excel spreadsheet that asked for people's names, addresses, contact information, and one line noting why they felt their lives were under threat). The email addresses of US embassy offices as well as Department of State offices changed each day due to an overload of evacuation requests. While forms were filled with alarming speed, for many people they diminished into the bureaucratic ether, never to be heard about again. Having to send such forms for the third or fourth time to government offices was unsettling.

At the same time, such bureaucratic tools and their repetitive appearances made people in AFBT feel a proximity to the state, giving organizers the impression that a resolution was close. But this was usually followed by a sense of disillusionment when requests were never met with a response. Neelab noted the frustration at how the process unfolded during this period:

> My mom's eldest uncle was [in Kabul], and he was like "The Taliban is coming, what do we do?" So I was trying to evacuate him and his family.

I had another uncle who was my dad's cousin, who is an American citizen, and his wife is a legal permanent resident but they were in Kabul when Kabul fell. They essentially became trapped and were not able to get on any plane. I worked around the clock to get them out. The fact that he had an American passport—he was at the top of the list—but because of the chaos at the airport he wasn't able to get out. I don't think I got much sleep in those two weeks. Not only worrying about my family, but also on a daily basis, adjusting advocacy points, call scripts for Congress, demand scripts for Biden, putting it out on social media, talking to other groups. In terms of evacuations, there was so much going on at that point in time. It was a whirlwind—very little sleep, stress, anxiety. Since then, as the months have progressed, there's still so much that feels frustrating. When it comes to immigration, when it comes to visas, when it comes to the resettlement process here in the US. Switching to more full-time advocacy in the US versus evacuations since then, but it's still a level of frustration, being upset at the systems in place. (Interview with Neelab, May 2022)

Here, Neelab narrates what it felt like to be on the other side of the crisis. This experience was marked by intensity, both in terms of humanitarian aid and advocacy. While she was trying to evacuate her father's cousin and his wife, she was also working with AFBT to advocate for changes to immigration policies—dealing with both the symptoms of an overwhelmed immigration system and its systemic blind spots. Neelab took part in campaigns calling on Congress to demand that US Citizenship and Immigration Services accelerate its review of humanitarian parole applications and hire more personnel. Being part of an unfolding humanitarian crisis while simultaneously trying to reform the systems that gave rise to it produced feelings of anxiety, stress, and anger.

Neelab's experience exemplifies the affect of operating within the institutional realities of imperial bureaucracy during times of crisis. This feeling is captured by Sunaina Maira's theoretical framework of "imperial feelings," which describes how South Asian Muslim youth in America come to see themselves as part of an imperial state. This affective response emerges as a result of their experiences of racialized discrimination following the events of 9/11 and through developing a stronger consciousness of historical regimes of border control and surveillance in the United States (2009). Maira defines "imperial feelings" through Raymond Williams's idea of "structures of feeling," which refers to the ways of life and affective experiences that emerge from and reshape structures of domination. Imperial feelings "unify the emotional and structural dimensions of citizenship, and the public and private domains of politics, for it acknowledges that like nationalism, political identification is based on subjective feelings as well as 'rational' discourse" (Maira 2009, 25).

For Neelab's own community of family and friends, the withdrawal illustrated what she had begun to suspect in 2018—that Afghanistan would be a pawn in a broader set of diplomatic and political maneuvers. Neelab herself came from a Shia Hazara background. Having faced systematic marginalization in Afghanistan and within the Afghan diaspora in the United States, Neelab played a role in leading the Shia Racial Justice Coalition in her local community. Neelab was particularly struck by how the US-led peace talks in Doha did not consider the voices of ethnic and racial minorities. She articulated the centrality of the United States' role in creating the political decisions that ultimately gave rise to such a chaotic withdrawal:

> The Trump presidency had folks tuned in and as the Taliban peace talks started to take shape under the Trump presidency, I remember with ADEP [Afghan Diaspora for Equality and Progress—an organization she was involved in before AFBT] we had a campaign around ensuring Afghan women were at the table for the peace talks. We were working closely with Afghan activists and civil society leaders and they were telling us, "Look, if we don't have a seat at this table, we can potentially expect the worst. This was 2017 or 2018. . . . We had action items for the community, to be like "Hey reach out to the community, hey this what we need." There was not much support there and I think one of the reasons was that people saw this as a far-fetched thing—like the US will not give power back to the Taliban, we had a twenty-year war with them. Fast forward to the withdrawal plans Trump announced, and then Biden taking over and saying, "Yes we are gonna do it," and then leading up to August of last year, I think that really riled up people. Whereas folks were more skeptical of the US giving the Taliban power again, I think when August rolled around, there was a lot of anger, disbelief, and all of that shifted into this more progressive mindset where now they understood that the US just doesn't care, this is part of their empire, and military exploits around the world. This is where the tide shifted, and people were connecting the dots a lot more. It's unfortunate it took such a tragic event and so much loss to reach that point, but I think it happened in that way as far as I can see with the folks that I know. (Interview with Neelab, May 2022)

Neelab describes the illuminating nature of the disillusioning withdrawal. For Neelab, the withdrawal reminded her of the political expediencies that preceded it, namely US diplomats' brokering of the Doha negotiations. In 2020, US diplomats met with Taliban leaders in Doha to develop an agreement that was designed to forge a path forward for peace in Afghanistan following the US/NATO withdrawal. Many critics of the Doha peace talks criticized it for its exclusion of the central government's representatives, and the absence of women and other ethnic minorities from the negotiating table (Jamal and Maley 2023). For Neelab, the peace talks represented one of several consecutive politically expedient moves led by the United States that rendered the most vulnerable, including ethnic minorities, afterthoughts.

For Tameem, the evacuation process solidified what had been a recent shift since 2018 in his own thinking about the twenty-year war, which he came to see as a form of occupation:

> For too long the Afghan diaspora in the US, including myself, we have been ignoring the Afghanistan question. We've been washing our hands of that situation and being quiet about it and not saying anything about it. I found that very strange actually. In 2018 specifically, Afghan women activists, like the Afghan Women's Network and Mary Akrami and Mahbouba Seraj [two well-known activists], they came to DC and met with all these legislators and they . . . reached out to the Afghan diaspora and no one showed up. I met them at the National Press Club, they were freaking out. [They were saying] "This is what's happening, Trump has put into motion this withdrawal and it's gonna' hand over the country to the Taliban." Everything they said in the spring of 2018 happened and some of those women still live there and some have been evacuated. I think that set into motion for me personally, we have to do something. So we started doing some congressional advocacy. . . . Did I think it was an occupation in 2012? Afghanistan did not live in my mind as something that was egregious in the way of the Palestinian occupation or the Iraq occupation. Some of that is sheer ignorance and maybe I was younger. I think its twofold. Even for them [Afghan Americans], perpetual crisis forces you to take part in harmful structures and some of it can be excused and some of it cannot be. . . . There's been some good [written] pieces about how that development money in Afghanistan, it creates this unequal power balance. Resources does not equal agency, equality, or equity. That's very much evident. We saw how quickly the country collapsed. . . . That is partially recreated here. We

are just a mirror reflection of what's happening at home. Some of the Afghan American community has been deeply complicit in not being critical enough of the twenty-year occupation. People made careers and money off this occupation; whether they served as cultural interpreters or actual interpreters, people have contracts with the DHS. . . . The war put us on the map. That invisibility within the structure of the US and also within other immigrant, Black, and Palestinian communities; it doesn't fit a narrative, our narrative is so complicated. (Interview with Tameem, April 2022)

Tameem notes that he did not always consider the war in Afghanistan an occupation. As he witnessed the withdrawal and connected it to previous instances in which Afghans themselves criticized the United States' role in bringing an authoritarian regime to power, the term *occupation* became a more apt way to describe what he had observed. He also expresses his belief that political consciousness has been shaped by the diaspora's complicated relationship to the American war economy, which offered tangible material benefits and forms of recognition for Afghan Americans but in the process shielded certain parts of the diaspora from its devastating effects, making it more difficult to question. According to Tameem, diasporic political consciousness has been limited by a sense of codependence on imperial powers for wealth, resources, and opportunities born out of a sense that crisis is imminent.

Tameem mentioned later in our conversation that the events of August 2021 made Afghan Americans feel like they could actually critique the war's foundational logics. Tameem noted that the events of 2021 marked a historical rupture in Afghan American political life in that Afghan Americans were being invited to "have a seat at the table unlike before, and maybe even to break the table." In August 2021, media outlets and immigration and legal advocacy organizations sought out Afghan American community leaders to lend their insights on the ever-changing situation in Afghanistan. Many took the opportunity to speak out on news shows, university-organized panel discussions, and social media about the underlying political and historical roots of the crisis and how it was being worsened by asylum procedures and immigration bureaucracies.

Tameem took up some of these invitations, seeing them as opportunities to change the narrative that Afghan Americans cared only about the evacuations and not the broader histories and imperial logics that gave rise to them. Tameem expressed that Afghans have a complicated relationship to the US state because US empire in Afghanistan has not primarily been a top-down imposition of political control—it has involved the participation of diasporic elites, exiles, and migrant returnees who have played key roles in the reconstruction of the country. While Tameem acknowledged that different figures have participated in imperial apparatuses to different extents, there was no easy divide between the colonizer and the colonized in a context where locals and diasporic subjects had benefited greatly by their relationships with the US humanitarian-development-military apparatus in Afghanistan. For Tameem, the evacuations and the ongoing shift in his views on the war culminated with him giving up his job and working full-time on organizing, advocacy, and humanitarian aid through AFBT.

As August 31 (the official withdrawal date) loomed ever closer, humanitarian parole emerged as another option to help Afghan nationals escape. Humanitarian parole is not a legal status but an authorization to enter the United States based on the Secretary of Homeland Security's determination that someone is facing a significant threat to their life. It offers temporary safety yet also demands that applicants prove they will not be public charges of the state. Illustrating that one would not be a public charge required that one find a financial sponsor, usually a US citizen, to demonstrate their capacity to financially support the applicant for approximately two years. For Tameem and Neelab, procuring such sponsors and collecting their financial information added a new layer to the evacuation process that felt punitive and restrictive. As Tameem noted, "Being Afghan is a lesson that things can get worse. Because the US supposedly cares about Afghanistan does not mean things will be okay. That's the 2001 lesson. We're all so easily disposable. That's the 2021 lesson." Witnessing the hurdles of finding refuge led AFBT to call for legislative and policy reforms.

In the months after August 2021, Tameem began to expand the work of AFBT and spearheaded a number of campaigns designed to turn attention to the root causes of the occupation as well as the ongoing problem of mass displacement. Many of AFBT's social media posts following the withdrawal directly called the US war in Afghanistan an occupation that was backed by war-profiteering corporations. In a post from October 2021, the organization included a graphic that noted, "No More Drone Strikes, No One Left Behind." In putting together both of these slogans, AFBT made a clear connection between the violence of aerial war and the violence of abandoning the displaced. In September 2021, AFBT also released a call to action that the United States repeal the 2001 and 2002 Authorizations for Use of Military Force Acts, which provided legal justification for the invasions of Afghanistan and Iraq, while also reemphasizing the need to welcome refugees. Here the injustices of the immigration system prompted a reflection on the legal foundations of the GWOT itself.

AFBT's activism around humanitarian parole was also a public statement on how managing the imperial core's borders is linked to both the political expediencies of imperial withdrawal and the foundational logics of the GWOT. In October 2021, AFBT arrived at the headquarters of the Department of Homeland Security with several boxes labeled "humanitarian parole" and demanded that USCIS's review of humanitarian parole applications be expedited. They then held a protest that featured newly arrived evacuees sharing their stories of filling out the daunting applications to secure some kind of temporary status. By holding a protest at DHS's headquarters, AFBT makes a claim on the US state, specifically the executive branch as accountable to the victims of imperial-driven mass displacement. As a powerful institutional symbol for the GWOT, DHS's formation in 2003 emerged out of the 2001 military intervention into Afghanistan and its premise that 9/11 was a symptom of the infiltration of religiously radical migrants into US borders. Such a premise led to the intensification of the securitization of migration in the United States. By bringing the conversation about humanitarian parole to DHS's headquarters, protestors showed that the fallout of the war in Afghanistan can be traced to domestic immigration bureaucracies.

These calls to action culminated in a larger AFBT campaign led by Tameem to pass what is known as the Afghan Adjustment Act (AAA) in Congress. The AAA would allow certain Afghan evacuees to apply for permanent residence after one year of being in the United States on humanitarian parole and would prevent them from being deported while their applications for permanent residence were pending review. AFBT members framed the Act as a responsibility of the United States to deal with the mass displacement born out of the hasty withdrawal and the twenty-year war that was continuing through ongoing drone strikes. In analyzing AFBT's efforts during the evacuation and its collective organizing, it becomes clear that the experiences navigating US bureaucracy became a galvanizing moment, an opportunity to rearticulate the links between displacement, exclusionary borders, and the institutional and theoretical justifications of war. Yarimar Bonilla's research on the rearticulation of political futures among labor activists in the French department of Guadeloupe is instructive here. Bonilla writes that the movement for national liberation must be understood not only in terms of its achieved outcomes but also for the ways in which it "transformed the landscape of political possibility" for Guadeloupe (2015, 4). While activists in the post-withdrawal landscape were not undertaking an entirely decolonial or anti-imperial politics, they still transformed the horizons of political possibility around justice for those displaced by imperial wars (5). The very attempt to reorient the public's attention to the laws that authorized the war, and to its effects on the displaced, changed the landscape of what could be said and thought when it comes to the United States' relationship with Afghanistan. It is now possible to consider the events of 2021 as part of a history of how imperial powers manage the human fallout of their political maneuverings.

Conclusion

This chapter has examined how moments of humanitarian crisis become the entry point for engaging in political forms of dissent by Afghan American community organizers in the wake of the 2021 US withdrawal from Afghanistan. Through their evacuation efforts, community organizers saw the difficulties Afghan civilians faced in finding refuge in a moment when they needed it most and when, ironically, the US military and humanitarian aid apparatus was most explicitly visible to and yet the least accessible to the Afghan people—as they were in the last two weeks of August. The question of refuge, then, has turned from a humanitarian question into a political one.

For those in the diaspora, the enduring effects of war and militarized humanitarianism make it difficult to see community building and connection as separate from collective political action. Being immersed in the crisis of the withdrawal galvanized people to engage in protests, collective vigils, and even art exhibits in which further dialogue and strategizing around refugee rights could take place. In this way, attempts to provide lifelines for displaced Afghans who sought refuge became entangled with critiques of US immigration policy toward Afghan civilians seeking evacuation and safe passage to transit countries. Organizations like AFBT, in calling for prompt assistance for displaced Afghans, also critiqued the institutions such as DHS that emerged out of the Global War on Terror and contributed to the securitization of borders that disproportionately affected postwar migrants. The call for humanitarian aid was paired with a call to provide Afghans with a pathway toward legal status, one way the US state could take responsibility for the mass displacement caused by the withdrawal.

Through this analysis, I have turned to how this moment allowed a diasporic collective to reframe the war not only as a humanitarian crisis but also as the human fallout of prolonged imperial intervention.

Note

1 The names of my interlocutors have been changed throughout this chapter. Both interlocutors have consented to their narratives and reflections of the evacuation being included in this analysis.

References

Ahmed-Ghosh, Huma. 2015. "Being a Woman, a Muslim, and an Afghan in the USA: Dilemmas of Displacements." In *Gendered Journeys: Women, Migration and Feminist Psychology*, edited by Olivia M. Espin, 123–141. London: Palgrave Macmillan.

Aseel, Maryam Qudrat. 2003. *Torn Between Two Cultures: An Afghan-American Woman Speaks Out*. Sacramento, CA: Capital Books.

Beydoun, Khaled. 2018. *American Islamophobia: Understanding the Roots and Rise of Fear*. Berkeley: University of California Press.

Bonilla, Yarimar. 2015. *Non-Sovereign Futures: French Caribbean Politics in the Wake of Disenchantment*. Chicago: University of Chicago Press.

Bonilla, Yarimar, and Marisol LeBrón. 2019. "Introduction: Aftershocks of Disaster." In *Aftershocks of Disaster: Puerto Rico Before and After the Storm*, edited by Yarimar Bonilla and Marison LeBrón, 1–17. New York: Haymarket Books.

Bonilla, Yarimar, and Jonathan Rosa. 2015. "#Ferguson: Digital Protest, Hashtag Ethnography, and the Racial Politics of Social Media in the United States." *American Ethnologist* 42 (1): 4–17.

Bose, Purnima. 2020. *Intervention Narratives: Afghanistan, the United States, and the Global War on Terror*. New Brunswick, NJ: Rutgers University Press.

Craig, Sienna. 2011. "Migration, Social Change, Health, and the Realm of the Possible: Women's Stories Between Nepal and New York." *Anthropology and Humanism* 36 (2): 193–214.

Crews, Robert D. 2015. *Afghan Modern: The History of a Global Nation*. Cambridge, MA: Belknap Press.

Daulatzai, Anila, Sahar Ghumkhor, and Saadia Toor. 2022. "Grievance as Movement: Conversations on Knowledge Production on Afghanistan and the Left." *Jadaliyya*, October 6. https://www.jadaliyya.com/Details /44486.

Fassin, Didier. 2011. *Humanitarian Reason: A Moral History of the Present*. Berkeley: University of California Press.

Feldman, Ilana. 2018. *Life Lived in Relief: Humanitarian Predicaments and Palestinian Refugee Politics*. Berkeley: University of California Press.

Gabiam, Nell. 2012. "When 'Humanitarianism' Becomes 'Development': The Politics of International Aid in Syria's Palestinian Refugee Camps." *American Anthropologist* 114 (1): 95–107.

Garelli, Glenda, and Martina Tazzioli. 2017. "Choucha Beyond the Camp: Challenging the Border of Migration Studies." In *The Borders of Europe: Autonomy of Migration, Tactics of Bordering*, edited by Nicholas De Genova, 165–184. Durham, NC: Duke University Press.

Gowayed, Heba. 2022. *Refuge: How the State Shapes Human Potential*. Princeton, NJ: Princeton University Press.

Green, Nile, and Nushin Arbabzadeh, eds. 2012. *Afghanistan in Ink: Literature Between Diaspora and Nation*. Oxford: Oxford University Press.

Gregory, Thomas. 2012. "Potential Lives, Impossible Deaths: Afghanistan, Civilian Casualties and the Politics of Intelligibility." *International Feminist Journal of Politics* 14 (3): 327–347.

Hakimi, Aziz A. 2023. "'Good Men Don't Elope': Afghan Migrant Men's Discourses on Labour Migration, Marriage, and Masculinity." *History and Anthropology* 34 (2): 260–283.

Hanifi, Shah Mahmoud. 2016. "The Pashtun Counter-Narrative." *Middle East Critique* 25 (4): 385–400.

Jamal, Ahmad Shuja, and William Maley. 2023. *The Decline and Fall of Republican Afghanistan*. Oxford: Oxford University Press.

James, Erica Caple. 2010. *Democratic Insecurities: Violence, Trauma, and Intervention in Haiti*. Berkeley: University of California Press.

Kessler, Glenn. 2022. "Numbers Behind Afghanistan Evacuation Come into Focus." *Washington Post*, May 25. https://www.washingtonpost.com/politics/2022/05/25/numbers-behind-afghan-evacuation-come-into-focus/.

Maghbouleh, Neda. 2017. *The Limits of Whiteness: Iranian Americans and the Everyday Politics of Race*. Palo Alto, CA: Stanford University Press.

Maira, Sunaina Marr. 2009. "'Good' and 'Bad' Muslim Citizens: Feminists, Terrorist, and US Orientalisms." *Feminist Studies* 35 (3): 631–656.

Maira, Sunaina Marr. 2016. *The 9/11 Generation: Youth, Rights, and Solidarity in the War on Terror*. New York: New York University Press.

Massoumi, Mejgan. 2022. "Soundwaves of Dissent: Resistance Through Persianate Cultural Production in Afghanistan." *Iranian Studies* 55 (3): 697–718.

Naber, Nadine. 2012. *Arab America: Gender, Cultural Politics, and Activism*. Berkeley: University of California Press.

Nojan, Saugher. 2022. "Racialized Hauntings: Examining Afghan Americans' Hyper(in)visibility Amidst Anti-Muslim Ethnoracism." *Ethnic and Racial Studies* 45 (7): 1347–1370.

Oeppen, Ceri, ed. 2010. *Beyond the "Wild Tribes": Understanding Modern Afghanistan and Its Diaspora*. New York: Columbia University Press.

Olszewska, Zuzanna. 2015. *The Pearl of Dari: Poetry and Personhood Among Young Afghans in Iran*. Bloomington: Indiana University Press.

Osman, Wazhmah. 2020. *Television and the Afghan Culture Wars: Brought to You by Foreigners, Warlords, and Activists*. Urbana: University of Illinois Press.

Osman, Wazhmah. 2022. "Building Spectatorial Solidarity Against the 'War on Terror' Media-Military Gaze." *International Journal of Middle East Studies* 54 (2): 369–375.

Qasmi, Hosai. 2020. "Representations of Gender Relations in Turkish Soap Operas and Afghan Audiences' Reception." PhD diss., University of Ottawa.

Redfield, Peter. 2013. *Life in Crisis: The Ethical Journey of Doctors Without Borders*. Berkeley: University of California Press.

Rokay, Moska. 2021. "Critical Ethnography as an Archival Tool: A Case Study of the Afghan Diaspora in Canada." *Archivaria* 91 (June): 176–201.

Rostami-Povey, Elaheh. 2007. *Afghan Women: Identity and Invasion*. London: Zed Books.

Sadat, Mir Hekmatullah. 2007. "Hyphenating Afghaniyat (Afghan-ness) in the Afghan Diaspora." *Journal of Muslim Minority Affairs* 28 (3): 329–342.

Shahimi, Farnaz, Karen Block, and Eva Alisic. 2023. "'Still Stood Adamant and Strong to Chase My Dream': Sense of Identity and Resilience Among Hazara Youth Following Childhood Experiences of Forced Migration." *Journal of Immigrant and Refugee Studies*. https://doi.org/10.1080/15562948.2023.2290644.

Ticktin, Miriam. 2011. *Casualties of Care: Immigration and the Politics of Humanitarianism in France*. Berkeley: University of California Press.

Zafar, Morwari. 2016. "COIN-Operated Anthropology: Cultural Knowledge, American Counterinsurgency and the Rise of the Afghan Diaspora." PhD diss., University of Oxford.

Zeweri, Helena, and Thomas Gregory. 2023. "'Outside the Wire': Brereton and the Dehumanization of Afghan Civilians." *Australian Journal of Political Science* 58 (3): 256–271.

Reflections
Afghan Literature and Politics
Under US Occupation

Drawing on short fiction written between 2001 and 2021, this chapter explores how Afghan writers chronicled and participated in the prolonged (globalized) Afghan Civil War. From 1979 to 1989, the Soviet Army occupied Afghanistan with the help of its domestic ally, the People's Democratic Party of Afghanistan (PDPA). Meanwhile the United States, Western Europe, the Arab (Gulf) States, and Afghanistan's neighbors funded and trained countervailing political forces within the country. The resulting war was a monumental event in the Cold War and in the contemporary history of Afghanistan. For the authors examined here, however, the Soviet withdrawal and the eventual collapse of the USSR did not constitute a rupture in their country's history. For Afghans, the war of "brother killing" continued in the form of the PDPA-mujahideen conflict (1989–1992), mujahideen infighting (1992–1996), Taliban hegemony (1996–2001), and the violence of the United States and NATO with their Afghan allies and the Taliban (2001–2021).[1]

Set in disparate historical moments and featuring subaltern as well as privileged characters, the literature examined here captures the waves of humiliation, torture, and massacre Afghans endured and exploited. Even if the authors' sociocultural orientations diverged and their political leanings conflicted, they shared a mutual target: the war *within* Afghan society and its different benefactors. The authors anchor this collective trauma in three interlocked threads: Afghans' intimate confrontation with war, gender dynamics, and poverty. They consign foreign interference to the background as one would discuss earthquakes—juggernauts that cannot be so much overcome as endured. By foregrounding Afghans' everyday survival strategies, they interrupt the hierarchical view of Afghanistan's history that progresses from such abstractions as the "Cold War" battleground to a "terrorist haven" and from "communists" to "mujahideen" and "Taliban."

Yet, I argue, the history of foreign involvement in Afghanistan is indelibly entwined with the universe of these texts, even if confined within fleeting sentences and words. These writers reached maturity during the Afghan Civil War that connected the eras of both the Soviet and the American occupations. Their experiences of these political orders profoundly impacted their literary voices. The war forced most, if not all, of these writers to seek refuge outside of Afghanistan on a temporary or permanent basis, primarily in Pakistan and Iran but also in the West, where they learned the local languages of these societies. Most of their literary output was, however, in Dari or Pashto, and the tales derive their force from an awareness of both attachment to and separation from their community of origin. They rely on a shared understanding among the author, their protagonists, and the readers, presuming an Afghan literary audience that is familiar with their country's history. While foreign aggression remains in the background, each story relies on that understanding, providing cues that are infested with the presence of imperial interventions.[2]

To provide a sequential history of the country's past, the texts are presented below in roughly the chronological order in which they engage with and periodize the war. Published shortly after the US invasion in 2001 and representing the contemporary war in Afghanistan as an episode in the broader region's history that stretches back centuries, it seems appropriate to begin our exploration with Rahnaward Zaryab's (1944–2020) novella *Gulnār va āyina* (Gulnar and the mirror) ([2003] 2016). The narrative follows an unnamed protagonist who embarks on a journey that spans from 1965 to the late 1990s. But the text also carries the burdens of the past from long-ago dynastic empires: the Maharajas, the Mughals, and the Manghits in the premodern era. As time passes, the political changes accelerate, and life becomes more dramatic and dangerous, especially in the late 1970s. In real life, the Sawr or April coup of 1978 mounted by the PDPA consumed more and more Afghans—participants as well as bystanders—as the new regime gave way to infighting and then political violence. Accordingly, the narrative mood darkens from excitement to anguish and bitterness.

At the heart of the story lies the encounter between the protagonist and Rubaba, a dancer who also embodies and is the iteration of the persona of Gulnar, an ancestral dancer in premodern Lucknow, India, where she was mistreated by a Maharaja and escaped to Kabul. The characters meet weekly at shrines in Kabul, one of which is the tomb of a Manghit ruler who had fled Bukhara following the Red Army's conquest of the city in 1920 (28–29). The story of this exile is engraved on the emir's tombstone, and the narrator vividly recalls the death date of that "padishah of Bukhara," Emir Sayyid Mir Muhammad Alim Khan, because it coincides with his own (and Zaryab's) year of birth in 1944 (29).

Written more than two decades after the Soviet occupation of Afghanistan, the emir's story chronicles the march of the USSR as an episode in the movement of dynasties and empires. In the broad stretches covered in the novella, however, powers collapse over time, yet the couple's story endures, as Rubaba urges the narrator: "'Start this moment!' . . . Write . . . write . . . write!'" (9). As the narrative progresses, we gradually realize that the migrations, separations, and humiliations experienced by the characters, including a pair of puppies, but particularly Rubaba and her family, are recurring motifs from the past. The initial sense of hopefulness proves to be momentary, an exception to the sufferings endured: The civil war and the Taliban's subsequent rise to power take the lives of Gulnar's family members one by one.

Though no specific dates are assigned to these events, readers with a working knowledge of Afghanistan's recent history will quickly identify very real years. The April coup claims one of Gulnar's brothers. This is followed by the disappearance of her cousin before another "king" (Zaryab is alluding to the PDPA leader Babrak Karmal) assumes control with Soviet support and releases prisoners in 1979.[3] To safeguard her remaining brother, they become refugees in Pakistan, but after financial hardships they return to Kabul, which is embroiled in mujahideen infighting in the early 1990s. Eventually, the Taliban kill Gulnar's remaining brother for playing the tabla (hand drums) (112–118).

Preceding the Sawr coup and the events that followed, however, there is a socially and culturally revealing moment when Rubaba and the narrator venture out in public together. This is the only occasion that the two do so, for their time is otherwise largely spent among shrines or family and friends. Surrounded by mostly unveiled individuals, Rubaba remains cloaked in her burqa throughout their outing. The narrator asks whether she would remove her veil to eat. But despite the perplexed gazes of passersby, she adamantly refuses to unveil herself (58–59). Later, during a performance, a drunken man inappropriately touches Rubaba (by now it is evident that she is an iteration of her ancestor Gulnar), driven by the delusion that a dancer is inherently promiscuous. In response, she explains to the narrator why, in public, she finds comfort beneath the veil: "They know me. Even if one of them recognizes me, it is as if every single one of them recognized me. Then, it is as if I have danced for every one of them; as if I have danced for the entire city; from the time of Adam until today I have danced. A big sinner . . ." (87–88).[4] We come to recognize that Rubaba/ Gulnar is not merely a representation of Afghanistan, but also that different cycles of the South/Central Asia's history are embodied within every different iteration of Gulnar.

Afghan women and the country itself are not only targeted by foreign powers and domestic rulers and abusers, but also fall victim to their own male-dominated culture.[5] And so, Zaryab chooses to spotlight a dancer, a figure historically subjected to contempt and ridicule in Afghan society even if intertwined with the country's social history. He reminds his readers to recognize that the dancer's struggles stem less from external influences such as foreign invasions and more from the entanglement of machismo and power within the Afghan social hierarchy and cultural framework. In other words, the underlying cultural upheaval looms larger than any economic or political turmoil within Afghanistan. The suffering of Rubaba, though centuries apart from the original ancestor named Gulnar, is shown as a single social catastrophe, grounded in gender-based violence. The narration, however, relies on the civil war as the engine of change, even if that change is but one link in the cyclical history of the region.

Beginning in 1979, the opposing factions in the Afghan Civil War were financed and trained by the Soviets and the Americans (and their allies). This support culminated in a significant expansion in their size and operational capabilities. Over the following years, Afghans witnessed the emergence of a formidable military presence in Kabul and other major cities, as well as the rise of well-funded rebel leaders within the opposition ranks. In "The Late Shift" (initially published as "The Decision"), Sharifa Pasun delves into the savagery of that militarized society ([2020] 2022). Set over the course of one day in 1985, the short story follows Sanga, a student at Kabul University by day, and by night, a TV anchor in the city's National Radio and TV headquarters. Balancing the roles of both student and mother, in Sanga the reader recognizes another gloomy product of Afghanistan's civil war. The moment she leaves her home, the reader is made aware that every step brings the risk of death. Refusing to use the word *mujahideen*, Pasun instead refers to the anti-Kabul forces as the "opposition," so denying those factions the ethical authority that come with the word's religious foundation in jihad or holy (thus justified) war.[6] She writes about the opposition's indiscriminate bombing of Kabul with an abstract malice, though the mujahideen never materialize as demons. The case is quite different for the victims. We hear the "screams" of Kabul's residents, left with injuries and deaths: "It was eleven o'clock; the dogs could be heard barking far away, the roads were busy with ambulances. The rockets couldn't be heard anymore. They must be tired like her, she thought. She thought they would be sleeping now and getting ready to launch fresh attacks the following day. But no one knew where the next attack would be and when it would happen" (65). Written with an understanding of one who has lived through the bombings of Kabul, the reader recognizes in "blind" rockets the infamously indiscriminating Egyptian-made Sakr, their whistling sounds before their loud explosion, Kabul's power going on and off, the residents' learned habit to tell one another to move to lower floors or basements for safety, and even the dogs' barks that grew louder after the rebels were done for the day. The globalization of Afghanistan's war, though left unmentioned, can be tracked in the hushed history behind the Sakr rockets. These weapons were not only funded by Western and Arab Gulf States and handed to Afghan rebels with assistance from Pakistan's intelligence agency. The very development of these rockets—adaptations of Soviet originals—was made possible through US funding to the neoliberal Egyptian government after 1979. We can, then, deduce, even if not see, the triangle of US dollars, Soviet knowledge, and Afghan bodies that produce Sanga's ominous fate. Yet, despite the global arms industry's rockets employed by domestic terrorists, Sanga continues to read the news, embarking on the same unpredictably dangerous road the next day.

At the same time, these authors trace imperial entanglement in Afghanistan aided by their country's own ruling elites, whose opportunism and foolishness opened the doors for domestic conflict and foreign invasions. Abdul Wakil Sulamal Shinwari (1964–) delves into the psychology of those rulers, the victimizers, and their role in creating the country's woes. In his four-page story "The Solution" set sometime in 1978, the focus is a brief conversation between a young woman and a newly appointed PDPA minister. One day, she comes into his office panic-stricken: "Last night they came to the house and took my father away." The minister is "shocked" and asks, "Who? The anti-revolutionary elements, or our security comrades?" (2017, 101).

Shinwari's style in "The Solution" is one of calculated simplicity, carried through jocular restraint. The author manages to establish an uneasy relationship among himself, his protagonists, and his readers. "The Solution" is intended to be read by the social groups that came to power: the intellectu-als- and academics-turned-politicians as well as students. Having worked in real life for the Ministry of Defense under the PDPA government, Shin-wari's satirical barbs against the "Minister" are personal. Specifically, PDPA members will recognize the grim parody in the minister's uncertainty sur-rounding the captors of the young woman's father. The minister's unaware-ness would be recognizable to those familiar with the events of 1978. That year, even high-ranking officials were uncertain about who would be the next one to stand trial, as the Sawr coup conspirators turned against their own comrades a few months after seizing power. Their infighting would draw in the Soviets a year later, turning Afghanistan into one of the Cold War's open hot spots.

The victim in Shinwari's story, however, is the young woman Gulalay (and parenthetically the minister's wife), even though she had done everything required of a Party associate, including joining "the Youth As-sociation" and being recommended by the minister himself for "a Party membership!" (103). Upon learning that Gulalay's father has been taken away by their own comrades, possibly for belonging to the landowning class, studying in the United States, or due to associations with Maoists or newly accused PDPA members or some other faction, the minister suggests that the "solution" to secure her father's release is to have a "strong rela-tionship between you, your father, and me." At first, Gulalay believes that the minister wants to pose as her uncle, but her superior swiftly corrects her, revealing that his intention is for them to wed. When Gulalay objects, stating that he is already married, the official responds, "To hell with her!"

> It is not a problem honey; I will send her to her father's. I'll take financial
> responsibility for her, and I will tell you this minute for certain that I'll
> never see her face again. I am a victim of feudalism. The revolution has
> handed me the opportunity to make my own choices, so why should I let
> it slip away? (104)

Juxtaposing an absurd character with serious sentiment, Shinwari portrays the internal conflict within the government, exemplified by the minister's obliviousness to the cruelties committed by his own administration. What is more, the minister's willingness to exploit the situation and manipulate the concepts of "revolution" and "feudalism" for personal gain reflects a disregard for his own colleagues and juniors. The Afghan reader also recog-nizes that the minister, unhappy with his own perhaps arranged marriage (alluding to it as a feudal contract), does not hesitate to force the young woman's hand into marrying him. Misogyny outlives feudalism as the left-wing official simultaneously opens the gates for a party career for Gulalay and moves to take advantage of his position.[7]

The majority of Shinwari's stories employ the same style, creating a dialogue between historical figures to criticize the right-wing groups. In his two-page "Statues and Records," Western imperial powers—Europe, the United States, and the Soviet Union—appear directly, but they are criticized circuitously through a specifically named Afghan Mujahid and later Taliban member (2009). Set sometime after the Taliban's rise to power in the mid-1990s, Mullah Abdul Baqi (b. 1962) is given a tour of Madame Tussauds in London by a British guide. Through the backdrop of the wax museum, the reader gains insight into Afghanistan's civil war and its position within the Cold War's key players. The mullah's observations regarding the contradictory actions of the West are suffused with his own self-awareness as a real-life player within those events. This provides the reader with a sense of the truly globalized nature of Afghanistan's civil war. During the tour, the mullah encounters a statue of Lenin and expresses astonishment, remarking, "On one hand, you pat us on the back in the fight against his followers, and with the other, you decorate your museums with his statues" (61–62). Mullah Baqi, then, comes across his own wax statue, which surprises him once again. He suggests that all Afghans should have statues in the museum for having fought the "big bear" (Soviet Union) and points out that there are numerous more renowned commanders deserving of recognition, including those whom the American president and the British prime minister hosted (62).[8] The British tour guide, however, claims that Mullah Baqi holds the "record" for large massacres in the recent past, adding that the plaque attached to his statue contains that information, for the record keepers know everything about him. Without the slaughter, the mullah says defensively, "it was impossible to defeat our common enemy," then tells himself: "Here you people know about my importance, and there my own countrymen and even companions in the holy war speak ill of me" (63).

The Americans, the British, and the Soviets thus loom in the background, indirectly criticized for benefiting from a war fought with Afghan bodies, one that continues to create victims but that has turned into a distant memory, an artifact showcased in a museum in the West. We witness the Western omission of its own accountability and the human cost of war in the commodified history present for Western public consumption. Even the British tour guide's character is robotic, as if operated by a machine.

Shinwari therefore reserves the sting of his story for Mullah Baqi, who is despised by not only his fellow citizens but even his allies. What's worse, he is elevated in London, one of the imperial centers, where Afghan deaths are reduced to a mere statistic.

"Statues and Records" depends for its effect on complicity between the author and his readers, in a comradely way (as opposed to a mocking way as is the case with the PDPA minister in "The Solution"). Mullah Baqi is the archetype, familiar to Afghans, of numerous right-wing individuals financed by the West who would become prominent Taliban members, later demonized by their former financiers. Such figures can only be honored with statues and plaques in the very countries that financed their early careers to defeat the Soviets. Through the mullah's surprised simplicity, the author both depicts the oppressive realities in Afghanistan under the Taliban and traces Western complicity in shaping the country's contemporary history.

While foreign backers of different sides in the Afghan Civil War are in the background, their actions, through aid in the form of weapons and propaganda—whether rockets or the support and glorification of certain leaders—are palpable in these stories. The story of Mullah Baqi receiving statues in the museum reveals the hypocrisy of right-wing individuals who denounce idol worship but embrace it when they become the subject, even when idolized by foreign powers. We could, indeed, read the story as a response to March 2001, when the Taliban destroyed the Buddhas of Bamiyan, the world's largest standing Buddha statues.

Zalmay Babakohi (1951–) makes these iconoclasts the central protagonists in "The Idol's Dust" ([2001] 2011), published a few months before the American invasion of Afghanistan (Ahmadi 2008, 141). If "Statues and Records" explores imperial machinations through the bind of a right-wing mujahid commander and his backers, "The Idol's Dust" can be read as a condemnation of the Taliban's self-destructive rule and its consequences beyond Afghanistan. The statues are blown up, covering the Taliban with their dust. The iconoclasts teasingly compare one another to the destroyed statues, but soon discover that the dust covering them cannot be washed away. Over time, they turn into silent, pale statues, with only their eyes remaining movable. But the shattered Buddhas produce miniature statues that are carried through air, water, and land.

The stunned leader of the iconoclastic mission, Mullah Janan Akhund, then calls Mullah Omar, who says to break everything that has "become an idol and demolish everything that already was one!" (Babakohi [2001]

2011). In line with the order, the Taliban, turned into statues, are also broken by their own comrades. The remains are spread across the country by rivers and wind, and even the clouds take statue-like shapes that move to remote corners of the sky. Finally, Mullah Janan Akhund, fearful and feeling his own fingers slowly turning cold, hard, and discolored, travels to Kandahar to see Mullah Omar. When the curtain is pulled aside, to his shock, the mullah sees dust crawling on the commander as well. Like the two Buddha statues, one large the other smaller, the small mullah and the head of the Taliban begin slowly turning into statues, thus heading toward their own deaths.[9]

If we stretch out this reading, one element of the story points to the consequences of these actions, or what is known as "blow back." While Mullah Baqi's story comments on US intervention in Afghanistan, Mullah Janan Akhund's demise foretells the impact of that intervention for the empire itself. The residues of the shattered statues, as if the residual consequences of the Cold War, cling to their surroundings, including to the Taliban, who destroy and are, in turn, destroyed themselves. But the particles of such destruction also travel through the porous boundaries of the valley into the rest of the world. Written in March 2001, the story warns that the destruction will not be limited to the Buddhas or Afghanistan. Afghanistan becomes both the hot core of the Cold War, where the Soviet Union supposedly collapsed as Mullah Baqi believes, and the place where imperial power and conceit to see and control are undermined. Six months after the Buddhas' destruction, the attacks of 9/11 on New York and Washington, DC, took place. A month later, in October 2001, the United States and NATO attacked and occupied Afghanistan. To the West, their former allies, the anti-communist "freedom fighters" of the 1980s were now labeled "enemy combatants" and accused of providing a haven "for international terrorism" (Crews 2015, 261, 283).

Yet, one wonders about the sociopsychology and humanity of those terrorists and iconoclasts. So far, we have read about the trauma of the Afghan people through cosmopolitan actors who reference abstract ideas like feudalism, who work as news anchors, and who know when their next meal is coming, equating their experiences with what we consider middle-class preoccupations (if not lives). But Afghanistan is home to largely marginalized subalterns living in dire poverty, including the foot soldiers belonging to the warring Afghan parties. In "Dasht-e Leili," Mohammad Hussain Mohammadi (b. 1975) delves into the last day of such a figure in December 2001: a tied-up Taliban fighter, stuffed in a metal container with his fellows, who are from other parts of the world ([2003] 2011). After finding a bullet hole in the container, the unnamed man inhales the air from outside, his lungs filling with dust and sand (as if breathing in the residues of the destroyed idols from Babakohi's story). While during the day the bodies around him die of heat, at night he fears that the cold will take him. Eventually, however, it is the Afghans (including the tale's other protagonist) allied with the occupying Westerners that drag him and start to bury him alive in a mass grave. The narrator offers his last words: "I open my mouth to inhale the sandy air, but instead, my mouth is filled with soil, and when I open my eyes they cannot close again, and soil and soil and . . . soil . . . soil . . . soil . . . soil . . . soil . . ."

Mohammadi takes us beyond the paralyzing Taliban rule and their leadership, drawing us into the final moments of a subaltern fighter. Through his first-person narration, we drift into a gray zone to understand, even identify with the Talib, into a body that bears the harsh weather, that slowly stops feeling his limbs, a mind in which hope blossoms until the moment soil closes his eyes to the world. But, like the other stories, Mohammadi's also relies on a shared understanding between the author and the readers to create its full impact, grounded in the knowledge of Afghanistan's civil war. Like the Taliban, the American-allied Afghans committing atrocities are that war's grim and globalized outcome. In fact, the Talib's executioners were part of an organization led by Abdul Rashid Dostum (b. 1954), who was once allied with the PDPA and funded through Soviet aid in the fight against US-backed mujahideen. He later joined the mujahideen and, after 2001, served under the Americans. The United States is also mentioned directly in the appearance of its soldiers as they give bread and water to the prisoners before they are transported to the burial grounds. Flitting by in three sentences, the soldiers in "camouflage" would have been US special forces.[10]

What is more, throughout his last hours, the narrator does not know the words spoken around him (likely Arabic, Chechen, and Uzbek), and Mohammadi once again draws us to the mortality we share with the dying man. The choking heat of the "tomblike container" makes the narrator angry at the weight of the bodies and sweat of those on top and next to him, exacerbated by their alien languages. He feels more in common with his jailors (whom he also does not understand) than fellow detainees, telling the former that he does not belong with the foreign fighters, that he is Afghan, like them. The captors, however, instinctively continue to bind the hands and feet of their victims, even as one of those inside the container and one outside recite the Quran. But as the bodies around him perish, and his own death nears, the narrator longs for human voices and touch: "If only he whose language I could not understand had been alive, he who had fallen over my legs, he whose chest I had felt ascending and descending as he breathed heavily." Beyond this shared human experience, the story repeatedly gives us cues about the global character of Afghanistan's war in the Taliban-associated foreign fighters. "All of us, including me," says the protagonist, "had come from different and faraway places to engage in jihad and to reach paradise."

But these brutalities of war and foreign intervention go hand in hand with another reality: the Talib's subaltern background. Undoubtedly born into a poverty-stricken family, he likely had to attend a Saudi-funded madrassa that taught him only the militant facet of Islam. The narration invites us to relate to this man—reduced to a Muslim chauvinist and murderer on our TV screens without context—and to feel with him as he lays dying. For the readers familiar with Afghanistan's lived history, the Talib is an irredeemably transformed character, an outgrowth from a devastating war and poverty. We can see his killing as well as his victimizers' act of murder as a collective tragedy, not some primordially tribal hatred among Afghans or the euphemistic "targeting" of "militant Islamists" by the United States and NATO forces. We are left to reflect on our separation from the Talib and his victimizers, and the moral obligation that this separation embodies. Even if Mohammadi's immediate focus is not on those whose daily struggles are a dialectic between slow suffering imposed by hunger and the violent deaths brought by explosion and torture, we can imagine that most foot soldiers—Taliban and their Afghan enemies alike—are from subaltern classes, relegated to the margins of fiction and nonfiction alike.

Like these stories, Masouma Kawsari's (1974?) "Dogs Are Not to Blame" serves as another reminder of the ongoing brutality of massacres and terrorism (2022). Yet, for all the similarities, Kawsari's tale is a break from the others considered so far. Its subject matter is the poor, and the attack on inequality appears directly in the narrative itself rather than mediated through style and language or an assumed knowledge on the part of the reader. Whether intentional or not, Kawsari homes in on poverty, which in turn represents the topsoil on which patriarchy thrives. If in Mohammadi's tale we can only tease out the Talib's impoverished background, in Zaryab's narrative, the impoverished make fleeting appearances. Once, we catch a glimpse of them near a shrine, and the narrator describes a "little farther, two dust-covered . . . children were walking among the graves. Maybe they were playing. Maybe this was their respite." But then, as if directly addressing his (surely educated, mostly middle-class) reader, Zaryab writes without elaborating: "They were the children of the cemeteries" ([2003] 2016, 38). Those with intimate knowledge of Afghanistan will know the reference to children who would venture into cemeteries to pass time hoping for alms from the families of the buried. The novella, however, leaves them unexplored.

It is this subaltern class in the margins, embodied in sentences unable to contain them, that Kawsari brings to life, Saber, the protagonist in "Dogs Are Not to Blame," is not a writer, a student, a young party member or journalist, or a commander or a politician. Set during the American occupation, Saber's education is no path for a career; he resorts to writing petitions on a street corner near Kabul's courthouse as there are no available jobs in carpentry or tailoring. Left behind by his father, his mother ekes out a living by doing chores in peoples' homes. She had given Saber the time to study, but because of that she had had no time to love him. It is through Saber's clients that we delve further into the world of the extremely marginalized, constituting the great majority of Afghans. We hear their stories as they ask Saber to write their grievances for the courthouse looming behind the wall. One of his clients is an illiterate man and his mother, who, like Saber's own family, have been left behind by the husband. The man is attempting to claim his and his mother's share of inheritance from his father's other family. When Saber asks why they didn't lodge an application to secure their rights, the client reveals that not only are they illiterate but his mother also refuses to tarnish her ex-husband's reputation, fearing that people would criticize her for not standing by him and enduring the hardships of married life (Kawsari 2022, 38).[11] Poverty and sexism interlock, one feeding off the other.

Having lost her husband in the war and thus a means to survive, another woman visits Saber seeking help. She hopes to protect her daughter from a forced marriage imposed as retribution for a murder committed by her brother-in-law. She too faces obstacles in completing a petition, since her family restricts her daughter from leaving the confines of their home; yet again, sexism cannot be separated from war and material conditions.

The story also demonstrates not only the war's ravages but its connection to capitalism. Likely financed by the United States and its NATO allies, a recently rebuilt section of Kabul featured in the story is distinguished by a high concrete wall they'd built around the courthouse a year ago, after a suicide bomb attack. The municipality had painted pictures of the old part of Kabul on it. One image was of Darul Aman Palace, which was rebuilt after the war. Another of a girl giving a flower to an Afghan soldier. At the bottom of the wall were urine stains, some of them still wet. (39)

The concrete wall creates a visible demarcation between those in power and the marginalized, making the already fragile livelihoods even more vulnerable despite the influx of capital from imperial centers that renovate palaces and erect barricades for their own (foreign and local) agents. Those familiar with the country's history will recognize the "green zones" behind the wall, set up by Western occupiers and their allies. By writing about Saber's clients, Kawsari does not need to describe the other side of the wall to help us imagine the foreign journalists and diplomats and the native professionals in safe and commercial neighborhoods.

The blast walls thus place Saber and his clients between Kabul's rulers and suicide bombers. In another episode, he fondly recalls a girl he once loved but knew that his poverty would forever prevent a relationship between them. Indeed, Saber's and his clients' material conditions place them in proximity to Afghanistan's street dogs, including one of the tale's main figures, a female dog with puppies (45). Saber and his clients will stoically continue to accept their poverty as chance or destiny, while the class of rulers behind those walls, oblivious and indifferent, will continue to devour the lives in their trust.

"Dogs Are Not to Blame" can be read on two levels: both as a realistic account of the fate that has overtaken individuals like Saber and his clients during the American occupation and as a microcosm of national politics. Symbolized by the walls, behind Saber are the contractors, the multimillionaire investors (foreign and domestic) who dominate the nation's economy, and the leadership of the judicial hierarchy in the courthouse. He is an image of those millions of Afghans who live hand to mouth, for whom the world has moved on from one form of organized injustice to another. At the mercy of the suicide bomber and invisible to the Kabul elite, Kawsari's protagonist has "long ceased to go to the mosque or pray. He had become uncertain of everything—even God" (39).

Kawsari's narrative is not, however, a voyeuristic journey into the miserable existence of the downtrodden in Afghanistan. Despite his struggles, Saber is not ashamed that his mother does laundry for people or takes their discarded clothes home, nor is he bitter, wishing happiness for the girl he had once loved (45). It is perhaps Saber's mooring in his social environment that lifts the mood by the story's end. In contrast to our conflicted characters, he appreciates the chill of the wind and fondly calls to mind "Meena, the girl he loved, smiling, dimples forming on both her cheeks" (46).

At the story's core, reaching us thirdhand, are the petitions submitted to Saber, and through them we glance at the confessions of the poor, held up as a mirror to that part of society's power structure backed by imperial powers. We can imagine Kawsari's marginalized characters anywhere in the world, but it is in the heart of an empire that Akram Osman (1937–2016) transplants a stoic hero in his short story "Bākara!!" (The virgin!!). Published in 2005, we can only guess that the story takes place in the years after 1992 (when the author himself became a refugee). Ghiyas, a twenty-nine-year-old refugee, is a character straight out of Dostoevsky.[12] He is called the "virgin!!" by some of those around him, a "venomous word" that hurts his soul and reminds him of his lack of a family and community. The story represents a break from Osman's encyclopedic writings that catalog Kabul's monuments, (colloquial) sayings, (disappearing) occupations, and folkloric characters that inhabit those streets. Ghiyas is a transplant from those streets into Palm Springs, California.

Osman describes the formation of Palm Springs as a tourist destination by a khar pūl (filthy rich) American that drew shopkeepers who "could smell prey from afar like a fox," and with the "beat of advertising" attracted foreign and American tourists. On the surface, Ghiyas and his coworkers, including Teresa, and the Mexican restaurant that employs them are responses to that tourist tide. On another level, however, the characters are representatives of the global crises of war, famine, and refugees. Parenthetically, Osman tells us that Ghiyas found himself in the United States by circumstances beyond his control. About Teresa, however, we learn that she was forced from a young age to join a gang, work in bars, and ended up a dancer before she escaped Ecuador through Mexico for the United States. Both Ghiyas and Teresa share similarities—their skin tone, and working-class conditions, and they are refugees. Unlike Ghiyas, however, who has never experienced physical intimacy, Teresa has been in many relationships from an early age. It is exactly Ghiyas's "childlike innocence" that Teresa finds captivating, which for her stands in contrast to the patriarchal machismo she has experienced in the United States and Ecuador. Slowly "two individuals, from two different worlds, became acquainted. One an amalgamation and crystallization of longing, deprivation, and unful-filled desires, the other absorbed and disheartened by indulgence in both wholesome and unhealthy pleasures" (Osman 2005).

Yet, the story's importance lies less in such reflections than in the con-text surrounding the globalized working class, the streets, and the city of Palm Springs as symptoms of the forces of capitalism. The moneyed have erected an unnatural city amidst the desert, driven by their ability to take risks, and lure the bourgeoisie seeking leisure. This very city, however, flourishes on the toil of those refugees whose own cities have been rav-aged. The protagonists' destinies reflect the contradictions of US global hegemony. Both Ghiyas and Teresa are drawn to Palm Springs for safety and jobs. Paradoxically, it is precisely the American-dominated system that has left behind carnage in their countries of origin and that now exploits their labor.

The US neoliberal empire, the Soviet geopolitical project, and even the distant dynasties of the Maharajas have shaped the lives of our characters. But the driving forces of the literature examined here were Afghans: from Ghiyas and Sabir to Gulalay and Gulnar. For these characters, Afghanistan's past was not merely an echo of foreign invasions and withdrawals that label the country a "tribal society" gripped in a primordial conflict, the "grave-yards of empires," or defined by "Islamic fundamentalism." What these authors, instead, highlight are the tremors of poverty and sexism, exacer-bated by domestic and foreign wars.[13]

Notes

1   The framing for this essay came to me after reading Benedict Anderson and Ruchira Mendiones's (1985) *In the Mirror*.
2   For an exploration of Dari literature, see Ahmadi (2008). To gain insight into various aspects of Afghan literature, see Green and Arabzadah (2013). For the historical contours discussed in this chapter, see Crews (2015). Translations from Rahnaward Zaryab's and Akram Osman's stories are mine.
3   A founder of the PDPA, Karmal (1929–1996) ruled the country from 1979 to 1986.
4   As one critic has pointed out, Gulnār is stuck in the mirror, in the male gaze; whether she dances or puts on the burqa, she is unable to escape patriarchy. See Mehrdad (2010).
5   Moored in gender-based violence, the cyclical nature of time, inher-ent in the narrative form, also resurfaces in the illustration of a group of

dervishes. Symbolic of the repetitive history of Afghanistan (and the broader region), they circle, smoke, and sing the same tune throughout the novella. The only site around which the narrator and Gulnar are at ease, they are also the only unchanging element in the entire novella.

6 For Western propaganda, see Fitzgibbon (2020).

7 In the context of this chapter, *left wing* refers to those advocating for the nationalization of resources, wealth redistribution, and socially liberal policies. Conversely, the right wing opposed these policies, encompassing not only resistance to economic restructuring but also to expansion of rights to women.

8 Shinwari is referring to mujahideen leaders invited to the White House in 1987.

9 By deconstructing the sovereignty of the Taliban, Babakohi inverts their relationship with the immobile and marionette-like Buddhas, for the statues take on a life of their own and, simultaneously, take on the life of their destroyers. For this reading, I am drawing on Derrida and Nicholson-Smith (1991, 82).

10 For more on the massacre, see Rashid (2008, 93–94).

11 Kawsari's story was published in English translation in 2022, though she had written it prior to the US withdrawal in 2021.

12 If Dostoevsky's "idiot" represents Jesus, whose simple goodness highlights the vulgarity and excesses of the Russian bourgeoisie, then Ghiyas's virtues—virginity before marriage, lack of swagger, a superlative understanding of romantic love—are considered shortcomings in his new environment.

13 For their helpful feedback on earlier versions of this chapter, I thank Robert D. Crews, Wazhmah Osman, Helena Zeweri, Tanvir Ahmed, Aaron Neimann, and Tess C. Rankin.

References

Ahmadi, Wali. 2008. *Modern Persian Literature in Afghanistan: Anomalous Visions of History and Form.* Abingdon, UK: Routledge.

Anderson, Benedict, and Ruchira Mendiones. 1985. *In the Mirror: Literature and Politics in Siam in the American Era.* Bangkok: Editions Duang Kamol.

Babakohi, Zalmay. (2001) 2011. "The Idol's Dust." Translated by Anders Widmark. *Words Without Borders,* May 1, 2011. https://wordswithoutborders .org/read/article/2011 05/the-idols-dust/.

Crews, Robert D. 2015. *Afghan Modern: The History of a Global Nation.* Cambridge, MA: Belknap Press.

Derrida, Jacques, and Donald Nicholson-Smith. 1991. "Geopsychoanalysis: '. . . and the Rest of the World.'" *American Imago* 48 (2): 199–231.

Fitzgibbon, Jacqueline. 2020. *US Politics, Propaganda and the Afghan Mujahedeen: Domestic Politics and the Afghan War.* New York: I. B. Tauris.

Green, Nile, and Nushin Arabzadah. 2013. *Afghanistan in Ink: Literature Between Diaspora and Nation.* New York: Columbia University Press.

Kawsari, Masouma. 2022. "Dogs Are Not to Blame." Translated by Zubair Popalzai. In *My Pen Is the Wing of a Bird: New Fiction by Afghan Women,* introduction by Lyse Doucet and afterword by Lucy Hannah, 35–48. London: MacLehose.

Mehrdad, Mujib. 2010. "Gulnār va āyina wa dīdgāhā-i muntaqedān." Review of *Gulnār va āyina,* by Rahnaward Zaryab. *Kabulnath,* February. https:// www.kabulnath.de/Salae_Panchoum/Shoumare_114/MojeebMredad -Golnar.html.

Mohammadi, Mohammad Hussain. (2003) 2011. "Dasht-e Leili." Translated by Anders Widmark. *Words Without Borders,* May 1, 2011. https:// wordswithoutborders.org/read/article/2011-05/dasht-e-leili/.

Osman, Akram. 2005. "Bākara!!" *Kabulnath,* April 26. http://www.kabulnath .de/Schankar%20Dara/Shamalie/Dr.%20Akram%20e%20Osman/Bakera .htm.

Pasun, Sharifa. (2020) 2022. "The Late Shift." Translated by Zarghuna Zargar. In *My Pen Is the Wing of a Bird: New Fiction by Afghan Women,* introduction by Lyse Doucet and afterword by Lucy Hannah, 57–66. London: MacLehose.

Rashid, Ahmed. 2008. *Descent into Chaos: The U.S. and the Disaster in Pakistan, Afghanistan, and Central Asia.* New York: Viking Penguin.

Shinwari, Abdul Wakil Sulamal. 2009. "Statues and Records." Translated by Rashid Khattak. In *Fifty Million: Short Stories by Abdul Wakil Salamal Shinwari.* Pittsburgh: Dorrance.

Shinwari, Abdul Wakil Sulamal. 2017. "The Solution." Translated by Noorullah Atal. *Asian Literature and Translation* 4 (1): 96–104. https://orca .cardiff.ac.uk/id/eprint/99681/1/645-1617-1-PB.pdf.

Zaryab, Rahnaward. (2003) 2016. *Gulnār va āyina.* 4th ed. London: Afghanān Muqīm-i London.

Imperial Remainders

Reconfiguring the Legacy of US Occupation in Contemporary Afghan Art

The ending, ultimately, could never justify the means: In August 2021, the last of thousands of US military officials climbed into fighter jets and departed from Kabul's international airport, two months shy of the twenty-year anniversary of the US invasion and subsequent occupation of Afghanistan in October 2001. To say that the withdrawal of the US military—officially begun during the twilight moments of the Trump administration in 2020 and continued through the transition to the Biden presidency—was a botched and blundered act would be an understatement, one that massively neglects the cataclysmic effects of the United States' departure on the lives of Afghan civilians left behind to face the resurgence of the Taliban and the cruel exigencies of their fundamentalist government.

A report made by US State Department's After Action Review committee on Afghanistan, declassified to the public in June 2023, noted that the initial departure plan was thoroughly rushed after the Taliban began to reclaim territories around Kabul. The report stated that both the Trump and Biden administrations' decisions to withdraw troops from Afghanistan failed to consider the security and viability of the Afghan government run by President Ghani, leaving thousands of Afghans employed by the US military and embassy as translators, interpreters, and other crucial employees at grave risk and also leaving the lives of Afghan civilians at the mercy of the Taliban (AAR 2022). A report by the White House published in April 2023 reached similar conclusions, though its rhetoric was far more geared toward excusing the Biden government and placing blame on the inefficacies of the Trump administration. The report concluded that though the State Department had prepared for evacuation months in advance, it failed to properly account for "high risk, low probability events" and was ultimately unprepared for the sudden collapse of the Afghan government and the ignominious departure of its leader (White House 2023).

As official state doctrine, these two reports share the clipped, official language of the imperial state with all of its pretensions toward objectivity and its erasure of the human costs of an endless war and protracted occupation. Nowhere in these reports can one find testimonies of the thousands of Afghan civilians, either employed by the United States or not, who gathered in massive throngs on the airport tarmac pleading to be evacuated alongside the US soldiers and employees who had been a fixture of their landscape and a reminder of their subjugation. Absent, too, from these reports is any mention of the desperate civilians who clung to planes taking off and fell to their deaths or who clung to the sides of a relief jet as it departed Kabul, whose remains were only found later in the wheel well after the planes landed at Al Udeid Air Base near Doha, Qatar (Associated Press 2022).

The haphazardness of the US withdrawal after two decades of occupation and attempts at state-building necessitates critical reflection on the nature of what remains—that which is left behind and that which becomes indelible—after imperialism. Artists in the Afghan diaspora have taken up this question in recent years, critically engaging with the material and psychic residua of US imperialism across their varied practices to render potent and vital excoriations of militarism, cultural degradation, and dehumanization. Drawing on creative modes that span documentary photography, installation and performance, and hybrid modes of printmaking and collage, Naseer Turkmani, Aziz Hazara, and Laimah Osman have each developed visual works which critically reflect on the legacy of the US occupation of Afghanistan and challenge mainstream narratives that frame Afghans as merely disempowered and dependent on US largess. As members of the Afghan diaspora, Turkmani, Hazara, and Osman have through their artwork grappled with and tried to make sense of their relation to US empire. Each navigates contours of their identity as Afghan artists within a complex matrix of forces that have subjected them to stereotyping and erasure.

Responding to the limited representation afforded to Afghans in the aftermath of the 9/11 attacks and the subsequent War on Terror, Turkmani,

Hazara, and Osman offer structural critiques of US empire through the formal and symbolic dimensions of their art practices. Across a range of aesthetic forms, they continually draw attention to how the Global War on Terror relies on and exacerbates political and economic inequality between the United States and Afghanistan. By mobilizing the material and psychic remainders of US empire as prisms that refract the reality of imperialism—in real time and in retrospect—these artists of the Afghan diaspora invigorate decolonization as an ongoing exercise. Through their work, we understand decolonization as a process of witnessing and rein-scribing history from ground-up vantages that have long been overshad-owed by mainstream narratives.

For Naseer Turkmani, the act of bearing witness defines both the form and force of his photographic practice. Turkmani's 2021 series *Khuda Hafiz* (May God protect you) is exemplary of how urgent political conditions— in this case, the evacuation from and resettlement of Afghans following the United States' withdrawal from Afghanistan in August 2021—shape his documentarian approach to photography. The digital photographs from this series were shot on a mobile phone, owing to Turkmani's inability to bring his camera as he evacuated, and they capture both the exceptional chaos in the immediate aftermath of the US military's declaration of with-drawal and the more quotidian moments in the lives of Afghan refugees after relocation. In one image, large crowds gather at Kabul International Airport on August 22, 2021, a stone wall with a moat dividing the photo-graphic composition in half (figure 13.1). On either side of this moat are crowds of people—men, women, and children—clutching suitcases and documentation of their citizenship and right to travel. A US soldier stands on the wall, while an Afghan man stands in the middle of the water. In this formal configuration, we can read a dichotomy of power and positionality that speaks on several levels. On the one hand, the composition visually establishes the impossible situation of the desperate Afghans who feared the uncertainty of their fates under the Taliban's impending rule. Simulta-neously, the spatial arrangement stages the imperial dynamics that estab-lish the material and psychological gulf between those in power and those subjected to power: an intractable distance that persists even (and perhaps especially) in moments of crisis.

In other photographs from the *Khuda Hafiz* series, Turkmani portrays evacuees, who are often artists like himself, documenting their journeys as they move from Afghanistan to temporary locations in the wake of the US exit from Kabul. Stops along this transit include the French embassy

13.1 Afghans at Kabul International Airport seek to flee the nation after the seizure of the capital by Taliban forces on August 22, 2021. Four days later, on August 26, 2021, two deadly explosions would rip through these crowds, reportedly injuring dozens and killing ninety people, including women, children and thirteen US military personnel. Photo by Naseer Turkmani, from the series *Khuda Hafiz* (May God protect you), 2021.

in Kabul; a refugee housing compound in Marseille, France; and the interior of a Paris apartment. Though not all of the images are despondent— the artists seated on a couch in Paris are all captured mid-laughter, for instance—Turkmani's observant and sympathetic documentary photography counters the medium's long history of exploitation and extraction, what Ariella Aïsha Azoulay has referred to as photography's role in the "scopic regime" of imperialism, transforming people and objects into private property from which profits can be extracted (2021, 47).

Instead, Turkmani's images draw on the emotional force of Afghan refugees' struggle to reconstitute their lives in the wake of US occupation, and this force is often heightened by the absence of the standard documentary portrait of a human figure. Consider, for instance, an untitled 2021 photograph depicting the belongings of the Hazara artist Mohsin Taasha and his wife, taken in a temporary shelter in France (figure 13.2). The image toggles between the generic and the particular: at the center of

13.2 The belongings of the Hazara artist Mohsin Taasha, 31, and his wife were photographed by Naseer Turkmani as Taasha and his wife moved from a temporary location to another location in France in December 2021. Mohsin and his wife, both artists, fled Afghanistan on August 12, 2021 after they were granted visas by the French government. This fulfilled a promise made to Mohsin in 2019 during an exhibition showing his work Kharmohra in Marseille, France. Photo by Naseer Turkmani from the series *Khuda Hafiz* (May God protect you), 2021.

a nondescript, black-tiled hallway stand a brown cardboard box, a wheeled bluish-gray suitcase, and two bags, a black duffle and a bundle of clothing with red plastic handles. Though these mundane objects are specific items belonging to a specific family—items that are perhaps long-cherished, laden with both utilitarian and sentimental value—their generic quality in this photograph alerts viewers to the enormity of imperialism's effects in Afghanistan. These are possessions that could belong to any number of refugees, at any number of transitory hubs. Stripped of affect in Turkmani's photograph, they emblematize displacement and dispersal as aftershocks of US occupation. In Turkmani's documentary images, forced migration is the crux of the Afghan diaspora, and what members of this diaspora are able to take with them on their journeys—the sundry objects required for day-to-day living, as well as the psychic weight of leaving behind one's home—are rendered as important as what is left behind.

Like Turkmani, the Berlin-based artist Aziz Hazara frequently makes use of the documentary photograph to consider the ramifications and remainders of the US military withdrawal from Afghanistan. Hazara, who has exhibited his work internationally and primarily works in video, installation, and performance, offers a strikingly materialist and structural critique of military occupation in his ongoing multimedia work *A Gift to the American People*.[1] Begun in 2021 as a commission for the 2022 Carnegie International in Pittsburgh, the conceptual project mobilizes both durational performance and the photographic documentation of this performance to examine the nonhuman detritus left behind by the US military as an extended analogy for the hidden costs and consequences of imperial occupation. Whereas the US government has limited media coverage and discussion of the residual effects of its weapons and bombs and the long-term environmental costs of war more generally (Osman 2022, 371), Hazara's *Gift* highlights it. Hazara began by shipping twenty tons of waste material from Bagram Air Base—once the largest US military base in Afghanistan—to the United States on the condition that it never be returned to Afghan soil. To do so, the jetsam was labeled as art, in order to skirt US regulations against the import of waste material. En route to Pittsburgh, the "gift" traveled through Karachi and the Gulf toward the United States, a movement that follows the same route soldiers and arms traveled during the 2001 Afghan invasion. Along this route, Hazara continuously received photographs documenting his shipment as it reached different intermediary stretches of the journey, producing a parallel archive of images that could be considered redundant, or "waste" material.

Accumulating along a predetermined path to an uncertain end, Hazara's *A Gift to the American People* serves as a stark reminder of the unintended material and consequences of the United States' military engagements. As both the subject and material of Hazara's artwork, waste functions as a critical gesture when considered in the context of "burn pits," the open-air sites used by US troops to incinerate waste in Afghanistan that have generated pollutants and released plastic derivatives into the air. A byproduct of the Afghan occupation, this well-documented phenomenon poses greater adverse health effects on Afghan nationals, who are more likely to have long-term exposure to their toxicity than occupying forces, as outlined in a 2015 report by the American Public Health Association (APHA 2015).[2] And, as the critic Rahel Aima (2022) has rightfully pointed out, Hazara's critique of the waste produced during the military occupation also encapsulates the waste laid to time—the "wasted childhoods and absent futures" of Afghan citizens, the disruption to the natural population cycles of plants and animals, and, of course, the plastic matter that will take centuries to degrade. In this way, Hazara's "gift" powerfully illuminates the lack of oversight within the bureaucracy of US militarism and lays bare the unequal structures of social and political organization that further subject occupied populations to death and harm beyond direct military violence. Engaging both long- and short-term impacts of the US occupation of Afghanistan as both the form and content of his artworks, Hazara demonstrates the urgency of decolonization as an active and persistent struggle that must be challenged on multiple fronts.

Laimah Osman's artistic practice addresses the enduring psychological violence of war and occupation through a feminist and reparative approach that seeks to name and understand trauma and build feminist solidarity by identifying and undoing the masculinist frameworks that have defined the War on Terror. For over a decade, Osman's multimedia practice has centered the experiences of women and children, who are often treated as expected casualties of war or as helpless victims in need of the "civilizing" mission of US empire—a narrative that was heavily promoted within Western media networks to justify extended occupation. The latter critique is most evident in Osman's *War on Terror* series (2001–2011), for which the artist took clippings from US news outlets that presented the ongoing military occupation as a matter of both Western saviorism and patriotic duty. Western saviorism was particularly mobilized in the realm of education, in light of the Taliban's ban on primary education for girls. For *Girls School (On the Outskirts of Kabul)*, 2010, Osman screen-printed portraits of six Afghani girls, each wearing a style of hijab, onto a long piece of white linen using natural pigments. When the piece is stretched horizontally on the wall, viewers engage in a face-to-face confrontation with these girls, but only two visages can be clearly made out. Osman has effaced four of the other figures as a haunting gesture of how the futures of these young girls—their very subjectivity—came under threat as a form of retaliation by the Taliban. Retaliation may be one of the costs of waging the forever wars, but the ghostly presence of these young women as rendered on the stark white linen sheet is a haunting reminder that for women and girls with real dreams and aspirations the cost is their lives and futures.

The *War on Terror* series allowed Laimah Osman, as an artist, to make sense of the anxiety and alienation that she and her peers in Muslim and Afghan communities experienced in the aftermath of the September 11 attacks, when the combined mission to "retaliate" against foreign perpetrators led to a widespread practice of labeling all Afghan men "terrorists" (Laimah Osman, email with author, August 10, 2023). At the same time, as feminist scholars have argued, issues particular to Afghan women—such as the role of women in public life and their rights to education, property, etc.—became contentious, often violent sites for the Taliban and other religious and political extremist groups to wage debates on national symbolism and their ideological separation from the perceived excesses of Western culture (Osman 2020, 169). However, as Lila Abu-Lughod (2002) has argued, the post-9/11 rhetoric of "liberating" Afghan women from cultural practices like veiling so quickly became the dominant discourse within liberal circles that it overshadowed the pursuit of establishing a fair and just society, ultimately becoming yet another weapon in the imperial arsenal of the United States.

Organizing protests, cultural events, and educational programs in schools to combat the negative stereotyping of Afghans, Osman and her peers demonstrated how the dehumanization of Afghans at home and in the diaspora was a psychological and social extension of US militarism abroad. Osman's art is no less an act of resistance against cultural stereotyping, and within more recent series, such as *Gaze* and *Letters to My Sisters*, 2023, both begun during the COVID-19 pandemic, Osman has developed a hybrid form of printmaking that asserts Afghan women's presence using the remainders of both physical material and historical legacies. For these works, Osman began by making drawings, which were then transferred onto woodblocks and carved so that she can print multiple impressions. Atop these layers of imagery, Osman inscribes poetry, having been inspired to write by women poets in Central and South Asia. After organizing a reading and translation group of medieval Afghan poets with family members, Osman collectively published a book of translated poems titled *Ishqnama/Book of Love*.

By centering the voices of women poets from Afghan's past in her visual art, Osman reaches into a long tradition of Persian poetics in Afghanistan. As the cultural anthropologist Omar Sharifi has argued, Persian poetry is not only a relic of Afghanistan's literary and historical past but also serves a sociopolitical function. While the people of Afghanistan speak many different languages, Persian and its many localized dialects—including the two official languages, Pashto and Dari, with the latter serving as the lingua franca of Afghanistan—evidence how the nation continues to celebrate its Persian roots while also maintaining its ethnic and linguistic diversity

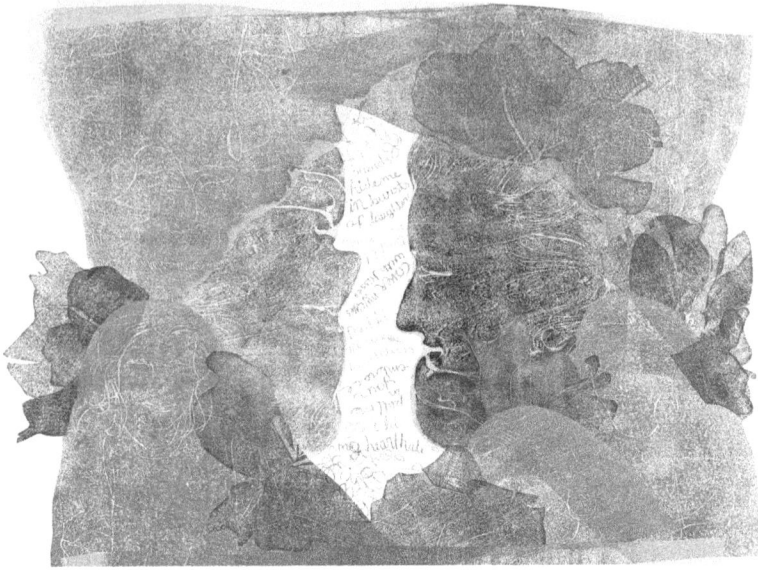

13.3 Laimah Osman, *Letters to Sisters: Don't Let My Hearthate*, 2023. Woodblock prints on Kitakata paper cut and pasted to Rives BFK paper, with graphite and colored pencils, 24 × 19 in.

(2018). Persian poetry's continued presence in Afghan society and the culture of its diaspora connects readers, listeners, and, indeed, viewers—as demonstrated by Laimah Osman's visual art—to a deep textual tradition that transcends both tribal and religious differences and allows for the expression of imaginative and idealized futures that are mediated by, but not beholden to, the past.

In this way, Osman's poetic inscriptions are an extension of the artist's collectivist and transnational feminist politics, connecting her work to the work of artist peers in the Afghan diaspora, as well as creating broader solidarity with feminist movements in oppressive regimes such as Iran's.[3] In works such as *Letters to Sisters: Don't Let My Hearthate*, 2023—a palimpsest of self-imagery, cherry blossoms, and original poetry—Osman enacts this solidarity by identifying love as a political force (figure 13.3). She commands her reader-viewer to "pull me in your embrace / don't let my hearthate," refusing the impulse to turn bitter from the abjection of masculinist militarism and choosing instead to remain loyal to her female comrades and the political solidarity they have engendered. Osman's integration of self with sisterhood is fashioned through fragments, each component contributing to the total understanding of a political self aligned with those whose histories have been denied, erased, and deemed whole. In the wake of the unraveling of social fabric and infrastructure and the decimation of the Afghan psyche by the machinations of war, Osman's art fiercely rejects the erasure of women and refuses to leave them behind in the pursuit of a decolonized and politically liberated future. Her art is an assertion that women *cannot* be reduced to remainders of war and militarism, and that their stories and experiences need to be centered in order for the dream of decolonization to become a practical reality.

Across documentary, performative, and poetic forms of creative expression, artists from the Afghan diaspora have demonstrated that the role of the artist is not merely to make sense of destruction but to critique the imperial grounds on which that destruction is wrought. In their varied practices, Naseer Turkmani, Aziz Hazara, and Laimah Osman each engage with the material and psychic remainders of the ill-fated goals of the US War on Terror in Afghanistan. As they sift through and repurpose more than two decades of occupation and destruction, these artists trenchantly ask us to imagine and reimagine what possible futures may yet take shape from the remnants of a dying colonialism.

Notes

1   For a brief overview of Hazara's practice, including discussion of *A Gift to the American People*, see Noor (2023).
2   For more on the environmental legacy of the United States' occupation in Afghanistan, see Atherton (2021). An earlier study of the environmental effects of burn pits can be found in Blasch et al. (2016).
3   For more on the feminist solidarities of Osman's work in relation to the art of the Afghan diaspora, see Saed (2021).

References

AAR (After Action Review team). 2022. *After Action Review on Afghanistan, January 2020–August 2021.* US Department of State, March. https://www .state.gov/wp-content/uploads/2023/06/State-AAR-AFG.pdf.

Abu-Lughod, Lila. 2002. "Do Muslim Women Really Need Saving? Anthropological Reflections on Cultural Relativism and Its Others." *American Anthropologist* 104 (3): 783–790.

Aima, Rahel. 2022. "To Know Which Way the Wind Blows." *Mousse*, November 1. https://www.moussemagazine.it/magazine/aziz-hazara-rahel-aima -2022/.

APHA (American Public Health Association). 2015. "Cleanup of U.S. Military Burn Pits in Iraq and Afghanistan." Policy statement. November 3. https://www.apha.org/policies-and-advocacy/public-health-policy -statements/policy-database/2015/12/16/08/56/cleanup-of-us-military -burn-pits-in-iraq-and-afghanistan.

Associated Press. 2022. "Air Force Clears Crew After Human Remains Found on Plane During Afghan Evacuation." NBC News, June 15. https://www .nbcnews.com/news/us-news/air-force-clears-crew-human-remains -found-plane-afghan-evacuation-rcna33703.

Atherton, Kelsey D. 2021. "U.S. Forces Are Leaving a Toxic Environmental Legacy in Afghanistan." Scientific American, August 30. https:// www.scientificamerican.com/article/u-s-forces-are-leaving-a-toxic -environmental-legacy-in-afghanistan/.

Azoulay, Ariella Aïsha. 2021. "Toward the Abolition of Photography's Imperial Rights." In Capitalism and the Camera: Essays on Photography and Extraction, 27–54. London: Verso.

Blasch, Kyle W., John E. Kolivosky, and Jack M. Heller. 2016. "Environmental Air Sampling Near Burn Pit and Incinerator Operations at Bagram Airfield, Afghanistan." Journal of Occupational and Environmental Medicine 58 (8): S38–S43. https://doi.org/10.1097/JOM.0000000000000792.

Noor, Tausif. 2023. "Aziz Hazara's Transformative Artworks Grapple with the Never-Ending Conflict in His Native Afghanistan." Art in America, July 5. https://www.artnews.com/art-in-america/features/aziz-hazaras -transformative-artworks-never-ending-conflict-afghanistan-1234673371/.

Osman, Wazhmah. 2020. Television and the Afghan Culture Wars: Brought to You by Foreigners, Warlords, and Activists. Urbana: University of Illinois Press. https://muse.jhu.edu/book/81069.

Osman, Wazhmah. 2022. "Building Spectatorial Solidarity against the 'War on Terror' Media-Military Gaze." International Journal of Middle East Studies 54 (2): 369–375. https://doi.org/10.1017/S002074382200037X.

Saed, Zohra. 2021. "'Heart Heat,' Ishq, Eros, and Radical Love in the Collaborative Artwork of Gazelle Samizay, Laimah Osman, and Sahar Muradi." In Muslim American Hyphenations: Cultural Production and Hybridity in the Twenty-First Century, edited by Mahwash Shoaib, 163–184. London: Lexington Books.

Sharifi, Mohammad Omar. 2018. "Language, Poetry, and Identity in Afghanistan: Poetic Texts, Changing Contexts." In Modern Afghanistan: The Impact of Forty Years of War, edited by M. Nazif Shahrani, 56–76. Indianapolis: Indiana University Press. https://muse.jhu.edu/book/58875.

White House. 2023. "The U.S. Withdrawal from Afghanistan." Public statement, April 6. https://www.whitehouse.gov/briefing-room/statements -releases/2023/04/06/the-u-s-withdrawal-from-afghanistan/.

Disrupting the Colonial Canvas
Afghan Art in the Wake of Withdrawal

In this chapter I focus on how artists, including myself, have attempted to speak back to hegemonic narratives about Afghans in the wake of the US/NATO withdrawal from Afghanistan in 2021. I explore themes of borders, mobility, displacement, and occupation through two approaches: autoethnographic reflection on my personal experience of the withdrawal, expressed in my art installation *With/Draw*; and analysis of *Emergenc(y): Afghan Lives Beyond the Forever War*, a group exhibition I cocurated with Iranian American artist Katayoun Bahrami. While I touch on the work of several artists, I specifically highlight the work of Amanullah Mojadidi, Elina Ansary, and Hamid Amiri. Working under conditions of crisis during the US/NATO withdrawal inspired me and other diasporic artists to challenge colonial narratives about Afghan experiences of war and displacement. The pieces I analyze not only counter oversimplified depictions of Afghans but also illuminate the structural inequalities that shape Afghan experiences of immobility.

As a multimedia artist who emphasizes community engagement in my work, I have sought to critically reflect on American involvement and interventions in Afghanistan. My artistic practice traces the history of my Afghan family and bears witness to the reverberations of historical and contemporary events. This began as a personal journey to put the pieces of my missing story together, as my family rarely discusses our time in Afghanistan. My earlier creative pursuits revolved around challenging oversimplified depictions, particularly media representations of Afghans, Afghanistan, and Muslims. One of my earliest projects, *Afghanistan Beyond the Burqa* (2005), emerged from my first visit to the country and sought to question the media's portrayal of Afghans through centering individuals' stories. In contrast to American headlines that focused on the burqa or terrorism, I observed that many Afghans were more concerned with economic issues affecting their families. This realization deepened my understanding of the complexities of Afghan experiences, prompting me to explore broader themes in my work.

My subsequent creative projects examined the complex effects of displacement on the diaspora, including the profound impact of trauma at both individual and collective levels. However, in 2021, a crucial moment unfolded when I became directly involved in assisting an Afghan artist and other vulnerable individuals as they sought to escape the country during the US/NATO withdrawal. This experience brought forth a series of profound realizations. Prior to this, Afghanistan had felt removed from my day-to-day life, but now I found myself in close contact with an Afghan artist living there, gaining a deeper understanding of the challenges they faced in surviving amid political instability. My previous skepticism about US involvement grew into consternation as I witnessed the reckless manner in which the American government handled the withdrawal. It became starkly evident that the assessment of the value of Afghan lives frequently hinged on their proximity to, and potential for, advancing the interests of the American government. For example, Afghans who had assisted Washington in its military or development projects as interpreters or NGO employees received priority for evacuation over those who had no such affiliation. Moreover, my experiences led me to a deeper understanding of the systemic inequalities embedded within the US immigration system, which exacerbate the difficulties, costs, and hardships faced by the very individuals it aims to assist. During the evacuations, this system mired Afghan diaspora leaders in bureaucratic busywork and opaque immigration processes, even as displaced Afghans faced mounting uncertainty and hardship. Furthermore, the enduring effects of intergenerational trauma stemming from displacement, conflict, and violence, often attributable in part to US involvement, have become an undeniable reality for resettled Afghans.

In the context of the withdrawal, the evacuations, and their aftermath, Afghan artists play a pivotal role in revising long held historical narratives that render Afghan life disposable, in preserving culture, and in shaping a collective identity that refuses long-standing colonial tropes. In her article "Transformation in Afghan Media and Culture Through Cycles of Upheaval," Wazhmah Osman (2022) demonstrates that, contrary to colonial stereotypes of Afghan backwardness and cultural immutability, Afghans and diasporic Afghan cultural workers have a long history and an active present of engaging in reformist and social justice movements, including speaking back to various empires. Following August 2021, Afghan artists who had personally experienced and witnessed the injustices of the evacuations used their work as a powerful tool to speak back to the violence of colonial representation.

From Curation to Crisis

My efforts to help Afghans leave the country began in July 2021, driven by my prior connection with an artist in Afghanistan. This artist had been featured in the exhibition *Fragmented Futures: Afghanistan 100 Years Later* (2019), a product of my collaboration with Helena Zeweri of the Afghan American Artists and Writers Association (AAAWA),[1] and Ara and Anahid Oshagan, the curators of the ReflectSpace gallery in Los Angeles. Originally titled *At the Crossroads of Empire and Independence: Afghanistan 100 Years Later*, the exhibit marked the centennial of Afghanistan's independence from British rule in 1919.[2] It aimed to creatively explore the impact of empire, colonialism, and independence on present-day Afghanistan. By examining everyday life, relationships, and the aftermath of displacement, the exhibit revealed the nuanced legacies of Afghanistan's struggle for self-determination within the ordinary experiences of its citizens and diaspora. It reflected on the present as an outcome of an interrupted future across multiple generations.

In July 2021, the artist wrote to me saying, "I think these are the last days of my life. In a few days Kabul will fall to the Taliban, and it will be gruesome. They've cut off electricity and there's no water. Our employer stopped paying us, and I don't have any income. I don't have anybody to help me. I'm just an artist like you, I'm sure you understand me."[3] His words resonated with me not only as an artist but also as someone whose family had also experienced the unsettling signs of political upheaval at the onset of the Afghan-Soviet War in 1979. The fact that essentials like electricity and water were inaccessible, coupled with the disconcerting news that institutions like Kabul University had stopped paying employees, indicated a looming crisis that many of us in the United States had not fully considered. This artist's situation was particularly concerning because he was from the Hazara ethnic minority and his work illuminated the discrimination and violence that Hazaras have historically faced, including by the Taliban.

Subsequently, AAAWA initiated a fundraising campaign aimed at facilitating his evacuation, along with his artist spouse. An Afghan American activist advised that the United States would not grant the artist refuge, and that his best option was to seek entry to Canada. Canada had established programs for refugees with UNHCR-processed cases in third countries, particularly for those with specific skill sets. As other Afghans reached out, our fundraising endeavor swiftly expanded to encompass a cohort of forty-four individuals, including artists, writers, filmmakers, cultural and civil society figures, and their respective families with whom members of AAAWA had previously been in contact. With the political landscape and immigration options rapidly changing, I found myself increasingly drawn into the unfolding events.

What began as a modest fundraiser to help the artist reach a neighboring country rapidly snowballed into an all-encompassing endeavor requiring ceaseless coordination and evacuation operations. As I scrambled to facilitate the entry of these artists through the gates of the Kabul airport, including military contacts, the cinematic depictions of military maneuvers had suddenly become an everyday reality for me and other members of the diaspora. The term *manifest* entered my lexicon, embodying the list of individuals slated for departure on evacuation flights—a word that still haunts me. The journey was both heart-wrenching and illuminating in how it revealed the fragility and cavalier abandonment of human life. My sorrow extended not only to the Afghans witnessing their futures disintegrate in a matter of moments but also to the troubling realities of the US immigration system. Each potential avenue for the artist's escape, and that of others, was entangled in intricate prerequisites. The Special Immigrant Visa (SIV) option, contingent on involvement with the US government or NGOs, did not align with the artist's circumstances. The emergence of the Priority 2, or P-2, program offered a glimmer of hope, but it required affiliation with US government–funded programs or American media organizations. Moreover, the process of evacuating an Afghan entailed filling out numerous forms, applications, and Excel sheets with dates of birth, passport numbers, and legal names, among other details. Nearly all of these submissions required succinct "vulnerability statements," condensing the essence of one's life and their justification to live into a mere two sentences. The United States seemed to categorize refugees, distinguishing those deemed significant from those considered expendable, contingent on their alignment with American interests or their susceptibility to the Taliban's violence. Here, there were not only hierarchies of suffering at play (Fassin 2012) but also what I would call hierarchies of labor and political alignment that determined who was worthy of another opportunity at life and a future.

Shouldering the responsibility for another person's life was an unforeseen commitment, causing each decision and action to be weighed down by a pervasive sense of fear, including that a mere technical discrepancy, such as the inconsistent spellings of "Muhammad" and "Mohamed" across different identity documents, could potentially undermine the entire claim for protection. After a failed evacuation attempt from the Kabul airport (a chaotic mess of people seeking unmarked gates among dirt, trash, and jostling crowds under a scorching sun), during which the artist's friend was beaten by the Taliban and his phone confiscated, the artist's well-meaning foreign exchange student friends residing abroad found another opportunity for escape via Facebook. A man with an Anglo name alleged he had a US military connection and could get the artist out for $3,000 payable upon his arrival in Europe. It was nearly a done deal—the date, time, and pickup location were set. But after I inquired about getting others out, he revealed a hefty fee of $20,000 per person payable upfront solely in cryptocurrency. Suspecting it was a scam, I questioned whether he was capitalizing on the misfortune of others or was a Taliban member gathering the artist's personal information, including his whereabouts, for potential retribution. Regardless, the situation left me deeply unsettled. It revealed the exploitation of Afghan suffering, highlighting how Afghans were ultimately treated as pawns in broader schemes, whether driven by financial or political motives. This exploitation extended to humanitarian parole applications, which provided a legal pathway for entry and temporary admission into the United States. These applications came with a staggering price tag of $575 per person, amassing roughly $19 million for the US government, with very few applications approved.

The Department of Homeland Security considered, but ultimately rejected, the idea of waiving fees for Afghan humanitarian parole applications. In contrast, the US government waived all fee requirements for Ukrainians seeking refuge from the Russian invasion through the Uniting for Ukraine program the following spring. As of February 2023, over 117,000 Ukrainians have entered the United States under the Uniting for Ukraine program, and no fees were collected (American Immigration Council 2023). The extensive obstacles placed in the path of Afghans, coupled with the comparatively smoother process for Ukrainians, prompted me to question whether the United States truly prioritized the welfare of Afghan refugees.

In the face of mounting challenges, the artist's quest for safety was met with a series of setbacks and disappointments. When Kabul was captured by the Taliban, the artist gave up all hope and decided to go into hiding. A potential avenue emerged through a military contractor, shedding light on the pivotal role of military connections in successful evacuations. The artist's pickup and evacuation were arranged and scheduled, but the next day, on August 26, 2021, the plan was canceled due to a suicide bombing at the Kabul airport. I reached out to the only military connection I had, who incidentally was now employed in a US Senator's office. Sympathizing with the dire circumstances, he advocated for humanitarian parole as the sole remaining option. Engaging a pro bono lawyer, we embarked on the complex paperwork process and prohibitive costs (application fees amounted to $4,950 for one family of nine we were assisting). This financial burden, coupled with the necessity of a US-based financial sponsor to shoulder the potential economic liability of the family, made the process very difficult to execute. By August 2023, we received a conditional approval letter for only one of the nine families we had applied for.

Statistics obtained through the Freedom of Information Act, requested by the International Refugee Assistance Project and American Immigration Council, revealed that US Citizenship and Immigration Services (USCIS) received 44,785 applications from January 1, 2020, to April 6, 2022. However, as of April 6, 2022, only 114 of these applications, a mere 0.25 percent, had been conditionally approved. Astonishingly, a staggering 94 percent of applications remained unadjudicated. On August 13, 2021, USCIS officials initiated expedited processing for Afghan humanitarian parole applications, but they quickly reversed this decision within hours. Following the conclusion of the withdrawal of US and NATO forces on August 31, 2021, USCIS temporarily suspended the adjudication of Afghan humanitarian parole applications. In September 2021, USCIS even contemplated creating a standard template for denying applications from Afghans, signaling a potential mass denial approach.

Although many members of the diaspora persisted in appealing to political institutions for help (such as asking for endorsement letters from members of Congress for potential evacuees to enter the United States), a considerable number of us were left shattered, deeply disillusioned with the American state, having realized that we could not count on political institutions for help during such an urgent crisis. This was exemplified by an Afghan American artist and social justice advocate with whom I frequently communicated; she vanished for two years as the stress of the evacuation process exacerbated her previously dormant fibromyalgia.

This experience magnified the dire consequences of a broken system that placed undue responsibility on ordinary individuals to provide aid and support, and disregarded the lives of those caught in the crossfire. Navigating complex military networks, bureaucratic obstacles, and financial constraints to save a life was compounded as Afghan Americans were thrown into the role of coaching distressed Afghans fleeing for their lives and running out of time. This unexpected humanitarian role compounded my own unresolved trauma and responsibilities, evoking collective family memories of our exodus from Afghanistan almost exactly four decades earlier—an experience I had lived through as an infant but now felt new. A profound sense of guilt and obligation stirred within me, rooted in my own privileged status as an Afghan refugee who "made it." I felt a responsibility to pay it forward during this critical juncture.[4] My own infant's cries for a diaper change blended with the ceaseless hum of my phone as I remained engrossed in the continuous monitoring of updates, chat groups, and other communications. One glimmer of hope emerged from the resilience of ordinary individuals from across the globe, Afghans and non-Afghans alike, uniting to coordinate flights out of the country, raise money, share resources, and more. That said, a profound sense of despair permeated the entire endeavor, and even now, several years later, that emotion persists, making it challenging to revisit or recount the experience.

As I found myself entrenched in these efforts, a parallel reality was unfolding in Afghanistan. Paintings were being effaced, sculptures destroyed, and artistic voices silenced as the Taliban regained control of the country. This cultural annihilation extended beyond the physical in that the Taliban were attempting to erase Afghanistan's history, cultural heritage, and diverse identities. They targeted art, a historically powerful tool for dissent, the celebration of diversity, and the challenging of societal norms, to eradicate narratives of the past. This would leave a void, as the Taliban's version of history claimed authoritative space, reestablishing its roots unopposed.

Artistic Reckoning

The events of 2021 were deeply illuminating. I began to grasp the severe flaws of the US immigration system and how it functioned as an extension of an imperial endeavor, using Afghans to advance its interests before ultimately discarding them. Consequently, I was inspired to develop a multimedia project called *With/Draw* (2022), which serves as a contemplation of how this complex framework has mishandled and manipulated Afghan lives.

With/Draw is the first chapter of a multiroom in-progress installation called *Chelah: 40 Years Later*. *Chelah*, from the word *chehel* (forty), is a term used to refer to different cycles of time, including celebrating a baby's fortieth day of life and mourning for forty days after death. August 2021 marked the US/NATO withdrawal, the subsequent Taliban takeover, and the forty-year anniversary of my own family's departure from the country, all in my fortieth year of life. *Chelah* features the afterlives of Afghan artists who have been displaced over multiple generations and the invisible labor of the Afghan diaspora as they aid Afghan refugees through a cruel immigration system. The project is meant to forge empathy and connection with the Afghans highlighted in the project, prompting the audience to relate to their stories and struggles. It seeks to humanize them and convey that they share universal desires to live their lives safely and see their children go to school, grow up, and be happy. The objectives of this project are to go beyond the often-forgotten headlines to see the real-world impacts of US immigration policy.

With/Draw featured messages exchanged between myself and the Afghan artist previously mentioned. Transcripts of these communications were written on the gallery walls with black acrylic marker but were erased at the end of the exhibition, reflecting the invisible labor of so many in the diaspora who have been working tirelessly to evacuate at-risk Afghans, in spite of a negligent and inaccessible state apparatus. In the center of the room, a single black analog telephone receiver hung, playing voice memos sent to me by the artist in the hopes of leaving Afghanistan to continue his life. Like a body in limbo, the phone symbolized a life on hold and someone desperately calling out for help to anyone who would listen. Speakers projected my voice memos and those of others involved in the evacuation. Video projections appeared on opposing walls, displaying texts, photos, videos, social media posts, and news articles (figure 14.1). The concurrent images, voice memoirs, and written texts represented the overwhelming and chaotic exchange of information I experienced at that time. The physical act of mapping that chaos through restless marks

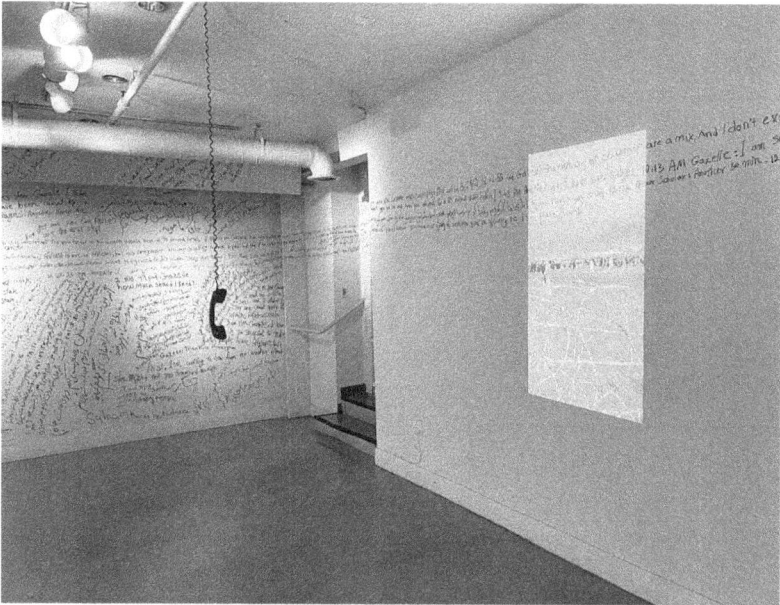

14.1 Partial view of Gazelle Samizay's installation *With/Draw*, LA Artcore, Los Angeles, 2022. Photo by author.

embodied the fragmentation and uncertainty experienced both by displaced individuals and by those, like me, aiding them.

With/Draw became a means for me to process my emotions on a personal level and to create a platform that would prevent this crucial sequence of events from fading away unnoticed in the collective memory of the American public. My feelings of anger were palpable—anger directed at the burdensome responsibilities the US government had imposed on the Afghan diaspora, compelling us to assume roles as impromptu immigration advocates, makeshift trauma counselors, and unplanned military operatives. In the end, many of us realized that despite our tireless efforts, we were met with more false promises. The harsh realities of border control became evident as request after request was denied.

As I set up *With/Draw*, I encountered moments that left me on the verge of nausea or reduced me to tears. Amid the installation process, I was struck by an unusual vision—an entrance to the past when my father left Afghanistan, four decades earlier. It linked me to the anguish my father experienced when departing from his homeland, a feeling I now experienced on a visceral level, whereas previously I had only comprehended it intellectually. It became evident that my intense present-day emotions were intimately entwined with the sorrow my father endured upon our departure from the country, magnifying the intensity of our shared experiences.

Anxiety gripped me over the potential reception of the project. It was raw and messy, a stark contrast to my previous projects, which had a clean, refined aesthetic and a measured approach. Nonetheless, I was inspired by fellow Afghan Americans entangled in the crisis who found that the project articulated their experiences of pain when they themselves were unready to confront them. For many, the installation created a space where collective healing and processing could unfold. As the intensity of the evacuations subsided toward the beginning of 2022, the frustration, anger, and disillusionment of the previous months began to set in. It also showed me how important it was to create a space in which the Afghan diaspora could collectively process what had happened.

Emergenc(y): Afghan Lives Beyond the Forever War

In 2022 AAAWA, in conjunction with the Worth Ryder Art Gallery at UC Berkeley, where I serve as the gallery director, put out a call for artists and writers to submit work that reflected on the events of August 2021 and beyond called *Emergenc(y): Afghan Lives Beyond the Forever War*. Playing on the words *emergency* and *emergence*, we sought to show how Afghans in the diaspora and within Afghanistan were using art as a tool to reclaim their humanity, to critique a world of impenetrable borders, and to reimagine and reconstruct their futures. We asked: How do Afghans, both those who remain in Afghanistan and those displaced waiting in limbo, make sense of twenty years of both prolonged intervention and sudden abandonment? What historical traditions and contemporary practices of art, writing, and advocacy were being resurrected in this moment when the language of policy, military strategy, and scholarship failed to understand the kinds of futures people imagined for themselves? How does the uncertainty of life become felt in new ways when an empire redraws its boundaries? (AAAWA 2022). The call for submissions required no entry fee and was circulated in English and Farsi to make it accessible to as many people as possible. The selected art and writing submissions reflected perspectives from Afghanistan, Pakistan, Iran, Europe, and North America and included twenty-four artists and twenty-nine writers, most of whom were Afghan.[5] By featuring contributors from diverse professional and geographic backgrounds, the exhibition not only centered Afghan perspectives but also exposed the gallery's false neutrality, recasting it as a space for dialogue, dissent, and collective reflection.

As Al-An deSouza notes, diaspora exhibitions strive to reclaim and re-define the gallery space "*as* contested territory; by making visible a political and social context within which the artwork may function, the diaspora exhibition not only allows the diasporic artist to 'speak,' it also allows for the possibility of intervention into the territories of visual culture and its attendant critical cultures by providing that elusive necessity, the justice/justification for speech" (2000, 17). DeSouza highlights the significance of diaspora exhibitions as platforms where artists in exile not only express themselves but also shape the broader discourse of visual culture and criti-cal analysis while validating their voices and perspectives. The public pro-grams created in conjunction with *Emergenc(y)* included Amanullah Mo-jadidi's lecture performance, a dance performance by Sarah Ramin Zamani, and readings by several anthology contributors, including virtual presen-tations from writers outside the United States. Together, these programs provided tools for the diasporic community to critically examine itself and imagine new constructs (deSouza 2000, 17). These gatherings also served as communal acts of remembering, enabling the collective processing and archiving of trauma within the Afghan community. Thus, exhibitions like *Emergenc(y)* transform the gallery into a space of political significance, en-abling intervention and representation that challenge traditional narratives.

Ronak Kapadia asserts that a thorough examination of "insurgent" art can uncover marginalized forms of knowledge pertaining to the United States and its forever wars, serving as a crucial asset for informing policy decisions, fueling activism, and fostering societal change (2019, 15). This approach enables the articulation of alternative social ideals and political visions that stand in contrast to prevailing counterinsurgency and coun-terterrorism strategies: "Under this formulation, diasporic visual art and related cultural forms are the sites where knowledge and meaning about the forever war are at once constituted and unraveled" (20). For Afghan diasporic artists, highlighting the suffering caused by the war while hold-ing empires accountable challenges and unsettles the prevailing narra-tives surrounding the conflict. Political philosopher Jacques Rancière has aptly characterized the political potential of art through the lens of the worker poet and his concept of the "distribution of the sensible" (2010, 141). He argues that the dominant social order determines who is a worthy political agent, and that politics occurs when those who do not have a recognized place in public discourse assert their presence and agency. They "demonstrate that their mouths really do emit speech capable of making pronouncements on the common which cannot be reduced to voices signalling pain" (Rancière 2009, 24). By speaking out in a way that cannot be dismissed as mere cries of suffering, they participate in political and artistic life and claim a role in shaping society. The "distribution of the sensible" also describes the critical potential of these art forms: "Critical art is an art that aims to produce a new perception of the world, and therefore to create a commitment to its transformation" (Rancière 2010, 142).

This notion of art as a catalyst for change and new perceptions is exemplified in the work of artist Amanullah Mojadidi. His interactive performance lecture and installation, *Remembering a Future #2*, delves into the concepts of home, migration, and the interplay between personal and political histories. Together with the audience, the artist explored the notion of a "post-9/11" world on an interactive chalkboard timeline that he cocreated with spectators. He asked, "The phrase signifies a world forever changed. But for who?" Built up over the series of performances, the timeline included significant historical and political events from 2001 to the present alongside personal details of both the artist's and audience's lives. In contrast to a colonial temporality in which time, narratives, and histories are manipulated to serve a teleological narrative that culminates in the US/NATO military intervention, Mojadidi challenges this temporal hierarchy managed by the US government. He achieves this by first populating the timeline with both personal and political events significant to him and relevant to writing an anti-colonialist history, including those shaped by a post-9/11 Islamophobic discourse (figure 14.2). Here is a sampling of events he included:

SEPTEMBER 11, 2001: American Airlines Flight 11 crashes into the north tower of the WTC in NYC. / I'm on a bus on my way to work.

DECEMBER 2001: U.S.-imposed leader Hamid Karzai becomes Interim President of the Afghan Transitional Administration.

2003: I begin work for an Afghan NGO in Kabul.

DECEMBER 2003: 2 police officers killed in 14-hour standoff with 3 self-proclaimed "sovereign citizens" in South Carolina.

JUNE 2006: U.S. F-16 airstrikes in Iraq kill Abu Musab al-Zarqawi, the leader of Al-Qaeda in Iraq.

2006: I hide from rioters in Kabul.

2007: I lose my mother to cancer.

DECEMBER 2009: A pig's foot is hung on the door and swastikas painted on the walls of a mosque in Castres, France.

JULY 2014: Eric Garner killed in a chokehold by NYC police officer— Garner is recorded saying "I Can't Breathe" 11 times before losing consciousness and dying.

JUNE 2016: 49 people are killed by a gunman at the Pulse nightclub in Orlando, FL.

SEPTEMBER 2019: A U.S. drone strike intended to hit an Islamic State hideout kills 30 pine-nut farmers in Nangarhar province, Afghanistan.

FEBRUARY 2020: The Taliban and the Trump admin. reach an agreement for U.S. troops to withdraw by May 1, 2021.

AUGUST 2021: The Taliban enter Kabul with no resistance as President Ghani flees the country leading to massive evacuation efforts at Kabul airport.

FEBRUARY 2023: We are all here now, together. What might be happening elsewhere today?

Mojadidi's timeline reframes history, decentering colonial narratives that position colonizers as the sole agents of progress and modernity. His work addresses amnesia and the reclamation of control over the collective memory of the events that have impacted Afghanistan since 9/11. Additionally, Mojadidi highlights the extensive global repercussions of the US empire's actions. By inviting viewers to contribute to the timeline, he involves them as active participants in broader social histories, allowing them to retain authority over how the Global War on Terror—as an imperial war that is deeply entangled with people's everyday lives—is remembered and narrated.

In one segment of his performance, Mojadidi prompted participants to contemplate the consequences of the US empire's negligence. By simulating the experience through sound and narration, he invited participants to imagine themselves as the drone pilot operating the misguided US military drone strike that killed ten civilians, including seven children, in late August 2021, from over seven thousand miles away in the Nevada desert (Schmitt 2021). He questioned, "Let's think about this—beyond the tragedy of the act itself, what kind of symbolic message does it convey to the Af-

14.2 Partial view Amanullah Mojadidi's timeline as part of the installation *Remembering a Future #2*, Worth Ryder Art Gallery, Berkeley, 2023. Photo by author.

ghan people that after fleeing the country from Bagram Military Base outside of Kabul under the cover of night without even informing the local Afghan military and/or police units, one of the last acts carried out by the US after twenty years of occupation, development, exploitation, and reconstruction is a drone strike that only kills civilians?" (Mojadidi 2023). His performance underscored the sobering message conveyed to the Afghan people in its last days of engagement, raising crucial questions about accountability, intent, and the human cost of the US government's foreign policy decisions.

Mojadidi's approach echoes Al-An de Souza's discussion on the decolonizing power of artworks that revisit and reclaim time, revealing intricacies and contradictions. Drawing inspiration from Homi Bhabha's exploration of temporal hybridity and reflecting on three diaspora exhibitions from the 1990s, deSouza posits:

> By locating art practice within social forces that operate across temporal Ambivalence—as I believe diaspora exhibitions are attempting to do—the concept of authenticity is again disrupted. Time is literally hybridized: reconfigured so that past, present and future are experienced not as linear, but as simultaneously occurring within the same moment. . . . This concept of simultaneity is crucial to the process of decolonization, invoking

the period of colonialism and its aftermath in a hybrid weave of forces and positionings both acting upon and enacted by the colonized subject. It is precisely those spaces and movements between such polarities as acting upon and enacted, subject and object, colonizer and colonized, where these exhibitions have attempted to intervene. (2000, 15)

Building on deSouza's notion of hybrid temporalities, the artists in *Emergenc(y)* occupy overlapping terrains. Their interventions disrupt linear narratives of rescue, progress, or defeat by holding multiple timelines in the same conceptual field. Rather than reinforcing fixed categories of colonizer and colonized, the works operate in the spaces between, where memory, grief, and critique converge. In doing so, they give rise to creativity, agency, and new imagined futures.

Mojadidi's *Rembering a Future #2* and Elina Ansary's *For What It's Worth* both employ what Kapadia calls "insurgent aesthetics." This approach "craft[s] a queer calculus of US empire that makes intimate what is rendered distant, renders tactile what is made invisible, and unifies what is divided, thereby conjuring forms of embodied critique that can envision a collective world within and beyond the spaces of US empire's perverse logics of global carcerality, security, and war" (2019, 10). Ansary painted intimate miniature portraits of Afghans killed across four decades of conflict onto US pennies and placed them in a repurposed antique box, lined with red velvet, adding a sense of sacredness and funerary reverence to the artwork objects (figure 14.3). Ansary challenges viewers to engage intimately with those memorialized. The small scale of the portraits demands deliberate observation, fostering a deeper connection than the fleeting images in the news cycle.

Inscribed with "Liberty" and "E Pluribus Unum" (Out of many, one), the penny evokes ideals of unity, freedom, and American democracy. Yet within the context of Ansary's work, these inscriptions take on an ambivalent tone—revealing how the language of faith and national virtue can mask the violence and disposability of lives sacrificed in the pursuit of imperial power. Ansary obscures Abraham Lincoln's image—a symbol of American pride and the contested legacy of emancipation—to highlight the contradictions at the heart of American empire. This intervention raises questions about whom these ideals serve and whose suffering is erased from state memory. By naming every victim in Farsi—echoing the memorial strategy of the 9/11 Memorial site—Ansary both embeds Afghan loss into American collective memory and symbolically effaces the Lincoln Memorial depicted on the coin's back.

14.3 Detail of Elina Ansary's *For What it's Worth*. Acrylic and resin on pennies. Dimensions variable. 2021–present. Photo by author.

Ansary's practice resonates with those of the artists Kapadia discusses in *Insurgent Aesthetics*, whose practices extend beyond gallery walls and "co-implicate" audiences,[6] "thus closing the distance between state violence and its afterlives" (Kapadia 2019, 13). Dressed in traditional Afghan attire but evoking a 1920s cigarette girl, Ansary has stood outside esteemed cultural institutions such as the Metropolitan Museum of Art in New York or the Art Basel art fair in Miami, offering the open penny box to passers-by. Her presence unsettles the quiet authority of these elite art spaces, inviting curiosity while offering onlookers the opportunity to "share in the burden of Afghan grief" (Ansary 2023).

Ansary uses everyday American currency to embody a critique of the commodification of Afghan lives—lives rendered disposable once their strategic utility ends. The penny's negligible worth contrasts sharply with the immense human and economic costs of war, exposing the profit-driven logics sustaining US intervention. By memorializing Afghan lives across four decades of conflict and presenting the work in public American spaces, Ansary binds histories of violence in Afghanistan to everyday material culture. In doing so, she collapses geographic and temporal distances, urging viewers to confront the enduring legacies of conflict, loss, and imperial entanglement.

Similarly, Afghan Canadian artist Hamid Amiri's artwork critically confronts the imperialist agendas and foreign interventions of the US government and other foreign powers. His *Trespassers* series seamlessly merges historical traditions with contemporary artistic practices to vividly capture the amalgamation of dreams and nightmares shared by displaced Afghans. Through this collection, Amiri vividly portrays the experiences of ordinary individuals who grapple with fear and trauma stemming from persistent conflict. Inspired by his own childhood memories in Afghanistan, the series captures the poignant realities and contradictions of those affected by the war (Hamid Amiri, comm. with author by video, July 12, 2023).

Play (2022) examines the interplay of power, freedom, and foreign influence on Afghan society (figure 14.4). The painting portrays a young Afghan boy balancing on a seesaw while a Western businessman stands on the opposite end, walking toward its edge. The seesaw straddles two worlds—on the left behind the boy is a natural, rural Afghan landscape, and on the right is a Western cityscape, characterized by the clean lines of buildings, paved freeways, and manicured shrubs. The composition captures a moment frozen in time, imbuing a sense of tension and precariousness.

The seesaw serves as a metaphor for the delicate balance of power between Afghanistan and foreign actors. The depiction of the foreign agent as a businessman underscores the lucrative nature of the US war industry and the profits made by its many private contractors and subcontractors in the forever war. The Afghan boy bearing the businessman's weight symbolizes the burden placed on Afghan society and future generations to accommodate and sustain foreign interests. Given that the boy's feet are not fully planted on the ground, this balance is tenuous. There is a sense of determination in the man's forward trajectory, though with one more step he would fall through the maze-like terrain of freeways and oil pipelines to the construction site below. In contrast, the boy's carefree stance and expression could symbolize a false sense of security.

The backdrop contextualizes the power dynamics between these two figures. Behind the seesaw, a grand piano is perched on the edge of the cavernous divide that separates the Afghan landscape and Western city. The piano symbolizes artistic freedoms that were accessible during a period

14.4 Hamid Amiri, *Play*, 2022. Oil on linen, 24 × 30 in. Photo by artist.

of relative stability and semidemocracy in Afghanistan, now suppressed under Taliban rule. It serves as a reminder of the aspirations and desires for creativity and self-expression that exist within Afghan society.

The beauty of the distant Afghan mountains is disrupted by a thick plume of smoke, presumably from an explosion. As the smoke drifts toward the Western city, it darkens the sky—signaling the deep interconnection between these geographically distant places. However, the construction of the Western city, with its pristine edges, immaculate structures, and well-maintained manicured shrubs, is sustained by oil funneled from Afghan soil, underscoring the exploitative economic interests that have long fueled foreign intervention.

Play explores the entanglement of space, time, and power through fragmented architectures whose twisted pathways terminate in illogical dead ends. These formal disturbances convey nonlinear temporalities that expose the personal and political dislocations of war, exile, and foreign intervention (Chakrabarty 2007). By undermining the illusion of progress, the painting prompts viewers to interrogate the true motivations and consequences of foreign involvement in Afghanistan. Its constructed incoherence renders reality both recognizable and estranged, foregrounding resource exploitation, asymmetric power relations, and the selective beneficiaries of intervention. Although the US invasion was framed as a mission of political stability, women's liberation, and nation building, Amiri exposes the contradictions that underwrite such rhetoric, disrupting the developmental and humanitarian narratives that legitimize imperial action (Mamdani 2004). The title *Play* offers a sharp double entendre—evoking both the innocence of a child's game and the calculated theater of global politics. In this context, the painting critiques how powerful nations "play" with the fates of smaller countries, reducing complex human realities to mere moves on a strategic board.

Conclusion

In the wake of the 2021 US/NATO withdrawal from Afghanistan, a sobering set of insights emerged, illuminating the interplay between policy decisions and their real-world implications. Through my artistic pursuits and community-driven initiatives, I have grappled with the multifaceted dimensions of American engagement in Afghanistan. This exploration, exemplified by projects like *Fragmented Futures*, led me to an unexpected juncture in 2021, where I found myself deeply involved in aiding an artist from that same exhibit—as well as other vulnerable Afghans—seeking refuge during the tumultuous withdrawal period.

The lessons drawn from these experiences are both instructive and disheartening. They reveal the fragility of Afghan lives within a fraught geopolitical system wherein competing stakeholders' agendas play out in the theater that is Afghans' everyday lives. It has become increasingly clear that the value attributed to Afghan lives often hinges on their utility in advancing the interests of the US government and its allies. This devaluation is operationalized through opaque immigration systems and inconsistent policies that privilege those aligned with US interests over others in need.

The labyrinthine US immigration system further exacerbates these inequalities, entangling the Afghan diaspora in bureaucratic challenges and robbing them of precious time, energy, and resources. While some of the diaspora's efforts were directed toward political change, the prevailing sentiment was one of depletion, leaving many broken and fatigued.

The enduring effects of intergenerational trauma, triggered by displacement, conflict, and violence—often influenced by US intervention—echo through the narratives of resettled Afghans. This struggle to cross borders appears in multiple generations of Afghans displaced by imperial wars, emphasizing the long-lasting impact of geopolitical conflicts on Afghan communities. This trauma can fuel a deep sense of obligation to address the pain of the past and may serve as the foundation for many diaspora activists' actions.

The role of artists emerges as pivotal, serving as historians, cultural architects, and storytellers who give voice to the silenced and challenge dominant narratives. This is evident in *Emergenc(y): Afghan Lives Beyond the Forever War*, a testament to the power of art as a vehicle for navigating and responding to the complications of US involvement in Afghanistan. It also acts as a means of collectively archiving and processing the trauma within the Afghan community. The selected works highlighted in this chapter—including those by Amiri, Ansary, Mojadidi, and my own—counter dominant colonial chronologies by weaving personal memory into global political events, offering an understanding of time rooted in lived experience rather than in imperial logics of progress (Fabian 1983). The work reveals how historical narratives, collective memory, cycles of violence, and ideas of progress are inseparable from physical space—unsettling colonial hierarchies between spatial and temporal registers and thereby destabilizing hegemonic narratives.

The US/NATO withdrawal served as a crucible for examining the geopolitical, economic, diasporic, and humanitarian consequences entangled within the US imperial project. The lessons drawn from this experience—shaped by the failures of the immigration system, the reverberations of intergenerational trauma, and the vital role of artists—reveal the power of creative practice to endure and to speak truth to power. Their creative practices and ongoing struggles collectively implore us to reassess the enduring impact of empire on the lives of Afghans, urging a more just and compassionate engagement with the complex realities faced by colonized and displaced communities.

Notes

1   AAAWA is a nonprofit organization that hosts community exhibitions, creative workshops, and public commentaries aimed at amplifying critical analyses of US mainstream discourse on Afghanistan. Contributors to

this volume, Wazhmah Osman, Gazelle Samizay, and Helena Zeweri, are members of the board of directors.

2   Known as Jashn-i Inquilab or the Festival of Independence, or simply Jashn, this annual national holiday in Afghanistan features multiday events and exhibitions celebrating the country's independence from British colonial rule.

3   The artist consented to the use of their remarks in this chapter.

4   For more on the connection between trauma and activism, see Haglili (2020).

5   The exhibit opened February 22, 2023, at the Worth Ryder Art Gallery at the University of California, Berkeley. An anthology, *Writing Afghan Lives Beyond the Forever War: An Anthology of Writing from Afghanistan and Its Diaspora*, accompanied the exhibit.

6   Instead of implicating a single entity or group, the term *co-implicate* suggests a more interconnected and interwoven understanding of how various elements, including individuals, institutions, and ideologies, are mutually implicated or involved in the issues and events being explored through art and culture.

References

AAAWA (Afghan American Artists and Writers Association). 2022. "'Emergenc(y): Afghan Lives Beyond the Forever War' Call for Art/ Writing Submissions." Last modified July 14, 2022. https://www.aaawa .net/emergency.

American Immigration Council. 2023. "Advocates Release FOIA Data, Seek Transparency for Thousands of Afghans Seeking Humanitarian Parole and the Extensive Delays They Are Facing." March 16. https://www .americanimmigrationcouncil.org/news/advocates-release-foia-data-seek -transparency-thousands-afghans-seeking-humanitarian-parole.

Ansary, Elina. 2023. Artist statement. Worth Ryder Art Gallery, University of California, Berkeley, March.

Chakrabarty, Dipesh. 2007. *Provincializing Europe: Postcolonial Thought and Historical Difference*. Princeton, NJ: Princeton University Press.

deSouza, Al-An. 2000. "The Flight of/from the Authentic Primitive (Revised)." Unpublished manuscript. https://www.academia.edu/35349757/THE _FLIGHT_OF_FROM_THE_AUTHENTIC_PRIMITIVE_revised_1.

Fabian, Johannes. 1983. *Time and the Other: How Anthropology Makes Its Object*. New York: Columbia University Press.

Fassin, Didier. 2012. *Humanitarian Reason: A Moral History of the Present*. Berkeley: University of California Press.

Haglili, Ronna Milo. 2020. "The Intersectionality of Trauma and Activism: Narratives Constructed from a Qualitative Study." *Journal of Humanistic Psychology* 60 (4): 514–524.

Kapadia, Ronak K. 2019. *Insurgent Aesthetics: Security and the Queer Life of the Forever War*. Durham, NC: Duke University Press.

Mamdani, Mahmood. 2005. *Good Muslim, Bad Muslim: America, the Cold War, and the Roots of Terror*. New York: Three Leaves Press.

Mojadidi, Amanullah. 2023. Performance lecture on "Remembering a Future #2." Worth Ryder Art Gallery, University of California, Berkeley, March.

Osman, Wazhmah. 2022. "Transformations in Afghan Media and Culture Through Cycles of Upheaval." *Current History* 121 (834): 135–140.

Rancière, Jacques. 2009. *Aesthetics and its Discontents*. Cambridge: Polity.

Rancière, Jacques. 2010. *Dissensus: On Politics and Aesthetics*. Edited and translated by Steven Corcoran. London: Continuum International.

Schmitt, Eric. 2021. "No U.S. Troops Will Be Punished for Deadly Kabul Drone Strike." *New York Times*, December 14.

An Other Afghanistan

Indigeneity, Migration, and

Belonging in Andkhoy (1973)

Afghan Turkestan, an Other Afghanistan

In 1973, my Baba, a twenty-five-year-old young dentist fresh out of manda-
tory military training, traveled through the remote towns, mountain villages, and countryside of Afghanistan to serve the people because there
was a scarcity of modern dentists. He went as far east as Shinwar, Dara i
Nur, a Pashai-inhabited area, Waigal, Salau, Kohistan, and north to Andkhoy and Kunduz, known as Turkestan. Living for months in each of these
border towns exposed him to the many ethnic minorities within the country. These remembrances were recorded for the Digital Archive of Turkic
Heritage in Afghanistan (DATHA). This interview focuses on his three-
month stay in Andkhoy.[1]

Andkhoy was the heart of carpet weaving in Afghanistan and a town
of mostly Turkmen and Uzbeks in what was referred to as Turkestan,
nestled near the border of Turkmenistan. In the nineteenth century,
'Abd al-Rahman Khan, who consolidated power with British backing
during the Great Game, divided the area into separate provinces—
Wilayat-i-Turkestan, Qataghan, Badakhshan, and Hukumati A'laye
Maimana (Shahrani 2002; Shahrani and Canfield 2022). Scholars have
extensively examined the complex history of Afghan Turkestan and
Qataghan.[2]

Although Afghanistan is often mythologized as an anticolonial force and
"the graveyard of empires," its actions in Turkestan during the Great Game
intertwined with British colonial strategy, receiving both funding and endorsement as reflected in archival correspondence. To ensure British interests

were safe, Colonel C. E. Yate pushed the Pashtunization (or Afghaniza-
tion) of the north, known as Yate's Policy (Lee 2018, 387). As Jonathan L.
Lee writes, "The mostly Durrani tribes who were relocated to the region
would have more loyalty to Afghanistan by dint of their ethnic and tribal
links with the ruling dynasty, a bond which was reinforced by the distribution of free land, houses and grazing rights seized from displaced populations" (Lee 2018, 388). The region underwent violent rearrangements.
Thousands upon thousands of people were massacred in the Hazara genocide and the "Turkestan Atrocity" in the late 1880s. 'Abd al-Rahman Khan
displaced thousands of local Uzbek and Turkmen families, all to ensure
that the northern borders remained loyal to the central government (Tapper 2011, 235).

Such policies of control, erasure, and redefinition persisted under later
rulers. In 1931, Nadir Khan abolished the name Turkestan; it no longer appeared on a map, and the province was changed to Mazar-i-sharif, with
Maymana as a separate *hukumat-i-aala*. Wilayat-i-Qataghan and Badakhshan were provinces on their own. Qataghan included Baghlan, Kunduz,
and Takhar, while Badakhshan was its own province (Mudessir 2024). Despite the multiple renamings, the people of Afghanistan still referred to the
region as Turkestan during Baba's time.

A Young Dentist's Journey from Jalalabad
to Andkhoy

Baba traveled to Andkhoy with a simple goal: to earn enough for his up-
coming betrothal. He packed his dentist's satchel, took a bus from Jalalabad to Kabul, then flew to Maimana before boarding a private bus to
Andkhoy. He had heard there were no dentists in the region and decided
to try his chances.

My grandfather had passed away when Baba was sixteen. So, as the
Uzbek saying goes, "Tal'yagh'och madang bolmidi amak'ng daday'ng
bolmedi" (A wood cannot be a lock and an uncle cannot be a father).
Baba traveled in search of belonging through service to the people of
Afghanistan in remote towns and villages. His work in Andkhoy was not
just about providing dental care; it was how he found himself by bridging
the gaps left by a state that had long marginalized the north.

In comparison, Baba grew up in Timurid-style houses in Jalalabad's
Old City before moving to new suburban homes, *hajhda famila*, under

government-supported housing programs in the 1960s, part of a broader initiative to modernize the city and encourage residents to settle in newly developed neighborhoods. Jalalabad had a medical college, high-ranking high schools, a hospital, and dental clinics. Meanwhile, Andkhoy had only primary education up to the sixth grade, forcing students to travel to Maimana or Kabul for further schooling. There were *layleeya* schools, or boarding schools, in Kabul and the eastern and southern provinces, but rarely was there such a boarding school to accommodate students from remote areas wishing to study in the north. Though Andkhoy was a center for carpet weaving and karakul production, it suffered from government neglect, particularly in education and healthcare.

Baba Tells His Story of Andkhoy

In 1973, they engaged me to your mother. They wanted us to have a party, so I had to raise money. I had just finished the army service, where I served for two years.[3] I couldn't run my business then, so I didn't have enough money. My friends told me to take my equipment and go to Turkestan because no dentists were there. "If you work there for a month or two," they said, "you will have money for your wedding." I went to Andkhoy via plane because they said the land routes were difficult. I traveled from Jalalabad to Kabul by bus, purchased the ticket, and went to the airport in Kabul. The airport was small in Khuja Rawash, which was made larger later. The flight to Maimana was on a fifteen-person airplane. When I sat down on my seat in the tiny airplane, under my feet, I could see the airplane floor was repaired with tin hammered in with nails. The other men on the flight were businessmen, and we were squeezed into this small plane. We were all nervous.

The other men in suits said in Farsi, "Agha, what work do you do?"

"I'm a dentist."

"What are you doing going here on this plane? I have no other choice but to go for business there."

"I am also going for business. I need to make money there."

And they nodded and said, "OK then, yes, business is good there."

Then the plane's *ghrr ghrrr* started, and we heard the noise all around us, but the plane was not moving. [Laughs.] The plane had a cleaner (technician), meaning a steward, but he was like a cleaner on the buses. The cleaner said, "Come, brothers, we have to get off and push the plane!"

So we all got on the runway, the pilot started the plane, and we pushed from behind. Once it started moving, the pilot stopped for us to catch up and get on the plane.

"Burroo Ba Khair! Let's go!" The cleaner said, and we were on our way. [Laughs.]

The plane was flying, but it kept sinking, flying up again, and going up and down like that, especially when we went over the mountain of Shiberr.

The cleaner said, in Farsi, "Don't worry, there is a gravitational pull over the mountains here, so it keeps pulling the plane, so the pilot has to fly up higher. Don't worry when it pulls us down. We will fly right up again!"

The plane kept going up and down. Some of us started reciting the Ayatul Kursi while others prayed aloud, "God protect us. We are going to fall."

It was like this until we reached the airport in Maimana. There were no direct flights to Andkhoy. As it landed, it flew down so fast it made our stomachs sink from the speed. The plane landed at Maimana airport, a tiny runway with a loud thump that shook us all. The plane bumped and thumped its way to finally stopping. We exited the plane and started prostrating in thanks for surviving the flight. Some kissed the floor in thanks for having survived. [Laughs.] And so, we ended up in Maimana safely. And from there, I got on a bus to Andkhoy. This was not technically a bus. They called it a bus and used it like a bus to move lots of people. It was a big truck to transport goods turned into a passenger bus. Benches were nailed into the truck back so many people could fit, but it was not a bus like we had in Kabul or Jalalabad. We sat in rows facing each other. During the ride, we stared at each other's faces, and many were just in disbelief at how we traveled. But we reached Khan Churwagh[4] and came to Andkhoy to Babai Wali Madrassa. The bus dropped passengers off there because it is where boys from all around were sent to school. In the normal shops, there were surprising things that were only available at supermarkets in Kabul and not available in Jalalabad: tissues, paper napkins, and toilet paper! Most likely for all the Americans and Europeans who came to study us then.

When I got off the bus, I went to the madrassa to ask where to find a place to stay and a clinic to set up. As I walked to the madrassa, a stream led to a *hawuz* [reservoir]. Water was being filled that day. While the water was filling and rising, there were *kulcha*-[cookie-] like things that were bubbling up to the surface from the force of the water and then sinking back down to the bottom. Mullah Sayib came out of the madrassa, and I greeted him, "Damla Sayib, do you see what is coming along with the water?"

"Oh, it is just dung. Don't worry so much it won't kill anyone. [Laughs.] I'm seventy years old and survived drinking this water. You will not die from this water!"

[Speaking in Uzbek.] "Do you boil this water?"

"Oh, we don't drink water. We drink tea!"

Then I thought, "Oh, they boil this water to drink."

He said, "You know this water in this stream comes from Maimana, that far place you came from as well on the bus. The stream the water travels through starts in Maimana and is filled once a month. It passes through many towns and villages where children and animals defecate in the dry stream until the water comes. The water coming in brought it all up from the bottom. Water is delivered to the towns this way once a month. The *hawuz* is ten meters deep and fifteen meters squared."

Damla Sayib continued, "The water is filled and is used by the people for a month until it dries. The people bring muslin fabric to filter out debris and bugs."

This method filtered out the worms and maggots. The *kulchas* brought on the maggots after they sank to the bottom of the water. Not only were these things in the water, but then the mullah *bacha* [students] started running and throwing themselves into the water before me to celebrate with a swim. This was the primary water source for the entire town.[5]

When I saw all this, I thought, "My God, I cannot stay here."

I said, "Damla Sayib, is there a malik or some leader here I can speak to?"

"Yes, of course, but he's Afghan."

"It's OK if he is Afghan."

"He's Afghan. He's not going to be helpful to us. They don't care for the Uzbeks here. They don't listen to us. Look at the condition of our water. Look at the condition of our streets. Nothing is paved, and everything is dirt roads. The main paths that lead out cause car accidents in the rain and snow, where they topple over at the turns because there is so much mud buildup. They don't care about fixing the roads. This Afghan sitting in the office now won't help or listen to you. They don't respect or value Uzbeks."

"Whatever it may be, I would like to meet him."

Damla Sayib called over one of the students at the madrassa and said, "Take him to the Hakim Sayib's home." Then, to me, "Remember what I told you. He won't help you."

I went to Hakim Sayib's home after leaving my suitcase with Damla Sayib.

Someone opened the door, looked at me dressed in a Western suit [*dirishi*], and immediately welcomed me.

Then he ran inside to say that an inspector was there.

The Hakim Sayib quickly rushed to meet with me, "Asalamalaykum, how are you?" and shook my hand warmly.

[Aside, to me.] I was not speaking Uzbek with him. I was speaking Farsi. So he heard my city accent. Then he said in Pashtu to his assistant, "Go get tea." I said to him in Pashtu, "You speak Pashtu?"

Hakim Sayib said, "You are Pashtun?" and embraced me. "You are the light of my eyes!"

"Come, my brother, come. Whatever you need, I will help you. And I will give you sweets with that as well." [In Pashtu.]

[In Uzbek translated for me.] He said "*Shirni*," or sweets, which means bribe. They don't say bribe, they say "sweets."

"I don't take sweets. I am a dentist!" [Laughs.]

"Ohh!" said Hakim Sayib, and his color returned to his face, relieved. He laughed. He thought I was an inspector from Kabul because of my Farsi and Dirishi.

"I heard there were no dentists here, so I came to serve the people."

"Yes, you are right. I am glad you came. Yes, you are very much needed here."

"I saw the water here, and it's in terrible condition."

"We won't let you drink that water. We will get you clean water! We get our water in a tank from Maimana, which is mountain water. When we get the water, you can send your men, and they can take it for you."

"I don't have any men."

"I have soldiers on duty who can bring water to your place."

I thanked him and left. I didn't see him again. The *hamshahrlar* [same city people] came together and set up a dental clinic for me. I only had my equipment. They came and celebrated the opening. They all started saying, "*Tufalam tufalam tuf*," and lightly spitting on me to keep the evil eye away. And they were all celebrating. I didn't understand and didn't like the sprays coming from them. I knew it was affectionate. My host, the *samowarchi*, a tea shop owner who was very fatherly, saw me flinching and said,

"Stand still and accept it. They are protecting you from the evil eye, and it is to celebrate. Some people put a streak of black on the face to keep away the evil eye. But here, the people say '*Tuvalem.*' We Turkmen say *Tuvalem*, and you Uzbeks say, '*Tuf Tuf.*' It is all the same gesture to show you love. Don't turn away from it."

Of course, when the mothers and grandmothers came to do *tufalam*, I had to stand still and accept out of reverence.

Hakim Sayib came at the opening and said, "Here, only barbers, *dalaks*, pull teeth. We will tell them that pulling teeth with their large pliers is illegal. Then all the people will have no choice but to come to you. I will send the police to reach out."

"No!" I was worried for the *dalaks*. "It's fine. Some people like to do things the old way. Let them be. I will have enough patients through word of mouth. I am sure. You don't need to get the police involved." [In Farsi.]

Word spread about the dental clinic, and people came with various pains. On the third day, the *dalaks* visited me. They came together to greet me and said, "We are pleased you are here! The people will get proper treatment now. We wanted to tell you that we are sending people who come to us straight to you. Now it will be done '*Osully*' the proper way."

"It's alright. I don't need more people to come. We can all practice in one big town."

"You didn't tell the Hakim Sayib to keep us from our work?"

"No, not at all. Keep your work as you have always done. I will tell him." I had German dental equipment, syringes, Novocain, and antibiotics, so it was a small clinic. "Come stay with me if you want and learn." So, I invited some of them because I wouldn't stay in Andkhoy for too long. Only a few stayed to learn. I sketched the anatomy of a mouth and showed them how to pull teeth at an angle outward rather than straight up.

This was one of the first times in my life that I had been in a town that mostly spoke Uzbek or Turkmen. It was straightforward to understand Turkmen, and I had no problems because we are originally from Marghelan. The Turkmen women wore cotton straight-leg pants and long tunics with splits so they could ride horses. They wore high hats. I would see them and the Uzbek women dye wool in many colors in their courtyards. Bright-colored wools were hung out to dry in separate groupings. They were very precise. The dry land was yellow, but everyone wore bright and colorful clothes. I still wore my suit, just no tie, even though it was scorching. Families who came to see me paid me double or triple and said it was because the only way they could receive proper medical services was by going to Kabul.

I was there for three months when I had a visit from the revered pir, Qizilayaq khalifa. I didn't know who he was at the time. His men came to take me to where he was staying in Khan Churwagh. But I said, "I can't make dentures at home. I need my clinic!" They were very shocked that I refused. The next day Qizilayaq khalifa came to me with armed guards in a *gadi* [horse-drawn carriage]. When it stopped before the clinic, his men rolled out a long red Turkmen carpet from the *gadi* to the clinic's doorstep! It was very muddy, and I saw he was an elder. I understand, but it seemed grand for such a small town.

When he came to sit in the chair, his men wouldn't leave him.

"This is my dental clinic. I can't work while people are standing around with guns." The Qizilayaq khalifa shooed away his men and sat with me. He was very kind, but I didn't understand the crowd and the commotion around him. He was my last patient, I told him. I was leaving. He asked who I was and who my father was. I told him. The khalifa asked if he had come from Marghelan. "Yes, his name is Mir Kaamil," I said. And he nodded and asked if he was a Basmachi, and I said, "Yes, we are descendants. My father escaped." And he was very gentle to me after that. Each time he came to see me, there would be crowds of people there to see him. But he joked with me, and we spoke very freely. After I completed his dentures, the khalifa gifted me 10,000 Afs for my wedding. He was very fatherly with me. His men would glare at me for having so much time alone with him, but I didn't pay attention to them.

The *hamshaharlar* came to bid me good wishes. I didn't want to leave them, but I had to go back. My fiancé was sending me letters so that I couldn't stay. I left behind all my German tools for the new *dandansaz* there so they could continue working for the community.

This time, I chose a land route to go back to Kabul.

[End of interview.]

The Dentist and the Apprentices: A Migration Story

My family's education, achieved despite a system that made it very difficult for minorities, particularly Turkic minorities, to obtain schooling, is a testament to our migrant history. Baba is the son of Mir Mohammad Kaamil, whose elder brother, Mir Fauziljan, was a Basmachi, a term used for insurgent fighters who resisted Russian Bolshevik rule and sought to preserve their autonomy against foreign domination. My grandfather was a teenager in 1923 or 1924 when he fled with his infant brother after surviving the massacre of his extended family in Tashkent. This massacre ended generations of his family line in one day due to their involvement in the Turkestan nationalist struggle. Mir Kaamil had fled to Kazakhstan and then to Ila in East Turkestan/Xinjiang before making his way to Bombay. In India, the British welcomed refugees from Turkestan. In British India, he suffered at first, but with some business acumen, he prospered. By the time he was in his forties, he had a few factories in India. This was when he visited Afghanistan with his younger brother, hearing that one could find the scent of homeland in Afghanistan's north, "watan'di isi." He planned to visit Baghlan but was stopped at the Torkham border, where he had to wait for special clearance because he had a British Indian passport. But because his birthplace was listed as Turkestan and his profession was listed as dentistry, it raised enough interest to allow him entrance. These details drew the attention of the prime minister, Sardar Mohammed Hashim Khan, who requested to meet Mir Kaamil in Kabul. He convinced my grandfather to stay a year in Kabul, where he trained an Afghan named Mohammad Ehsan in dentistry. Ehsan served in Kabul.

Mir Kaamil attended a medical college in Hong Kong that had a dental program. In the early twentieth century, early in the history of dentistry, it was common for those who graduated to train apprentices who became known as *dandansaz* in Afghanistan, someone who "makes or fixes teeth,"

15.1 Portrait of Mir Mohammad Kaamil by Gholam Ali Omid, painted in 1973.

a denturist with extraction skills. This training in Afghanistan and the rest of Asia included extractions and fillings but not more complicated surgical processes like root canals.

Mir Kaamil did not stay in Afghanistan; he left his brother, whom he had trained as an apprentice, in his place. Farsi was taught in the schools of West Turkestan, as well as in schools in East Turkestan, so both were literate in the language. Mir Mohammad Hussayn Hashem, *dandansaz*, was Jalalabad's sole dentist from 1934 to the 1960s.[6] After this period, more dentists graduated from Kabul, and more *dandansaz* began serving in various provinces.

During the anti-colonial movement and Hindu-Muslim battles in India just before partition, Mir Kaamil lost his businesses in 1946 and returned to Afghanistan with his pregnant Uyghur wife. In Kabul, he had a stroke and was treated in Aliabad Hospital, where Sardar Hashim Khan called in German doctors to help him walk again. Baba was born in Kabul and missed being Indian by a few months.

This is the story of our migration. For a while, Mir Kaamil's name and photo were in the school textbooks as the first dentist in Afghanistan; later,

15.2 Family photo in Jalalabad, circa 1972. *Left to right*: Abdulsamad Saed (Baba) with nephew, Mir Mohammad Husayn Hashem, Rahim (standing), and Ahad.

in the 1960s, they replaced him with the apprentice he had trained, who was then named the first Afghan dentist. My grandfather's contribution was erased from the history books because he was Turkestani and not Afghan.

Until the 1960s, one could become a *dandansaz* or assistant dentist in Kabul after graduating from a dental high school and one more year of certification. The 1960s also saw a successful Turkestani *dandansaz* opening a dental supplies shop, helping local dentists and denturists order supplies from within Afghanistan rather than from Germany. Until the imports, dentists used local materials like *choona* (known as quicklime) for molds, which were used in modern dentistry but heavily processed.

Baba obtained permission to practice dentistry by presenting his degree. He had graduated from the International Dental College in 1970. He was an endodontist. When my father returned from his studies, there were five dentists, not including his uncle, in Jalalabad, so there was a lot of competition. When he went to Andkhoy, his practice thrived because wealthy residents generously supported him, and he was also able to serve those who couldn't afford dental care.

On Turkic Families in Eastern Provinces

A minority of Uzbeks and Turkmen lived in the eastern provinces. From the 1930s to the 1980s, the few families in these traditionally Pashtun-speaking lands highlighted the rarity of finding Uzbek or Turkmen communities. Turkic people had been present in these areas since the Mughal era, but these families primarily spoke Pashto, like the Sikh communities in Shinwar.

Jalalabad, a cosmopolitan gateway to South Asia, is predominantly Pashtun but also home to vibrant Pashai, Chalasi, Kohistani, Sikh, and Hindu communities. Wealthy Kabuli families often spent winters in this resort town, enjoying its streams, orange groves, and gardens.

In the late 1960s, Abdul Rahim Khan, a Turkmen from Andkhoy, became the police commissioner of Laghman and regularly visited Baba's family. Naim Khan, an Uzbek from Mazar-i-Sharif, was the police commandant in Nangarhar. These three families and Baba's family formed the Turkic community in the eastern provinces as part of Zahir Shah's integration program, though they often felt like token representatives. Living in Jalalabad, a two-hour bus ride from Kabul, meant they were connected to larger Turkestani communities in the capital.

On Gender

In Baba's reminiscences, women often dominate decision-making and sometimes rescue him and his friend Kabir from difficult situations. For instance, in Dara i Noor, Pashai women, instead of carrying kindling, transported Baba and his friend in their baskets after they were stranded on a mountaintop. In Andkhoy, matriarchs led the inaugural celebration of Baba's dental clinic, a community effort. Grandmothers blessed the new beginning and were the first patients transitioning from the old practice of visiting the barber for tooth extractions. The town's mothers also approached him with matchmaking intentions.

During a time when carpet weaving and karakul production were lucrative, families and women enjoyed relative wealth and mobility. Despite the government's heavy taxation on the north, the market remained strong. However, with the onset of war, the loss of men, displacement, and economic uncertainty, women's burdens increased. Even during the era of the Republic, as the carpet market declined, women faced significant challenges. In recent years, opium addiction among children rose as a drop of opium became a way to soothe children while mothers worked. The disruption of traditional family structures and the loss of support systems for weavers has come at the cost of women and children. Baba remembers an Afghanistan where women's roles and contributions were the community's spine.

On the Khalifa Qizilayaq, Pir, Spiritual Leader, and Baba

The Qizilayaq khalifa was a revered Naqshbandi pir and spiritual leader of the north. A pir is a saintlike figure who advises political leaders. This inherited title represented a multigenerational lineage of anti-colonial spiritual leaders who fought significant wars against the Russian Soviets: one in the early twentieth century and another in the 1980s following the Soviet invasion.

The original Qizilayaq khalifa, Abed Nazar, was a prominent figure in Turkestan. Lee is one of the few scholars who write about his impact: "The Turkman pir and former Basmachi leader, the Khalifa of Qizil Ayaq . . . commanded an army of 12,000 murids." Lee's account is one of the rare English texts mentioning the khalifa and the history of northern Uzbeks and Turkmen siding with Habibullah Kalakani against Amanullah Khan and Nader Shah. Lee continues, "In Qataghan, Ibrahim Beg, the Turkish [Uzbek] Basmachi commander, also declared for Habib Allah" (Lee 2018, 495). This political alignment created rifts (if not outright enmities) with the central government. Nadir Shah exiled Ibrahim Beg over the border, where the Bolsheviks executed him.

Government officials were met with distrust by the locals. Spiritual leaders advocated for the exploited and marginalized northern community. The original Qizilayaq khalifa hailed from Greater Turkestan across the Amu Darya, in the area now known as Turkmenistan. In Jauzjan, Khoja Du Koh, there is a village called Qizilayaq. In 1968, during his time in Aqcha, Mark Slobin photographed a younger Qizilayaq khalifa. The title was handed down to a few male family members.

During Baba's stay in Andkhoy, there are several moments where distinctions are made between "Afghans" and "us," Uzbeks. The Afghans are the ones in power as administrators and government officials. There were no Pashtun families in these parts yet since they were resettled in more fertile

15.3 Baba with dentist satchel, on his way to Waigal from the outskirts of Laghman.

areas with access to water. Tapper writes that conflicts in the Turkestan area "have generally been perceived as interethnic disputes (dawa) and as evidence of a polarization of 'Afghan' versus 'Uzbek' in local political affairs." The pir intervenes and protects the people in cases of confrontations with "Afghans" and offers social services that the government cannot or will not provide for the locals (Tapper 2011, 233). Just as Baba had gone to serve, so had the community come together to care for Baba. It was the elders of the town who gave him rent-free space and helped him set up his clinic. Baba says all he did was come with his dental instruments and the medication he had brought. The community was especially generous toward him, knowing he was there to earn enough for his wedding. Baba would return a few years later before leaving the country to see his friend, the *samowarchi*. During the Soviet-Afghan War, the descendants of the Qizilayaq khalifa led battles against the invading Russian forces and helped families flee to Turkey.[7]

On American Researchers in
Afghan Turkestan

Baba often humorously remarked that no matter how remote the location, in the 1970s, one could turn over a rock and find an American researcher with a notebook. This observation held some truth. Following Zahir Shah's visit with John F. Kennedy in 1965, a wave of researchers and developers, primarily American, arrived in Afghanistan. This was also when artists, scholars, and scientists came to study in the United States in larger waves. Turkestan in the north became a significant focus of these studies, beginning with Hiromi Lorraine Sakata's ethnomusicological research. Sakata provided a clear analysis of the ethnic stratification in Turkestan, noting, "The Pashtun is unquestionably conceptualized as the most native of all ethnic groups living in Afghanistan. After all, the term 'Afghan' is traditionally applied to Pashtuns alone; other groups still prefer to be identified by their group affiliations, such as Hazara, Tajik, Uzbek, etc." She states that Sunni Pashtuns "constitute the politically dominant group in Afghanistan. This group lends its name to the whole country" (1985, 133–134). Sakata's observations highlight the political dominance of Pashtuns over other ethnic groups in Afghanistan, most noticeable in interactions with Hazara and Turkic communities.

Other visiting researchers also observed the region's power hierarchies. From the 1960s to the 1970s, scholars like Richard and Nancy Tapper, John Baily, Jonathan L. Lee, and Mark Slobin commented in their scholarly works on internal colonization and forced displacement. Slobin conducted dissertation research in Andkhoy, focusing on marginalized music.[8] He highlighted the north as a cultural touchpoint, especially in Tashkurghan, where Uzbek and Tajik cultures mingled through music like that of the ghijak and dombra. This contrasted with the Indian-influenced music of Radio Kabul.

These researchers' works underscored the evident inequities in power structures within Afghan society. It was also in Afghan Turkestan that my father became acutely aware of his position as an ethnic minority in Afghanistan and the enduring struggles faced by Turkic people.

Notes

1   Abdulsamad Saed, oral history interview for the Digital Archive of Turkic Heritage in Afghanistan (DATHA), November 24, 2022.

2   For in-depth analysis see Shahrani (2002), Mudessir (2022), Lee (1996, 2018), Bleuer (2012), and Noelle-Karimi (1997a, 1997b). See Lee (1996, xxxi) for British terminology.

3   Baba had filed paperwork to serve as a dentist in the army. But it was rejected by Minister Kobra Noorzai. He expressed anger at the unfairness of the decision, since most were able to provide medical service as military service. He had been stationed at Ghazni instead. His outburst had given him *shaaqa*, or an extra punishment year of military service.

4   Charbagh. The Farsi names are pronounced with an Uzbek accent.

5   In Andkhoy and some of the surrounding towns, even wells pull up salt water. Andkhoy later had so much salt deposit from the Namaksar Lakes (salt lakes) that they were able to mine. See Sakata (1985) on the water in Andkhoy and recent research on the water situation.

6   In the Afghan tradition, the families in Jalalabad who knew our patriarchs' history were these families who served as town elders, councils, and government officials: Leewal Sahib, Shaal Pacha, Maama Zarghunshah, Kalantar Nazeer, Haji Zahir, and Wazir Gholam Faruq Khan.

7   The Qizilayaq khalifa's descendant, Abdulkerim Mahdum, started the first Turkic political party in Afghanistan. They later resisted the Soviet regime. See his biography, in Turkish (Mahdum 2020).

8   Mark Slobin, interview for the Digital Archive of Turkic Heritage in Afghanistan (DATHA), October 1, 2022.

References

Bleuer, Christian. 2012. "State-Building, Migration and Economic Development on the Frontiers of Northern Afghanistan and Southern Tajikistan." *Journal of Eurasian Studies* 3 (1): 69–79. https://doi.org/10.1016/j.euras .2011.10.008.

Lee, Jonathan L. 1996. *The "Ancient Supremacy": Bukhara, Afghanistan and the Battle for Balkh, 1731–1901*. Leiden: E. J. Brill.

Lee, Jonathan L. 2018. *Afghanistan: A History from 1260 to the Present*. London: Reaktion Books.

Mahdum, Osman. 2020. *Orta Asya'da Bir Turan Lideri—Afganistan Türkleri'nin Lideri Abdulkerim Mahdum*. Istanbul: Kitap Arasi.

Mudessir, Moheb. 2022. "The Nation-Building Policies of the Afghan Governments and the Ethno-Cultural Identity of Turkic People in Afghanistan." Lecture and Q&A, Central Asia Research Forum, University of Illinois at Urbana-Champaign, November 2–4. Zoom.

Mudessir, Moheb. 2024. "The Accommodation of Turkic Peoples in Politics and Public Life in Afghanistan: A Rights-Based Approach." PhD diss., University of Sussex.

Noelle-Karimi, Christine. 1997a. "Amir Dost Muhammad Khan's Policies in Turkistan." In *State and Tribe in Nineteenth-Century Afghanistan: The Reign of Amir Dost Muhammad Khan (1826–1863)*. Oxford: Taylor and Francis.

Noelle-Karimi, Christine. 1997b. "Appendix E: The Population in the Towns of Afghan Turkistan and Badakhshan as Reflected by Reports of the Nineteenth and Early Twentieth Century." In *State and Tribe in Nineteenth-Century Afghanistan: The Reign of Amir Dost Muhammad Khan (1826–1863)*. Oxford: Taylor and Francis.

Sakata, Hiromi Lorraine. 1985. "Musicians Who Do Not Perform; Performers Who Are Not Musicians: Indigenous Conceptions of Being an Afghan Musician." *Asian Music* 17 (1): 132–142.

Shahrani, M. Nazif. 2002. "War, Factionalism, and the State in Afghanistan." *American Anthropologist* 104 (3): 715–722. http://www.jstor.org/stable/3567249.

Shahrani, M. Nazif, and Robert L. Canfield, eds. 2022. *Revolutions and Rebellions in Afghanistan: Anthropological Perspectives*. Bloomington: Indiana University Press. ProQuest Ebook Central.

Slobin, Mark. 1968. *Qizilayaq Khalifa*. Photograph. https://www.markslobin.com.

Tapper, Nancy. 2011. "Abd Al-Rahman's North-West Frontier: The Pashtun Colonisation of Afghan Turkistan." In *Tribe and State in Iran and Afghanistan (RLE Iran D)*, edited by Richard Tapper, 233–261. London: Routledge

Coda

Colonialism, however, is not satisfied by this violence against the present. The colonized people are presented ideologically as people arrested in their evolution, impervious to reason, incapable of directing their own affairs, requiring the permanent presence of an external ruling power. The history of the colonized peoples is transformed into meaningless unrest, and as a result, one has the impression that for these people humanity began with the arrival of those brave settlers.

—FRANTZ FANON

In the face of all this death, Palestinians offer lessons on life, on how to cherish it even in the midst of relentless horror. Fathers like Ahmad Imteiz navigated bullets and survived hunger on and through love. On the day of the Flour Massacre, when throngs of hungry people at the Nabulsi roundabout in Gaza City were subjected to live Israeli ammunition, Imteiz crawled for a kilometer as bullets rained down around him. He clung tightly to four cans of fava beans and a chicken. Once he was far from the Israeli attack that would take 115 lives that hour, he stood up to run. A journalist would later ask him if it was worth it. "Yes," he answered, "to save my hungry children, yes." In the face of Israel's engineering of social collapse, Palestinians shape and reshape a resilient social cohesion. In the face of death, life, Palestinian life and Palestinian futures continue.

—SHERENE SEIKALY

Early in *The Wretched of the Earth* (1963), psychiatrist and political philosopher Frantz Fanon writes of the "ruling species" or the "outsider from elsewhere" who governs through violence. Drawing from his experience with both settler colonial rule in Algeria and the legacy of transatlantic chattel slavery in the Caribbean where he was born, Fanon argues that modern Western civilization is rooted in a nonredemptive colonial racial violence. Fanon theorized the politics of racial violence just as the initial optimism about the promise of postcolonial freedom in the 1950s began to lose some of its luster. By 1961, it was clear to Fanon that anti-colonial liberation movements would trigger the brutality of proxy forever wars, while democratic electoral victories that dared to challenge colonial corporate power, as in the cases of Iran and Guatemala in the 1950s and the Congo in 1960, would be met with US-backed coups propping up national elites who would happily impose *post*colonial authoritarian racial violence against their own people.[1] Fanon allows us to recognize how "the ruling species," both at "home" and in the colonies, account for the racial logic of occupation and the fact of "total violence"—a violence that does not distinguish between civilian and soldier/police officer—as always already justified.[2] With our eyes on the unfolding devastation of Gaza, what does it mean to "decolonize" Afghanistan, and specifically, what lessons do the authors of this volume offer in terms of how we contend with the colonial racial present?

As a media studies scholar I am struck by an empirical reality as I write this coda in the summer of 2024. It seems clear to me that the asymmetrical and largely invisible (to the West) violence that the US-led Wars on Terror unleashed on Afghans, Iraqis, Pakistanis, Yemenis, and others for two decades has become momentarily visible to a significant number of US citizens watching this war on social media, reckoning with Israel's US-funded daily assault on Gaza. In this sense the illogic of "total violence" is also *momentarily* exposed to those who are not only its victims. As we know, colonial amnesia is a national condition. And yet, its double standards and false neutrality are not unquestionable, as the protests on college campuses and elsewhere since October 2023 have shown. Fanon's analysis helps to explain why it is that we as university faculty, students, and staff are encouraged by our institutions to condemn (rightfully) the unjust Russian war in Ukraine, but when it comes to thousands of our students protesting the US-backed Israeli massacre of Palestinian civilians, the same universities, and conservative and liberal politicians alike, insist on silencing, disciplining, and violently arresting their own students.[3] Likewise, it helps account for the bombings of hospitals and schools in Gaza or drone attacks on Afghan wedding parties. Fanon helps make sense of the senseless and unhinged state-sanctioned violence that kicks down doors of homes of women and children in the middle of the night whether in Afghanistan or Palestine, or the filming and sharing of videos by American soldiers urinating on dead Taliban fighters, or the strapping of Palestinian civilians on trucks as "human shields" by Israeli soldiers, or the body camera footage of the execution of a Black woman (Sonya Massey) by police whom she had called for help.[4] There is an unrelenting archive of such examples.

Fanon also helps us account for the slower violence of US economic sanctions and immigration policies. Following centuries-long Western traditions, the colonial violence of US military occupation disproportionately targeted the rural poor, which includes a majority of Afghan women and girls (Bose, chapter 9 in this volume); the violence of war has been followed by the violence of hunger, displacement, and untold environmental devastation. The effects of these include the astonishing fact that since 2022 92 percent of Afghans have faced hunger (Savell 2023), with almost no meaningful pathway to refugee status in the United States (in stark contrast to Ukrainian refugees). In other words, returning to Fanon is helpful in reminding us that the objective of colonial racial violence—whatever the purported motive for a "good" or "well-intentioned" colonial occupation and war might be—is based on logics of *excessive* forms of extraction, exploitation, and extermination—mechanisms that have sustained Western imperialism broadly, and US empire in particular, over the last century.

But in 2025, US empire is in a state of decline, even as its logics continue to unleash their over-the-top forms of violence around the world. In fact, as historian and editor of the *Journal of Palestine Studies*, Sherene Seikaly, pithily writes, "If the history of Israel and Palestine traces the rise of U.S. hegemony, it will also be one site of its erosion" (2024, 3). The Afghanistan catastrophe has been another such site.

Decolonial theories based on centuries-long histories and contemporary manifestations of settler colonialism in the Americas and Oceania engage discussions about twentieth- and twenty-first-century settler colonialism as well as extraterritorial colonial occupations, whether in Kashmir or Palestine, or in Afghanistan and Iraq. Many such approaches emphasize indigenous positionality and voice, ethical research methodologies, and politically oriented scholarly interventions (Lugones 2010; Byrd 2017; Coulthard 2014). As useful as these ideas are in their original context, when we turn to South Asia or West Asia (the Middle East), we find that indigeneity itself can be a troubled category, cynically mobilized against subaltern indigenous groups by the Right, whether by Zionists in Israel or Hindu nationalists in India.

Careful to avoid such essentialist traps and centering Afghan experiences and perspectives that are attentive to power differentials within Afghan society across gender, class, rural and urban, and ethnic differences, *Decolonizing Afghanistan* challenges decades of skewed academic and military knowledge production about Afghanistan and its peoples. The authors in this volume confront not just the legacy of military occupations and war, but also the legacy of ontological and epistemological violence. It is the first book of its kind written by an interdisciplinary group of Afghan diasporic and area studies scholars, journalists, artists, and activists who engage critically and reflexively in the colonial and racial history of modern Afghanistan and the Afghan diaspora. The authors examine the last four decades of colonial racial violence keeping in mind the earlier history of Afghanistan as a colonial frontier, which was on what the authors of the introduction call the "edges of British and tsarist Russian expansionism."

Colonial temporality and historiography are purposefully tricky. The authors in this volume speak back to what Nivi Manchanda calls "imperial negligence" and "lazy historiography" rearticulated through the "racial arsenal" (Ferreira da Silva 2007) that has conveniently rendered Afghanistan as intrinsically "ungovernable" and hopelessly "traditional." The chapters in the volume manage to account for centuries of British and Russian imperial power, while most focus on the more contemporary period following the decade-long Soviet invasion of 1979 to the US-led "War on Terror" that ended in the media spectacle of the catastrophic "withdrawal" in August 2021.

Decolonizing Afghanistan speaks to contemporary scholarly debates that are challenging Cold War framing of twentieth-century historiography and social theory, foregrounding the context of anti-colonial "worldmaking after empire," when across much of the world the foundational violence of colonial power was contested by newly sovereign nations (Getachew 2019). We see glimpses of this era in Afghanistan in the 1960s and 1970s, a transformative period from constitutional monarchy to electoral democracy that "inspired robust sociopolitical movements" that pushed for and gained democratic reforms, as noted in the introduction. As Robert D. Crews points out in chapter 2, already in 1919, "Lenin's Soviet government was the first to recognize the independence of Afghanistan," an act that would be "tout[ed] for decades as a symbol of the special relationship that bound the two states together in 'friendship' and anti-colonial solidarity." In 1979, as the Soviet military invaded Afghanistan in the name of said friendship, their solidarity and Soviet exceptionalism became cover for colonial racial violence. The decade of war that followed, against the CIA-, Pakistani-, and Saudi-supported mujahideen resistance to Soviet intervention (as Manchanda explores in chapter 1), led to the loss of hundreds of thousands of lives and the displacement of some 5 million Afghans (as

Crews notes in chapter 2). "Soviet Orientalism" would justify the scale of violence against the "irrational" Pashtun majority on the grounds that "Afghanistan was a space in which Soviets felt compelled to suspend conventional morality," as Crews goes on to note. Thus, the first part of this book establishes that there is more continuity between the racist motives and brutal legacies of the Soviet colonial occupation of Afghanistan and the US-led occupation than most Western scholars and policymakers would like to admit.

Many of the chapters in the volume remind us that the racial and gendered arsenal of colonial violence is exemplary in Western discourse about "premodern" Afghanistan. As the discussion of Fanon with which I began this essay notes, this discourse justifies the most extreme acts of violence and humiliation through the recurring logic of a "people arrested in their evolution and impervious to reason" (Fanon 1963, 755). As Purnima Bose argues in chapter 9, in Afghanistan the "status of women has become a dominant trope to periodize history" with US occupation signaling a "feminist war" even though "Afghans of all genders lacked access to such basic necessities as nutritious food, healthcare, sanitation, clean water, and adequate housing, all of which the United States failed to deliver in twenty years of occupation." The chapters in the middle parts of the volume each address the "infrastructures," "optics," and "framing" of Afghanistan as a project of Western imperial cultural and technological intervention. Morwari Zafar's chapter offers a particularly chilling account of the performative violence of Afghan Americans who had little lived experience in contemporary Afghanistan but would be employed by the US government as "cultural experts" to provide the "skeleton key" unlocking "tribal, premodern" Afghan culture.

Against the deluge of what Morwari Zafar refers to as "hyper-Orientalized perceptions," the last part of the volume "speaks back" in the realm of art, poetry, literature, and biography. In the closing chapter of the volume "An Other Afghanistan: Indigeneity, Migration, and Belonging in Andkhoy (1973)," Zohra Saed attempts to recover a history of "intercommunal difference" between the Uzbek, Turkmen, Pashtun, Hindu, and Sikh communities from her New Jersey–based Baba's experience in northern Afghanistan. In this sense, Saed's chapter along with chapters by Marya Hannun, Sabauon Nasseri, Tausif Noor, and Gazelle Samizay all complicate, challenge, and recover Afghan voices and lives, including those of women and sexual and ethnic minorities, against the monolithic racist tropes of Afghans and Muslims that continue to haunt global discourse, whether produced by media organizations in London and New York, film studios in Mumbai, or think tanks in DC. Today, even as total violence is repeatedly justified against the "barbarians" in Gaza and the nonviolent student protestors in the United States are censored and punished as supporting "terrorists,"[5] it is apparent to much of the world, including critics in Israel and the majority of the US public, that the United States and Israel have lost the global war of public opinion on Gaza.[6]

The authors of this volume remind us that colonialism and racial violence are not historical artifacts, nor can meaningful scholarship on decolonization and decolonial futures hide in the obscurity and safety of ivory towers. Fanon would have perhaps predicted the events over the last two years in the Western academy where liberal university presidents would call in the police and the military on their own campuses against peaceful anti-war student protesters, precisely because our students were able to see and name the colonial racial present. What the International Court of Justice has determined to be a "plausible genocide" against Palestinians by Israel[7] has been met in the heart of a declining empire, the United States, through the barrel of a gun and authoritarian silencing of critics. This violence "at home" must be seen as a response to the moral failures of the United States and its "good wars of empire," including the "feminist and humane" war in Afghanistan characterized by the "doublespeak" of destruction and development (Osman, chapter 3 in this volume). In her chapter about humanitarian efforts by Afghan American organizations in the wake of the United States' chaotic exit from Kabul, Helena Zeweri (2025) asks a resonant question. Echoing Sherene Seikaly's assertion that "in the face of death, life, Palestinian life and Palestinian futures continue," Zeweri asks, "How does the process of witnessing suffering in the form of mass displacement produce the collective will to address injustice?" *Decolonizing Afghanistan* is an act of will in its attempt to answer such an enduring question.

Notes

Epigraphs are excerpted from Fanon ([1960] 2018, 654) and Seikaly (2024, 4).

1   In the first section of *Wretched of the Earth*, Fanon references what historical sources have long revealed as US-led coups in Iran (1953) and Guatemala (1954); he writes specifically about Patrice Lumumba's assassination, which archival records have confirmed as also led by US and UN forces, in "Lumumba's Death: Could We Do Otherwise?," published in 1961.

2   Despite the known limitations of his writing that feminist critics among others have addressed (Gordon et al. 1996), Fanon is critical in accounting for what Denise Ferreira da Silva (2007, 2022) refers to as "total violence," whether in its manifestation of police violence against Black and Brown persons in the United States or Brazil, or military violence in Afghanistan and Palestine.

3   Censorship of speech that is critical of Israel's occupation and apartheid policies has been a long-standing challenge to academic freedom in the United States. Since the October 7 Hamas attacks in Israel and the subsequent ongoing war in Gaza, universities and other institutions across the United States have significantly restricted speech and activism that is critical of the political project of Zionism and the state of Israel. For more, see Chakravartty and Nesiah (2024). Since April 2024, an unprecedented 3,100 people have been arrested or detained in connection with pro-Palestinian protests in U.S. colleges. See *New York Times* (2024).

4   The above examples of such "excessive" violence in the war in Afghanistan are from authors in this book. For the current context of Israeli occupation of the West Bank, see Sawafta (2024) and Frankel and Alleruzzo (2024); on Sonya Massey, see Keck (2024).

5   For example, see Israeli Prime Minister Benjamin Netanyahu's speech to the US House and Senate on July 24, 2024 (*Haaretz* 2024).

6   For example, see Serhan (2024). Resisting the implications of facing this reality, in May of 2023, the US Congress passed a bipartisan bill barring the State Department from citing the Gaza Health Ministry, the only organization tracking the death toll on the ground in Gaza, from providing data to the US government. See Robertson (2024).

7   International Court of Justice, Order of 26 January 2024, Order No. 192–20240126-ORD-01-00-EN, *Application of the Convention on the Prevention and Punishment of the Crime of Genocide in the Gaza Strip (South Africa v. Israel)*, January 26, 2024, https://www.icj-cij.org/node/203447.

References

Byrd, Jodi A. 2017. "American Indian Transnationalisms." In *The Cambridge Companion to Transnational American Literature*, edited by Yogita Goyal, 174–189. Cambridge: Cambridge University Press.

Chakravartty, Paula, and Vasuki Nesiah. 2024 "Is This the End of Academic Freedom?" *New York Times*, April 5.

Coulthard, Glen Sean. 2014. *Red Skin, White Masks: Rejecting the Colonial Politics of Recognition*. Minneapolis: University of Minnesota Press.

Fanon, Frantz. (1960) 2018. "Why We Use Violence." In *Alienation and Freedom*, by Frantz Fanon, edited by Jean Khalfa and Robert Young, translated by Steve Corcoran. London: Bloomsbury Academic.

Fanon, Frantz. 1963. *The Wretched of the Earth*. Translated by Constance Far-
rington. New York: Grove.

Ferreira da Silva, Denise. 2007. *Toward a Global Idea of Race*. Minneapolis:
University of Minnesota Press.

Ferreira da Silva, Denise. 2022. *Unpayable Debt*. Cambridge, MA: MIT Press.

Frankel, Julia, and Maya Alleruzzo. 2024. "A Palestinian Was Shot, Beaten
and Tied to an Israel Army Jeep. The Army Says He Posed No Threat."
AP News, June 28. https://apnews.com/article/israel-palestinians-rights
-human-shield-jeep-8e8ed63bda65383e38e4dd52d239e319.

Getachew, Adom. 2019. *Worldmaking After Empire: The Rise and Fall of Self-
Determination*. Princeton, NJ: Princeton University Press.

Gordon, Lewis R., T. Denean Sharpley-Whiting, and Renée T. White, eds.
1996. *Fanon: A Critical Reader*. Oxford: Wiley Blackwell.

Haaretz. 2024. "Netanyahu's 2024 Address to Congress." July 25. https://
www.haaretz.com/israel-news/2024–07–25/ty-article/full-text
-netanyahus-2024-address-to-congress/00000190-e6c0-d469-a39d
-e6d7117d0000.

Keck, Patrick M. 2024. "Everything to Know About Illinois Bodycam
Laws After Fatal Sonya Massey Shooting." *Springfield State Register-
Journal*, July 24. https://www.sj-r.com/story/news/state/2024/07/24
/sonya-massey-shooting-prompts-questions-of-body-cam-use-training
/74505904007/.

Lugones, María. 2010. "Toward a Decolonial Feminism." *Hypatia* 25 (4):
742–759.

New York Times. 2024. "Where Protestors on U.S. Campuses Have Been Arrested or Detained." July 22. https://www.nytimes.com/interactive/2024
/us/pro-palestinian-college-protests-encampments.html.

Robertson, Nick. 2024. "House Votes to Ban State Department from Citing
Gaza Health Ministry Death Toll Statistics." *The Hill*, June 27. https://
thehill.com/homenews/house/4744241-house-amendment-gaza-death
-toll/.

Savell, Stephanie. 2023. *How Death Outlives War: The Reverberating Impact
of the Post-9/11 Wars on Human Health*. Costs of War, Watson Institute,
Brown University. https://watson.brown.edu/costsofwar/files/cow/imce
/papers/2023/Indirect%20Deaths.pdf.

Sawafta, Ali. 2024. "Israel Army Raids West Bank's Jenin, Palestinians Say
Seven Killed." *Reuters*, May 21. https://www.reuters.com/world/middle
-east/israeli-army-raids-west-banks-jenin-palestinians-say-three-killed
-2024–05–21/.

Seikaly, Sherene. 2024. "From the Editor." *Journal of Palestine Studies* 53 (1):
1–6.

Serhan, Yasmeen. 2024. "How Israel and Its Allies Lost Global Credibility."
Time, April 4. https://time.com/6963032/israel-netanyahu-allies-global
-standing/.

Acknowledgments

The post-9/11 American "forever war" in Afghanistan and its real and representational violence, along with its developmental and nation-building interventions, have left a confusing and mixed legacy. My own refugee story as an Afghan who grew up in the United States began with the Soviet invasion, during the Cold War, when more than half of Afghanistan's population fled. Prior to that, during the heyday of British and Russian imperial rivalry, Afghans were caught in the Great Game and subjected to three Anglo-Afghan wars. Over a century of imperial wars and at least fifty years of direct US interventions have irrevocably impacted the lives of Afghans and the Afghan diaspora in a variety of ways. Thus, this project of decolonizing Afghanistan and, by extension, the US imperial apparatus was always looming in my mind and in conversation with other hyphenated Afghans in the diaspora and with Afghans in Afghanistan.

First and foremost, I am grateful to Amahl Bishara, Paula Chakravartty, Faye Ginsburg, and Radha Hedge not only for encouraging and inspiring me to embark on this challenging and multifaceted project but for modeling what decolonial cross-cultural exchange and global engagement could look like through their publications and praxis. I am also grateful that Robert D. Crews accepted my invitation to coedit this volume with me. The book has benefited tremendously from his historical knowledge and nuanced and thoughtful feedback. When we reached out to Afghan, diasporic, and non-Afghan colleagues to submit their new research on Afghanistan and think through decolonizing Afghanistan with us, we were amazed by the responses and depth of scholarship people shared. The innovative research projects that we received, pushing Afghanistan studies forward and speaking back to empire, spanned disciplines and methods, including rich on-the-ground and ethnographic case studies, journalistic accounts, and art and literary criticism. Therefore, the bulk of the thanks belongs to the contributors for bringing the volume together and working with us to shape its critical and conceptual framework.

At Duke University Press, we are grateful for the generous support of Gisela Fosado and Elizabeth Ault and for the thoughtful copyediting by Christopher Hellwig, production management by Ihsan Taylor, and assistance of Benjamin Kossak. A special heartfelt thanks goes out to Tess Rankin, whose editing and organizational talents were integral in making the book happen. Miri Powell and Craig Willse also made valuable editing suggestions. We would also like to thank the book's designer, Matt Tauch, and my sister, Laimah Osman, whose painting graces the cover. We are also indebted to the proofreaders, Nora Lambrecht and Mark Mastromarino, and the anonymous reviewers.

My sincere gratitude also belongs to Barbie Zelizer and Aswin Punathambekar and their respective centers, the Center for Media at Risk and the Center for Advanced Research in Global Communication, at the Annenberg School for Communication, for providing me with institutional support and space during my sabbatical to complete this book. Other colleagues who deserve mention for moral support, collegiality, and intellectual community include Amita Manghnani, James Ryan, Michael Kennedy, Bilge Yesil, Christa Salamandra, Joe Khalil, Hatim El-Hibri, Ted Magder, Christina Dunbar-Hester, Shirly Bahar, Narges Bajoghli, Tilottama Karlekar, Zahra Ali, Manijeh Moradian, Manan Ahmed, Durba Mitra, William Carrick, Sarah Jackson, Juan Llamas Rodriguez, Eszter Zimanyi, Madison Miller, Jo Birkner, Jessa Lingel, John Jackson, Deborah Thomas, Alissa Jordan, Sarah Banet-Weiser, Karen Redrobe, Paul Cobb, Fatemeh Shams, Rahul Mukherjee, Brooke O'Harra, Sharon Haze, Eva Boodman, Whitney Howell, Larisa Mann, Andrea Wenzel, Lauren Kogen, Tauheedah Shukriyyah Asad, and Sezgi Başak Kavaklı.

Lastly, we dedicate this book to the diverse people of Afghanistan and other war-torn countries who, despite having had to pick up the pieces of their lives from the ruins of too many wars too many times, have always held out hope for a peaceful future to come.

Wazhmah Osman with Robert D. Crews

Contributors

MATTHIEU AIKINS is a Pulitzer Prize–winning journalist and author who has reported from Afghanistan and the Middle East since 2008. He is a contributing writer for the *New York Times Magazine* and a Puffin Fellow at Type Media Center. His first book, *The Naked Don't Fear the Water* (2022), about an undercover journey to Europe with Afghan refugees, has been translated into seven languages. Aikins received the 2022 Pulitzer for International Reporting as part of a *New York Times* team that investigated civilian casualties from US air strikes. The video investigation that he and his colleagues produced won two Emmy Awards. He has also received the National Magazine, Polk, and Livingston awards. He is a past fellow at the Harvard Radcliffe Institute, New America, the Council on Foreign Relations, and the American Academy in Berlin, and his work has appeared in the *New Yorker*, *Harper's*, and the anthology *The Best American Magazine Writing*. Aikins grew up in Nova Scotia and has a master's degree in Near Eastern studies from New York University.

DAWOOD AZAMI, PhD, is an award-winning senior journalist and academic. As a multimedia editor at the BBC World Service (London), he leads a team of journalists in covering international news and current affairs. He is also an associate fellow at the International Institute for Strategic Studies (IISS), London, contributing to research and analysis of geopolitical and developmental issues. In 2010–2011, he was the BBC World Service bureau chief and editor in Kabul, Afghanistan. He also worked as a visiting lecturer/scholar at The Ohio State University (USA) and the University of Westminster (London), teaching on globalization, conflict, and resource politics, as well as culture and politics in South and Central Asia and the Middle East. He received his PhD in politics and international relations and holds three master's degrees in various fields including politics, science, law, literature, and diplomacy. Dr. Azami speaks five languages and has written several book chapters and articles in various languages.

PURNIMA BOSE is a professor and chairperson of the English Department at Indiana University, where she also serves as the academic director of the IU India Gateway Office. She is the author of *Organizing Empire: Individualism, Collective Agency, and India* (Duke University Press, 2003) and *Intervention Narratives: Afghanistan, the United States, and the Global War on Terror* (2020). With Laura E. Lyons, she coedited *Cultural Critique and the Global Corporation* (2010), along with a special issue of *Biography* on corporate personhood. Her essays on Indian nationalism, globalization, and feminism have appeared in *The Global South, The Journal of South Asian History and Culture,* and *Critique of Anthropology,* among other venues.

PAULA CHAKRAVARTTY is James Weldon Johnson Professor of Media Studies at New York University. She has published widely in leading journals and is author/editor of *Race, Empire, and the Crisis of the Subprime* (2013), *Media Policy and Globalization* (2006), and *Global Communications: Toward a Transcultural Political Economy* (2007). Her current projects include a monograph titled *Media as Economic Violence,* and a forthcoming coedited volume, *An Anti-Colonial Feminist Critique of Capital* (Duke University Press). She is the editor of the the journal *Communication, Culture and Critique* and is the codirector of the Critical Racial Anti-Colonial Study Co-Lab at NYU.

ROBERT D. CREWS is a professor of history at Stanford University. He is the author of *Afghan Modern: The History of a Global Nation* (2015) and *For Prophet and Tsar: Islam and Empire in Russia and Central Asia* (2009) and coeditor of *Under the Drones: Modern Lives in the Afghanistan-Pakistan Borderlands* (2012) and *The Taliban and the Crisis of Afghanistan* (2008).

MARYA HANNUN is a postdoctoral researcher at the University of Exeter's Institute of Arab and Islamic Studies. Her current research project is a history of Afghanistan's first women's movement in the early twentieth century and its connections to gendered reforms across the transregion of South/West Asia and North Africa.

ALI KARIMI is an assistant professor and Canada Research Chair (Tier II) in the Department of Communication, Media, and Film at the University of Calgary. His research focuses on critical information studies, particularly surveillance, privacy, and data justice. He is currently writing a book on the history of information in Afghanistan, showing how numerical data—or lack thereof—shapes the state, society, and markets.

NIVI MANCHANDA is a reader (associate professor) in international politics at Queen Mary, University of London. She is interested in questions of racism, empire, and borders and has published in, among other journals, *International Affairs, Security Dialogue, Millennium, Current Sociology*, and *Third World Quarterly*. She is the coeditor of *Race and Racism in International Relations: Confronting the Global Colour Line* (2014). Her monograph *Imagining Afghanistan: The History and Politics of Imperial Knowledge* (2020) was awarded the L. H. M. Ling First Outstanding Book Prize by the British International Studies Association. She is currently on an AHRC-funded fellowship for her next project on borders and is a 2024 Philip Leverhulme Prize winner in Politics and International Relations.

SABAUON NASSERI studies the political and cultural history of Afghanistan and South and West Asia in the twentieth and twenty-first centuries. He has taught courses on Islam and literature, globalization, intellectual history, and environmental history at Beloit College.

TAUSIF NOOR is a critic, curator, and PhD candidate in the history of art at the University of California, Berkeley. His research interests broadly concern modern and contemporary art's imbrications with nationalism, internationalism, and postcolonialism with a focus on South Asia and its histories of decolonization. His criticism and essays have appeared in journals and periodicals including *Art History, ARTMargins, Artforum*, and the *New Yorker*, as well as in various exhibition catalogs and edited volumes.

WAZHMAH OSMAN is a filmmaker and associate professor in the Klein College of Media and Communication at Temple University. Her research and teaching are rooted in feminist media ethnographies that focus on the political economy of global media industries and the regimes of representation and visual culture they produce. She is the author of *Television and the Afghan Culture Wars: Brought to You by Foreigners, Warlords, and Activists* (2020), which won the 2021 Activism, Communication, and Social Justice Outstanding Book Award of the International Communication Association. She has published in leading journals, including the coauthored article "Decolonizing Transnational Feminism" (2024) in the *Journal of*

Middle East Women's Studies. Osman has appeared as a commentator on Democracy Now!, NPR, and Al Jazeera, among other news outlets.

HOSAI QASMI, PhD, cofounded Hosa Counselling and Research, an organization committed to providing culturally responsive mental health services and conducting research through decolonial and anti-racist methodologies. She is also a gender studies professor at Saint Paul University in Ottawa. Her academic interests include postcolonial feminism and gender relations, as well as the interplay between culture and media representations. She has been actively engaged with international feminist organizations, collaborating with Afghan women human rights defenders and other Indigenous-owned and women-led organizations as a research consultant focusing on women's empowerment, immigration, resettlement, reintegration, and the promotion of equality, diversity, and inclusiveness.

ZOHRA SAED is the coeditor of *One Story, Thirty Stories: An Anthology of Contemporary Afghan American Literature* (2010) and the editor of *Langston Hughes: Poems, Photos, and Notebooks from Turkestan* (2015). She is a Distinguished Lecturer at Macaulay Honors College and Lost & Found Faculty Editor and Mentor at the CUNY Graduate Center. She cofounded UpSet Press with fellow poet Robert Booras. She received an MFA in poetry from Brooklyn College, and a PhD in English literature from the City University of New York Graduate Center.

GAZELLE SAMIZAY is a multimedia artist, curator, and community organizer who uses personal narrative and experimental media to unpack the layered politics of gender, cultural memory, and national belonging. Her work has been exhibited internationally, including at the Gwangju Biennale (South Korea), Linden Museum (Germany), and the de Young Museum (San Francisco), and is collected by institutions including the Los Angeles County Museum of Art. Her writing appears in *One Story, Thirty Stories: An Anthology of Contemporary Afghan American Literature* (2010), and she has been featured on NPR and in the *Los Angeles Times* and *Hyperallergic*. She has received awards and residencies from the Princess Grace Foundation, Craft Contemporary, and the San Francisco Arts Commission. Samizay earned her MFA from the University of Arizona and directs the Worth Ryder Art Gallery at UC Berkeley.

MORWARI ZAFAR is an applied anthropologist and the founder of the Sentient Group, a research, education, and training consulting firm in Washington, DC. She is also an adjunct assistant professor at Georgetown University's Security Studies Program. Morwari has worked in both the international development and defense sectors, focusing on the use of cultural knowledge in US security force trainings. Her research has focused on US foreign policy in Afghanistan, militarism, and gun rights activism and militias in America. She has a PhD in anthropology from the University of Oxford, an MA in anthropology from George Washington University, and a BA in English from the University of Puget Sound.

HELENA ZEWERI is an assistant professor of anthropology at the University of British Columbia and faculty affiliate at the UBC Centre for Migration Studies. She is the author of *Between Care and Criminality: Marriage, Citizenship, and Family in Australian Social Welfare* (2024). Her current research examines deterrence-based border regimes and refugee-rights advocacy in the Afghan diaspora in Australia and the United States. Zeweri's work has been published in the *Journal of Refugee Studies*, the *International Feminist Journal of Politics*, and *Ethnos*, among other periodicals. She is also a member of the Afghan American Artists and Writers Association, a collective that aims to amplify diasporic art, writing, and scholarship. She received her PhD in anthropology from Rice University.

Index

Page locators in italics indicate figures.

art, Afghan, 9, 24, 88, 284–294; act of bearing witness, 286; autoethnographic reflection, 24, 295, 303–304; censorship and destruction of, 14, 19, 293, 301–302; colonial narratives challenged by, 295; documentary photographs, 286–289, 287, 288; gallery as contested space, 305; humanization of the deceased in, 309–311, 310; self and sisterhood in, 292–293; in the wake of withdrawal, 295–316; waste as critical gesture, 289–290. See also image/photography; media

Asad, Talal, 10

atrocities, 234–237; Dasht-e Leili massacre, 275–277; Gaza genocide, 14, 25, 90, 223, 335–337, 341n3; Hazara genocide, 7, 318; Tashkent massacre, 325; Turkestan Atrocity, 318

Authorizations for Use of Military Force Acts, 261–262

autoethnography, 24, 72, 218, 295, 303–304

Azoulay, Ariella Aisha, 287

Babakohi, Zalmay: "The Idol's Dust," 274–275, 282n9

Babri Masjid, 177

bacha bazi (pedophilia), 21, 105, 107

bacha posh (girls dressing as boys), 21

backwardness, tropes, 11, 12, 17, 44, 88–89, 170, 194, 199–203, 202, 214n6, 297

Bahrami, Katayoun, 295

bakhshish (donation, handout, or bribe), 109

Baluchistan, 58, 124

Barakatulla, Muhammad, 59

Barakzai, Shukriya, 205, 207

Basmachi (insurgent fighters), 324, 325, 329

Beg, Ibrahim, 329

benevolent imperialism, 18, 56, 73–78; doublespeak, 74, 76, 87, 90, 340; humanitarian justifications for military intervention, 75, 197, 290; rebranding as kinder and gentler, 76–78; United States as "empire lite," 77. See also development; imperialism

Bhabha, Homi, 47, 49

Bharatiya Janata Party (BJP), 175, 177, 182, 337

Biden, Joe, 110, 112

Biden administration, 5, 11, 69, 112, 247, 284–285, 7110; Afghan assets seized by, 7, 87; announcement of withdrawal, 255

bin Laden, Osama, 77

biometric technologies of identification, 23, 136–140, 141; Afghan-Automated Biometric Identification System, 143–144; Biometric Automated Toolset (BAT), 136, 139; Biometric Enrollment and Screening Device, 137, 138; iris scans, 137, 138, 140; women, biometric data collected from, 141. See also surveillance infrastructures

Black Lives Matter movement, 255

"blow back," 275

Bolsheviks, 46, 56–61, 325, 329

Bonn meetings, 78

Booth, Marilyn, 156, 163

borders and borderlands: Afghan Turkestan, 57; British India, 10, 38; colonial tropes of, 10; critiques of politics of, 249–250; Durand Line, 38; Indo-Afghan frontier, 16; northern border, 10; Pakistan, 83, 124–125; racist tropes of, 10; Turkestan, 325

Britain, 5–7, 57; attempts to situate Kabul in the geopolitics of empire, 156; colonial knowledge production, 14–15; "forward" and "close" policies, 38; media and empire, 156; press of 1920s, 156–160, 169. See also Anglo-Afghan wars

British (East India Company) Army, 38

British India, 6, 10, 156–158, 325; Durand Line, 38

Buddhas of Bamiyan, 274–275, 282n9

burn pits, 289

Bush, Laura, 75, 161–162

Canada: Haiti invasion, backing of, 13; programs for refugees, 298

cartoons and political satire, 42, 43, 121, 202, 202

Central Afghanistan Bank, 7, 87

Central Intelligence Agency (CIA), 40–41, 83, 118, 125

children: abuse of, 107; addicted to opium, 329; as child brides, 197; child soldiers, 175; encoded as unseen threat, 66; injured by land mines, 54

cinema, Indian, 23, 174–193; complicity with right wing, 185–186; *Dharmatma* (Khan 1975), 184–185; filmed in Afghanistan, 175, 177; inaccurate portrayals of Afghanistan, 181–187; Islamophobia in, 175–177, 182, 185, 188; *Kabul Express* (Khan 2006), 177, 180–182, *181*; *Khuda Gawah* (Anand 1992), 178–180, *180*; medieval wars portrayed in, 186–188; Orientalist depictions in, 23, 176–177, 180–185; *Panipat* (Gowariker 2019), 183, *183*; Pathans as characters, 174–175, 178–182; period films, 175; present-day Hindu-Muslim conflict rationalized in, 187; present-day situation of Afghanistan portrayed in, 183–184; Self/Other binary in, 176–177, 179–181, 184; shaped by Indian political scenario, 175, 178, 182–183, 188–189; shift in portrayal of Afghan characters, 175, 178–182. *See also* India; media

civilian casualties, 15, 23, 81–83, 123, 222–226, 233. *See also* human costs of war

"civilian," figure of, 66

"clash of civilizations," 105, 188

COIN FM-24, 49

Cold War, 15, 17, 24, 54, 309, 338; and Afghan Civil War, 40, 267, 273; Afghanistan as hot spot, 267–268, 275; as frame for twentieth-century scholarship, 338; and global private security industry, 117; imperialism denied, 77; Soviet viewpoints, 56, 66. *See also* Afghan Civil War (1992–1996)

colonialism: amnesia of, 44, 336; censorship and erasure of histories, 2, 18, 21; demasking, obsession with, 160–161; exceptionalism, notions of, 55, 68, 88, 338; exogenous domination, 5; gender

as justification for, 197; governance through violence, 335–336; in historical perspective, 5–7; internal, 6, 24; media representations of, 156; mystifying metaphors, 46–47; power relations normalized, 47; real-world consequences of, 3; reimagining of narratives, 309–311, *310*; "ruling species," 335–336; Soviet Union and United States compared, 12

colonial knowledge production, 2–4, 14–18, 50, 136–137; silencing effect of, 17–18; top-down imperial narratives, 4, 105–106, 110–111, 144–145

commander networks, pre-2001, 116–117

communism, 62–63, 116

"comprador intellectuals," 99–100, 111

corruption, 9, 17, 67, 78, 81, 86, 105, 107–110, 112n5, 127–128; in Afghan military, 142–143; pedophilia (*bacha bazi*), 21, 105, 107; produced by Western intervention, 109–110, 115; "state-sponsored protection rackets," 127; under US occupation, 209–210

Costs of War Project, 81, 82, 285

counterinsurgency, 81; "accidental terrorists" produced by, 87–88; Afghanistan as testing ground for, 82; defense contractors, 99; medical lexicon used, 49

counterinsurgency training, 23, 25, 97–114, 112n3; imperial gaze perpetuated by, 98; pretext of curated "native perspectives," 100; rotations, 101; skeleton key concept, 103; social and cross-cultural impediments addressed, 97–98; three-week training exercises, 97–98. *See also* Afghan American contractors; role-playing, by Afghan Americans

Crews, Robert D., 6, 254, 338

critical political geography, 42

"cross-cultural competence" (3C), 102

cultural expertise, 22, 98, 100, 102–103, 247–248

cultural relativism, 102, 107, 108

culture: Afghan as antagonist, 106–112; in borderlands, 10; commodification of, 23;

cultural awareness, 228–232; religious proselytizing as crime, 236–237; violation of cultural norms by Taliban, 228–232; violation of cultural norms by United States/NATO, 232–238; weaponization of, 99

Daoud Khan, Mohammed, 8, 39, 175, 184
Dasht-e Leili massacre, 275–277
Daulatzai, Anila, 3, 20, 198, 210
"death of dreams" rhetoric, 200
decoloniality, Afghan: alternatives and futures, 18–22; in global comparative perspective, 12–14
decolonial studies, 2, 18–19, 337; methodological issues, 3–5; right-wing attacks on, 18, 21
decolonization, 336; as active and persistent struggle, 290; artworks, power of, 308–309; future grounded in shared humanity, 89–90; of knowledge, 1, 195; in practice, 22–25; Third Worldist struggle, 40
defense contractors, 99
dehumanizing rhetoric, 11, 72
democracy-development projects, 78
Democratic Republic of Afghanistan, 60–61, 68. See also People's Democratic Party of Afghanistan (PDPA)
dentistry: dalaks (barbers), 323–324; dandansaz, 325–326; training, 325–326, 327
Department of Homeland Security (DHS), 262, 299
detritus of war, 83–84, 289–290
development, 9–10; corruption in, 78; "extended family" trope, 196, 213n2; failures of, 86; foreign assistance, 7, 9, 115, 116, 127, 199; good aspects of, 78–80, 88; inequalities exacerbated by influx of aid workers, 210; "militarized management of humanitarianism," 75; and private security industry, 115, 116, 119, 125; undermined by imperial violence, 84–87; during war, 72–75, 81; women and girls as focus of, 198–199. See also benevolent imperialism; nation-building projects

developmental idealism, 23; conflation of historical eras, 195, 210–211; history of, 195; modernity equated with Northwest European societies, 195–196, 209; teleological progression narrative, 194, 195–197, 306; why withdrawal narratives matter, 208–213; and women as civilizational indices, 195–199
development gaze, 9, 88
diaspora, Afghan, 1, 247–248; artists, 285; critiques of war, 24, 248–250, 260; elite, 251; forced migration, 288; nineteenth-century collaboration with Russia, 57; pastoralists in nineteenth century, 57; spectrum of discrimination and privilege in United States, 250–251. See also Afghan Americans; literature, Afghan
diasporas: art exhibitions and "insurgent" art, 305; comparative perspective, 12–13, 252–253
Digital Archive of Turkic Heritage in Afghanistan (DATHA), 317
disappeared, 42, 82, 138, 269
disarmament, 117–120
displacement, 12–14, 54, 89; of Afghan artists, 302; critiques of, 249–250; in Turkestan, 318; post-US withdrawal of 2021, 14; violence of abandonment, 261; war as problem of, 250. See also refugees
dissent: 2012 reaction to US disrespect, 236; erasure of, 14, 82, 90, 340; Kabul protest (1980), 63; led by women, 87; protest by AFBT, 262; violent crackdowns on, 14, 90. See also protests
"distribution of the sensible," 305–306
"divide and conquer" strategies, 16, 84, 89, 123, 127
Doha negotiations, 259
Dostum, Abdul Rashid, 276. See also Dasht-e Leili
drone warfare, 7, 74, 81–82, 306, 307–308
dual-identity narrative, 253. See also hybrid/hyphenated voices
Durand Line, 38

East India Company (EIC) Army, 38
Ebtikar, Munazza, 17
Edwards, Holly, 162
Egypt, 164, 168
Elphinstone, Mountstuart, 15, 17
Elphinstone, William, 37
Emergenc(y): Afghan Lives Beyond the Forever War (group exhibition), 295, 304–313; call for submissions, 304–305; temporality of art practices, 308–309
Emirate of Afghanistan, 38
empowerment, 13, 24, 79–80, 198, 201, 203–205, 252
environmental destruction, 54, 82, 84, 289–290
erasure: of Afghan heritage scholars, 4, 17, 19, 20–21; of Afghan women, 17, 293; amnesia of colonialism, 44, 336; "calculated forgetting," 44; of civilian assistance to United States, 285; in colonial histories, 2, 18, 21; of dissent, 14, 82, 90, 340; heritage destruction, 4, 174, 177, 274–275, 301–302; of human costs of war, 81–83, 273, 285, 289; media censorship, 82, 86; occlusion of Afghans in war commission, 20–21
ethnic groups, 58, 63, 297–298. *See also* "divide and conquer" strategies; Hazara; media, ethnic unity programs, 79–80; Pashtun; *qaum/quowm*; Tajik; tribes; Uzbek; violence
ethnic/sectarian violence, 81, 84, 297–298. *See also* atrocities
evacuations of Afghan nationals, 13–14, 89, 247, 254–256, 259, 261; artists, 287–288, 296, 297–298; bombing of crowds, 287; desperation of attempts, 285–286; interpreters privileged, 13–14, 296; and military connections, 300; mundane objects in, 288, *288*
"evil" occupation rhetoric, 68–69

Fabian, Johannes, 196
failure tropes, 5, 7–11, 338; "failed state" paradigm, 11, 13, 89, 128. *See also* backwardness tropes; unruly tropes

Fanon, Frantz, 3, 335–337, 340, 341n2; *The Wretched of the Earth*, 335–336, 340n1
fatwas (religious edicts), 224–228; counter-fatwas, 227; on suicide attacks, 230. *See also* religious scholars and clerics
feminism: colonial, applied to Afghanistan, 162–163; effect of scholarship, 160; support of war in Afghanistan, 197–198, 340; United States as feminist utopia, 195, 211–212
Feminist Majority Foundation, 197–198
Ferreira da Silva, Denise, 338, 341n2
flowers, soldiers greeting with, book cover art, *64*, 279
forward operating base (FOB), 97, 112n2
Fragmented Futures: Afghanistan 100 Years Later (exhibition), 297, 313
framing, 98
Freedom of Information Act (FoIA), 78, 300
"friendship": assumptions about shared ethnicity, 61–63; Soviet rhetoric of, 15–16, 56–63, *64*, 66, 338

Garner, Eric, 307
Gaza genocide, 25, 90, 223, 335–337; Flour Massacre, 335; student protests silenced, 14, 336, 340, 341n3. *See also* Israel
gender and sexuality: "Bākara!!" (The virgin!!) (A. Osman), 280–281; and coding of photographs, 155–156; colonial feminism applied to Afghanistan, 162–163; egalitarian ideologies, 206–207, 209; and family structure, 328–329; fashion and competing visions of the future, 165–167; "gender apartheid in Afghanistan" campaign, 197; global cultural scripts, 206; honor (*namus/namoos*), 21; Orientalist tropes of sexuality, 107–108; repetitious vocabulary used, 200–201; systems of difference critical to empire, 155–156; Western misrepresentations of, 21, 23, 160. *See also bacha bazi* (pedophilia); *bacha posh* (girls dressing as boys); women, Afghan

genocide, 6; Gaza, 14, 25, 90, 223, 336–337, 341n3; Hazara, 7, 318

George W. Bush administration, 75, 77, 237

Getachew, Adom, 338

Ghani, Ashraf, 81, 126, 209, 284–285, 307

Ghobar, Ghulam Mohammad, 154–155

"ghost" problem, 142

global arms industry, 271

Global War on Terror, 3, 7, 22; Afghan American relationship to, 247–248; "Afghanistan Papers," 78; asymmetrical violence of, 336; cracks in mission, 77–78; discursive and technological infrastructures of power, 16, 23; failures of concealed, 86; "forever war," 73; "good war" rhetoric, 68–69, 77–78, 248, 340; and Hollywood films, 11, 176, 188; international development aid tied to, 9; and internet era, 219; masculinist frameworks, 290; multipronged US approach, 16–17; waning enthusiasm for, 69; as War *of* Terror, 83. *See also* US/NATO intervention in Afghanistan

Goffman, Erving, 98, 99, 102, 103

"good war" rhetoric, 68–69, 77–78, 248, 340

"graveyard of empires" tropes, 11, 22, 68, 317; ahistoricism of, 35, 42; Anglo-Afghan wars, 36–38, 37; "highway of conquest" as counter to, 36; in media, 42; military, political, and economic withdrawal equated, 41; as politically charged trope, 35; as racialized, 36; Soviet-Afghan War, 35–44; Soviet invasion of 1979, 36, 38–40

"Great Game" tropes, 22; ahistoricism of, 46–47; "New Great Game," 45; trivialization of Afghan politics, histories, and lifeworlds, 47

green zones, 72, 83, 89, 279

grievability, 14, 28

Guadeloupe, 262–263

Guantanamo Bay, Cuba, 77, 223

Guatemala, US-led coup in, 336, 340n1

Haiti, 12–13, 252

Hamidi, Ghulam Haidar, 232

Hamid Karzai International Airport (HKIA), 256

Handheld Interagency Identity Detection Equipment (HIIDE), 139

Hanifi, Shah Mahmoud, 14–15

Haqqani, Sirajuddin, 231

Haqqani Network, 231

Hashem, Mir Mohammad Hussayn, 326–327, 327

Hazara, Aziz, 285–286; *A Gift to the American People*, 289–290

Hazara (ethnic group), 6, 258, 297–298. *See also* Hazara, Aziz; Taasha, Moshin

Hazara genocide, 7, 318

hearts-and-minds campaigns, 214n7; cultural awareness and the violation of cultural norms, 228–232; "good news stories" and "positive information," 228; in media, 23–24, 86; radio and newspaper as tools of, 219–220, 221. *See also* information warfare, media

Helmand Province, 142

heritage destruction, 4, 174, 177, 274–275, 301–302

Hikmat, Mawlawi Hikmatullah, 232

Hindutva (Hindu nationalism), 185–188, 337

Holbrooke, Richard, 48

Hollywood cinema, 11, 174, 176, 188

home front, as term, 205

home invasions (night raids), 81, 82, 222–23, 235, 336

honor, 36, 66, 80, 104, 183, 222, 274; Hindu, 196; *namus/namoos*, 21; and suicide bombings, 231

housing programs, 318–319

Hudson, Peter James, 12–13

human costs of war, 81–83, 273, 289, 310. *See also* civilian casualties

humane war notion, 74

humanitarian aid, 247–266; and anti-war critique, 24, 248–249; move toward policy advocacy from, 255–263; and social media platforms, 255

humanitarian government, 249

humanitarianism, as justification for military intervention, 75, 197, 208, 251, 290

humanitarian parole, 261–262, 299–300

human rights, exportation of, 74

human rights abuses, 80–81

"Human Terrain System," 16, 107–108

hunger, 277, 335, 337

Hurricane Maria, 252–253

Hussein, Saddam, 77

hybrid/hyphenated voices, 4, 21. *See also* dual-identity narrative

Illustrated London News (ILN), 157–158, 159, 160, 161

image/photography, 154–155; as "anchorage," 161; captions and text, 161; encoding of imperialist views, 155–156; and "scopic regime" of imperialism, 287. *See also* art, Afghan; Suraya, Queen (Suraya Tarzi)

immigration system, US, 24, 89, 256–257, 298, 314; and evacuations of Afghan nationals, 13–14, 89, 247, 254, 255–256, 259, 261; financial costs of applications, 299–300; hierarchies of labor and political alignment, 13–14, 249, 296; humanitarian parole, 261–262, 299–300; imperial endeavor extended by, 302; International Refugee Assistance Project, 300; mass denial approach, 300; obstacles for Afghans compared to Ukrainians, 299–300; US Citizenship and Immigration Services (USCIS), 257, 300; "vulnerability statements," 298. *See also* migration

imperialism: afterlives and deaths of empire, 84, 87–90; "civilizing" mission, 290; coerced dependency, 12–13; colonial power's ways of knowing preferred, 136–137; complex relations with colonized, 76; developmental idealism as foundational to, 195; "divide and conquer" strategies, 16, 84, 89, 123, 127; failures of US foreign policy, 89; Gaza

genocide, sponsorship of, 25; gender as justification for violence, 197, 290; "imperial feelings," 257–258; imperial formations, 12, 25; imperial gaze, 9, 23, 88, 90, 98; and the metaphoric, 49–50; multinational collective of countries involved, 13; racist tropes, 6–11; "reluctant imperialists," 87; twenty-first-century warfare, 80–84; United States as successor to British, 198; "victim/savior" script, 15, 18, 49, 75, 107, 161–162, 169, 194, 197–198, 290; violence of as norm, 87, 89. *See also* benevolent imperialism

imperial negligence, 43–44

India: British India, 6, 10, 38, 156–158, 325; goodwill and peace agreements with Afghanistan, 188; Hindi and Urdu languages, 174; Hindu nationalism, 185–188; partition, 326; support for Soviet Union, 59. *See also* cinema, Indian

information communication infrastructure, 135

information warfare, 63, 86, 218–220; casualty figures inflated, 224; controversial leaflets, 233–234; exploiting United States/NATO's follies and vulnerabilities, 232–238; slogans, symbols, and labels, 221–224, 222; in Spanish-American War, 218–219; and three C's of effective communication, 22, 238; "war of fatwas," 224–228. *See also* biometric technologies of identification; hearts-and-minds campaigns; media

"insurgents," 75

intergenerational trauma, 296, 303–304, 314

International Court of Justice, 340

International Criminal Court (ICC), 83

International Security Assistance Force (ISAF), 220

International Ulema Conference on Afghanistan Peace and Security, 226–227

internet, 219; escape scams on, 299; "internet mullahs," 225; social media, 219, 238, 255 interpreters, 13–14, 249, 260, 296

Iran, 18, 19, 253, 336, 340n1

Iraq, 3; "Critical Studies of Iraq" initiative, 19; US invasion of (2003), 74, 248, 262

Islam: Marxist attacks on, 39; rise of extremism, 68; Wahhabi, 36. *See also* Jamiat al-Islam; Jamiat-i Islami

Islamic State, 209

Islamophobia, 11, 76, 175–177, 182, 306–307; furthering of through cinema, 185–188

Israel, 83, 89, 223, 341n3; student protests against silenced, 14, 336, 340, 341n3. *See also* Gaza genocide

Jalalabad, 318–319, 328

Jamiat al-Islam, 164

Jamiat-i Islami, 119–121, 164. *See also* mujahideen; Tajik

jihad, 15, 225–227, 239n1; slogans of, 232–233; against Soviet Union, 15, 39–40; as "standard occurrence," 39. *See also* mujahideen; warlords

jirga (council or assembly), 106, 229; loya (grand) jirga, 78

Journal of Palestine Studies, 337

Joya, Malalai, 17, 209

Kaamil, Mir Mohammad, 325–326, *326*

"Kabubble," 89

Kabul Bank, 124, 128

Kabul International Airport, 142, 286, 287; suicide bombing, 300

Kabul–Kandahar route (Highway 1), 123

Kabul University, 199, 297

Kalakani, Habibullah, 329

Kandahar Province, 115–117, 123; peripheral rents and neopatrimonial governance, 127–128

Karmal, Babrak, 39, 269

Karzai, Ahmed Wali, 124–126, 232

Karzai, Hamid, 81, 124–128, 181, 209, 307; condemnation of US military, 235–236

Karzai, Seelai, 110

Katz, Elihu, 158

Kawsari, Masouma: "Dogs Are Not to Blame," 277–281

Kemal, Mustafa, 165, 167–168

Key Leader Engagements (KLEs), 99, 103, 104–106

Khalilzad, Zalmay, 68, 99–100

"Khan," as honorary title, 179

Khan, Emir Sayyid Mir Muhammad Alim, 269

Khan, Ismail, 119

Khan, Matiullah, 123

Khan, Nadir, 119, 318

Khan, Naim, 328

Khan, Sardar Mohammed Hashim, 325, 326

Khyber Pass, 36, 158

Kim, Jodi, 13

Kipling, Rudyard, 46

knowledge: Afghan American production of, 98–99, 102; challenges to academic and military production of, 337–338; critical intervention in production of, 19; decolonizing, 1, 195; illusion of, 144; performances of, 99; postcolonial literature, 160; vertical nature of surveillance, 136. *See also* colonial knowledge production

komandan, 116–117

Kosovo, 136

Kunar Province, female suicide attacks, 230–231

land mines, 54, 83, 85

Lee, Jonathan L., 318, 329

Lenin, Vladimir, 55, 59, 61

Lichtner, Giacomo, 186

lightness and darkness metaphors, 200

L'Illustration, 153

Lincoln, Abraham, 309

literature, Afghan, 24, 267–283; denial of ethical authority of mujahideen, 270–271; output in Dari or Pashto, 268. *See also* Afghan Civil War (1992–1996); specific authors and works

Lumumba, Patrice, 340n1

madrassa (religious school), 15, 225, 227, 277, 320–322

Maghbouleh, Neda, 248

Maira, Sunaina, 257–258

Malalai of Maiwand, 202

Manchanda, Nivi, 15, 19, 68, 155, 338

manifest, as term, 298

Mansfield, David, 124, 127

marginalized communities, 14, 20, 24, 250–251; poverty and violence experienced by, 275–280. *See also* Hazara; Shia; Uzbek

Marxist political ideology, 39

Massey, Sonya, 337

Massive Ordnance Air Blast (MOAB), 73, 82, *83*

Massoumi, Mejgan, 8–9

Mattis, James, 74, 226

Mbembe, Achille, 56, 89, 137

McChrystal, Stanley, 68

McClintock, Anne, 196

McGranahan, Carole, 12

media, 11; Afghan, 8–9, 79, 82, 296–297; Afghanistan encoded as "non-imperial counterspace," 156; Amanullah and Suraya's tour covered by, 153–170; backlash against military mistakes, 140; British press of 1920s, 156–160, 169; cartoons and political satire, 42, 43, 202, *202*, 212; critical coverage of Amanullah's apparel, 165; documentation of Taliban by women, 207–208; elections campaigns, 78; ethnic unity programs, 79–80; "formal news" stories, 158; global imperial scale of, 155, 158–159; hearts-and-minds campaigns, 23–24, 86; international connections, 156; journalist expertise, 256; "lateral cosmopolitanism" of Eastern Mediterranean print culture, 156; mediascape of South/West Asia and North Africa (SWANA), 163–164; military industrial media complex (MIMC), 82; out-groups portrayed in, 189; pictorial magazines, 157–158; radio, 8–9, 207, 210, 219–220, 221;

repetitious vocabulary used for women, 200–201; stereotypes of Afghans critiqued, 295–296; systems of gender differences encoded by, 155–156; Taliban tactics, 86–87; on Taliban treatment of women, 162, 200; television, 79–80, 110, 207, 210–211, 219; tour of Amanullah and Suraya as global "media event," 155, 169; translations and reprints, 163–164, 171n14; violence against makers of, 86; women's empowerment programs televised, 79–80. *See also* art, Afghan; cinema, Indian; information warfare; popular culture

Mignolo, Walter, 19

migration, 325–327; forced, 89, 288; of pastoralists, 57. *See also* displacement; immigration system, US; refugees

military industrial media complex (MIMC), 82

military personnel: Special Operations Forces, 104, 105, 109; as "warrior-diplomats," 102

Ministry of Defense, 121, 143–144

Mishra, Smeeta, 160

Mishra, Vijay, 186

Moby Media Group, 79

modernity, 8–10, 213–214n2; attire as vehicle for addressing, 156, 158, 160, 162, 165–170; and developmental idealism, 194; equated with Northwest European societies, 195–196, 209; "extended family" trope, 196, 213n2; "modern societies," 195–196; Western views of, 160, 169. *See also* Amanullah Khan (King); Suraya, Queen (Suraya Tarzi)

Modi, Narendra, 177

Mohammadi, Mohammad Hussain: "Dasht-e Leili," 275–277

Mojadidi, Amanullah, 295; *Remembering a Future #2*, 305–308, *308*

Moniri, Mohammad Anwar, 144

moral sentiment, 249

Morgan, Gerald, 46

Mujahid, Zabihullah, 199, 230, 239n1

mujahideen, 15, 39–41, 267–271; Basmachi, 324, 325, 329; and commander networks, 116–117; and corruption, 108–109; denial of ethical authority in fiction, 270–271; former leaders in transitional government, 80–81; "freedom fighters" labeled "enemy combatants," 275, 277; infighting (1992–1996), 267, 272; and sexual violence, 108; US support for, 41, 68, 80, 108, 276, 282n8. See also Dostum, Abdul Rashid; Jamiat-i Islami; jihad; Khan, Ismail; Rabbani, Burhanuddin; warlords
mullahs, 223–226; "internet mullahs," 225; role-playing, 101. See also religious scholars and clerics
multiculturalism, 21
museums, 4, 84, 85, 273–274, 310

Naber, Nadine, 248
Nahid-i-Shahid, 202
nahża (awakening), 164
Nasseri, Sabauon, 62
National Directorate of Security (NDS), 231
"nationality question," 16
National Security Agency, 141
National Security Entry-Exit Registration System (NSEERS), 248
National Ulema Council (Afghanistan), 226
nation-building projects, 7, 9, 11, 13, 75; Afghan American expertise limited, 99; failures due to private security companies, 115–116, 128–129; good aspects of, 78–80, 88; and US Global War on Terror, 16–17. See also development
Nawid, Senzil, 154, 171n14
Nazar, Abed, 329
Nazauna, 202
necropolitics 42, 89, 137
neopatrimonial governance, 127–128
New York Times Magazine article, 48
night raids (home invasions), 81, 82, 222–223, 235, 336

Nojan, Saugher, 250
"No More Drone Strikes, No One Left Behind" slogans, 254, 255–257, 261
nongovernmental organizations (NGOs), 214n4; and corruption, 109; inequalities exacerbated by influx of aid workers, 210; women and girls as focus of, 198. See also development; humanitarian aid
North Atlantic Treaty Organization (NATO), 14, 23, 38, 75, 81, 86–87; Article 5 invoked, 220–221; International Security Assistance Force (ISAF), 220–221; restrictions on surveillance, 139. See also US/NATO intervention in Afghanistan; US/NATO withdrawal from Afghanistan (2021)

Obama, Barack, 42, 48, 68–69, 74, 82, 235–236; apology for cultural insults, 236
occupation, war in Afghanistan as, 259–260
Office of the President of Afghanistan, 49
Olszewska, Zuzanna, 253
OMAR Mine Museum (Kabul), 85
Operation Enduring Freedom, 75
opium, 66–67, 124, 127, 329
Organisation of Islamic Cooperation (OIC), 226–227
"Orientalist scholar," 100
Orientalist tropes, 5, 11, 63–66; and Afghan American knowledge production, 98–99; European, 56; hyper-Orientalized perceptions, 106, 339; in Indian cinema, 23, 176–177, 189–185; performance of in role-playing scenarios, 106; of sexuality, 21, 107–108; Soviet, 16; "Soviet," 339; "tropics," discourse of, 42; of Vietnam and mujahideen, 40. See also racist imperial tropes
Oshagan, Anahid, 297
Oshagan, Ara, 297
Osman, Akram: "Bākara!!" (The virgin!!), 280–281

Osman, Laimah, 285–286, 290–293;
Ishqnama/Book of Love, 291; *Letters to
Sisters: Don't Let My Hearthate*, 291, 292;
They will be greeting by flowers, book
cover art
Osman, Wazhmah, 7, 9, 72, 110, 141, 210–
211, 214n6; on colonial feminism, 162; on
"good war" and War on Terror rhetoric,
248; *Postcards from Tora Bora*, 72, 84, 85;
Television and the Afghan Culture Wars,
207, 239n1; "Transformation in Afghan
Media and Culture Through Cycles of
Upheaval," 296–297
"other": Afghan, racialized, 11, 36, 42,
44; colonial construction of, 187; and
graveyard of empires tropes, 22, 35,
42; mystifying metaphors of, 46–47;
ostensible demystification of, 44; Self/
Other binary in Indian cinema, 176–177,
179–181, 184; and veiling, 160–161
Ottoman Empire, 163

Pakistan, 68, 177; Baluchistan, 124;
Deobandi clerics in, 225; status of
Afghan refugees, 89; suicide attack
volunteers, 230
Palestine, 12, 89, 166, 252, 335; Gaza geno-
cide, 14, 25, 90, 223, 336–337, 340, 341n3
Pandolfi, Mariella, 75
Panetta, Leon, 236
Parks, Lisa, 136
Pashto and Dari languages, 57, 291
Pashto film and music, 10
Pashtun (ethnic group): Alokozai, 124–125;
colonial and neocolonial stereotypes
of, 15–16; Durrani, 123, 318; in eastern
provinces, 330; as focus of anti-British
schemes, 58–59; irredentists, 60–61;
"Pashtunistan" proposal, 58; Pashtunization, 317–318
Pashtunwali, 36, 44, 178, 229; as Pathan
characters in Indian cinema, 174–175,
178–182; Popolzai, 124–125; as "traditional" rulers, 63; tsarist treatment of,
58–59

pastoralists, 57
Pasun, Sharifa: "The Late Shift," 270–271
pathology/disease tropes, 47–50
patriarchy, 10, 201–202, 277, 281n4
Patriot Act, 248
patronage, 6, 9–19, 109, 116–118
Payenda, Khalid, 142
peace process, 111, 258
pedophilia (*bacha bazi*), 21, 105, 107
People's Democratic Party of Afghanistan
(PDPA), 267, 271–272; coup of 1978, 5–16,
39, 60–62, 116, 268, 272; Khalq and Parcham factions, 39. *See also* Amin, Hafizullah; Daoud Khan, Mohammed; Democratic Republic of Afghanistan; Karmal,
Babrak; Taraki, Nur Muhammad
performance, 97–99, 102–104; of hyper-
Orientalized perceptions, 106, 339; rein-
forcement of top-down ideas, 105–106
Persian language, 291
Pierre, Jemima, 12–13
pir (saintlike figure), 329–330
Plastun, Vladimir, 62–63
pluralism, 11, 20, 79, 84, 90
pluriverse, 21–22, 90
poetics, Persian, 291–292
policy documents, 42
Pompeo, Mike, 83
popular culture, 11, 174, 185. *See also* media
Powell, Colin, 77
power relations, 47, 108; critiques of, 22,
286, 313; and evacuation, 286
Price, David, 108
Priority 2 (P-2) program, 298
prisons, 7, 83, 137–38; Abu Ghraib, 49, 77,
223; black sites, 7; Guantanamo Bay,
77, 223
private security contractors (PSCS), 115–133;
Afghan-owned, 118, 122; Afghan port
security contracts in United States, 122;
Afghan staff, 118; Amtex Global, 122;
ArmorGroup, 119; Asia Security Group,
122; Blackwater, 118; casualties, 123; and
failure of disarmament, 117–120; and
failure of Western state-building project,

115–116, 128–129; in "global security assemblages," 122; Jamiat-linked PSC north
of Kabul, 120–121; linked with smuggling
and organized crime, 121; links with
informal armed groups, 115, 118–119;
peripheral rents and neopatrimonial governance, 127–128; political settlements in
Kandahar, 124–126; and *qaum/quowm*
networks, 116–117, 121; and "securitization
of aid," 119; and surge of forces, 122–123;
United States inadvertently funding
enemy, 123; Western managerial elite, 118
Project Maven, 142–143
propaganda. *See* information warfare;
media
protests, 8, 63, 80, 87, 236, 250, 251, 255, 263,
291, 336
public charge of the state requirement,
261
public sphere, 8, 79, 86, 206–208;
television as, 207
Puerto Rican diaspora, 252–253
Puerto Rico, 13
Pulse nightclub shooting (Orlando, FL),
307

qaum/quowm, 80, 116–117, 121.
See also ethnic groups; tribes
Qizilayaq khalifa, 329–331, 332n7
queer, 21, 108, 308. *See also* gender and
sexuality

Rabbani, Burhanuddin, 232
racist imperial tropes, 6–11, 36, 42. *See also*
backwardness tropes; failure tropes;
unruly tropes
Radio Afghanistan / Radio Voice of
Sharia, 219–220
Rahnama, Sara, 165
Rancière, Jacques, 305–306
Rangers (US Army), 97
Raziq, Abdul, 126, *126*
Reagan, Ronald, 15, 40
refugees, 14, 25, 58, 90, 249–250, 255, 263;
Afghan refugees in Iran, 89, 253; Afghan

refugees in Pakistan, 89, 269; Canadian
programs for, 298; in fiction and artworks, 269, 280–281, 286–288, *287*, *288*;
mass displacement after 2021, 14; Palestinian camps, 252; recruitment of child
soldiers, 15, 175; Ukrainian, 299–300.
See also displacement
religious scholars and clerics, 223–228;
Deobandi clerics, 225; "grand gathering"
(2018), 227; madrassa (religious
school), 15, 225, 227, 277, 320–322; mullahs, 101, 223–225; pir (saintlike figure),
329–330; Taliban retaliation against,
227–228. *See also* fatwas (religious
edicts); mullahs
Revolutionary Association of the Women
of Afghanistan (RAWA), 203, 207
Rida, Rashid, 166–168
role-playing, by Afghan Americans, 16–17;
"Afghans" and "Americans" rather than
"subjects" and "occupiers," 105–106;
corruption and pedophilia, 105, 107;
"cross-cultural competence" as goal,
102; experiences of, 100–101; Key Leader
Engagements (KLEs), 99, 103, 104–106;
overlapping dimensions of, 101–103;
performance aspect, 98, 99, 102–104;
scripted performances, 97, 101; shuras
and jirgas, 106; in theater of operations,
100–106; villages staged, 97, 101, 103,
106. *See also* counterinsurgency
training
Rumsfeld, Donald, 42–43, 67
Russia: Asia, unique place in, 56–57; tsarist
expansionism, 5, 56–59, 338. *See also*
Soviet Union
Russo-Ukrainian conflict, 112
Ryan, Mick, 136

Sada-e-Azadi (The voice of freedom),
220, 222
Saed, Abdulsamad (Baba), 327; Andkhoy
experience, 319–325; migration story,
325–327
Saed, Zohra, 339

161; travel to India, Egypt, Turkey, and Iran, 163–164. *See also* image/photography

surveillance infrastructures, 134–149; aerial technologies of surveillance and strike, 136; capacity building not intended, 137, 139, 144–145; for crime fighting, 143–144; detainees and prisoners managed by, 136–137; fetishistic data collection, 141–142; friends and foes, colonial classification of, 139–140; "ghost" problem, 142; "identity dominance," 139–140; for military purposes only, 137, 144; participatory, 143; people turned against each other, 137–138; "social radar," 139; too much information and too little knowledge, 135, 142–144. *See also* biometric technologies of identification

Taasha, Moshin, 287–288, *288*

Tagore, Rabindranath, 178

Tahzib-i Niswan (women's newspaper), 164

Tajik (ethnic group), 57, 58, 61–63, 104, 119–121, 331

Tajikistan, 10, 60, 61

Taliban, 11; assassinations by, 207–208; attacks on PSCs, 123; capture of Kabul (2021), 247; conflation of historical eras, 195, 210–211; consolidation of central authority under in 1990s, 127; co-optation of commander networks, 117; cracks and fissures in ignored, 195; cultural annihilation by, 301; current generation of, 210; differences in post-2021 regime, 206; electricity and water cut off by, 297; information warfare by, 221–224; internet use, 225, 238–239; labeled insurgents and terrorists, 15, 80; "martyrdom brigade," 231–232; media rhetoric about, 200; media usage, 210–211; narrative of saving women from, 18, 75, 160–162, 197–198; outlawed from civil society, 80; return to power, 11, 86, 199, 211, 247, 284, 307; right-wing individuals financed by the West, 274, 282n8; self-destructive rule critiqued, 274–275; and suicide attacks, 229–234; Supreme

Court compared to, 212, 212–213; treatment of women, 87, 199–201, 290–291; US surveillance infrastructures used by, 145; warlords deposed by, 80; War on Terror targeting of, 77–78; women's resistance to, 23, 87, 195, 200, 202–203

Tapper, Nancy, 330, 331

Taraki, Nur Muhammad, 138

Tarzi, Suraya. *See* Suraya, Queen (Suraya Tarzi)

Tatar Soviet Socialist Republic, 62

technologies: of war, 1, 7, 23, 73, 81–83, 90, 136. *See also* biometric technologies of identification; drone warfare; land mines; Massive Ordnance Air Blast; surveillance infrastructures

television, 79–80, 110, 207, 219; Taliban on, 210–211

temporality: "Afghanistan is going back in time" narrative, 194, 199–203, *202*; "Afghanistan is *not* going back in time" narrative, 194, 203–208; and diasporic art practice, 308–309; generations of women in narratives, 200–201, 204–206; "post-9/11" world, timelines of, 306–307; premodernity attributed to non-Western societies, 195, 339; teleological progression narrative, 194, 195–197, 306

terrorism: as cancer, 49; counterterrorism strategy, 118–119, 128; as haven of, 2, 24, 90, 268, 275; "rent dispersion," 118; Soviet versus US designations, 15. *See also* Global War on Terror

terrorists, 75, 80, 175, 182, 223–224, 251, 291

theater of operations, 100–106

theater of war metaphor, 44, 84, 99, 230

Third Anglo-Afghan War (War of Independence), 6, 7, 38, 59–60, 297, 315n2, 338

Thompson, Elizabeth Southerend (Lady Butler): *Remnants of an Army*, 37, *37*, 42

Thomson Reuters Survey, 210, 212

Thornton, Arland, 194, 195–196, 213n2

222–223; feminist support of, 197–198, 340; first decade, 9, 81; as "first social media war," 219, 238; as "first tri-media war," 219, 238; justifications for, 18, 98, 107, 261–262, 290, 311, 313; life portrayed as ideal under, 209; as longest war in US history, 220; loss of civilian support for US/NATO, 233–238; mass displacement after 2021, 14; military mistakes, 140, 307–308; multiple dimensions of, 72; as occupation, 259–260; Operation Enduring Freedom, 75; second decade, 77–81, 233; testing ground for war technology, 82, 84; women as justification for, 107, 161–162, 197–198, 340. *See also* development; Global War on Terror; information warfare; private security contractors (PSCs); September 11, 2001; surveillance infrastructures; United States; US/NATO withdrawal from Afghanistan (2021)

US/NATO withdrawal from Afghanistan (2021), 2, 5, 14, 44, 75, 80, 89, 340; "Afghanistan is going back in time" narrative, 199–203, 202, 208–209, 214n6; "Afghanistan is *not* going back in time" narrative, 203–209; agreement of 2020, 307; Biden comments on, 5, 11, 69, 110, 112; disillusionment of, 258–259; evacuations of nationals, 13–14, 247, 254, 255–256, 259, 261, 285; haphazardness of, 83, 87, 284–285, 296; "imperial remainders" of, 84, 286, 289, 291, 293; nonhuman detritus left behind, 83–84, 289; official state doctrine, 284–285; as part of imperial management of fallout, 263; politically expedient moves, 259, 263; rhetorical clean-up, 83; transit countries, 247; tropes used to justify, 69, 110–111; war debris and residuals left behind, 83–84; why narratives matter, 208–213. *See also* US/NATO intervention in Afghanistan

Uzbek (ethnic group), 24, 61–63, 329–330. *See also* Dostum, Abdul Rashid

Uzbekistan, 60, 61

veiling, 154–155; colonial obsession with, 160–161, 166; as comforting, 269–270; presence and absence of, 160–163, 169; as source of anxiety about modernization, 165; unveiling coded as liberation, 161, 291

Veracini, Lorenzo, 5

Vietnam War, 17, 40, 77, 219

Village Stability Operations (VSOs), 99, 109

violence: of abandonment, 261; Abu Ghraib prison abuse, 49, 77, 223; against Afghan citizens, 81, 210, 222–223; colonial governance through, 335–336; development undermined by, 84–87; ethnic/sectarian, 81, 84, 297–298; extrajudicial, 82, 209; gender as justification for imperial, 197, 290; gender-based, 270, 281–282n5; at Guantanamo Bay, Cuba, 77, 223; imperial and national linked, 89; intergenerational trauma, 296, 303–304, 314; against media makers, 86; as norm, 87, 89; *post*colonial authoritarian racial, 336; privatized, 115; psychological, 290–293, 292; racial, 335–336; slow, 337; "total," 336

Wahhabi Islam, 36

walls, 89–90, 138–139; blast walls, 278–279

Walsh, Catherine, 19

war: Afghanistan as first major twenty-first-century war, 136; Afghanistan as testing ground for technology, 82, 84; automation of, 136; development during, 72–75, 81; discarded remainders of, 83–84; "green-on-blue attacks," 234; humaneness narratives as misleading, 88; official government narrative, 82; as problem of occupation and displacement, 250; traditional Afghan rules of, 228–230, 232. *See also* afterlives and deaths; technologies: of war

Wardak, Abdul Rahim, 68

warlords, 48, 79, 80–81, 84, 87, 105, 110, 117, 126, 175; in government, 81, 108, 120, 209; and private security companies, 120, 129. *See also* jihad; mujahideen

War on Terror. *See* Global War on Terror

warriors, Afghan, stereotypes of, 36, 39–40, 59

Watan Risk Management, 126, 128

"We Are All Afghan" campaign videos, 80

women, Afghan: agency denied to in developmental idealist narratives, 201–202, *202*; Amanullah's reforms, 154; assassinations of by Taliban, 207–208; biometric data collected from, *141*; as civilizational indices, 197–199; dancers, historical subjection of, 270; and development projects, 84–86; empowerment programs for, 78–80, 198–199, 203–205, 252; female suicide bombing, 230–231, 239n2; generational differences in narratives of, 200–201, 204–206; as justification for US intervention, 107, 161–162, 197–198, 340; labor force participation, 198–199; mothers, survival strategies of, 204–205; newspapers for, 164, 168; poets, 291–292; protests led by, 87; psychological violence to, 290–293, *292*; (mis)representations of, 155–156; resistance to Taliban, 23, 195, 200, 202–203; silencing of leaders, 18; Taliban treatment of, 87, 199–201; on *Time* magazine cover, 170; urban/rural disparities, 23, 84–85, 195,

210; US/NATO withdrawal, 194–217; "victim/savior" script, 18, 75, 107, 161–162, 169, 194, 197–198, 290; violence against media makers, 86; world's most dangerous countries for, 210, 212–213. *See also* gender and sexuality; saviorism/saving

World Bank, 119

World's Most Dangerous Countries for Women (Thomson Reuters Survey), 210, 212

World War I, 59, 76

World War II, 60, 76

Worth Ryder Art Gallery (UC Berkeley), 304

Yaqub (Emir of Afghanistan), 38

Yate, C. E., 317–318

Yeğenoğlu, Meyda, 160–161

Young Pioneers, 60, *61*

Yousafzai, Malala, 17

Yugoslavian Civil Wars of the 1990s, 219

Zafar, Morwari, 97, 248, 339

Zakaria, Rafia, 197–198

Zamani, Sarah Ramin, 305

Zaryab, Rahnaward: *Gulnār va āyina* (Gulnar and the mirror), 218–212n5, 268–270, 277

Zero Units, 83

Zeweri, Helena, 18, 110, 198, 340

www.ingramcontent.com/pod-product-compliance
Lightning Source LLC
Chambersburg PA
CBHW051434270326
41935CB00019B/1825